American Indian Tribes

American Indian Tribes

Volume 2

Tribes and Traditions

Miwok—Zapotec

Appendixes

edited by
The Editors of Salem Press

project editor
R. Kent Rasmussen

Salem Press, Inc.
Pasadena, California   Hackensack, New Jersey

Essays originally appeared in *Ready Reference, American Indians*, 1995; new material has been added.

∞ The paper used in these volumes conforms to the American National Standard for Permanence of Paper for Printed Library Materials, Z39.48-1992 (R1997).

Library of Congress Cataloging-in-Publication Data
American indian tribes / edited by the editors of Salem Press ; project editor, R. Kent Rasmussen.
    p.   cm. — (Magill's choice)
Includes bibliographical references and index.
ISBN 0-89356-063-4 (set : alk. paper) — ISBN 0-89356-064-2 (v. 1 : alk. paper) — ISBN 0-89356-065-0 (v. 2 : alk. paper)
1. Indians of North America. I. Rasmussen, R. Kent. II. Series.
E77.A53 2000
970'.00497—dc21

                                                                00-044659

Fourth Printing

Contents – Volume 2

Contents

Appendixes

Contents – Volume 1

Culture Areas of North America

Tribes and Traditions

Contents

Tribes and Traditions

Miwok

CULTURE AREA: California
LANGUAGE GROUP: Miwok-Costanoan
PRIMARY LOCATION: Western central California
POPULATION SIZE: 3,381 (1990 U.S. Census)

Miwok Indians lived in western central California. They are divided into three groups: the Lake, Eastern, and Coast Miwok. Miwok Indians hunted, gathered, fished, and traded for food. Both men and women fished using nets, baskets, spears, and their bare hands. Men used bows and arrows to kill waterfowl and large game such as deer, elk, and bear. Surplus meat and fish were mixed with salt and dried for winter use. Men and women made baskets which were used in ceremonies as well as for gathering, storing, and preparing food. The Miwok harvested numerous types of acorns, nuts, berries, roots, and other vegetation for food, medicine, and basketweaving materials.

The Miwok Indians lived in large, permanent multifamily homes covered with brush, leaves, tule, and dirt. A basket was set over the small doorway opening at night. Women wore deerskin apron skirts and men wore loincloths of the same material. Animal skins were cut into strips and sewn together for winter robes.

The shaman was the tribal doctor as well as a ceremonial and religious leader. There were two kinds of shaman: power (or singing) shamans and sucking shamans. Sucking shamans sucked on the skin to extract foreign bodies that were believed to cause illness. Power shamans danced and prayed to guardian spirits for cures. Many superstitions and taboos were observed to ensure health and good luck.

In 1595, Spanish explorers met the Coast Miwok. In the early 1800's, missions were established and Miwok Indians were forcibly taken there for conversion. Many ran away but were captured and returned by Spanish soldiers. Disease epidemics and warfare with the Spanish decimated and weakened the tribe. When white settlers arrived in California, hostilities were aimed at the ranchers. In 1850, federal troops from Sonoma killed a large number of Miwok. In the early 1900's, the federal government purchased land for a small reservation. Many Miwoks found seasonal work on local ranches.

Mixtec

CULTURE AREA: Mesoamerica
LANGUAGE GROUP: Oto-Manguean
PRIMARY LOCATION: Guerrero, Oaxaca, and Puebla, Mexico

The Mixtec people shared a common language and a distinctive Meso-american culture. Unlike many Mesoamerican societies, there was never a Mixtec empire with a capital city. Rather, numerous, small, politically independent kingdoms characterized the Mixtec political landscape. Each kingdom was headed by its own prestigious royal dynasty, centered in its own town boasting public buildings, temples, ball courts, hieroglyphic writing, luxurious royal residences, and elaborate tombs. The mountaintop sites of Monte Negro, Yucuñudahui, and Huamelulpan are examples of such royal centers in the Mixteca Alta.

The social system was one of the most rigidly hierarchical in Meso-america, with clear class divisions between nobility and commoners as well as ranked divisions within each of these broad classes. Mixtec royalty were among those in Mesoamerica who claimed (possibly fictional) descent from the Toltec of Central Mexico. A small but professional military helped maintain social order and was sometimes used for territorial expansion at the expense of neighboring Mixtec kingdoms. Agricultural produce (maize, beans, and squash) and crafts were extracted from the commoners as tribute.

The Mixtec were divided into three principal groups. The most northerly group inhabited the Mixteca Baja, a series of hot, humid valleys descending toward the Gulf Lowlands. Kingdoms within the Mixteca Baja flourished from 600 to 900 C.E., after the decline of Teotihuacán and Monte Albán and before the rise of Tula. A second Mixtec group, the Mixteca de la Costa, occupied the Pacific coastal lowlands of Oaxaca state, where cacao (chocolate bean), a valuable trade item, was grown. The third group lived in the Mixteca Alta, the cold, high mountains and upland valleys west of Oaxaca. The Mixteca Alta lies near the Zapotec Valley of Oaxaca, and this group had the closest relationship with the Zapotec kingdoms, especially in the Late Postclassic period (after 1200 C.E.), when the Mixtec expanded and royal intermarriage was common.

The Mixtec were highly skilled craftsworkers. Elaborate luxury goods were produced for the Mixtec nobility and for trade with the elite of other regions. Gold and silver were worked with amber, turquoise, jade, pearl, jet, coral, and shell to produce exquisite necklaces, bracelets, and ear and nose ornaments. Craftsworkers producing such luxury goods and working with such valuable materials may themselves have been part of the nobility.

The Mixtec developed their own unique script. In addition to stone slabs, the Mixtec wrote codices—books with accordion-shaped paper pages with elaborately painted pictures in vivid colors. The codices contain genealogical and historical records as well as religious information related to Mixtec deities and divination. Although the Mixtec script resembles Mesoamerican script symbols in general, it remains only partially deciphered.

Beginning in the late 1400's, most Mixtec kingdoms fell prey to the powerful and expanding Aztec empire. Less than twenty-five years later, the Mixtec kingdoms again fell prey to the Spanish. An estimated 260,000 people still speak Mixtecan languages.

Mobile

CULTURE AREA: Southeast
LANGUAGE GROUP: Muskogean
PRIMARY LOCATION: Choctaw Bluff on the Alabama River

Despite extensive historical data on the Mobile, there is little prehistoric information. In 1540, Hernando de Soto first fought with the Mobile, who were under the leadership of their chief, Tuscaloosa, who rallied his people and neighboring groups to oppose the Spanish successfully.

Later, many Mobile moved south to Mobile Bay, where the French encountered them in 1700. The Mobile appealed to the French for protection from their traditional enemies, and in 1708 they were settled near Fort Louis, along with the Tohome. French Roman Catholic missionaries were relatively successful in Christianizing the Mobile, who were absorbed into the Choctaw Nation. By 1758 there remained fewer than two hundred Mobile.

In addition to their own language, the Mobile spoke a so-called Mobilian lingua franca, or trade language, which actually was a corrupted Choctaw jargon used by most tribes from Florida to Louisiana, and north along the Mississippi.

Modoc

CULTURE AREA: Plateau (some authorities indicate Great Basin)
LANGUAGE GROUP: Klamath-Modoc
PRIMARY LOCATION: Northern California, southwestern Oregon, Oklahoma
POPULATION SIZE: 574 (1990 U.S. Census)

Modoc, California's northeasternmost county, is named for a Native American tribe whose ancestors arrived in that area not later than 6100 B.C.E. By that date, the Modoc (which means "southerner") also inhabited the nearby Tule Lake region (presently in Siskiyou County, California), as well as south-central Oregon's Klamath Lake and Lower Klamath Lake region. Archaeological discoveries in the Surprise Valley of northeastern California, as well as near Oregon's Klamath lakes, indicate the occupancy of large semi-subterranean lodges (or pit houses), suggesting old, well-established societies that were at least partially sedentary. Around 2500 B.C.E., however, the appearance of brush wickiup housing, denoting adaptations to a less settled life, suggests changes in Klamath-Modoc cultural conditions or a shift in the ranges of the Modoc.

Generally, the Klamath-Modoc were hunter-gatherers; that is, they specialized in fishing, fowling, and plant gathering, particularly along lake shores. Their legacy of artifacts consists of leaf-shaped and large side-notched projectile points, which at later dates changed to smaller, notched and barbed arrowheads. Mortars and pestles, knives, scrapers, twined basketry, and sagebrush sandals have also been found in abundance, although the archaeological record for relatively more recent ancient times has been destroyed by modern relic collectors.

Since the Modoc inhabited a relatively isolated region of rich grasslands and lava beds, unlike other Plateau tribes they remained relatively unaffected by extensions of the nineteenth century European mining frontier and the ruthless search for gold and other precious metals that characterized it. Nevertheless, trouble began in the early 1860's when Modoc grasslands began attracting white ranchers who were eager to clear Indians from their path. Under pressure from the ranchers, the federal government negotiated a treaty with the Modoc in 1864 that resulted in the Modocs' movement to a reservation north of Tule Lake. Whatever advantages the treaty brought to white ranchers, it brought little solace to the Modoc, for they were obliged to share the reservation with the Klamath tribe among whom, despite their language affinities, the Modoc were both culturally alien and badly outnumbered.

Late nineteenth century sketch of an 1873 skirmish in the Modoc War.
(Library of Congress)

Faced with these disabilities, Captain Jack (Kintpuash), a Modoc leader, encouraged his people to return to their original homes around Tule Lake, an area that in the meantime had been occupied by white settlers who were panicked by the Indians' reappearance. Initial efforts by whites to persuade Captain Jack to remove his people to the reservation once again failed. The appointment in 1869 of Alfred B. Meacham, a staunch Oregon Republican and a reformer, as superintendent of Oregon's Indian affairs, soon resulted in the Modocs' reluctant return to the reservation. There, faced once again with the hostilities of the Klamath as well as with pressures from other Indian agents, the Modoc for a second time left the reservation and returned to their homeland.

By 1872, federal efforts to force the Modoc back to the reservation brought on the Modoc War. For a year, the military campaign against the Modoc proved an embarrassing stalemate to federal troops led by General Edward R. S. Canby, whom Captain Jack treacherously murdered during peace parleys. Simultaneously, the war deeply divided the Modoc themselves. Confronted in the aftermath of Canby's murder with national outrage and intensified federal military operations, the Modocs swiftly surrendered. Captain Jack and three associates were hanged. The surviving 153 Modocs were exiled under the aegis of the Department of Interior to Oklahoma Indian Territory, where subsequently they farmed peacefully. In 1909, those who remained were given the option of returning to Oregon's Klamath reservation.

The Modocs' contacts with whites proved disastrous. The Bureau of Indian Affairs counted four thousand Modocs in 1873. By 1994, between three hundred and five hundred of their descendants lived near Chiloquin, Oregon, and a few hundred more in Oklahoma (the 1990 U.S. Census gave the Modoc population as 574). In 1986, through the Modoc tribe of Oklahoma, the tribe was restored to direct federal recognition and government-to-government relations with the United States. The Modoc's rich cultural tradition lives on in its myths about Kmukamch, the ancient creator, and Loon Woman.

Clifton K. Yearley

Mogollon

DATE: 200 B.C.E.-1000 C.E.
LOCATION: Arizona, New Mexico
CULTURES AFFECTED: Western Pueblo tribes

The Mogollon tradition represents the emergence and florescence of agricultural village life in central and eastern Arizona and western New Mexico, especially in mountainous, highland regions. It begins with the appearance of pottery and ends with the transition from pit house villages to a Western Pueblo settlement pattern. Definitions of the Mogollon cultural sequence have become very complex with the proliferation of regionalized phases, and there is a lack of agreement on a generalized nomenclature.

Excavations at Tularosa Cave and Bat Cave (New Mexico) have provided evidence for the local development of the Mogollon tradition from Archaic period Cochise cultures, signaled by the emergence of pottery and increased sedentation. The timing of this transition is still poorly understood, and interpretations of dates for the beginning of ceramics in the Mogollon region range from 600 B.C.E. to 200 C.E., with most scholars favoring the later date. The earliest Mogollon pottery is plain, with a red wash or slip. Red-on-brown and black-on-white styles appear around 650 C.E., with a red-on-white type appearing around 800.

Early Mogollon villages were situated on mesas and high ridges, close to cultivable alluvial valleys, possibly for defensive purposes. The earliest dwellings were pit houses with central posts and circular or D-shaped layouts, entered via sloping ramps. Over time, these became more rectangular in shape. In the final Mogollon phase before the transition to the Western Pueblo tradition (circa 800-1000), pit houses were often lined with stone masonry and occasionally had roof entries instead of inclined ramps. Typical Mogollon villages were small, averaging about six to eight houses, although larger examples may have had as many as fifty dwellings. At larger villages, especially large pit houses were used for ceremonial rather than residential functions, and some scholars have identified these as "great kivas."

Mogollon farming was based on the use of rainfall rather than irrigation, as with the Hohokam tradition. Given the proximity of highland forest regions, hunting remained an important adjunct to Mogollon agriculture. Typical subsistence technology included digging sticks, milling stones, bows and arrows, fine baskets, and pottery.

By the year 1000, the Mogollon tradition had given way to that of the Western Pueblo pattern of aboveground, multiroomed structures with great kivas (subterranean ceremonial structures with circular plans). As population density grew, reaching a peak in the late thirteenth century, populations in the northern Mogollon area coalesced into large pueblos such as Point of Pines, Kinishba, and Grasshopper. To the south, in the Mimbres Valley, the Mogollon tradition evolved into the Mimbres phase (1100-1150), characterized by large pueblos of several hundred inhabitants and beautiful black-on-white Mimbres pottery. This was followed by the Animas phase (1150-1300), during which the southern pueblos had close ties to cultures such as that of Casas Grandes in Chihuahua, Mexico.

Casas Grandes, also known as Paquimé, was a large pueblo occupied between 1060 and 1350 c.e. At its height, the site had a central core of sixteen hundred rooms and an estimated population of twenty-two hundred people. There is abundant evidence at Casas Grandes for craft specialization, especially in the working of marine shell. The people of this site engaged in long-distance trade with Mesoamerican cultures to the south, exchanging painted pottery and turquoise for marine shells, macaws, and exotic bird feathers.

Mohawk

Culture area: Northeast

Language group: Iroquoian

Primary location: Northern New York State, Ontario, Quebec

Population size: 15,490 in U.S. (1990 U.S. Census); 9,305 in Canada (Statistics Canada, based on 1991 census)

The Mohawks, the eastern-most tribe of the Iroquois Confederacy, originally called themselves Kaniengehaga, the "flint people." Among the most warlike of the eastern Indians, the Mohawks in prehistoric times fought with all their neighbors, both fellow Iroquoian Indians and the Algonquians living to the east of them. They, according to legend, were the source of the idea of the Iroquois Confederacy. It vastly reduced the amount of intertribal warfare among the Iroquois of New York State, though not that with their non-Iroquois neighbors.

Mohawk leader Joseph Brant urged the Iroquois to side with the British in the American Revolution. (Library of Congress)

According to legend, two men of peace, Deganawida and Hiawatha came to the Mohawks and convinced them to spearhead a proposal of peace among the tribes in what is now New York State. It took a considerable amount of persuasive argument, but eventually the Seneca, the Oneida, the Cayuga, and (most reluctantly) the Onondaga agreed to join in a confederacy. The tribes of the confederacy retained total independence in internal affairs, but "foreign relations" were to be conducted by a council composed of the chiefs of all the tribes. The confederacy was probably founded between 1400 and 1600.

Hiawatha, again according to legend, was also responsible for introducing wampum to the Mohawks and, through them, to the other tribes of the confederacy. Hiawatha persuaded the Mohawks to use monetary compensation, to be paid in wampum, instead of the blood feud to compensate the family of the victims of murder. This practice helped materially to reduce the murder rate among the Iroquois.

Iroquois society was matrilineal. The sachems, or tribal leaders, were selected by otianders, the matriarchs of the tribe. The organizational system of the Iroquois was the clan system, each of which had a natural figurehead, such as a wolf or an eagle. The strength of the clans was maintained through the practice of adoption; that is, Indians captured in war were adopted by the captor, becoming an integral member of the adopting clan.

The Mohawks were a very religious people, attributing success in the harvest or in warfare to the invisible spirits of nature. As agriculture spread among them, they began holding feasts to commemorate the harvest of squash, beans, and corn. The Green Corn Festival celebrated the corn harvest.

The Mohawks were the "Keepers of the Eastern Door of the Lodge" of the Iroquois Confederacy. As such, they were the first to become involved with the European settlers. They were allied with the Dutch and the English and were, except for brief intervals (especially during the first half of the eighteenth century), at war with the French in Canada. They aided the British during the American Revolution.

Following the American Revolution, the new American government concluded the Treaty of Fort Stanwix (1784) with the Mohawks. This treaty eliminated almost all Mohawk land claims in New York State, and most of the Mohawks retreated to Canada, where the British offered them a reservation on the Grand River. A few Mohawks remained in New York, many on the St. Regis Reservation along the shores of the St. Lawrence River.

In 1802, under pressure from the U.S. government, the Mohawks agreed to adopt a "democratic" system of government for the tribe, with first three, later twelve, elected "trustees." This system persists to this day, but alongside it has grown a revival of the old system under which tribal leaders are selected by the matriarchs of the tribe. The Mohawks have become known for their skills in high-rise steel construction, and many are employed in building modern skyscrapers.

Mohegan

CULTURE AREA: Northeast
LANGUAGE GROUP: Algonquian
PRIMARY LOCATION: Connecticut
POPULATION SIZE: 674 (1990 U.S. Census)

The Mohegans occupied the Thames River valley and its tributaries in Connecticut. Originally, they were part of the Pequot Nation, but they formed their own separate entity in the early seventeenth century. Their original name before the division, "Pequot," means "destroyers," while the name "Mohegan" means "wolf."

The Mohegan lived in palisaded villages, with bark houses clustered around an open area for games and gatherings. Women planted corn and beans, while men hunted deer and other wild game. Their chiefs were called "sachems."

No tribe in the Northeast has been the subject of so much confusion and so many differing interpretations as the Mohegan. Part of the confusion stems from James Fenimore Cooper's famed novel *The Last of the Mohicans*, published in 1826. The author was from New York, and he probably patterned his Indians after the Mahican of that region, an entirely separate tribe. Cooper spelled the name "Mohican," and the Connecticut Mohegan's name was sometimes spelled in that way. Cooper made the confusion worse by naming one of his characters "Uncas," the name of a real-life Mohegan subchief.

It was the sachem Uncas who led the Mohegans in their split with the Pequots. A figure of controversy, Uncas generally remained an ally of the English. In fact, the Mohegans joined the English in the Pequot War of 1637, a conflict that led to the virtual destruction of the Pequot tribe.

There is also some debate over when Uncas finally severed the Mohegan's connection with the Pequot. He married a daughter of Sassacus, a prominent Pequot chief, but a rebellion against Sassacus led to Uncas' defeat and banishment. The Mohegans escaped destruction in King Philip's War of 1675-1677, thanks largely to their alliance with the English. In 1721, the Mohegan still owned 4,000 acres of the Thames Valley, though it had been reduced to 2,300 by 1850.

The tribe entered into a long and steady decline. Some Mohegans left New England and settled in the Oneida region of New York, while others migrated to Wisconsin, where a small reservation was created in 1832.

In 1861, Connecticut took over many unoccupied Mohegan lands. Though descendants have scattered all over the country, the Mohegan never entirely abandoned their ancestral enclaves around Uncasville, Connecticut. The Uncasville region boasts a Mohegan church and the Fort Shantok Point burial grounds, where members of the tribe are interred. The Mohegans could not stand the pressure of the dominant white culture and eventually assimilated. Extensive intermarriage produced a population that is mainly of mixed ancestry.

Mojave

CULTURE AREA: Southwest
LANGUAGE GROUP: Yuman
PRIMARY LOCATION: Lower Colorado River
POPULATION SIZE: 1,386 (1990 U.S. Census)

The name Mojave comes from a native word meaning "three mountains." These people have lived along the lower Colorado River since the 1100's. The early people had sprawling encampments scattered throughout the valley near cultivable land, and their mud-covered houses were above the floodplain on low rises. Most of the year the Mojave slept under flat-topped shades (ramadas), using the houses in winter months.

The Mojave considered themselves one nation and one territory, regardless of the location of the residence. They had loosely defined bands and local groups. Warfare was common, and in war they presented a united front. The hereditary tribal chief was expected to look after the welfare of the tribe and exert a moral influence.

Farming was the principal occupation, and maize was the chief crop. Other products included beans, pumpkins, and melons. The diet was supplemented by fishing, hunting, and wild plants, especially the mesquite bean and screwbean. The men cleared the land, planted, and cultivated, while women did most of the harvesting. Soil fertility depended on the silt deposited by yearly flooding of the Colorado River.

Dreams were the most important part of the Mojave religion; it was believed that special skills, talents, and success in life depended on dreams. Ordinary dreams were considered to be omens; the few individuals who had great dreams became the leaders.

The traditional Mojave culture had mostly vanished by the early 1970's as the people became assimilated into American culture. Pride in tribal identity remained, but the old way of life had gone, the language was being forgotten, and much intermarriage had occurred. The last hereditary chief died in 1947.

The Colorado River Reservation, with 225,995 acres, was established in 1865, and Fort Mojave in 1880. In 1940, part of the reservation was taken for Parker Dam and its reservoir. The acreage in the early 1990's was 22,820. Both reservations are shared with other tribes. The present tribal offices are in Needles, California.

Mojave boy photographed around 1903.
(Library of Congress)

Molala

CULTURE AREA: Plateau
LANGUAGE GROUP: Molale (Penutian)
PRIMARY LOCATION: Oregon
POPULATION SIZE: 14 (Molala, 1990 U.S. Census)

The Molala (or Molale), a poorly recorded tribe, lived in the interior of Washington and Oregon. Their language, while related to that of the Cayuse, was quite distinct. Cayuse tradition suggests that the Molala once lived with them on the Deschutes River but that the two tribes were driven apart and to the west by hostile neighbors. "Molala" is the name of a creek in the Willamette Valley, which a Molala band occupied by joining with the Klikitat to drive out its former inhabitants. Other bands settled on the Umpqua and Rogue rivers to the north. The Molala were greatly feared because they raided neighboring tribes to capture people as slaves. In 1855, the Molala joined with a number of other Willamette Valley tribes in two treaties. They agreed to give up their lands and move with other small tribal groups to a reservation. Many moved to the Grande Ronde Reservation in Oregon, where they adopted European American clothing and customs. They intermarried freely with other tribes and were considered by official enumerators to have been absorbed by other tribes. In 1881, as many as twenty Molala were living outside the reservation in the Cascade Mountains. In 1964 the tribes of the reservation formed the Confederated Tribes of Grande Ronde. The 1990 U.S. Census listed the Grande Ronde tribal population as 1,230.

Moneton

CULTURE AREA: Northeast
LANGUAGE GROUP: Siouan
PRIMARY LOCATION: West Virginia

The Moneton, a branch of the Siouan family, lived in West Virginia. As is the case for many of the eastern Sioux, there is no information about the Moneton language. Evidence suggests they lived in matrilineal clans and that they conducted harsh initiation ceremonies. They wore long hair and tattoos—decorations which set them clearly apart from their Iroquoian neighbors. Probably the Sioux had been in what is now the southeastern United States for hundreds or even thousands of years before the first Europeans arrived. Scholars have struggled to learn about the prehistoric migrations of the Sioux, but without much success. What is clear from oral tradition and the records of early white settlers is that through the fifteenth, sixteenth, and seventeenth centuries the southeastern Sioux suffered greatly. Constant attack by Iroquoians and the introduction of new diseases by Europeans decimated the tribes. Many people fled and disappeared from record, while others were absorbed into other tribes; many died. In 1671, the Moneton were visited by the trader Thomas Batts. Three years later they were visited again by Gabriel Arthur, who reported finding them living in "a great town." They were not heard of again and are assumed to have united with Siouan groups in the Piedmont region of Virginia.

Montagnais

CULTURE AREA: Northeast
LANGUAGE GROUP: Algonquian (Cree)
PRIMARY LOCATION: Labrador Peninsula, Newfoundland, Quebec provinces
POPULATION SIZE: 12,025 (combined Montagnais/Naskapi population, Statistics Canada, based on 1991 census)

The Montagnais have resided north of the St. Lawrence River on the Labrador Peninsula since before Europeans arrived in North America. Living to their southwest is a culturally and linguistically related but distinct group, the Attikamek, who were decimated by smallpox and Iroquois warriors late in the seventeenth century and seem to have been confused with the Tête de Boule until the 1970's, when the Attikamek name was revived concurrent with rising Attikamek political awareness. Both the Montagnais and Attikamek lived by hunting, trapping, and fishing prior to the Europeans' arrival as well as by fur trading afterward. Both were organized in bands loosely tied by marriage and proximity and, in the seventeenth century, by the Iroquois threat. The Labrador Peninsula had abundant game, and the residents were well adapted to it, moving seasonally with what the environment provided. They transported themselves and supplies in canoes during summer and by snowshoes and toboggans in winter. The basic traveling unit was a band of three to four families (fifteen to twenty people), typically led by older men with practical knowledge or religious charisma rather than by a formal or elected chief. Band membership could easily change if a need arose. One effect of the advent of trading posts in the region was an evolution toward bands associating with trading posts and defining band hunting territories. Marriages became opportunities for alliances between families with neighboring hunting territories.

European influences on the Montagnais and Attikamek were limited primarily to the fur trade until the mid-nineteenth century, when the area was invaded by loggers, and the early twentieth century, when there was railroad and dam construction. White hunters and trappers, combined with the construction projects, reduced fur-bearing animals and forced Montagnais into wage employment, which, along with local schools, interrupted seasonal migrations. World War II drew away the loggers, opening jobs for residents of the Weymontachingue reserve. The traditional conical lodges housing fifteen to twenty people were replaced with prefabricated houses. Montagnais religious practices have been influenced by Christianity but still include the shaking tent rite, various feasts, and ceremonial drumming. Religion is very personal, with some individuals gaining considerable power and becoming shamans—men or women with especially close relations with spirits and able to influence people's health or success in hunting. Despite the increasing presence of non-Indians, the Montagnais and the Attikamek retain their identity.

Montauk Confederacy

TRIBES AFFECTED: Corchaug, Manhassett, Massapequa, Matinecock, Merric, Montauk, Nesaquake, Patchogue (Poospatuck), Rockaway, Secatogue, Setauket, Shinnecock, Unquachog
CULTURE AREA: Northeast
LANGUAGE GROUP: Algonquian
PRIMARY LOCATION: Central and eastern Long Island

The Montauk Confederacy was formed as a protective league against mainland tribes, primarily the Pequot and Narragansett. All of its member groups shared essentially the same culture patterns and language. Thus, they may have been loosely connected elements of one group or tribe. The Montauk were the most powerful and controlled the others. Montauk may mean "fortified place."

The Montauk subsisted on plant, land, and sea animals. Food cultivation required a complex and frequent pattern of seasonal shifting of residences, from the summer fields to the deep forests in the winter. A trade network linking regional and adjacent groups was also developed. Trading with Europeans began in the sixteenth century.

The tribes lived in villages of small circular houses holding two families during the temperate seasons. In winter they lived in large longhouses that held forty to fifty people. Villages were relocated when the supply of firewood was depleted.

Each village was presided over by a hereditary chief or sachem. Sachems had limited power and always made decisions in consultation with a council of "great men." Women also held respected positions. Quahawan, the sister of Nowedonah and Paygratasuck, Shinnecock and Manhassett sachems, became a Shinnecock sachem around 1667. The confederacy was presided over by the Montauk sachem, the grand sachem or great chief. Wyandanck (mid-seventeenth century), brother of the above three named sachems, was the most famous leader of the confederacy.

The confederacy population was about six thousand in 1600. Because of white diseases, alcoholism, and raids, numbers rapidly declined. Around 1788 most of the one hundred or so remaining members joined the Brotherton Indians in New York and moved with them to the Oneida reservation in Wisconsin about 1833. The handful of remaining Montauk and Shinnecock, the last representatives of the Long Island tribes, preserved tribal organization into the nineteenth century. Their last hereditary grand sachem, David Pharaoh, died about 1875. The old customs and native language were lost soon thereafter.

Limited hunting, fishing, crop cultivation, and sale of craft items on the 400-acre Shinnecock Reservation provided subsistence. Limited financial support from New York State and off-reservation, low-wage jobs provided additional income. The encroachment of suburbia and tourists wanting to see "real Indians" rekindled an interest in traditional tribal customs and dress, self-respect, and group pride beginning in the 1900's. Renewed interest in tribal incorporation occurred in the 1930's. Intertribal associations, such as the Algonquin Council of Indian Tribes (1926), were formed. The Shinnecock are represented by an elected council in their dealings with New York State.

Mountain

CULTURE AREA: Subarctic
LANGUAGE GROUP: Northeastern Athapaskan
PRIMARY LOCATION: Mackenzie Mountains, Northwest Territories, Canada

The Mountain Indians, commonly associated with the Goat Indians, lived in semi-permanent winter camps in the mountains. They depended on hunting moose, Dall sheep, woodland caribou—and trapping of ground squirrels—for subsistence and utilitarian by-products. Some fishing was done. Mooseskin boats were essential to river travel and trading, particularly after European Canadian contact. As a composite band, Mountain people had much knowledge of their terrain and good mobility. They sometimes faced starvation, which reduced their number, as did internal feuds and hostilities with the Yukon peoples.

Canadian trappers and traders knew of the Mountain Indians as early as 1789, but it was not until 1822 that they interacted with them. The building of Fort Simpson in 1822, and Fort Norman in 1823, brought sustained European contact and trading with many Mountain Indians. The introduction of influenza and measles reduced their population. The signing of Treaty 11 in 1921 created a chief and council who represented their people at Fort Norman. Most modern Mountain employment is local, with some involvement in Canadian government programs. The Mountain population has been estimated to be between 100 and 150.

Muckleshoot

CULTURE AREA: Northwest Coast
LANGUAGE GROUP: Salishan
PRIMARY LOCATION: White and Green rivers, Washington
POPULATION SIZE: 985 (1990 U.S. Census)

The Muckleshoot comprised four separate territorial groups: Sekamish, Skopamish, Smulkamis, and Dothliuk. They had complex ceremonialism, part of which regulated their yearly pattern of moving to obtain subsistence, which was basically maritime and riverine in orientation. They had guardian-spirit beliefs and used shamans for curing, making predictions, and maintaining social control. Decisions were by group consensus and advice of elders.

The Muckleshoot Reservation was established in 1857 by executive order after an 1855-1856 war, but many did not move to the reservation. In the early 1880's the Indian Shaker Church was established as a reaction against the U.S. government's "peace policy" of 1869, which had favored Roman Catholic missionaries among the Muckleshoot.

The modern Muckleshoot have established their own business enterprises, planning department, tribal government, and school system on the reservation. In the late 1970's the Muckleshoot sued for damages created by diversion of water from the reservation and its fishery by a hydroelectric plant. There exist several reservation programs for revitalizing myth, art, and language.

Multnomah

CULTURE AREA: Northwest Coast
LANGUAGE GROUP: Chinookan
PRIMARY LOCATION: Sauvie Island and Columbia River, Oregon

The Multnomah, living in a densely populated stretch of riverside villages, were composed of ten separate territorial bands, situated between the Clackamas to the south and the Cathlamet to the north. Their stratified society was based on ocean and river harvesting as well as hunting and trapping on land. They had well-developed trading relations within the region. Chinookan jargon was a lingua franca (trade language) on the Northwest Coast and along the Columbia River.

The first European American contact was probably by John Boit and Robert Gray in 1792, but by the time of first contact, the Multnomah population had already been drastically reduced by epidemics, particularly smallpox. Population reduction and the effects of trade created demographic changes for the Multnomah and other groups, causing the merging of certain groups. Some Multnomah lived on the Grande Ronde Reservation along with the Clackamas, and some lived off-reservation in the Willamette Valley.

Nabedache

CULTURE AREA: Southwest
LANGUAGE GROUP: Caddoan
PRIMARY LOCATION: Oklahoma

The Nabedache were the westernmost of the nine tribes of the Hasinai Confederacy in East Texas, linguistically related to the Caddo. Their homeland was west of the Neches River; they lived in scattered rancherias, farming and hunting.

During the two Spanish occupations (1690-1693 and 1716-1821), missions were established for the Nabedache. They refused to Hispanize, however, maintaining good but reserved relations with the Spanish. They retained their own culture and independence. Between the 1750's and 1799 the Nabedache were the dominant tribe among the Hasinai. Leaders Bigotes, or Sauto (to 1778), and Baltasar Bigotes (post-1778) interacted with the Spanish regarding French trade, war with the Apache, and relations with the Comanche and other tribes to the west. In 1800 they were faced with Indian and American encroachment and the effects of disease. Within seven years they were reduced to 120 people.

During the period of the Texas Republic (1836-1845), their fortunes waned further. They were forced into central Texas, where they faced hostile Comanche raiders and Texans. Under U.S. control after 1846, the Nabedache were removed to Oklahoma in 1859. The Nabedache survived the Civil War and, after 1870, entered a period of peace and stability. Today they are listed under Hasinai and Caddo but are governed by their own tribal government.

Nanticoke

CULTURE AREA: Northeast
LANGUAGE GROUP: Algonquian
PRIMARY LOCATION: Delaware, New Jersey
POPULATION SIZE: 1,471 (1990 U.S. Census)

The Nanticoke originally inhabited the eastern shore of Chesapeake Bay along the Nanticoke River in Maryland. Culturally, they were closely associated with surrounding Algonquian-speaking groups such as the Conoys. Unfortunately, only a few details survive about traditional lifeways. Men hunted and fished, and women practiced maize horticulture. The Nanticoke were adept at the production of shell beads for peake (wampum) and at the processing of furs. A hereditary chief ruled over several villages and, with elders, formed an upper social stratum. Individuals traced their ancestry through women. The Nanticoke buried their dead in ossuaries (mass graves) after lengthy interment in aboveground mortuary structures.

Sustained contact with white settlers began after 1608. By the early eighteenth century, the Nanticoke had suffered greatly from disease and from harassment by colonists. To lessen conflicts, they agreed to live on two reservations along the Nanticoke, known as Broad Creek and Chicacoan. This greatly reduced their territory and limited their ability to support themselves. During this period, the Nanticoke became tributaries of the powerful Five Nations of the Iroquois of New York.

By the mid-1700's, because of further interference by colonists, the Nanticoke petitioned the Iroquois for protection. Several hundred migrated to Iroquois territory in Pennsylvania before regrouping at Otsiningo, near present-day Binghamton, New York. By then, they had merged with the Conoys. After the American Revolution they moved west, finally settling in Oklahoma, where they became identified with and absorbed into the Delaware (Lenni Lenape) tribe.

By the 1760's, the Nanticokes who remained in Maryland had abandoned their land. In the succeeding years, they settled with members of local tribes on Indian River Hundred near Millsboro, Delaware. In 1903, after many attempts, they gained official recognition as Nanticoke Indians from the state. The formation of the Nanticoke Indian Association furthered tribal causes during the twentieth century. A separate organization, known as the Nanticoke-Lenni Lenape Indians of New Jersey, developed in 1978 near Bridgeton, New Jersey, where members of the two tribes had settled. Both organizations strive to preserve community history, revive traditional ways, and educate the public through museums and annual pow-wows.

Narragansett

CULTURE AREA: Northeast
LANGUAGE GROUP: Algonquian
PRIMARY LOCATION: Rhode Island
POPULATION SIZE: 2,456 (1990 U.S. Census)

The Narragansett were a powerful tribe of southern New England. They spoke an Algonquian language, and their territory encompassed much of present-day Rhode Island. Recent estimates suggest that there may have been as many as sixteen thousand Narragansetts in 1600. The name "Narragansett" is usually translated "at the narrow point of land."

Narragansett culture and lifeways were similar to those of other tribes in the region. They were adept at agriculture, regularly planting corn, beans, squash, and sunflowers. The diet was supplemented by hunting and trapping. The wigwam, a circular shelter of bent poles covered with bark, was the typical dwelling.

Sachems (chiefs) wielded authority in Narragansett society, aided by councilors, usually warriors of distinction. Powpows were also important, healers with great spiritual powers. First white contact came with Giovanni da Verrazano in 1524, though permanent white settlement did not come until a century later.

In 1616-1617, a devastating plague (probably smallpox) decimated neighboring tribes, but the Narragansett were spared. The Narragansett warred with their neighbors and dominated such tribes as the Wampanoags. In 1633 the plague, long delayed, finally struck the Narragansett, killing at least seven hundred.

White-Narragansett relations were cordial at first; Rhode Island founder Roger Williams championed Indian land rights. Yet though the Narragansett helped the English in the Pequot War of 1637, the colonists were suspicious of their allies; they were also hungry for more land.

When King Philip's War broke out in 1675, the Narragansett maintained neutrality, though they sheltered Wampanoag women and children. When the English demanded the surrender of the Wampanoag fugitives, Narragansett sachem Canonchet refused. The English assembled the largest colonial army up to that time—a thousand men—and launched a surprise attack on the Narragansett. On December 19, 1675, the English assaulted a large Narragansett fort near present-day Kingston, Rhode Island. The resulting battle, called the Great Swamp Fight, was one of the bloodiest of the war. At least six hundred Narragansett were killed, and three hundred were taken prisoner. Most of the Indian casualties were women and children.

King Philip's War destroyed the Narragansett as a distinct tribal entity. Some survivors joined the Niantic, and in time the combination was called Narragansett. A reservation was established in Rhode Island. In the eighteenth and nineteenth centuries, assimilation seemed the only alternative to extinction. The last full-blooded Narragansett died in the nineteenth century, and the language died out about that time as well.

In 1880, the Narragansett were detribalized and their reservation sold. Though the remaining people were of mixed Indian-white-black blood, and the culture was virtually dead, some measure of Narragansett identity survived. Beginning in the 1920's, pan-Indianism caused the embers of the Narragansett heritage to flare again.

The culture was revived, and activists such as Ella Thomas Sekatau and Eric Thomas Sekatau managed to secure federal recognition of the tribe in 1983. In 1978, as part of the Rhode Island Indian Claims settlement, the state gave the Narragansett 1,800 acres of wooded public and private land that was once part of tribal territory. Every year, the tribe holds an Annual August Meeting.

Naskapi

CULTURE AREA: Subarctic
LANGUAGE GROUP: Algonquian
PRIMARY LOCATION: Labrador Peninsula
POPULATION SIZE: 12,025 (combined Montagnais/Naskapi population, Statistics Canada, based on 1991 census)

The Naskapi, closely associated with the East Cree and Montagnais, lived in semipermanent winter villages in rectangular, split-log lodges. During the rest of the year, temporary hide-covered conical dwellings were used during the subsistence round, which focused upon hunting and trapping caribou, moose, and Dall's sheep. Nearly every species of bird was also hunted. Watercraft were usually made of birchbark, although some moose-skin boats were utilized, mostly for load transportation.

The first sustained European Canadian contact was with the trapper-traders of the Hudson's Bay Company, who introduced considerable change to aboriginal settlement patterns, subsistence orientation, and eventually to the Naskapi religion. The once highly mobile Naskapi developed ties to trading posts and became dependent on the exchange of furs for trade goods.

The traditional self-sufficient Naskapi culture no longer exists; Naskapis are dependent on the European Canadian market economy, and most earn a living by wage employment. They are served by government schools and health programs.

Natchez

CULTURE AREA: Southeast
LANGUAGE GROUP: Natchez
PRIMARY LOCATION: Natchez, Mississippi
POPULATION SIZE: 98 (1990 U.S. Census)

Natchez social complexity fascinated early explorers of the Mississippi River as well as later ethnographers and archaeologists. For this reason, much has been written on these Native Americans.

The Natchez occupied an area east of the Mississippi River, centered at modern Natchez, Mississippi. They raised corn, beans, squash, and other crops in addition to hunting, fishing, and gathering wild plants. The agricultural surplus permitted a sedentary lifestyle, and their villages impressed European visitors, as did the lavish material culture, both of which were complemented by an elaborate sociopolitical system. Natchez social organization was hierarchical, with numerous low-level positions overseen by the tribal leader, known as the Great Sun. The Great Sun controlled events during peaceful times; however, he relinquished command to a male relative (brother or uncle) in times of war. These ruling titles were inherited, and visitors remarked upon the elaborate funerary rituals (including human sacrifice and burial in mounds) which accompanied the death of one of the leaders.

European contact was initiated with René-Robert Cavelier, Sieur de La Salle's visit of 1682. By the early 1700's, a French priest was residing in their midst (Jean François Buisson de Saint-Cosme, who was later killed by the Chitimacha), and they received regular visits from Jesuits and other dignitaries, such as Pierre LeMoyne, Sieur d'Iberville in 1700, and Penicaut in 1704, all of whom wrote of their experiences. By 1713, a French trading post was established among the Natchez. After some minor social unrest, Fort Rosalie was constructed in approximately 1716 to demonstrate French dominion.

During the mid-1720's, two minor uprisings occurred among the Natchez. In both cases, the French overpowered them and reinforced their control. The major Natchez Revolt of 1729, however, resulted in many deaths among both the French and the Natchez, and this sealed the fate of the remaining Natchez; the French were determined to quell the insurrection forcefully. By 1731, approximately four hundred Natchez were enslaved and sent to the Caribbean colonies, while the remainder escaped to seek refuge among the Chickasaw, some ultimately joining the Creek or the Cherokee. Ultimately, the remaining Natchez took part in the enforced migrations of 1830-1839 known as the Trail of Tears. The last speakers of the Natchez language died in the 1940's in Oklahoma. In 1990, fewer than one hundred people identified themselves as Natchez.

Nauset

CULTURE AREA: Northeast
LANGUAGE GROUP: Algonquian
PRIMARY LOCATION: Cape Cod, Massachusetts

The Nauset, a branch of the Algonquian family, lived on Cape Cod in Massachusetts. The meaning of their name is not known; they were also commonly known as Cape Indians. They were related to or controlled by the Wampanoag ("eastern people"). Evidence suggests they had lived in the area for thousands of years. Because of their coastal location, they probably came into contact with white traders and navigators very early. In 1614, seven Nauset were kidnapped and sold into slavery by Captain Thomas Hunt of England. They were also visited early in the century by the French explorer Samuel de Champlain.

For the most part, the Nauset were friendly with English settlers in the area, and many adopted Christianity. Most stayed friendly even through King Philip's War between the settlers and Indians, and some went so far as to aid the white settlers. The Nauset lived in permanent villages and ate a diet of fish and seafood as well as maize, beans, and pumpkins. They cooked food in clay pots, stirred it with wooden utensils, and created beautiful woven fabrics and leather goods. In 1622, the Nauset shared corn and beans with starving Plymouth colonists. In 1617, they escaped the great pestilence that killed many Indians along the East Coast, but around 1710 they lost many people to fever. By 1802, only two Nauset were still alive.

Navajo

CULTURE AREA: Southwest
LANGUAGE GROUP: Athapaskan
PRIMARY LOCATION: Northeastern Arizona, northwestern New Mexico, southern Utah
POPULATION SIZE: 219,198 (1990 U.S. Census)

There has been disagreement among scholars regarding when the ancient ancestors of the Navajo (or Navaho) migrated to North America. Some believe that they came in a relatively recent migration across the Bering Strait, about three thousand years ago. The linguistic designation of the main group is Na-Dene. This grouping contains several subgroups, the largest of which is Athapaskan. These hunting and gathering peoples, who once occupied Alaska and northwestern Canada, also began moving south. How and why the Athapaskans migrated into the Southwest is still a matter of discussion among scholars. As they did, they called themselves Diné (the people). The Navajo and their linguistic cousins, the Apache, reached the Southwest sometime in the mid-fourteenth century, with the Navajo occupying the area of the Gobernador and Largo tributaries of the San Juan River some 75 miles north of Santa Fe. This became the traditional homeland, the *Dinetah*, which means "among the people" in the Navajo language.

Prehistory. Anthropologists have pointed out a major difference between the Puebloans and the Navajo in prehistory. By the time the Navajo arrived in the Southwest, the Puebloans had been there for centuries and were firmly committed to the traditions of their ancestors, one of which was putting the good of the group or village as a whole above that of the individual. The Navajo, on the other hand, considered the individual to be of primary importance. They were also not as resistant to change as the Puebloans were.

The first Navajo in the Southwest were organized into fairly small groups, each with a headman whose duties consisted of leading his people to places where water, game, and wild grains and berries were plentiful. As they tended to move with the seasons, following the game, they built semipermanent circular wooden dwellings called hogans. Excavation of several prehistoric hogan sites has established that the Navajo were in the area at least as early as 1540.

Most scholars agree that the Navajo were greatly influenced by the culture of the Puebloans, which they recognized as more advanced than their own. Many Navajo myths and folk tales portray the Puebloans as sophisticated, rich, and powerful. Apparently, the Navajo were especially impressed by Pueblo religion and the complexity and power of its ceremonials, which surpassed anything in their own culture at the time. Their first rudimentary efforts at agriculture were also inspired by the Puebloans.

Manuelito, who led the Navajo fight against U.S. forces during the 1860's and later became a leader on the newly created reservation. (National Archives)

The Spanish-Mexican Period. The first Spanish colonists in northern New Mexico, who came with Don Juan de Oñate in 1598, recorded that many raids on their settlements were carried out by "Apache or Apachean" peoples. In 1626, Fray Zárata Salmerón was the first to designate the Navajo as a specific Apachean group. By this time the Navajo had become a large and powerful tribe, whose various bands were led by both war and peace chieftains. They traded with and raided both the Puebloans and the Spanish settlers equally. As the numbers of the Spanish colonists increased, they became more demanding and cruel, especially to the Puebloans, attacking and burning the pueblos and killing or enslaving the people. As a consequence, the Puebloans began to encourage Navajo and Apache raids on the Spanish. By the mid-seventeenth century, the Spanish effort to convert all the Indians to Christianity had driven both the Puebloans and Navajo to conduct their own religious rituals in secret.

Navajo-Pueblo Contact. After the Pueblo Revolt of 1680 and the Spanish reconquest of 1692, many Puebloans fled north to the San Juan River area, which brought about greater contact with the Navajo. It has been established that, as a result of this interaction, the Navajo continued to learn much from the Puebloans: more sophisticated agricultural practices, styles of architecture, manufacturing techniques, and art forms such as weaving and improved pottery-making. Pueblo and Navajo ceremonial articles have been found in the same caches in the upper San Juan, establishing that Navajo religious practices were also greatly influenced by the Puebloans.

In the last decade of the seventeenth century, in the upper reaches of the San Juan, the Navajo and some of the Pueblo refugees built both open clusters of hogans and small masonry pueblos (*pueblitos*) consisting of fewer than six rooms each. Then, moving south into the Gobernador and Largo canyons, they built large masonry compounds and pueblitos, where they lived by hunting and gathering, herding, and dry farming. By the end of the century, they had acquired horses, cattle, sheep, and goats by trading with or raiding the Spaniards. In the next fifty years or so, they moved into Chaco Canyon and the Big Bead Mesa area, and then into Canyon de Chelly in northeastern Arizona.

Although the first bands of Navajo to reach the Southwest had been patrilineal, the close contact with the Puebloans in the late seventeenth century led the Navajo to adopt a matrilineal system of descent, with matrilocal residence, a characteristic they have retained into the modern period. The Navajo also adapted the Puebloan idea of clans into their own cultural pattern.

1700-1845. Throughout the eighteenth century, the Navajo continued their raids on Spanish communities and the Puebloans in the Rio Grande Valley, greatly aided by their acquisition of the horse. As many scholars have pointed out, the Navajo considered these raids to be an economic pursuit rather than war, and they were therefore never as anxious to drive the Spanish out as the Puebloans were. Although the Navajo in the Mount Taylor region rejected the Spanish attempt of 1745 to establish missions among them, for example, they remained friendly to the Spanish. On the other hand, Spanish and Mexican reports on the Navajo in the eighteenth and early nineteenth centuries were contained largely in official government documents and therefore dealt mostly with warfare, describing countless Navajo raids and Spanish or Mexican reprisals.

The fact that the horse gave the Navajo greater mobility, increasing their range for hunting, raiding, and trading, has led some to think that the Navajo reverted to nomadism, which was not the case at all. The horse made the Navajo more mobile, but that mobility was confined, in almost all cases, to specific areas where a family might build one or more houses which would serve as fixed centers of family life. With these centers as a permanent base, some family members might follow the sheep herds from their summer to winter grazing lands or go off to hunt or trade while others remained behind to tend the crops. The fact that clan names are almost always place names as well also reinforces the fact that Navajo nomadism in the historic period is largely a myth.

Sheep and goats were also important to the growth of the Navajo population, providing not only a more dependable food supply but also a renewable source of trade goods, such as raw wool and woolen textiles, that could be exchanged for other necessities.

The U.S. Period. When the United States took possession of the southwestern territories from Mexico in 1846, General S. W. Kearny, arriving with his armies in August of that year, declared that he would stop all Indian raids. After a military expedition against the Navajo in November, 1846, Colonel A. W. Doniphan signed a treaty with thirteen Navajo leaders, among whom were Zarcillos Largos, Antonio Sandoval, and Narbono. This was only the first of many treaties into which the United States entered with local headmen in the mistaken belief that they were tribal "chiefs" who could speak for the entire Navajo Nation. Thus, when these treaties were broken by Navajo from groups not led by the signers, United States authorities, completely misunderstanding Navajo social and political organization, concluded that the Navajo were without honor and could not be trusted. In an attempt to control the Navajo, the United States mounted numerous campaigns against them and built military posts in their territory.

With the outbreak of the Civil War in 1861 and the resultant decrease in U.S. troop strength in the Southwest, both the Navajo and Apache took advantage of the opportunity to increase their raids on settlers and Puebloans. The government reacted by adopting a merciless policy of resettlement developed by General James Carleton. In June, 1863, Colonel Kit

Carson was sent into Navajo country to order the Navajo to surrender at Fort Defiance in Arizona. Many fled and were pursued, and many were killed in the fighting which followed. In the end, however, Carson did not subdue the Navajo by military actions but by destroying their crops and livestock, the economic basis of their lives. Finally, on March 6, 1864, twenty-four hundred people, thirty wagons, four hundred horses, and three thousand sheep and goats began the "Long Walk" of 300 miles to Fort Sumner in eastern New Mexico. In April, thirty-five hundred more Navajo were forced to make the same trek. Ultimately, more than eight thousand Navajo and four hundred Mescalero Apache were held in captivity at Bosque Redondo Reservation, just outside the fort. Several thousand Navajo avoided capture by hiding in the Grand Canyon, on the top of Black Mesa, north of the San Juan River, and in other inaccessible areas of Navajo country.

The Return Home. Now totally impoverished and not understanding their group captivity and the loss of their freedom to roam where they pleased, the Navajo suffered greatly from humiliation and homesickness, illness from an alien diet and bad water, and new diseases caught from their captors. Many died.

Finally, the United States government admitted that the resettlement had been a horrible mistake, and Carleton's despotic regime was ended in the fall of 1866. Custody of the Navajo was given to the Bureau of Indian Affairs in January of 1867. Late in 1868, after the signing of a treaty which created a 3.5-million-acre reservation for the Navajo within their old territory, they were allowed to return home. Although this was only a small part of their previous holdings, the Navajo were happy to be going back. They soon found that their troubles were far from over, however, as they struggled to make a living in a land that had been devastated by Carleton and Carson. All their homes had been razed, they had no livestock, and their fields had been destroyed. Fort Wingate and Fort Defiance served as distribution centers for the rations which the government eventually agreed to issue to help them, but there were many delays and shortages.

More stable conditions were finally established, however, and the Navajo enjoyed a short period of prosperity and growth. About 1870, the first schools promised in the Treaty of 1868 were established, although with mixed results. Some of these boarding schools were run more like reformatories than schools and produced graduates who were prepared neither for life in white society nor life back on the reservation. In the 1880's, the building of the railroad across New Mexico and Arizona brought new problems to the Navajo in the form of liquor, diseases, and economic exploitation. They were forced to give up much of their best range land and water to the railroads in exchange for less desirable areas. Since 1868, the most persistent factor of Navajo life has been the struggle with whites for land. From time to time, the Navajo reservation has been extended, from the original 3.5 million acres to about 15 million acres located in an area bounded on the northeast by the Continental Divide, on the southeast by the Rio Puerco, on the south by the San Jose and Puerco rivers, on the west by the Little Colorado and Colorado rivers, and on the north by the San Juan River. The area contains more spectacular scenery than good farming and grazing land; thus, increases in land holdings have never kept pace with the needs of the people, who depend upon sheep and cattle as the basis of their economy.

The Twentieth Century. The Navajo population increased from an estimated twelve thousand to thirty-five thousand by 1930, the beginning of the so-called stock reduction period. (The first attempts at stock reduction had actually begun in the 1920's, when the Navajo were told that they would not be given new grazing lands through congressional approval of boundary extensions until they had reduced the number of horses on the reservation.) In 1930, Indian Service foresters reported that the Navajo range was seriously overgrazed and that land erosion was an immediate problem. When the government instituted a stock reduction program, the Navajo equated it with the destruction of their culture because it affected not only their economic life but also their religious life. Sheep were essential to their entire ceremonial process, being used to pay the medicine men and to feed the large crowds who assembled for many days at a time for each ceremonial. Navajo resistance to and governmental insistence upon stock reduction caused additional misunderstanding and bitterness between the Navajo and non-Indians for many years.

The twentieth century has also seen the discovery of oil, uranium, and coal on the Navajo Reservation. It was the discovery of this mineral wealth that prompted the creation of the Navajo Tribal Council in 1938 as a major governing body authorized to decide how these new resources could be put to the best use. Prior to that, the only entity that represented the interest of all the Navajo was the Business Council, which first met in 1923. The Business Council consisted of three influential men, including Henry Chee Dodge. Dodge, an intelligent, well-educated man with great leadership abilities, helped guide the Navajo for more than seventy years.

As many scholars have observed, World War II marked the beginning of the modern Navajo world. As thousands of Navajo who served in the armed forces or were recruited to work in defense industries were exposed to life beyond the reservation for the first time, they realized that formal education and more consistent economic development were necessary for their survival. Consequently, they built a system of public schools across the Navajo Nation and, utilizing funds from the Navajo-Hopi Long Range Rehabilitation Program, provided highways and other programs to improve their economic development. Their industrial and commercial enterprises include those involving the arts and crafts; timber, oil, and gas production; power plants, and a parks and recreation department with a corps of Navajo Rangers. The center of their tribal government is housed in an attractive complex of buildings in Window Rock, Arizona.

Until recently, the Navajo did not live in groups large enough to be called villages or towns; they settled in smaller family groups in desirable locations dispersed throughout the reservation. In their matrilineal society, the grandmother is the central person in the family, and the children belong to her clan. Since it is taboo for a Navajo man to look upon or socialize with his mother-in-law, a woman and her husband do not live with the wife's mother but have their home nearby so that mother, daughter, and grandchildren can spend much time together. The typical Navajo dwelling is still the hogan, which is round or hexagonal and built of logs and adobe, with an air vent in the center of the roof.

Navajo mother and child photographed by Ansel Adams at Canyon de Chelly, Arizona.
(National Archives)

Among the Navajo, ownership of property is individual, so that wife and husband have their own to do with as they choose. The wife usually owns the house and has her own crops and livestock, which she and the children tend. Additionally, the money she makes from her pottery and weaving is hers to keep. The husband has income from his own livestock and crops, plus whatever money he earns from his jewelry making or any other kinds of employment. It is he who represents the family at ceremonials and other public functions.

Weaving and Silversmithing. Traditionally, it is the women who make the pottery and weave the textiles. The earliest Navajo weavings were woolen wearing blankets, made on an upright loom which was adapted from one used by the Puebloans to weave their own cotton textiles. After the establishment of trading posts on the reservation in the early 1870's, the traders persuaded the Navajo to weave heavier textiles which could serve as rugs, having discovered that there was a market for these in the eastern United States. At the time, Turkish carpets were very popular with eastern buyers but were fairly expensive, so Turkish designs had been reproduced on linoleum—a less costly floor covering. Each trader provided the weavers in his area with samples of different Turkish designs on linoleum, declaring that he would henceforth buy nothing from them but rugs woven in these patterns. The Navajo weavers made their own adaptations from these designs, which have since evolved into the beautiful and exquisite Navajo rug of the present day.

Navajo men have always excelled in silversmithing and have led the way in the overall development of this art in the Southwest. The first smith was Atsidi Sani, who learned to work iron from a Mexican smith around 1850. He made knife blades, bits, and bridles, which he sold to earn his living. During the Bosque Redondo captivity, he taught other Navajo to work with iron, copper, and brass. After returning home, Atsidi Sani learned to work silver from the same Mexican smith and then taught his sons and other Navajo. The forms and the decorative styles originated by the Navajo have been adopted by other tribes, but Navajo silver has remained the most widely known and is the badge of distinction among the Navajo themselves.

LouAnn Faris Culley

Bibliography

Bahr, Howard M., and J. Lee Correll, comps. *Dine Bibliography to the 1990s: A Companion to the Navajo Bibliography of 1969.* Lanham, Md.: Scarecrow Press, 1999.

Bial, Raymond. *The Navajo.* New York: Benchmark Books, 1999.

Dutton, Bertha P. *American Indians of the Southwest*. Rev. ed. Albuquerque: University of New Mexico Press, 1983. An authoritative introduction to the subject, this book covers the history, contemporary tribal affairs, cultural and social characteristics, and arts and crafts of each group in the Southwest.

Dyk, Walter. *Son of Old Man Hat: A Navajo Autobiography*. New York: Harcourt, Brace, 1938. The classic autobiography of a Navajo from childhood to maturity in the late 1880's. The narration is chronological and vivid, recording a Navajo's relations with his kinsmen in daily life, his marriage, his accumulation of property in sheep, cattle, and horses, and the importance of religion and ceremonies in his life.

Faris, James C. *Navajo and Photography: A Critical History of the Representation of an American People*. Albuquerque: University of New Mexico Press, 1996.

Halpern, Katherine S., and Susan B. McGreevy, eds. *Washington Matthews: Studies of Navajo Culture, 1880-1894*. Albuquerque: University of New Mexico Press, 1997.

Howard, Cheryl. *Navajo Tribal Demography, 1983-1986: A Comparative and Historical Perspective*. New York: Garland, 1993.

Kluckhohn, Clyde, and Dorothea Leighton. *The Navaho*. Cambridge, Mass.: Harvard University Press, 1974. In a thorough and readable manner, the authors consider four aspects of Navajo life: history, economic situation, cultural heritage, and social structure.

Levy, Jerrold E. *In the Beginning: The Navajo Genesis*. Berkeley: University of California Press, 1998.

McPherson, Robert S. *The Northern Navajo Frontier, 1860-1900: Expansion Through Adversity*. Albuquerque: University of New Mexico Press, 1988. A well-documented and thorough study of the history of the northern Navajo frontier. This is an aspect of Navajo development which has been passed over by most scholars in their study of the Navajo.

Page, Susanne, and Jake Page. *Navajo*. New York: Harry N. Abrams, 1995.

Towner, Ronald H. *The Archaeology of Navajo Origins*. Salt Lake City: University of Utah Press, 1996.

Trennert, Robert A. *White Man's Medicine: Government Doctors and the Navajo, 1863-1955*. Albuquerque: University of New Mexico Press, 1998.

Underhill, Ruth M. *The Navajos*. Norman: University of Oklahoma Press, 1967. Underhill, professor emeritus of anthropology at Denver University, was associated with the United States Indian Service for thirteen years. Her book offers many insights into the history and rich cultural background of the Navajo.

Neutral

CULTURE AREA: Northeast
LANGUAGE GROUP: Iroquoian
PRIMARY LOCATION: West of Lake Ontario

A large sedentary tribe occupying palisaded villages north of Lake Erie and west of Lake Ontario in the early 1600's, the Neutral tribe was closely related to the Huron and other Iroquoian tribes. Like these other tribes, they were organized into matrilineal clans and lived matrilocally in female-headed, extended-family longhouses and had an economy based on tobacco, corn, beans, and squash. These crops were produced by the women; men hunted and fished to round out this healthy diet. There were about fifteen thousand Neutral people by the early 1600's. A major economic boon to these people was their monopoly on a regional supply of flint near Lake Erie. Perhaps because of this singular access to an important trade commodity, they remained neutral in the rivalry between the Hurons and the Iroquois, hence the name given to them by the French. The Hurons called them Attiwandaron, or "people who speak a language slightly different from ours."

Despite their monopoly on an important trade item, the Neutrals were prevented from trading directly with the French by the Hurons, who wanted to preserve their middleman role between tribes to their west and the French. In addition, despite the Neutrals' neutrality in the battle for control of trade between the Hurons and the Iroquois, the Iroquois attacked and destroyed them as a nation along with the Huron, Erie, and Tobacco tribes in 1650-1651. A few Neutrals survived as refugees along with the Hurons in the area around Lake Huron (later migrating to Quebec), but most were absorbed into Iroquois tribes by being adopted into Iroquois families by clan mothers.

Nez Perce

CULTURE AREA: Plateau
LANGUAGE GROUP: Sahaptin (in Sahaptian language family)
PRIMARY LOCATION: Idaho
POPULATION SIZE: 4,113 (1990 U.S. Census)

Nez Perce is the French name (meaning "pierced nose") for one of the Sahaptin tribes located in what became Idaho. The term seems to be a misnomer, since few if any members of this Native American tribe actually pierced their noses.

The Nez Perce were the largest and most powerful component of the Sahaptin. "Sahaptin" (also spelled Shahaptin) is a collective term for a group of Indian tribes that share linguistic commonalities. All Sahaptian languages are of Penutian stock. The Sahaptin, as a collective group, inhabited an area which later became southeastern Washington, west-central Idaho, and northeastern Oregon. The Sahaptin may be divided into two major groupings, the western tribes (Molala, Tenino, and Yakima), and the eastern tribes (Nez Perce, Palouse, Cayuse, and Umatilla). The eastern and western groups differ culturally. The western Sahaptin constitute a loose tribal confederation and are generally pacifistic. The eastern tribes marry intertribally, share stronger intertribal relations, and tend to be more warlike than their western counterparts.

The Nez Perce themselves originally thrived along the lower Snake River and along its tributaries in what is now central and western Idaho, northwestern Oregon, and southeastern Washington. The staple food of the Nez Perce was dried salmon and other fish, as the Columbia River is the greatest producer of freshwater salmon in the world. In addition, their diet consisted of berries, roots, and small game, as well as deer and elk. Housing consisted of both square houses and long A-frame communal sleeping rooms that could house up to thirty families and were approximately 150 feet in length. This living style, in addition to other customs and conventions of the Nez Perce, was influenced by the Plains Indians; the Nez Perce were one of the easternmost Sahaptin tribes.

During the eighteenth century the Nez Perce became more involved in intertribal affairs, including wars with Plains tribes. This was attributable especially to the introduction of the horse around 1730. As a result, the Nez Perce participated in more distant hunting expeditions and in trade with Plains tribes beyond the Rockies. Frequently, the Nez Perce allied themselves with such groups as other Sahaptin tribes and the Umatilla, Cayuse, Walla Walla, Flathead, Spokane, and Coeur d'Alene. At various times, the enemies of the Nez Perce included the Blackfoot, Shoshone, Bannock, Crow, and Gros Ventre. Along with a greater frequency of warfare there were ushered in subsequent cultural adaptations such as war dances, equine tactics and maneuvers, and the introduction of the tipi.

The Nez Perce are particularly known for their selective breeding of horses to produce better stock. This resulted in raids upon the Nez Perce from Plains tribes so that they could improve their own herds. This selective

Joseph the Younger was chief of the Nez Perce during the turbulent 1870's, when he tried to lead his people to Canada to avoid confinement on a U.S. reservation.
(National Archives)

breeding facilitated more distant intertribal relations of which the Nez Perce became a dominating force.

The first contact with European explorers and settlers in the early nineteenth century evidently affected the Nez Perce. Shortly after the expeditions of Meriwether Lewis and William Clark between 1810-1815, traders and fur trappers flocked to the region of the Nez Perce. Later, missionaries began their influx. During the 1820's and 1830's, the Nez Perce themselves engaged in fur trading. This prolonged contact with foreigners contributed to epidemics among the Nez Perce, whose numbers dropped to under two thousand by 1850. This was a marked reduction in population compared with the early nineteenth century census yielding a population estimate of six thousand for the Nez Perce.

In 1855 the Nez Perce, along with other Sahaptin tribes, were pressured to sign a treaty which entitled them to a reservation consisting of various parts of their former ancestral land. Several reservations were formed for the Sahaptin peoples: Nez Perce Reservation, Colville Reservation, Yakin Reservation, Umatilla Reservation, and Warm Springs Reservation, plus other smaller reservations. Tribes were frequently broken up and collected indiscriminately when placed on reservations. It is difficult to distinguish among modern Sahaptin tribal groups or determine the ancestral traditions that were original to each.

The Nez Perce condition considerably worsened in 1860 with the discovery of gold in the Salmon and Clearwater rivers. This event led to a redrawing of reservation boundaries in 1863 by U.S. commissioners. With the loss of the Wallowa and Grande valleys, the acreage of the Nez Perce Reservation was reduced by an estimated three-fourths. There was an enormous influx of miners, settlers, and homesteaders into the area.

A period of increasing hostility and intolerance culminated in the Nez Perce War of 1877. A militant band of Nez Perce—numbering between 250 and 450—led by Chief Joseph and Looking Glass resisted U.S. Army attempts to force them onto reservation land. The Nez Perce resistance held off five thousand U.S. military troops, headed by General Oliver O. Howard, for five months. On October 5, 1877, Chief Joseph surrendered to the U.S. forces, with each side having suffered approximately 250 casualties. The 1877 surrender took place near the Montana-Canada border. The Nez Perce were subsequently sent to the Indian Territory of Oklahoma, where many perished from malaria.

In the 1970's the Nez Perce Reservation in Idaho consisted of a total population of fifteen hundred to seventeen hundred. The reservation comprised 34,000 acres of tribal land and 53,000 acres of land for individual use. Many of the surviving Nez Perce have left the Idaho reservation to join the general U.S. populace. On the reservation, cultural traditions such as ceremonial dances and ceremonies of the Seven Drums Society are still observed. As mentioned above, the existing reservations containing Sahaptin peoples are somewhat syncretized, since many tribes were incorporated by force into the various reservations, not necessarily according to tribal distinctions.

Daniel L. Smith-Christopher

Bibliography

Hampton, Bruce. *Children of Grace: The Nez Perce War of 1877*. New York: Henry Holt, 1994.

James, Caroline. *Nez Perce Women in Transition, 1877-1990*. Moscow: University of Idaho Press, 1996.

Lavender, David S. *Let Me Be Free: The Nez Perce Tragedy*. New York: HarperCollins, 1992.

Moeller, Bill, and Jan Moeller. *Chief Joseph and the Nez Perces: A Photographic History*. Missoula, Mont.: Mountain Press, 1995.

Stadius, Martin. *Dreamers: On the Trail of the Nez Perce*. Caldwell, Idaho: Caxton Press, 1999.

U.S. National Park Service. Division of Publications. *Nez Perce Country*. Washington, D.C.: U.S. Department of the Interior, 1983.

Walker, Deward E. *Nez Perce Coyote Tales: The Myth Cycle*. Norman: University of Oklahoma Press, 1998.

Niantic

Culture area: Northeast
Language group: Algonquian
Primary location: Connecticut, Rhode Island

The Niantic, a branch of the Algonquian family, lived on the coasts of Rhode Island and Connecticut. Their name means "at a point of land on an estuary." Evidence suggests they had lived in the area for thousands of years. They lived in permanent villages and ate a diet of fish and seafood as well as maize, beans, and pumpkins. They cooked food in clay pots, stirring it with wooden utensils, and created beautiful woven fabrics, splint baskets, and leather goods. Their houses, called wigwams, were made on a bent and lashed pole framework; in later years they often included European furniture. During the sixteenth century, the tribe was divided into the Eastern

Niantic and the Western Niantic by a series of Pequot attacks. The Western Niantic, who numbered about 600 in 1600, lived on the coast between the Connecticut River and Niantic Bay. This land was much desired by white settlers, who continually tried to take it. After their population was decimated by a series of epidemics in 1616-1619, the Western Niantic were all but wiped out by the Pequot War in 1637. Those who survived became subjects of the Mohegan. Since the nineteenth century, no one has claimed Western Niantic as his or her tribal identity. The Eastern Niantic merged with the Narragansett in the 1670's. Population counts after the merger treated the two tribes as one group.

Nipissing

CULTURE AREA: Northeast
LANGUAGE GROUP: Algonquian
PRIMARY LOCATION: Ontario

The Nipissing, a branch of the Algonquian family, were so named because the French found them in 1613 living on the shores of Lake Nipissing in Ontario, Canada. The name means "little-water people." From the first contact with French missionaries, the Nipissing were friendly with them. They accepted Christianity but without giving up their traditional shamanism. They had steady contact with British traders after 1610 but remained allies of the French through the French and Indian War. The Nipissing lived in permanent villages along the lake, traveling throughout the fall to gather food. They grew a few crops, but fished in southern waters and traded with Cree neighbors to the north. Chiefs were elected from a group of eligible males. The Nipissing had great skill as jugglers. Reliable population counts are unavailable. Their numbers were small through recorded history. Many were killed by Iroquois attackers in the middle of the seventeenth century, and at various times groups moved away and disappeared from record. In the late nineteenth century, the last known group of Nipissing were living with other Algonquians at Lake of Two Mountains in Quebec. When the church and its records burned in 1877, the last register of Nipissing families was destroyed. Probably Nipissing descendants are included among recent counts for other tribes, but no separate population figures for the Nipissing are recorded.

Nipmuck

CULTURE AREA: Northeast
LANGUAGE GROUP: Eastern Algonquian
PRIMARY LOCATION: Central Massachusetts
POPULATION SIZE: 376 (1990 U.S. Census)

The Nipmucks relied upon moose, deer, black bear, and numerous fur-bearing mammals for food and utilitarian by-products. Smaller animals, such as the hare, squirrel, weasel, and rabbit were trapped and snared, as were certain birds. Stream fishing and the gathering of roots, berries, and nuts, which stored well, supplemented the Nipmuck diet. Birchbark and willow were used extensively for containers, dwellings, and sundry other products. Winter travel was by snowshoe and toboggan. Permanent villages exercised control over an area's resources and territory, particularly its sugar groves.

The first European American contact was with the Pilgrims at Plymouth Rock. Though little is recorded, by 1674 the New England Mission had converted some Nipmucks to Christianity. In 1675, however, many Nipmucks fought against the colonists in King Philip's War, with many then fleeing to Canada or to tribes on the Hudson River. Their population was estimated to be five hundred in 1600 but had declined in 1910 to eighty-one, largely because of European American diseases, conflict with settlers, and low birthrates.

Nisqually

CULTURE AREA: Northwest Coast
LANGUAGE GROUP: Salishan
PRIMARY LOCATION: Washington State
POPULATION SIZE: 447 (1990 U.S. Census)

The socially stratified Nisqually lived in permanent winter villages of split-planked rectangular houses. They were dependent upon both marine and land resources for food, practiced a definite yearly subsistence round of travel, and observed a strict division of labor.

The 1850 Donation Act of Oregon allowed settlers to acquire and settle on lands belonging to the Nisqually and others. The 1855 treaties of Point No Point, Point Elliott, and Medicine Creek reserved small tracts of land that eventually became reservations, including the Nisqually Reservation.

Chief Leschi, who incited unrest among numerous groups, refused to accept the 1855 Medicine Creek Treaty. The U.S. Army occupied and eventually expropriated two-thirds of the Nisqually Reservation in 1917, forcing some inhabitants to relocate on other reservations. Other tribes lost valuable waterfront property to the expanding city of Tacoma. Many Nisqually live on the Chehalis Reservation, along with some Clallam, Muckleshoot, Quinault, and Chehalis.

Nooksack

CULTURE AREA: Northwest Coast
LANGUAGE GROUP: Salishan
PRIMARY LOCATION: Washington State
POPULATION SIZE: 840 (1990 U.S. Census)

The Nooksack were a little-known tribe of the Central Coast Salish, who once had close socioeconomic relations with the contiguous Upriver and Downriver Halkomelem. All the twenty permanent winter villages were river-oriented for travel and subsistence. Sea mammals were prized, along with eulachon, for oil. Land animals were hunted and trapped by men, whereas women gathered and collected roots, tubers, berries, fruits, and nuts.

The peoples of the Strait of Juan de Fuca were first contacted in 1787 by Charles Barkley, and in 1808 Simon Fraser of the North West Company charted the river which now bears his name. By 1811 land-based fur traders established themselves at the mouth of the Columbia, bringing considerable change to the Nooksack. By the 1870's and 1880's some Nooksack acquired homesteads in the Nooksack Valley, but considerable damage was done to salmon fishing—by 1900 there were at least seventy canneries at the mouth of the Columbia River.

Nootka

CULTURE AREA: Northwest Coast
LANGUAGE GROUP: Wakashan
PRIMARY LOCATION: West coast of Vancouver Island
POPULATION SIZE: 4,325 (Statistics Canada, based on 1991 census)

The Nootka tribe may be an isolated representative of early Mongoloid hunters and fishers. The Nootka and the Nitinat subtribe are referred to as the "West Coast People." They have increasingly disliked appellations imposed by outsiders, however (Nootka is a white name), and since 1980 they have referred to themselves as "Nuu-chah-nulth."

At the first contact with Europeans in 1778, the Nootkans numbered about nine thousand to ten thousand and lived in twenty-five villages of different sizes along two hundred miles of coastline. The Nootka were a technologically capable people who were skilled hunters, fishers, and whalers. Land animals were a secondary food source. They amassed an abundance of food, which permitted lavish ceremonial feasts (convivial social gatherings) and potlatches. The potlatches allowed the host to distribute surplus wealth and gain honor status.

There was a highest-ranking chief for all the Nootka villages, a position obtained through titles and wealth. Maquinna and Wickanninish of the Clayoquet subdivision were two powerful chieftains. (Chiefs acted more as representatives of the various villages than as absolute rulers.)

Social and political life centered on the extended family, which lived together. The extended family cooperated to meet its needs and to amass wealth and status. Slaves were also kept. The family was presided over by a hereditary (patrilineal) chief. Although the extended family unit was autonomous, a number of families often wintered together, sometimes forming confederacies.

Nootka fisherman in a canoe carved from a tree trunk. (Library of Congress)

The spirit world was very much a part of Nootkan culture, and Nootkans often prayed for power to the Four Chiefs of Above, Horizon, Land, and Underseas. Two major ceremonies were the Wolf Ritual, to initiate a son or young relative, and the Doctoring Ritual, to help sick people.

A combination of disease, warfare, and integration into the white- controlled commercial economy caused a significant decline in population beginning in the late 1700's. A population low of 1,605 occurred in 1939, but numbers have gradually and steadily increased since then. The Nootkans' integration into the commercial economy capitalized on their native ways. They supplied furs, dogfish oil, seal pelts, and curios as well as becoming involved in commercial fishing and logging.

In 1871 the Nootkans became part of the Canadian Indian reserve system; missionary work began in 1875. By 1900 about 60 percent were at least nominally converted. During the 1960's and 1970's a pan-Nootkan or independence movement developed in order to establish a positive identity, control Nootkan affairs, and act as a counterpoint to assimilation into Canadian society. From the 1930's to 1958 the Nootkans belonged to the Native Brotherhood of British Columbia. In 1958 they formed their own organization, the West Coast Allied Tribes, later changed to the West Coast District Council, then to the Nuu-chah-nulth Tribal Council. A primary goal has been to obtain recognition of aboriginal land titles and to pursue land claims settlements.

Nottaway

CULTURE AREA: Northeast
LANGUAGE GROUP: Iroquoian
PRIMARY LOCATION: Virginia

The Nottaway, a branch of the Iroquoian family, lived in southeastern Virginia on the Nottaway River. They called themselves Cheroenhaka but were known to the Algonquians as Mangoac and Nadowa ("adders," a common name for non-Algonquian neighbors). They lived in permanent villages and maintained little contact between villages. They lived mainly by growing crops but were also skilled hunters and gatherers. Corn was the most important crop, and women and girls seem to have done most of the field work. The Nottaway dialect was similar to that of the Tuscarora, the largest of the early Iroquoian tribes of the Virginia-North Carolina coastal plain. The Nottaway were not much affected at first by the expanding of the Jamestown colony in the seventeenth century. As trade grew after 1650, however, and as a major trade route passed through Nottaway lands, tensions increased. In the aftermath of Bacon's Rebellion in 1677, the Nottaway and their neighbors became subject to the dominance of the Virginia colonists. Through the next century they were pushed onto smaller and smaller allotments of land. They intermarried with free blacks and adopted

European ways of life. In 1824 the Virginia legislature officially voted to terminate legal tribal status for the Nottaway. They tried for many years to maintain their identity and lasted longer than many of their neighbors, but intermarriage and geographical displacement made it impossible. William Lamb, the last person claiming Nottaway identity, died in 1963.

Ocaneechi

CULTURE AREA: Southeast
LANGUAGE GROUP: Siouan
PRIMARY LOCATION: Virginia, North Carolina

The small tribe of river-oriented Ocaneechi were horticulturalists about which little is known ethnographically. They had two chiefs, one who presided over warfare, and the other over matters concerning planting and hunting. Their so-called tribal symbol was a serpent. They are first recorded in 1670 as inhabiting a large island in the Roanoke River. Apparently, they later established and maintained close socioeconomic relations with the Tutelo and the Saponi, who shared the same language and who settled on two adjacent islands. In 1676, the Conestoga sought protection from the Ocaneechi against the English and Iroquois, but later the Conestoga attempted to dispose of their benefactors and were driven away. In time, after continual conflict with the Iroquois and Virginians, the Ocaneechi left their island and settled in North Carolina.

Ofo

CULTURE AREA: Southeast
LANGUAGE GROUP: Siouan
PRIMARY LOCATION: Mississippi

Beginning in 1673, under pressure from the Iroquois, a Siouan tribe of eight villages moved in successive stages from the area of the upper Ohio River to land located on the Yazoo River in Mississippi. They were known as the Ofogoula (translated by some as "Dog People" and by others simply as "People"), Ofo (a contraction of Ofogoula), and Mosopelea. The first historical reference to the Ofo, in 1699, refers to a village of Ofogoulas among six river villages. In 1721, a mixed village of Ofogoulas and Curoas, consisting of approximately 250 persons, was reported.

In 1729, the Natchez Revolt against the French occurred; the Ofo refused to participate, moved south, and became allies of the French. In 1739, they joined the French in attacking the Chickasaw, and in 1764, they participated in a French attack on an English convoy on the Mississippi River. Many of the Ofo were killed. In 1784, a dozen or so were found with the Tunica Indians in a village on the Mississippi, eight miles north of Point Coupée. Following 1784, no mention is made of the Ofo in books. In 1908, the last surviving Ofo speaker was discovered. The woman, named Rosa Pierrette, had been taught the language by her grandmother, and all other remaining members of the Ofo tribe had died when she was young. She was interviewed, and she confirmed the name of the tribe and many of its cultural practices. She also provided a substantial amount of the Ofo language, enough to enable the publication in 1912 of an Ofo dictionary by the Smithsonian Institution.

Ojibwa

CULTURE AREA: Northeast

LANGUAGE GROUP: Algonquian

PRIMARY LOCATION: Minnesota, Wisconsin, Michigan, upper Great Lakes area, southern Ontario

POPULATION SIZE: 103,826 in U.S. (1990 U.S. Census); 76,335 in Canada (Statistics Canada, based on 1991 census)

The Ojibwa, ancestors of the modern Chippewa, Ojibwa, Mississauga, and Saulteaux, resided along the eastern shore of Georgian Bay, the north shore of Lake Huron, and west onto Michigan's Upper Peninsula before European contact. Changing residence with the seasons, they depended on hunting, fishing, and trading. The Ojibwas' basic sociopolitical units were small bands that traveled after game. No overall political organization united the bands. In the early 1600's, the Ojibwa encountered Samuel de Champlain, Jesuit missionaries, and *coureurs de bois* (French trappers).

After 1650, the Ojibwa suffered setbacks from Iroquois raiders and their number declined substantially; however, they recovered before the century ended and pushed their way south, actively involved in the fur trade. Antoine Laumet de Lamothe Cadillac helped draw the Ojibwa south by establishing Detroit in 1701. One effect of the fur trade was growth in band populations and concentrations around trading posts; another was expansion of the band leader's authority and the evolution of leader into a hereditary position. The Ojibwa joined Pontiac in his war against the British in 1763.

In the late 1700's, Ojibwa began ceding land to the British and then to the Americans in the 1800's. Between the 1820's and 1860's, Michigan, Wisconsin, and Minnesota Ojibwa ceded much of their lands and were confined to small reservations; only a small number acquiesced to being removed to Kansas. Through the nineteenth century, non-Indians acquired and exhausted many of the natural resources upon which the Ojibwa traditionally depended. Between 1820 and 1840, some Ojibwa adjusted by becoming farmers, raising hay, wheat, oats, peas, Indian corn, and potatoes, and keeping livestock; others found wage opportunities in the lumber industries.

Ojibwas adapted in many ways to the changing world during the nineteenth century. They integrated Victorian fashions with traditional dress of buckskin breechcloth, leggings, and moccasins, sold native-made goods to non-Indians, and built log cabins to replace the dome-shaped wigwam covered with birchbark and cattail matting. Still, many continued to draw a living from what they gathered and continued to construct wooden utensils, birchbark containers, canoes, and cedar cradleboards.

Traditional Society. Status was earned in Ojibwa society through success as warriors, civil leaders, or shamans. Marriages were usually monogamous; polygyny was acceptable but rare. Individuals belonged to clans which were exogamous and patrilineal—children were born into their father's clan and could not marry another of the same clan. Clan rules remain important into the twenty-first century. Children are highly valued, and child rearing was traditionally permissive. Fathers prepared sons, and mothers prepared daughters for adulthood. The most significant event in a

Flat Mouth, an Ojibwa principal chief during the nineteenth century. (National Archives)

child's life came at puberty, with boys making a vision quest for a guardian spirit. It was not expected, but girls could also have a vision at this phase. Kinship continues to be a strong binding force in Ojibwa society.

According to the Ojibwa religion, spirits reside in most things and places, and a supreme spirit presides over all. One can satisfy spirits with offerings to avoid suffering the consequences of offending them. Dreams are interpreted as revelations from the spirits. The Midewiwin, or Medicine Dance, existed before the Drum Dance and peyote cult were introduced around the beginning of the twentieth century.

Twentieth Century. The most significant change to occur in the twentieth century was the move to urban centers. The Depression struck the Ojibwa hard because they were already poor, but World War II offered economic opportunities as factories turned to war production, drawing Ojibwa away from their homes and into the cities. The trend continued under the federal government's relocation policies during the 1950's. During the 1960's and 1970's, many Ojibwas were involved in Indian activism and began to demand that the state and federal governments uphold the treaties they had signed. Many Ojibwa continue to be involved in gaining federal recognition in order to benefit from the promises made to their predecessors.

Sean O'Neill

Bibliography

Brill, Charles. *Red Lake Nation: Portraits of Ojibway Life.* Minneapolis: University of Minnesota Press, 1992.

Broker, Ignatia. *Night Flying Woman: An Ojibwa Narrative.* St. Paul: Minnesota Historical Society Press, 1983.

Child, Brenda J. *Boarding School Seasons: American Indian Families, 1900-1940.* Lincoln: University of Nebraska Press, 1998.

Clifton, James A. *People of the Three Fires: The Ottawa, Potawatomi, and Ojibwa of Michigan.* Grand Rapids, Mich.: Grand Rapids Inter-Tribal Council, 1986.

Jiles, Paulette. *North Spirit: Sojourns Among the Cree and Ojibway.* St. Paul, Minn.: Hungry Mind, 1996.

Johnston, Basil. *The Manitous: The Spiritual World of the Ojibway.* New York: HarperCollins, 1995.

Kugel, Rebecca. *To Be the Main Leaders of Our People: A History of Minnesota Ojibwe Politics, 1825-1898.* East Lansing: Michigan State University Press, 1998.

Landes, Ruth. *The Ojibwa Woman.* Lincoln: University of Nebraska Press, 1997.

Lantz, Raymond C. *The Potawatomi Indians of Michigan, 1843-1904: Including Some Ottawa and Chippewa, 1843-1866 and Potawatomi of Indiana, 1869 and 1885.* Bowie, Md.: Heritage Books, 1992.

Peers, Laura L. *The Ojibwa of Western Canada, 1780 to 1870.* St. Paul, Minn.: Minnesota Historical Society Press, 1994.

Schmalz, Peter S. *The Ojibwa of Southern Ontario.* Toronto: University of Toronto Press, 1991.

Okanagan

CULTURE AREA: Plateau
LANGUAGE GROUP: Salishan
PRIMARY LOCATION: British Columbia, Washington State
POPULATION SIZE: 2,275 in Canada (Statistics Canada, based on 1991 census); smaller population in U.S.

Initially the Okanagan (also spelled "Okanogan" and "Okana-gon") comprised two groups, the Northern Okanagan and Southern Okanagan (also known as the Sinkaietk). The Northern Okanagan lived near the Canadian boundary in the present province of British Columbia, and the Southern Okanagan inhabited the area around the Okanagan River, a tributary of the Columbia River, in north-central Washington.

The Southern Okanagan practiced the culture of the Plateau tribes, and their interaction with coastal tribes was minimal. The Okanagan followed a seasonal cycle. In the winter they lived in permanent camps, some in subterranean housing but most in a long mat lodge. A few lived in tipis. During the winter, they depended on the resources they had collected during the spring, summer, and fall, supplemented by whatever they could hunt or fish. Their principal food source was salmon, but deer were also important to their diet.

With the coming of spring, the gathering of food began to replenish the exhausted winter supply and the tribe became mobile, breaking up into different groups. One of the first activities was fishing for suckers, followed by steelhead trout. The most important fishing, however, took place in the summer salmon camps. Weirs were built to aid the capture of large catches. The salmon that were caught were either dried or frozen. All the available salmon were taken, and the old women of the camp would even pick up the dead salmon that had spawned and prepare them. Almost the entire salmon would be used, including the head.

Another food source was the variety of available roots and berries. Camps were established to gather the camas root, along with the numerous berries, including huckleberries, red or orange foam berries, and serviceberries. By fall, the Okanagan hunted deer, from which they used not only the meat but also the skins for clothing. Preparations were under way for winter camp by late fall.

Other aspects of Okanagan culture included a shaman and a dream cult. Sweat lodges were also used. Aboriginal culture persisted throughout the nineteenth century, and although the horse probably was introduced by the 1840's, it did not appear to have much effect on Okanagan culture. The Okanagan traded with the Hudson's Bay Company in the nineteenth century, which is probably how they acquired the horse.

Unlike many of the other Plateau tribes, the Okanagan did not enter into a treaty with the United States government until 1891—and this treaty was never ratified. In addition to the fur traders, their contacts with European Americans were through Roman Catholic missionaries, miners, and settlers. The Okanagan did not fight in any of the major Plateau wars with the whites, such as the Yakima War. They were unhappy, however, with the creation of the Moses Reservation in the 1860's; it was located on their land, but it only lasted until 1884. Upon termination of the reservation, many Okanagans remained in the area. Others lived in the area of the Colville Reservation, which also included traditional Okanagan land. The Colville Reservation was first established in 1872 and became a home to the descendants of the Southern Okanagan, Colville, Sinkiuse, Senijextee, Nez Perce, Methow, Entiat, Nespelem, Sanpoil, Wenatchi, and Palouse. Its official governing body is the Business Council of the Colville Reservation.

Numerous claims have been filed by Salish and other Northwest tribes with the federal government for compensation regarding land and fishing rights. One of the claims dates back to the 1891 treaty, which was never ratified, in which the Okanagan were one of the tribes that agreed to cede 1.5 million acres for $1.5 million. An additional payment was awarded. Other claims concern lost fishing rights with the construction of dams, such as the Grand Coulee. The present-day economy derives revenue from timber and gambling.

Old Copper culture

DATE: c. 3000-700 B.C.E.
LOCATION: Wisconsin, Upper Peninsula of Michigan
CULTURE AFFECTED: Late Archaic

Approximately 3000 B.C.E., there appeared in the region from the Great Lakes to New York State and in the St. Lawrence River valley a culture known as Lake Forest Late Archaic. Within that cultural tradition, there was a subtradition known as Old Copper. In a few areas of the world, native outcroppings of relatively pure copper occur at or near the surface of the earth. One of those areas includes the Brule River basin of northeast Wisconsin, the Keweenaw Peninsula of Michigan, and part of the northern shore of Lake Superior and its Isle Royale.

Approximately 3000 B.C.E., natives of that area began to exploit these natural copper resources and a wide variety of western Lake Forest peoples continued to use those resources for more than two thousand years, and even to some extent until the arrival of white fur-traders in the area after 1650 C.E. The copper was used to make a wide variety of items. These included axe and adze blades, gouges, *ulus* (curved blade knives), wood-splitting wedges, and many types of awls. Fishhooks and gorges, and even gaffs for landing the catch, have also been found. Most common in the early period were the socketed and tanged spearheads and arrow points and barbed harpoons of a hunting culture. Though made of a very different and usually superior material, these copper items bear a striking resemblance to the slate tools of the Lake Forest peoples. It is almost certain that the lifestyles of the groups were very similar.

The Old Copper peoples learned to quarry the relatively pure copper sheets and nuggets from under moderately thin layers of soil. They then heated the copper, just as stone was sometimes heated prior to chipping. The copper then would be hammered into the shapes desired. Since many of the recovered designs are quite delicate, the technical ability of the Old Copper metal workers must have been quite skillful. Finally, the material would be annealed—slowly cooled, probably in water to increase strength and reduce brittleness.

The Old Copper culture exhibited one of the best evidences of transition from the Late Archaic period to the Early Woodland after 2000 B.C.E. Burial practices became much more elaborate, including a characteristic use of red ochre to cover the burial materials. This type of burial spread throughout the eastern United States, including into the celebrated Adena area of Ohio. Copper axes and adzes became common burial items, and thousands of copper beads indicate personal decoration was quite important. These copper items were spread throughout the eastern Woodlands areas by trade routes that dominated that society. When the copper items appeared outside the immediate Old Copper area, they were highly prized, and the appearance of copper burial items is one of the best indications of the social prominence of the person being buried.

After about 700 B.C.E., the amounts of readily available copper decreased and the Old Copper subculture disappeared. Some items, however, were still being made of copper when the French fur traders first reached the Lake Superior area in the 1650's.

Olmec

CULTURE AREA: Mesoamerica
LANGUAGE GROUP: Olmecan
PRIMARY LOCATION: Southeastern Mexico

The Olmecs flourished between 1200 and 400 B.C.E. in the humid tropical lowlands of what is now the state of Veracruz in southeastern Mexico. The name "Olmec" was given arbitrarily to these ancient people by twentieth century archaeologists. It means "the people of rubber" in Nahuatl, the language of the Aztecs. The Olmecs were probably the first true civilization of ancient Mexico. Olmec culture spread throughout Mesoamerica, a region that includes southern Mexico and parts of Central America, and had great influence on later civilizations. Unrecognized before the middle of the twentieth century, the first evidence of Olmec culture was uncovered by José María Melgar in 1862. He found a gigantic carved stone head with features similar to those of Africans. It took nearly one hundred years, however, and many more discoveries of large and small artifacts, to convince archaeologists that this was a distinct and original culture.

While the large stone heads, measuring as much as 10 feet in height and weighing up to 20 tons, have sparked theories of African contact with prehistoric America, there is no consensus on their purpose or their meaning. Other, smaller statues depict individuals with different features, and the image most often found is that of a creature half jaguar and half human.

Although the land was fertile (the staple of the Olmec diet was maize), evidence suggests that the population was relatively small and not clustered into true cities. Archaeological remains show, instead, ceremonial centers, where conical-shaped pyramids and burial mounds were located. The Olmecs may have performed human sacrifices to a jaguar deity who was seen as a creation god. There is also evidence of a fire god as well as an early form of the Feathered Serpent deity that would play such an important role among later indigenous populations.

One of the most startling discoveries associated with the Olmecs was a system of mathematical symbols. Archaeologists had believed that the "long count" calendar, based on counting time from a base year, was developed by the Maya. In 1939, however, Matthew Stirling discovered a recorded date that was centuries earlier than the Maya, showing that the Olmecs had first developed this method of counting years. Using a bar for five, dots for ones, and a shell symbol for zero, the Olmecs had a numerical system that could go into the thousands. The Olmecs also produced an early form of hieroglyphic writing. One hundred and eighty-two symbols have been identified as having some form of specific meaning.

The spread of Olmec culture in art, religion, writing, and mathematics throughout coastal regions and into Central America has led to the belief that the Olmecs created the "mother civilization" of the region. Nevertheless, arguments persist as to whether the Olmecs conquered and controlled an empire or whether trade and other contacts spread their accomplishments.

Omaha

CULTURE AREA: Plains
LANGUAGE GROUP: Siouan
PRIMARY LOCATION: Nebraska, Iowa
POPULATION SIZE: 4,143 (1990 U.S. Census)

The Omaha moved from the eastern forests to the Missouri River between Iowa and Nebraska shortly before their first contact with European Americans. They became part-time buffalo hunters but clung to their Woodland agricultural practices as well. The Sioux and Pawnee were their most consistent enemies, and the Ponca were their closest relatives and allies. Their relationships with whites were often strained, but they were never at war with the colonial powers or with the United States. They have recently reclaimed their most sacred tribal symbols from the museums in which they were placed in the late nineteenth century.

Early History and Traditional Lifestyle. The Omaha lived in the forests of eastern North America with four related tribes until around 1500, at which time the tribes moved west to the Mississippi and Missouri rivers. The Omaha became established on the Missouri near Omaha, Nebraska, probably pushing the Arikara north in the process.

They continued to grow corn, beans, squash, and other vegetables in the river's flood plain, but also moved into the Plains twice a year (spring and autumn) to hunt buffalo. Buffalo provided many of the tribe's needs: meat;

hides for robes, clothing and tipi covers; shoulder blades for hoes; and more. The Omaha lived in earthlodges in their villages along the river, but in tipis while hunting buffalo. Dogs pulling travois carried their belongings in migrations across the Plains until the Omaha obtained horses in the middle of the eighteenth century.

The Omaha hunted over most of Nebraska. There they encountered Sioux or Pawnee hunting parties, with whom they often fought over hunting rights. Each of those tribes occasionally attacked the Omahas' earthlodge villages as well. The Ponca were usually allied with the Omaha against the Sioux and Pawnee. Occasionally, the Ponca joined the Sioux against the Omaha, or Pawnee and Omaha hunted together, reversing the more common relationships.

The social and spiritual life of the Omaha was more or less typical of Plains Indians. Men hunted, butchered, made and decorated their shields, bows and arrows, and fought to defend the tribe. Women cooked, preserved meat and other foods for future use, gardened, made and decorated clothes and tipi covers, and raised the tipi at a new campsite and took it down in preparation for a move. Both sexes participated in building the earthlodges.

To the Omaha, all aspects of nature were sacred and part of a vast network of natural interactions, with which they interacted through elaborate rituals and symbols. They did not develop the Sun Dance, which nearly every other Plains tribe practiced, but had other dances and ceremonies. A sacred pole and white buffalo robe were the tribe's most important spiritual symbols. Each of the two main divisions of the tribe, the earth people and sky people, had a sacred pipe.

The vision quest, in which a young man fasted in the wilderness hoping for a spiritual experience to give him special power, was a part of growing up for most Omaha boys. Men belonged to warrior societies, some of which were made up of men who had similar vision quest experiences. For most societies, however, eligibility depended on age, bravery, and service. At one time, Omaha chiefs were determined by hereditary lineages, but this changed to the more typical Plains system of choosing chiefs according to the criteria above.

Transition and Modern Life. The Omaha were never at war with the United States. They agreed to a series of treaties that eventually left them with a small reservation in Nebraska and Iowa. Their transition to the agricultural context of reservation life was probably easier than that of other Plains tribes, because they were part-time farmers before the accompanying restrictions were imposed. They share many of the problems of Indian tribes throughout the country, however—lack of education, poverty, and loss of native culture.

In the last half of the twentieth century, the Omaha have initiated several efforts to overcome these problems. They have regained possession of their sacred pole and sacred white buffalo robe, and have taken steps to preserve the Omaha language. They have sued the United States to recover a small portion of tribal land. Not every effort can be expected to succeed, but these and other efforts indicate the determination of the Omaha to maintain their culture and improve conditions for tribal members.

Carl W. Hoagstrom

Oneida

CULTURE AREA: Northeast
LANGUAGE GROUP: Iroquoian
PRIMARY LOCATION: New York State, Ontario, Wisconsin
POPULATION SIZE: 11,564 in U.S. (1990 U.S. Census); estimated 5,000 in Canada

One of the five (later six) tribes of the Iroquois Confederacy, the Oneidas were ancestrally located between the Onondagas to their west and the Mohawks to their east in what is now central New York State. Their language is very similar to other Iroquois languages; the name "Oneida" means "people of the standing stone." The Oneidas were at times overshadowed by the larger Onondaga and Mohawk tribes, and they attempted to rectify this imbalance at times in the Grand Council of the Confederacy when it met at Onondaga. The Oneidas held nine of the fifty seats in the Grand Council. Like all other Iroquois tribes, they adhered to a matrilineal clan system in which the matron of each clan appointed the sachem (chief) for each clan. The sachem participated in political activity at both the local and confederacy levels. The three Oneida clans are the Turtle, Bear, and Wolf clans.

Oneida society was traditionally matrilocal in that a marrying couple would live with the wife's family in her extended-family longhouse. A longhouse was made of poles or saplings as a frame, with the walls filled in with bark. These dwellings could be up to 70 feet long and could house up to thirty people or more. There were anywhere from ten to fifty longhouses in a village. Particularly after contact with Europeans, the villages were female-oriented places, as the men were often traveling for purposes of hunting, fishing, trading, and warfare. Women were the main breadwinners, growing and harvesting corn, beans, and squash, the staples of Iroquoian horticulture. The ceremonial cycle of Oneida (Iroquois) life made plain this orientation toward horticulture: the Maple Sugar Festival, the Green Corn Ceremony, the Strawberry Festival, the Harvest Festival, and the Midwinter Festival framed the religious year.

Increased contact with the French, Dutch, and English in the 1600's meant that Oneida society changed greatly. In addition to the escalation of warfare over the seventeenth and eighteenth centuries, disease epidemics took their toll on the Oneida people. They numbered about one thousand in 1677 but probably had much greater numbers before European contact. The patterns of warfare changed during the American Revolution when most of the Oneidas broke with the rest of the confederacy and sided with the Americans. Following this war, the Oneidas assumed that they would be able to retain their homeland, but they were increasingly marginalized by the U.S. government, which tried to convince them to move to Kansas. This was unsuccessful, but one faction of Oneidas did purchase a tract of land in Wisconsin and moved there in the 1820's. Others moved to Ontario and resided on an Oneida reserve on the Thames River near the Six Nations reserve, and still others moved to the Six Nations reserve itself. All the Oneidas—in Ontario, New York, and Wisconsin—have seen their landholdings dwindle at the hands of various governments and land speculators. The Ontario and New York Oneidas have remained more traditional than their Wisconsin counterparts. They still have matron-appointed sachemships and include some fluent Oneida speakers. Many of the traditional ceremonies, along with newer ones incorporated in the Handsome Lake religion (Longhouse religion), are still practiced. Oneidas living at the Six Nations reserve and on the Onondaga reservation in New York are minorities within these larger communities. The tiny remaining Oneida reservation in the ancestral homeland east of Syracuse, New York, is the site

Oneida woman standing beside a house made of bark—a material that Iroquoian people used to make dwellings, canoes, and carrying utensils. (National Museum of the American Indian, Smithsonian Institution)

of the first tribal casino to open with the sanction of the New York state government, made possible partly because of a land claims case won by the Oneida tribe.

Oneota

DATE: c. 800-1500

LOCATION: Upper Mississippi River valley

CULTURES AFFECTED: Early Iowa, Missouri, Oto, Winnebago; later Osage, Sioux

The Oneota are considered both a people and a cultural tradition. This tradition appears to have developed from the Late Woodland or Upper Mississippian tradition by times variously given as 400 to 800 C.E. The sites identified as emergent Oneota are located in Minnesota, Wisconsin, and Illinois, but later sites occur in Iowa, Missouri, North Dakota, Indiana, and the near corner of Michigan. The society was a mixture of hunter-gatherer and agricultural, with permanently established villages and houses. The houses, usually of wattle and daub construction with sod roofs, were single-family dwellings only 6- or 8-feet square in the early settlements; but some of the later ones featured longhouses as much as 90 feet in length. A late site near Cahokia, Illinois (a few miles from East St. Louis), had some twelve to fifteen hundred inhabitants and appears to have been a center for barter with other tribes. This was the exception, however; most villages had only one or two hundred residents, although they spread out to as much as a hundred acres in cultivated area.

The artifacts most often used to distinguish the Oneota tradition from others are their pottery vessels, which are smooth and globular with handles in pairs (when present), and with the upper half of the vessel decorated with line patterns of various sorts. Stone artifacts are found also: scrapers, drills, knives, and characteristic small, unnotched projectile points. Animal bones were used for needles, beads, fishhooks, and flint flakers, with scapulas of elk and buffalo serving as hoes. Some metal was used, mostly for personal ornaments.

The Oneota appear to have had extensive contact with surrounding Indian groups, including the trade already mentioned. At some time after 1400 or 1500 C.E., when written history in the European style commences, the account of the Oneota becomes that of the individual tribes in the Upper Mississippi area.

Onondaga

CULTURE AREA: Northeast
LANGUAGE GROUP: Iroquoian
PRIMARY LOCATION: New York State, Ontario
POPULATION SIZE: 1,500 in U.S. (1990 U.S. Census); estimated 3,000 in Canada

In the Onondaga language, the name "Onondaga" means "people of the hill"; the main Onondaga village was on a hill southeast of present-day Syracuse, New York. The Onondaga tribe was the geographically central tribe of the Five (later Six) Nations of the Iroquois Confederacy. The capital of the confederacy was therefore at this main Onondaga village, and the Onondagas were the Keepers of the Council Fire of the confederacy. The main speaker of the council was always an Onondaga, as was the keeper of the council wampum. The Great Council of the Confederacy, which met each autumn and in emergency situations, was composed of fifty sachems (chiefs) from the five tribes. The Onondaga held fourteen of these hereditarily chosen sachemships, more than any other tribe. These rules were set down some time before European contact (estimates vary widely, from the 1300's to the 1500's) by the founders of the Iroquois League or Confederacy, Hiawatha and Deganawida.

The Onondaga tribe was organized into matrilineal clans: Wolf, Bear, Beaver, Turtle, Deer, Eagle, and Heron. Clan sachems were appointed by the clan matrons, the senior women of each clan. The Onondagas were also matrilocal, in that a marrying couple would live with the wife's family in an extended-family longhouse made of poles and bark. Each longhouse accommodated up to thirty people, and there could be from twenty to fifty longhouses in a village. The Onondaga population around 1600 was probably more than two thousand.

While men hunted for game and practiced warfare and trade at great distances, Onondaga women tended the fields adjacent to their villages, carrying on the main economic subsistence of the community. Corn, beans, and squash, along with sunflowers and tobacco, were the main crops grown by the women. The seasonal cycle of religious ceremonies reflected the importance of agriculture to the Onondagas: the Maple Sugar Festival, the Strawberry Festival, the Green Corn Ceremony, the Harvest Festival, and the Midwinter Ceremonies.

The Onondagas, along with the other Iroquois tribes, became involved in a spiral of warfare and imperialism in the seventeenth century which did not end until the war of the American Revolution. In the latter conflict, the vast majority of them, including the Onondagas, sided with the British and lost most of their ancestral lands across New York State. The Onondagas did manage to retain a reservation southeast of present-day Syracuse, but many Onondagas settled instead on the Six Nations reserve along the Grand River in what is now Ontario, Canada. Many who remained in what is now New York State were living at Buffalo Creek, a predominantly Seneca community. Eventually, most Onondagas at Buffalo Creek made their way back to the Onondaga reservation near Syracuse.

The issue of rightful location of the seat of the Iroquois Confederacy became one of great contention among the Iroquois; the Grand River Onondagas claimed that the seat was at their Six Nations reserve, but the Buffalo Creek community also claimed the seat. The Buffalo Creek group acceded to the group at the Onondaga reservation, but a conflict still exists between the Onondagas (and all Iroquois) of the Grand River (Canadian) reserve and the Onondagas in their ancient homeland as to which council fire is the legitimate one.

The New York Onondagas still use the traditional method of deciding political leadership; the matrons of each clan appoint leaders. They are involved in ongoing negotiations with New York State and the federal government over sovereignty issues. The Canadian Onondagas are split into two governmental factions, traditional and elected leadership, and the Canadian government recognizes only the latter. The Onondaga language is still spoken by many older tribal members, and children learn it in school. Some adhere to Christian denominations, but at least a quarter of Onondaga people in both Ontario and New York practice the traditional Iroquois religion, the Longhouse religion, which is a mix of pre-contact belief systems and Christian ideas institutionalized by the prophet Handsome Lake in the early nineteenth century.

Osage

CULTURE AREA: Plains
LANGUAGE GROUP: Siouan (Dhegiha)
PRIMARY LOCATION: Oklahoma
POPULATION SIZE: 9,527 (1990 U.S. Census)

The Osage are one of five tribes in the Dhegiha group of the Siouan linguistic family. Osage is a French corruption of the tribal name Wazha'zhe. At the time of first white contact, the Osage lived primarily in western Missouri. Tribal legend and archaeological evidence suggest, however, that the ancient Osage lived east of the Mississippi River.

Traditional Life. Among early Plains tribes (before the introduction of the horse), the Osage held high rank. Although they depended heavily on the buffalo, the Osage also developed a strong agricultural base; they relied on dogs as beasts of burden before the horse. Their villages were permanent. Their lodges were wood frames covered with woven mats or bark, and they ranged from 36 to 100 feet long. As buffalo grew scarce in the Mississippi Valley, bands were forced to extend hunting trips farther onto the Plains.

The Osage comprised two divisions (moieties): the Tzisho, or Sky People, and the Hunkah, or Land People. These moieties were then divided into twenty-one clans, with each person inheriting his or her father's clan. The chief of the Tzisho division was the peace chief, while the war chief came from the Hunkah. Since the early nineteenth century, there also existed three political groups: the Great Osage, the Little Osage, and the Arkansas Osage. In marriage, spouses were required to be from opposite moieties, and a man who married an oldest daughter also held marriage rights to his wife's younger sisters, a form of polygamy. The Osage believed in a supernatural life force, Wakonda, which they believed resided in all things. Shamans provided religious leadership, although there also existed a religious society to which both men and women belonged. Physically, the Osage have been a noticeably tall tribe; they often adorned themselves with tattoos.

History. The first recorded contact with the Osage was by French explorers Father Jacques Marquette and Louis Jolliet (1673). The French subsequently established a lucrative trade and a strong alliance with the Osage. Trade made the Osage a significant force among Plains tribes. The Osage recognized their strategic position in the Plains trade as middlemen and as gatekeepers to the region and were persistent in protecting that advantage. Trade rivalry existed within the tribe, however, and ultimately caused factionalism. In the mid-1790's, trader Auguste Chouteau established a post on the Arkansas River in Oklahoma and persuaded a large faction to locate there permanently, thus creating the Arkansas Band.

In 1808, the Osage ceded the northern half of Arkansas and most of Missouri to the United States, and the Great and Little Osage bands moved to the Neosho River in Kansas. This area became the center of tribal life. As the government removed eastern tribes to Indian Territory, however, clashes between the Osage and removed Cherokee over hunting rights to the region escalated into a long, bloody war. United States agent William Lovely finally convinced the Osage to cede the region to the Cherokee in 1817. Still, hostilities continued, including one of the bloodiest Indian battles in Okla-

An Osage leader during the late nineteenth and early twentieth centuries, Bacon Rind was elected the Osages' principal chief in 1909. (Library of Congress)

homa history, the battle of Clare-more Mound.

By 1825, the Osage had ceded all their lands to the United States through treaties and were given a reservation (in present-day southern Kansas) in Indian Territory. During this time, Protestant missionaries established among the Osage some of the first missions and schools in the region, though later they were replaced by Roman Catholic missionaries.

After the outbreak of the Civil War, Confederate commissioner Albert Pike was able to secure the allegiance of many Osage to the south, though many sided with the Union as well. This factionalism created tension among tribal members, already suffering from the ravages of white guerrilla raiders. After the war, the Union used the tribe's Confederate allegiance to secure large land cessions through Reconstruction treaties. Ultimately, the Osage were forced to sell all their lands to the government and use the proceeds to purchase a new reservation in the eastern end of the Cherokee Outlet (all of present-day Osage County, Oklahoma).

The post-Civil War years were hard on the tribe, bringing a nearly 50 percent decline in the tribe's population because of poor medical aid and a scarcity of food and clothing. The buffalo were gone, and the land given the Osage was the poorest in Indian Territory for agriculture. The range-cattle industry of the 1880's, however, offered some economic relief for the tribe; they leased grazing rights to cattlemen. Some very lucrative oil and gas deposits were then discovered under the barren Osage lands. The royalties received from the leases on these resources catapulted the Osage from an impoverished to an indulgent lifestyle and have since provided the financial foundation of the Osage Nation. Because of their shrewd leasing arrangements, the Osage have become one of the wealthiest of Indian nations on a per capita basis.

Modern Life. Osage interests are governed by an eight-member tribal council, along with the principal chief and assistant chief, with the ever-present supervision of the Bureau of Indian Affairs. The Osage Agency, located at Pawhuska, Oklahoma, is unlike other agencies in Oklahoma in that all expenses accrued are paid with tribal funds. One of the biggest issues the tribe has had to confront in the twentieth century has been tribal membership: The tribe's wealth has made citizenship in the nation an enticing relationship. Because of the wealth that oil brought to the tribe, the name Osage was once synonymous with profligate spending. Wealth also brought conflict, and many tribal members have been torn between modernity and traditional ways. Ultimately, the tribe realized the necessity of moderation, and in that light the oil industry has given the tribe economic independence and great advantages in educational and societal matters. Even with the wealth and modernity which have threatened to eradicate the traditional Osage ways, the tribe has retained interest in its culture, arts, crafts, and language.

S. Matthew Despain

Bibliography

Baird, W. David. *The Osage People*. Phoenix: Indian Tribal Series, 1972.

Din, Gilbert C., and Abraham P. Nasatir. *The Imperial Osages: Spanish-Indian Diplomacy in the Mississippi Valley*. Norman: University of Oklahoma Press, 1983.

La Flesche, Francis, and Garrick A. Bailey. *The Osage and the Invisible World: From the Works of Francis La Flesche*. Norman: University of Oklahoma Press, 1995.

Matthews, John Joseph. *Sundown*. Norman: University of Oklahoma Press, 1934.

_____. *Wah'Kon-Tah: The Osage and the White Man's Road*. 1932. Reprint. Norman: University of Oklahoma Press, 1981.

Rollings, Willard H. *The Osage: An Ethnohistorical Study of the Hegemony on the Prairie-Plains*. Columbia: University of Missouri Press, 1992.

Tallchief, Maria, and Larry Kaplan. *Maria Tallchief: America's Prima Ballerina*. New York: Henry Holt, 1997.

Wilson, Terry P. *The Osage*. New York: Chelsea House, 1988.

_____. *The Underground Reservation: Osage Oil*. Lincoln: University of Nebraska Press, 1985.

Wolferman, Kristie C. *The Osage in Missouri*. Columbia: University of Missouri Press, 1997.

Oto

CULTURE AREA: Plains
LANGUAGE GROUP: Siouan
PRIMARY LOCATION: Oklahoma
POPULATION SIZE: 1,840 ("Otoe-Missouria," 1990 U.S. Census)

Oto (or Otoe) tradition indicates that these people lived at one time with the Missouri, Iowa, and Winnebago tribes somewhere in the upper Great Lakes region. Probably pushed by other tribes squeezed from the east, they began moving west and south, perhaps in the 1500's, leaving the Winnebago in the Green Bay, Wisconsin, area, and the Iowa people at the confluence of the Mississippi and Iowa rivers. The Oto and Missouri continued south along the Mississippi and west along the Missouri until reaching the confluence of the Missouri and Grand rivers. At this point there was a conflict between the two groups involving a romantic relationship between the Missouri chief's daughter and the Oto chief's son. Consequently, the Oto continued west along the Missouri while the Missouri people remained. This conflict explains the Oto tribal name, originating from the Chiwere word *wahtohtata*, meaning "lovers" or "lechers." (The Oto and Missouri shared the Chiwere language with the Iowa.)

In the late 1600's, the Otos lived in what is now the state of Iowa, on the Upper Iowa and the Blue Earth rivers, but they were not numerous. Their population at that point was probably about 800. For most of the eighteenth century, they lived further west, along the Platte River near its mouth at the Missouri River. The Otos benefited from trade with the French and later the Americans, but they were also devastated by disease and warfare brought by these outsiders. Their rivals in warfare were mainly the Pawnees, Mesquakies (Fox), and Sauks. The Pawnees at times dominated the Otos militarily.

By 1829, the Otos and Missouris had merged, both having suffered greatly, and having had their populations shrink, from smallpox and other diseases. The following decades were difficult, as they and other beleaguered tribes fought for scant food resources. By 1854, the Oto-Missouris (or Otoe-Missourias) had ceded all of their lands to the United States and moved to a reservation on the Big Blue River, near the Kansas and Nebraska territories. Eventually, one faction split off and moved to Indian Territory (Oklahoma) in 1880. A decade later the rest followed them. In 1907, the Oklahoma reservation was allotted to individual tribal members.

Oto culture of the prereservation era reflected an adaptation to a Plains environment from the eastern woodlands. While women cultivated corn, beans, squash, and melons in the bottomlands along the rivers, men spent much time hunting. Major buffalo hunts were carried on in the spring and fall, with deer, turkey, raccoon, and rabbit hunting occupying other times. While on hunting trips, the Otos stored their food in underground bell-shaped caches and used skin tipis for shelter. Their villages, however, were quite substantial. Depending on the population of a village, there were forty to seventy earthlodges 30 to 40 feet in diameter. Each lodge had a heavy wooden framework filled in with brush and grass and covered with an outer layer of earth or clay. Villages were divided socially into ten clans, each clan representing several related extended households. Oto society was patrilineal (one belonged to one's father's clan), but the lodges and all other household property were owned by the women. Different clans were responsible for various seasonal celebrations or leadership for particular hunts, and clan chiefs, war chiefs, and spiritual leaders were hereditarily chosen. Curing societies and dance societies such as the Medicine Lodge and the Buffalo Doctors Lodge specialized in particular ceremonies necessary for communication with the spiritual world. Mourning practices were highly ritualized, sometimes involving the killing of a horse so that the deceased person could ride to the afterlife.

Although loss of their homeland and reservation has resulted in some acculturation, the Oto-Missouri tribe still has some tribally owned land in Oklahoma and holds ceremonies and traditional dances each year. Oto-Missouri children started, in the 1970's, learning their Chiwere language in school, with the aid of a published grammar of the Chiwere language.

Ottawa

CULTURE AREA: Northeast
LANGUAGE GROUP: Algonquian
PRIMARY LOCATION: Michigan, Oklahoma; Ontario, Canada
POPULATION SIZE: 7,522 in U.S. (1990 U.S. Census); estimated 3,500 in Canada

The Ottawa, members of the Algonquian language group, came from north of the Great Lakes with the Chippewa (Ojibwa) and Potawatomi; they formed the Council of Three Tribes. By the 1600's, the tribes had separated, with the Ottawa controlling the northern shore of Lake Huron and Manitoulin Island in the lake and the other two tribes settling farther south and west. "Ottawa" means "to trade" in Algonquian, and tribal members controlled commerce in furs, skins, corn, sunflower oil, tobacco, roots, and herbs among the Native American tribes in the northern Great Lakes region before the coming of Europeans. They were famous for the quality of their birchbark canoes and their abilities as businessmen.

Contemporary depiction of a meeting between Ottawa leader Pontiac (right) and a British major named Rogers during the 1760's. (Library of Congress)

The Ottawa were skilled hunters and fishermen, though in the harsh winter months they had to eat bark to survive. Women gathered blueberries and strawberries and tapped trees for maple syrup while the men hunted. Samuel de Champlain, the French explorer, made contact with the Ottawa in 1615, and he reported that they tattooed their bodies, painted their faces, pierced their noses, and had very long hair. They hunted mostly deer and small game with bows and arrows, and they wore no clothes in warm weather, although in the winter they put on buffalo robes. Jean Nicolet, a French trader, met the Ottawa in 1635 and exchanged guns and powder for furs. The Ottawa lived in small villages in bark- and skin-covered homes.

They divided into four bands, named after the places they lived: the Kiskakon, the Outaouae Sinago, the Sable, and the Nassawaketon. Traditional Ottawa religion stressed belief in a spirit world governed by Manitou, the "Great Spirit."

Contact with the French eventually led to displacement and disaster for the Ottawa. In 1649 and again in 1660, the Iroquois from New York attacked in Michigan and southern Canada as they sought expansion of their trade empire. After this attack, the Ottawa retreated to the area of Green Bay, Wisconsin, where they remained until 1670 when, under French protection, they returned to the Lake Huron region. Ten years later, the Ottawa moved again, this time to Mackinaw Island and St. Ignace, Michigan, where they joined temporarily with the Huron and were converted to Christianity. A smaller band moved south to the southeastern shore of Lake Michigan where they remained until 1769, when they moved again after warring against the British.

A key event in Ottawa history took place in 1720 with the birth of the great chief Pontiac. Little is known of his early life. During the French and Indian War (1756-1763), Pontiac led the combined forces of Ottawa, Chippewa, and Potawatomi in the battle against British occupation of the Great Lakes region. When the French surrendered, he organized a "conspiracy" to continue the war against the British. Pontiac assembled a large force of Indians in a siege of Detroit, the main British outpost in the west, that lasted from May to December, 1763. Influenced by the "Delaware Prophet," a holy man who claimed direct contact with the Manitou, Pontiac called for a return to traditional Indian lifestyles and a rejection of white trade goods, except for guns. The siege ended, however, after traitors told the British of the Indians' plan of attack and a supply ship managed to reach Detroit with food and ammunition. Over two thousand settlers and Indians died during the "conspiracy," which the British blamed on the French. Pontiac escaped and went to Illinois, where he was killed in 1769 by a Peoria Indian, probably in the pay of the British.

In 1831, tribal leaders accepted lands in Kansas under provisions of the Indian Removal Act. Fifteen years later, however, this cession became more valuable to white farmers, and the Ottawa ceded them back to the United States in exchange for land in Indian Territory (Oklahoma). Only a few Ottawa moved to this new reservation, and many others returned to Michigan. By 1910, more than twenty-four hundred of the 2,717 members of the tribe resided in Michigan, and not on reservations. Of the Ottawa population of the early 1990's, more than half lived in Michigan, three thousand lived in Ontario, and fewer than five hundred lived on the Oklahoma reservation. Many made their livings as farmworkers, sawmill laborers, and fishing guides. The Ottawa of Ontario still spoke the tribe's language, though it had largely disappeared among American-born tribal members.

Leslie V. Tischauser

Paiute, Northern

CULTURE AREA: Great Basin
LANGUAGE GROUP: Uto-Aztecan
PRIMARY LOCATION: Nevada, California
POPULATION SIZE: 11,142 (total Paiute population, 1990 U.S. Census)

The Northern Paiute, or Paviotso, a branch of the Shoshonean division of the Uto-Aztecan language group, originally occupied the far western region of Nevada, the southeastern part of Oregon, and the far eastern fringes of central California. "Paviotso" is actually a derogatory Shoshone word meaning "root digger," so members of the tribe prefer to be called Paiute, which means "pure water." The Southern Paiute spoke the same language but inhabited the deserts of northern Arizona and western Utah and had little contact with their northern brothers.

Traditional Lifeways. The Northern Paiute fished, hunted deer, antelope, and bighorn sheep, and gathered piñon nuts. During harsh winters, the women dug plant roots to eat (the derivation of the name Paviotso). In winter, the Paiute lived in grass-covered, cone-shaped structures that had a smokehole at the top. In summer, they moved outside and lived in areas surrounded by trees to protect them from the hot winds. Usually no more than fifty persons, or three or four families, lived in each campsite, with the winter homes widely scattered. In the summer, women wore aprons of rabbit skins, but changed to buckskin dresses in the winter. Men wore rabbit skin shirts in the hot months and buckskin leggings when it started to get cold.

The eldest males usually made key decisions, though each village had a "headman" who enforced law and order. Paiute religion stressed belief in a world inhabited by many spirits. These spirits could be found almost everywhere in nature: in animals, plants, stones, water, the sun, moon, thunder, and stars. Individuals prayed to these spirits for help in hunting and food gathering. These supernatural powers gave orders that had to be followed, such as how to divide the remains of a hunted animal, or who to marry. Failure to follow these instructions could be punished by sickness, misfortune, or death. Contact with the spirits could be sought by anyone. Usually a seeker had to visit a dark and dangerous cave or spend the night on a remote mountaintop to get the spirit's attention, but if contact was made the seeker would receive great powers to heal sicknesses or become a successful hunter. If a Paiute obeyed the spirits, upon death his soul would be rewarded by being taken to another world filled with dancing, food, and gambling.

Post-contact Life. The Paiute acquired horses sometime in the early 1700's, although they did not make contact with whites until 1804, when a few Paiute hunters came upon the Lewis and Clark expedition exploring the Louisiana Purchase. In 1827, an expedition led by the famous explorer Jedediah Smith began trading furs for guns in western Nevada. In the 1830's and 1840's, thousands of white settlers poured through the region on their way to gold strikes in California and farms in Oregon. They brought chaos with them as their wagons, horses, and cattle destroyed meager food supplies in the Great Basin. In response, Paiute bands attacked the wagon trains and killed dozens of migrants. Not until after the Civil War did U.S. Army forces "pacify" the territory by killing hundreds of Indians.

Government officials established a reservation in Oregon in 1874, but thousands of Paiutes refused to go. They did not want to become farmers, especially on land that was almost desert. Many Paiutes became ranch hands, cowboys, and sheepherders for area whites. Paiute women worked as housekeepers or servants. In 1887, a Paiute holy man named Wovoka ("the Cutter") had a vision which he described to Indians throughout the Great Basin and beyond: If Indians could dance for five nights and listen to the drums, the fish and wildlife would return, dead Indians would rise

Wovoka, the Paiute whose Ghost Dance religion rapidly spread throughout the Great Plains, in an 1892 photograph. (National Museum of the American Indian, Smithsonian Institution)

from their graves, and whites would disappear from the earth. This "Ghost Dance" movement had spread all the way to Wounded Knee, South Dakota, by the winter of 1890. It led to the last great massacre in Indian history, when army troops killed more than two hundred men, women, and children who were trying to dance whites out of the world.

In the 1930's, cattle ranching became the most important economic activity on the reservation. Paiutes either leased their land to whites or tried to raise their own herds. Paiute cowboys have a reputation for being excellent horsemen and dedicated workers. Most Paiutes do not live on the reservations in Nevada and Oregon, preferring to find jobs for themselves on the cattle and sheep ranches in the area.

Leslie V. Tischauser

Paiute, Southern

CULTURE AREA: Southwest
LANGUAGE GROUP: Uto-Aztecan
PRIMARY LOCATION: Northwestern Arizona, southern Nevada, southwestern Utah
POPULATION SIZE: 11,142 (total Paiute population, 1990 U.S. Census)

The Southern Paiutes belong to the Numic-speaking group of the Shoshonean branch of the Uto-Aztecan family. They call themselves *nuwu*, which literally means "human being." The Paiutes spread across the Great Basin into the northern portion of the southwestern United States around 1000 C.E., replacing prehistoric Pueblo-like peoples who had inhabited the region. Similarities in agricultural production and pottery making indicate that the Southern Paiutes must have learned much from the Pueblos they replaced. Defensive structures and artifacts dated at mid-twelfth century suggest that strife may have existed between the groups, causing the Pueblos to flee the region and allowing the Paiutes to expand their territory eastward. By the eighteenth century the Paiutes were living in a great crescentic region from southeastern Utah to northeastern Arizona to the deserts of Southern California and Nevada.

Aboriginal Paiute Culture. During their aboriginal period the Paiutes were primarily gatherers of wild plants, roots, berries, and seeds, supplemented by some hunting of rabbits, deer, mountain sheep, and some insects and lizards. Farming was severely limited and included only corn, beans, and squash. During this early period the Paiutes traded with nearby tribes including the Hopi, Havasupai, Walapai, and Mojave. There is evidence to suggest that these groups existed peaceably with one another.

It is doubtful that the Paiutes had any tribal/political organization binding them into one nation during aboriginal times. Shortages of food and water forced the dispersion of the Paiutes into small family groups. Occasionally, larger social groups came together to harvest piñon nuts or to hunt for rabbits; however, these groups remained together only until the task was completed, then dispersed again. Political or social leadership is evident in the form of praise given to a respected person, a good hunter, or a great dance leader. Religious and other cultural developments were severely limited among the Paiutes because they spent virtually all of their time searching for food and pursuing the other necessities for survival.

Paiute basketry seed beater

Their tools included bow and arrows, hunting nets, seed beaters, gathering baskets, flint knives, digging sticks, and flat grinding stones. Their clothes consisted of rabbit-skin robes, bark or hide aprons, and sandals or moccasins. Their dwellings were rudimentary, constructed mainly of grass, sticks, and mud. Every aspect of their development manifests of the Paiutes' marginal subsistence pattern.

European Contact. The Southern Paiutes, historically, were one of the last Indian groups to have sustained contact with whites. While other southwestern groups experienced early contact with the Spanish, the Paiutes' first contact was with the Dominguez-Escalante expedition of 1776. The Spanish explorers described the Paiutes as the lowliest of peoples, destitute and degraded. The Spanish had a number of significant effects upon the Paiute peoples. The spread of horses to neighboring tribes facilitated trade with such tribes as the Ute and Navajo. The most devastating effect was the beginning of slave trading in the Southwest. Small Paiute bands were prey to Ute and Navajo raiding parties in which they would steal children, especially young girls, and trade them to the Spanish for goods. In some instances, the Paiutes would trade their own children to the Utes for horses (which they would later kill and use for food) or other necessary goods. This slave trade led to a severe depopulation of the Paiutes but also led to their acquisition of material goods such as horses, guns, knives, tipis, kettles, and dogs. This trade persisted well into the nineteenth century, when the Mormons, under Brigham Young, caused it to end.

During the first half of the nineteenth century the Paiutes also came into contact with fur trappers and explorers because of their position along the

Old Spanish Trail. Notable among these were Jedediah Smith, Peter Skene Ogden, James Ohio Pattie, and John C. Frémont. These men, too, were critical of Paiute culture and wrote degradingly of them as savages. Indian-white contacts intensified greatly when the Mormons began to settle in southern Utah in 1850. John D. Lee was the church's recorder and wrote extensively of the Paiute Indians. He seemed much less critical of their nature than were the Spaniards or the trappers. Relations between Paiutes and Mormons were generally peaceful and respectful. Although the Mormons subscribed to many of the stereotypes of Indians as lazy, thieving, and savage, because of their theological beliefs they also believed that they had the responsibility to teach the Paiutes to be civilized. The Mormons taught the Paiutes farming and other useful skills. Because of their ever-increasing contact with whites and their low immunity to European diseases, the Paiutes were struck heavily by measles and smallpox. A smallpox epidemic in which hundreds died was recorded in 1877.

Modern Movements and Civilization. In 1873 the Bureau of Indian Affairs sent a special commission, headed by John Wesley Powell, to Utah to suggest the removal of the Southern Paiutes away from the white settlements. They had recommended removal of the Paiutes to the Uintah reservation in northeastern Utah, but because of the Paiutes' animosity with the Utes it was decided to create the Moapa Reservation in Nevada. Many groups resisted and tried to subsist in their old ways, but the expansion of white farming and grazing made this impossible. The bureau's concern for Paiute welfare also expanded into issuing cattle to the Indians because they could not survive solely on farming. The Paiutes later became fine ranchers.

Other reservations, closer to their traditional lands, were later created by the bureau; among them were the Shivwits reserve in 1891, near Santa Clara, Utah, and the Kaibab reserve in northern Arizona, near Fredonia, in 1907. Many Paiutes, however, unaided by the federal government, were given assistance and protection by nearby Mormon settlements. Drastic changes were taking place among the Paiutes in different degrees depending on contact with whites. Some adopted white culture readily, while others resisted and became hostile. Many smaller family groups formed large bands for the first time in an effort to stop the white intrusion. The Kaibab, Moapa, and Shivwits were among the most notable of these newly formed bands.

Southern Paiute children began attending federal day schools in the 1890's, and some have attended colleges and universities in Arizona, Utah, New Mexico, and California. During the first half of the twentieth century the Paiutes simply existed and continued to be dependent on the charity of the Mormons and others around them; however, three pivotal events occurred that improved the circumstances of the Paiutes. In 1946 the Paiutes filed suit against the federal government for their lands that had been unlawfully taken. The issue was hotly debated, and finally, in 1970, the Paiutes were awarded a settlement, bringing needed money into the reservations. Second, in 1951, the Paiutes established their official constitution and bylaws "to improve our civilization." This allowed them to elect a tribal council and to have a more secure land base. Finally, in 1957, the Southern Paiutes were voluntarily terminated from federal control. In these reforms, the Kaibab band has been the most progressive.

Income-producing opportunities are scarce on the reservation. The tribal chairman is the only paid employee of the tribe, and the federal government employs only a few people for maintenance purposes. Most obtain part-time work at locally white-owned ranches. Most of the cultural traditions of the early periods are remembered only by a few older individuals, and the majority of the children do not hear their native language spoken at home. Nevertheless, the Paiutes' continued survival is a direct result of their successful attempt to join together their voices and fight for survival.

Robert E. Fleming

Bibliography

Dutton, Bertha P. *The Rancheria, Ute, and Southern Paiute Peoples.* Englewood Cliffs, N.J.: Prentice-Hall, 1975.

Euler, Robert C. *The Paiute People.* Phoenix: Indian Tribal Series, 1972.

Fowler, Catherine S., and Don D. Fowler. "Southern Paiutes and Western Shoshonis." *Utah Historical Quarterly* 39 (April, 1971): 95-113.

Hittman, Michael, and Don Lynch. *Wovoka and the Ghost Dance.* Rev. ed. Lincoln: University of Nebraska Press, 1998.

Holt, Ronald L. *Beneath These Red Cliffs: An Ethnohistory of the Utah Paiutes.* Albuquerque: University of New Mexico Press, 1992.

Kelly, Isabel Truesdell. *Southern Paiute Ethnography.* Salt Lake City: University of Utah Press, 1964.

Knack, Martha C. *Life Is with People: Household Organization of the Contemporary Southern Paiute Indians.* Socorro, N.Mex.: Ballena Press, 1980.

Knack, Martha C., and Omer C. Stewart. *As Long as the River Shall Run: An Ethnohistory of Pyramid Lake Indian Reservation.* Reno: University of Nevada Press, 1999.

Liebling, A. J. *A Reporter at Large: Dateline—Pyramid Lake, Nevada.* Reno: University of Nevada Press, 1999.

Manners, Robert A. *Southern Paiute and Chemehuevi: An Ethnohistorical Report.* Vol. 1 in *American Indian Ethnohistory: California and Basin-Plateau Indians.* New York: Garland, 1974.

Martineau, LeVan. *The Southern Paiutes: Legends, Lore, Language, and Lineage.* Las Vegas, Nev.: KC Publications, 1992.

Sapir, Edward, and William Bright. *Southern Paiute and Ute: Linguistics and Ethnography.* Berlin, N.Y.: Mouton de Gruyter, 1992.

Paleo-Indian

DATE: 10,000-7500 B.C.E.
LOCATION: North, Middle, and South America
CULTURES AFFECTED: Pancultural

There is artifactual evidence of human occupation throughout the Americas by Paleo-Indians by 9500 B.C.E. They hunted large Pleistocene (Ice Age) animals. The Paleo-Indian fluted points were finely made spear points chipped on both sides, with a distinctive flute removed from the base on both sides. The fluted points were hafted to the end of a spear. Spears were thrown with the aid of a spear thrower, or "atlatl," which increased the throwing distance.

The Paleo-Indian period is divided into the Early Paleo-Indian period, consisting of the Clovis tradition (9500-9000 B.C.E.) and the Folsom tradition (9000-8000 B.C.E.), and the Late Paleo-Indian tradition. The Clovis tradition is named for the discovery site of Clovis, New Mexico, and their environmental adaptation focused on hunting Pleistocene mammoths and mastodons. The Folsom tradition, named for the Folsom site in New Mexico, emphasized the hunting of extinct bison, *Bison antiquus*. Clovis points are relatively large, with a flute that extends only part way from the base toward the point tip, whereas Folsom points are smaller and have a flute that extends almost to the point tip. Late Paleo-Indian points lack the distinctive flute of the earlier periods. The adaptation of the Late Paleo-Indian people was more regionally diversified, as reflected in their greater variety of point styles. The Paleo-Indian tradition is marked by fluted points as found at such sites as Clovis, Folsom, Lindenmeier, Olsen-Chubbuck, and Casper in the western United States; Debert, Bullbrook, Shoop, Parkhill, Udora, and Sandy Ridge in the Northeast; Ladyville, Turrialba, and Los Tapiales in Middle America; and Monte Verde in South America.

The Paleo-Indians were descendants of hunting people who followed Pleistocene animals across the land bridge, Beringia, from Asia. At various times during the Pleistocene period when the glaciers advanced, the sea level was lowered, providing the opportunity for people to travel from

Siberia to Alaska. During the late Pleistocene, Beringia consisted of a 1,000-kilometer (600-mile) land bridge between 75,000 and 40,000 B.C.E. and between about 23,000 and 12,000 B.C.E. Once in Alaska, early humans were blocked from southward travel by the Laurentide ice sheet to the east and the Cordilleran ice sheet to the west. The occurrence of Paleo-Indian artifacts in the continental United States by 9500 B.C.E. indicates that people were able to penetrate the ice barrier, either by a Pacific coast route or through the "ice-free corridor" between the ice sheets. With the extinction of more than thirty genera of animals at the end of the Pleistocene (associated with the climatic changes and, in some instances, perhaps related to Paleo-Indian hunting overkill), people changed their subsistence adaptations to emphasize hunting smaller animals and collecting wild plants throughout the Americas in what is termed the Archaic tradition.

Palouse

CULTURE AREA: Plateau
LANGUAGE GROUP: Sahaptian
PRIMARY LOCATION: Washington State

Traditionally the Palouse lived along the lower Snake River and its tributaries, including the Palouse River. The Palouse are considered a Plateau tribe. They organized into three independent groups and lived in villages during the winter months in wooden houses.

Similar to other Columbia Basin Indians, their economy depended on salmon fishing in the Columbia River, gathering roots (such as the camas) and berries, and hunting. The area in which they lived was arid and flat, broken by steppes. Hunting increased in importance after the horse was introduced in the mid-1700's. The Palouse became excellent horsemen, and their economy expanded to include horse trading in the early nineteenth century. Their first European American contact was with the Lewis and Clark expedition in 1804, followed by fur traders exploring the area in the early 1800's.

Friction with whites began almost immediately and persisted throughout Palouse history. Of any of the Plateau tribes, the Palouse were the most resistant to U.S. government plans to resettle them on reservations. In one of their initial contacts with fur traders, one of their members was found guilty of stealing from a Pacific Fur Company manager. For this crime the thief was executed, much to the horror of the Palouse and nearby Nez Perce.

413

After the incident, the Palouse and Nez Perce kept their distance from the traders.

Further contact with white people was inevitable as white settlers sought to settle eastern Washington and Oregon. In 1855, Washington Territorial Governor Isaac Stevens held the Walla Walla Council to negotiate with tribes throughout the Columbia Plateau. Stevens wanted to confine the Indians to a limited area and open the region to homesteaders. During the treaty negotiations, the Palouse tribe was considered part of the Yakimas. The council was concluded with the Yakima Treaty. The treaty was signed by Kamiakin, who was chosen Yakima headman by Stevens; it included the Palouse as being one of the signatories who made up the Confederated Tribes of the Yakima Indian Reservation. Kamiakin claimed that he never signed the treaty. The Palouse also had their own representative, Koo-lat-toosa, again appointed by Stevens to act as chief.

Dissatisfied with the treaty, the Palouse joined in the Yakima War, led by Kamiakin, who was part Palouse. Despite defeat in 1856, the Palouse refused to move to the reservation and occupied their ancestral lands, located between the Nez Perce, Umatilla, and Yakima reservations. White settlers, however, wanted the land, and the Palouse population, which had dwindled to less than two hundred, still posed a threat. Some members of the tribe, remembering the Yakima War, did move to either the Yakima, Nez Perce, Warm Springs, or Umatilla reservations, while others remained off the reservation.

In 1863, problems ensued when gold was discovered in the Clearwater River on the Nez Perce reservation. Trying to stave off a gold rush, the government negotiated the Lapwai Treaty with the Nez Perce, in which the Nez Perce ceded more land. Although the nearby Palouse did not sign the treaty, the federal government insisted that they follow treaty provisions. Thus the Palouse were treated as a subtribe of the Nez Perce. Part of the Nez Perce (about one-third), however, did not abide by the treaty and lived off the reservation in the Wallowa Valley. By the 1870's, white settlers wanted these lands as well, and in 1877, the army ordered Nez Perce Chief Joseph and his tribe to return to the Nez Perce reservation. While moving to the reservation, hostilities occurred and several whites were killed. Chief Joseph and his band of eight hundred, which included a small number of Palouse, fled to Montana and tried to reach Canada. The army defeated them, however, and the remaining Nez Perce and Palouse were forced to move to Oklahoma Territory and finally to the Colville Reservation. The Palouse tribe has no official population figures; many Palouse Indians undoubtedly intermarried with surrounding tribes and have thus kept their ancestry alive.

Pamlico

CULTURE AREA: Southeast
LANGUAGE GROUP: Algonquian
PRIMARY LOCATION: Pamlico River, North Carolina

Though there are numerous references to this tribe, little is known about them. The Pamlico were horticulturalists whose subsistence base consisted essentially of maize, beans, squash, and a wide variety of cultivated foods, supplemented by men's hunting, trapping, and fishing. Women dug roots and gathered berries and nuts, some of which were dried for winter storage.

The first mention of the Pamlico was by the Raleigh colonists in 1585, who called them Pomouik. The population of the Pamlico was estimated to be nearly one thousand in 1600. The Pamlico suffered a devastating small-pox epidemic in 1696 that left only seventy-five survivors, who by 1710 were living in a single village. In 1711, the Pamlico participated in the Tuscarora War, at the end of which the Tuscarora, under treaty with the English, agreed to exterminate the remaining Pamlico. Those not killed were incorporated as slaves by the victorious Tuscarora.

Passamaquoddy

CULTURE AREA: Northeast
LANGUAGE GROUP: Algonquian
PRIMARY LOCATION: Maine
POPULATION SIZE: 2,398 (1990 U.S. Census)

The Passamaquoddy tribe has many similarities to the Abenaki tribes of Maine, New Hampshire, Vermont, and southern Quebec. All these tribes referred to themselves as Wabanaki.

The first contact with Europeans occurred in the late 1400's, when English, Scandinavian, Spanish, and French fishermen discovered the great quantities of cod along the Maine coast. Giovanni da Verrazano left the first written descriptions of the Maine natives in 1524. Both the English and the French tried to colonize the area, and the contact with new people brought devastating epidemics of smallpox and other diseases to the natives.

Fur trading changed the traditional life by introducing guns, alcohol, and new religions. Many Native Americans converted to Roman Catholicism and were sympathetic toward the French and supported the colonists during the American Revolution. The Passamaquoddy tribe was one of three Maine groups who remained in their original land, although for economic reasons they ceded more than a million acres of it to Massachusetts by treaty in 1794.

The Passamaquoddy followed the traditional lifestyle of the Abenaki. They had summer fishing villages and moved to northern hunting territory in the fall and late winter months. Winter clothing included skin leggings and a long cloak of beaver fur with sleeves tied on separately, with fur-lined moccasins or boots and tapered snow shoes. Traditional utensils and lightweight canoes were made from waterproof, durable, white birchbark. Ash provided the material for splint baskets, later an important item in trade. Beads made of quahog shell were woven into decorative items of clothing and also used for currency and in treaty negotiations.

It was not until 1980 that the Passamaquoddy and their Maine neighbors, the Penobscot, were recognized as a tribe by the federal government and became eligible to receive health and welfare services. The Maine Indian Claims Settlement Act in 1980 established an $81.5 million fund for the tribes, which has been used to repurchase 300,000 acres of land, to work toward economic independence through such businesses as a blueberry farm, and to preserve culture with school education and a radio station.

Patayan

DATE: c. 500-1600

LOCATION: Western Arizona, southeastern California, northern Baja California

CULTURES AFFECTED: Havasupai, Mojave, Yuman language groups

Patayan, as a designation for the ancestors of the Yuman-speaking peoples of the Colorado River Basin from the Grand Canyon to the Gulf of California, along with the surrounding upland areas, first appeared in the 1930's, when a familiar division of prehistoric Southwest cultures emerged: Anasazi, Hohokam, Mogollon, and Patayan. Since the 1950's, there has been support for an overall designation of Hakataya, with Patayan to be restricted to the upland regions of Arizona and Laquish to be used for the lower Colorado Basin area. Some scholars, however, continue to use Patayan as an overall designation.

The key to understanding the Patayan is their extremely dry and rugged country, which receives less than ten inches of rain a year. The terrain is rocky with sparse vegetation. It was the most difficult terrain of any of the southwestern cultures, and one of the most difficult in America for a hunting, gathering, and marginally farming people.

Culturally, the Patayan had certain common traits, including a predominance of hunting and gathering. There is considerable evidence that the Patayan peoples, particularly in their Patayan I phase (up to 1100 C.E.), remained almost as nomadic as their desert culture ancestors or their Great Basin cultural relatives to the north. They used stone-lined roasting pits for food preparation, sealed vessels for food storage, percussion-flaked choppers, mortars and pestles (which are found in great numbers), and circular rock shelters of a type of construction known as jacal (but not pueblo-like apartment structures). They almost all cremated their dead, though some burials are known.

Traditional method of firing pottery. (Library of Congress)

One of the most identifiable characteristics was the use of ceramics that were finished by paddle and anvil technique, and were of varying colors resulting from uncontrolled firing, with no further decoration. The most typical was a buffware jar with tapered chimney neck and a rounded Colorado shoulder. Only the northeastern area near the Grand Canyon showed any gray coloration from anoxic firing of the clay, which was common among other southwestern cultures.

Certainly the most possibilities for economic advances were found in the lower Colorado River basin, where inundation (flooding) irrigation was used to produce a much stronger agricultural base. The tidal bores of the river regularly caused problems, however. Because the Gulf of California is a long narrow body of water, a combination of high tides and southern winds could drive a twenty-foot high wall of water up the river almost to the Grand Canyon before modern breakwaters prevented the problem. Though the roar, similar to a locomotive, gave ample warning to evacuate to the hills, crops, homes and cultural items often were washed away.

Linguistic evidence indicates that the modern Yuman-speaking peoples of the Colorado basin are direct descendants of the Patayan. Along with the Pueblo to the east, the Patayan-Yuman represent one of the longest-term sequences of one people in one area in the United States.

Patwin

CULTURE AREA: California
LANGUAGE GROUP: Wintun (Penutian)
PRIMARY LOCATION: From Suisun Bay to Little Snow Creek, California

The patrilineal Patwin were divided by territory into Hill and River Patwin, whose villages were always located on streams. A single village constituted a tribelet. They had a diversified subsistence base that included fishing, hunting, trapping, gathering, and collecting. Though they had four types of structures, all were earth-covered and semi-subterranean, with either circular or elliptical ground plans; each housed several families. Their sweathouses were also subterranean. They had numerous rites of intensification, but rituals of particular importance were the Kuksu and Hesi cult systems. The Kuksu cult, in all its ritual complexity, may in fact have originated among the Patwin.

Prior to 1800, there were numerous Spanish missionary accounts and vital statistics concerning the Patwin. After coming into contact with European Americans, they became serfs and a valuable labor force to Mexicans. Several Indian leaders arose in opposition, forming alliances with other Indian groups. The Patwin suffered greatly from epidemics and conflict with settlers, miners, and the military; eventually they were forced onto reservations. The decline in Patwin population and ethnographic identity continued into the twentieth century, and by 1972 the Bureau of Indian Affairs could locate only eleven people who claimed Patwin ancestry.

Pawnee

CULTURE AREA: Plains
LANGUAGE GROUP: Caddoan
PRIMARY LOCATION: Oklahoma
POPULATION SIZE: 2,892 (1990 U.S. Census)

Early accounts indicate that the Skidi Pawnees, as early as 1600, first came into the region that would become known as Nebraska from the south. Their previous home was a "place where sugarcane grew," possibly in the lower Mississippi Valley. It was not until the eighteenth century that other Pawnees entered the Nebraska region to join the Skidi. The Pawnees' northernmost extension was into South Dakota.

By about the 1760's, a situation that would dominate Pawnee existence for a full century began: warfare with Siouan tribes over hunting in many of the same areas. Many experts believe that, had it not been for their continual struggles against the Sioux, the Pawnees would not have had a single name describing them as "one." Their tradition usually emphasizes separate exploits by key groups: the Skidis, Chauis, Kitkehahkis, and Pitahauerats. Common cultural elements, however, mark the Pawnees. Well-known religious symbols included the star deities—the Morning and Evening Stars—whose daughter was betrothed to the son of Sun and Moon, called "Closed Man." This couple was instructed by four gods whose special knowledge (in lodge building and ceremonies) was passed on to all Pawnee tribes.

In 1749-1750, French traders arranged a peace between the main Plains tribes, allowing them to penetrate Pawnee territory. Wider trade relations increased Pawnee access to guns, at least until the French and Indian War (between the English and French) ended with France's defeat in 1763. Thereafter, the Pawnees lost their dominance in Kansas and reconcentrated farther north along the Platte River in Nebraska. After the late 1760's, three tribes (the Grand Pawnees, the Kitkehahkis, and the Pitahauerats) began attacking their Skidi predecessors in this area. By the time the expedition of Meriwether Lewis and William Clark followed the Platte River (in 1804), they found that the Skidis had become increasingly subordinate to the Grand Pawnees.

Inevitably, the entire area inhabited by the Pawnees and Sioux attracted the attention of American military outposts (specifically at Fort Atkinson, near Omaha). In 1825 the Pawnees signed a fateful treaty promising safety for settlers along the Santa Fe Trail in return for (undefined) "benefits and

419

acts of kindness" from the U.S. government. When what were assumed to be Pawnee raids continued, chances of more forceful intervention by Washington policy makers mounted.

Escalation grew from the government's post-1830 decision to relocate eastern tribes into the vast open areas west of the Missouri. Before long, newly relocated tribes such as the Delawares and Shawnees clashed with the Pawnees over hunting grounds. Warfare was "settled" only temporarily by the signing, in 1833, of a treaty giving up Pawnee claims to territories south of the Platte. By the 1833 treaty, the Pawnees received paltry payment ($1,600) and were promised a twelve-year annuity of goods and cash plus "advantages" (such as agricultural instruction and the construction of mill sites) for agreeing to settle in the North Platte Loup Fork area. Soon afterward, missionaries and traders arrived in the area to settle Fort William (later Fort Laramie). American officials intended to bring Oglala Sioux elements from the Black Hills into this "neutral" zone—a move that inevitably heightened hostilities with the Pawnees along the North Platte.

After this turning point, Pawnee prospects for an independent existence declined steadily. Increasingly they found that they could not survive without the government annuity promised (but not always given) in 1833. Worse still, the Pawnees suffered defeats dealt them by the Great Sioux between 1842 and 1846 and were driven to refuges south of the Platte. There they became so destitute that they sold the best land they occupied for the construction of Fort Kearney.

Pawnee family at the entrance of their central Nebraska earthlodge, around 1870.
(National Archives)

It was not until four years after the Kansas-Nebraska Act of 1854 that a special Pawnee treaty was ratified by Congress. This treaty determined that the Pawnees were to return north to resettle Loup Fork as a Pawnee Indian reservation with government aid. As late as 1865, President Abraham Lincoln's Pawnee Agent, Benjamin Lushbaugh, tried to obtain congressional money to help resolve pressures affecting Pawnee security. A so-called great peace treaty of 1868, however, apparently only helped their Sioux enemies to obtain guns and press toward Loup Fork.

Rather than continue to commit Indian Agency funds to help Pawnees on Loup Fork, policy makers decided to move them again—this time to undeveloped Indian territory farther west. By 1874 the movement to a new reservation had begun. The area reserved was west of the Arkansas River in what became Oklahoma. Although some two thousand Pawnees were relocated in the 1870's, by the 1890's there were only about eight hundred left. In the meantime, their agency had been combined with that of the Ponca and Oto tribes.

The sad state of Pawnee marginality was to continue until, under the Roosevelt administration in 1932, special attention was given to their case. In the June, 1936, Oklahoma Indian Welfare Act, they were allowed to elect their own tribal council. It was not until 1957, however, that Pawnees gained effective rights to use lands on their reservation as they saw fit. Receipt of federal partial payment for lands taken away from them nearly a century earlier came in 1964. Four years later, actual ownership of their reservation lands was turned over. From the middle of the 1970's the Pawnees began to register gains, partially as a result of the Indian Self-Determination Act of 1975, partly because of the dynamic leadership of Council Chairman Thomas Chapman.

Byron D. Cannon

Pennacook

CULTURE AREA: Northeast
LANGUAGE GROUP: Algonquian
PRIMARY LOCATION: New Hampshire

The Pennacook are part of the western branch of the Abenaki family. Their name means "bottom of the hill," and they encompass a number of Algonquian-speaking bands, seventeen tribes of which were united as the Pennacook Confederacy by their best-known leader, Passaconaway, in the early seventeenth century. In 1614, there may have been as many as twelve thousand people in thirty villages along the Merrimack River.

In 1675, their chief, Wanalancet, led the Pennacook deep into the woods to avoid becoming involved in King Philip's War. In 1689, the last chief of the Pennacook, Kankamagus (also known as John Hawkins), under threat of Mohawk attack, led the tribe north. Many tribespeople joined French mission villages in Canada (such as St. Francis), where their tribal identity was lost. Metallak, said to be the last of the Pennacook, returned to the United States and died in New Hampshire in 1848.

In the summer, family groups lived together in sturdy bark-covered, domed, rectangular longhouses with separate fires for each family. As many as sixty people lived in a house. In hunting seasons, smaller groups lived in conical moveable wigwams.

Religious beliefs and traditions, handed down by oral tradition to those who now identify themselves as descendants of the Pennacook and other New Hampshire Abenaki, had led to conflicts between state officials and the 2,134 Native Americans (1990 census figure) living in New Hampshire. Burial sites are protected by federal law. Early Abenaki custom, however, was to bury the dead in unmarked sites near their homes; thus, all former homesites are considered sacred burial sites. The state has generally not recognized these claims. There is no reservation land in New Hampshire.

Penobscot

CULTURE AREA: Northeast
LANGUAGE GROUP: Algonquian
PRIMARY LOCATION: Maine
POPULATION SIZE: 2,173 (1990 U.S. Census)

The Penobscot, of the eastern branch of the Abenaki family, whose name means "the rocky place," live along the river and the bay that bear their name on the Maine coast.

Tradition says that prophesies foretold the coming of white men who would bring a time of trouble because of their desire for the land. Unlike some other Abenaki groups that gave up their New England homelands and migrated north under pressure from white settlers, the Penobscot remained in their original area. During the American Revolution, the Penobscot helped turn back the British, and Chief Joseph Orono was rewarded with a visit to Boston and Newport, Rhode Island.

Their traditional lifestyle began to die out in the early 1800's, as over-hunting and increased lumbering diminished the profitable fur trade and traditional game hunting. The Great Miramicki Fire in 1825 destroyed much of the Maine woodland; disease also took its toll on the tribe. Under economic and political pressure, the Penobscot sold much of their land. The last lifetime chief was Joseph Atteau, chosen in 1858, who is mentioned as a guide by Henry David Thoreau in his book *The Maine Woods* (1864).

By the beginning of the twentieth century, many of the Penobscot lived in poverty and isolation on an island in the river near Old Town. The state granted Indians voting privileges only in 1954—the last state to do so. In 1965, Maine became the first state to establish a Department of Indian Affairs, and in 1980 a long legal battle resulted in the Maine Indian Claims Settlement Act, which allocated $81.5 million to the Penobscot and two other Maine tribes. The money has been used to purchase land, improve housing and schools, and build a factory and a gambling casino to provide employment. About a quarter of the population lives on reservation land, where the schools teach traditional arts and language.

Pequot

CULTURE AREA: Northeast
LANGUAGE GROUP: Algonquian
PRIMARY LOCATION: Connecticut
POPULATION SIZE: 536 (1990 U.S. Census)

In the early seventeenth century, the Pequot, probably numbering about thirteen thousand persons, occupied a territory on the lower Thames River in present-day Connecticut. The Pequot were a horticultural people, subsisting chiefly on corn, beans, and squash raised by the women. Men hunted to supplement these foods, and both sexes harvested the rich resources of fish and shellfish available nearby. There were two large, fortified villages with about seventy wigwams each, several smaller, unfortified ones, and a number of scattered hamlets. Sassacus, who became chief sachem in 1634, lived in the principal village, Weinshauks, in present-day Groton. The chief sachem, chosen from a chiefly lineage or family, exercised a limited, traditional authority through persuasion and influence rather than through direct power. Each subsidiary village had one or more local sachems. There were said to be twenty-six lesser sachems under Sassacus. This no doubt included those of conquered, tributary peoples. Considered

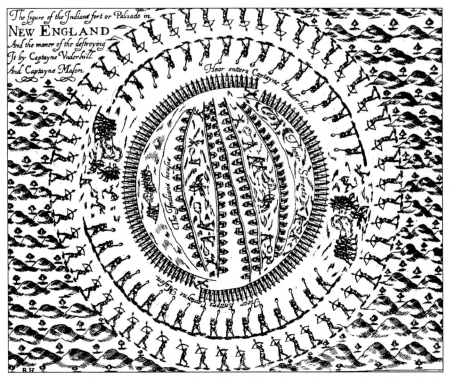

Contemporary engraving of the 1637 defeat of the Pequots at Fort Mystic, their fortified village. (Library of Congress)

the most warlike tribe in southern New England, the Pequot had forced a number of small tribes in the valley of the lower Connecticut and on Long Island to become their tributaries.

In 1633, a smallpox epidemic ravaged the region, reducing Pequot numbers to about three thousand. The severe population loss among the tribes of the lower Connecticut River encouraged English settlers from Plymouth and Massachusetts Bay colonies to move into the area, disrupting native political arrangements. This, along with trade rivalries and attribution to the Pequot of the murder of several English traders, precipitated the Pequot War of 1636-1637. Crushed in that war, many of the one thousand to fifteen hundred Pequot survivors were divided among the colonists' Indian allies. Others found a haven with distant tribes, and for some years the Pequot were forbidden to have an independent existence. In time, several small villages were permitted to reconstitute themselves. Their modern descendants, largely assimilated and no longer speaking the Pequot language, occupy two small reservations: Mashantucket, in Ledyard, and Paucatuck (or Lantern Hill), at North Stonington, Connecticut.

Petun

CULTURE AREA: Northeast
LANGUAGE GROUP: Iroquoian
PRIMARY LOCATION: South of Georgian Bay

Located just west of the Hurons, the Petun Nation (also known as the Tobacco tribe) were very closely related culturally and linguistically to the Hurons, particularly the Attignaouantan band. Tionontati was the name for them in the Attignaouantan language, meaning "people of the place where the hills are." The other distinctive geographic feature of the Petun region was its microclimate, which made possible the cultivation of highly specialized varieties of tobacco. The neighboring Hurons were not able to grow tobacco in this fashion; therefore, the Petun people had an economic advantage.

The basis of the Petun economy, however, was rooted in corn, beans, and squash grown by the women of the tribe. Men hunted and fished to complement these products, and fruit was gathered for variety. In all other ways, including village habitation, matrilineal and matrilocal longhouse dwelling, dress, and spiritual practices, the Petun seem to have been highly similar to the Huron peoples. In one respect they differed slightly, in that they divided their tribe into two groups, the Deer and the Wolves.

Population figures for the Petun tribe are difficult to discern, since the French often grouped them together with the Hurons. They may have numbered as many as eight thousand before contact with these Europeans. The French Jesuits set up missions to the Tobacco people in the 1630's, and smallpox epidemics reduced the population, probably to about three thousand. The Petun people were caught in the Huron-Iroquois rivalry, and after the Iroquois destroyed Huronia in 1649-1651, some Huron survivors took refuge among the Petuns, only to come under attack again when the Iroquois subsequently turned their wrath on the Petun nation. The few surviving Petuns and Hurons who were not adopted into Iroquois families traveled further north and west after 1652. A few of them later journeyed to the St. Lawrence Valley with Jesuits, but others remained in the Michigan-Wisconsin area and eventually, by about 1870, acquired lands in Indian Territory, now Oklahoma. In the twentieth century, the Wyandot tribe of Oklahoma included some people who were partly of Petun ancestry, but their ancestors were absorbed into the Huron-Wyandot group and are not distinguishable from them.

Pima

CULTURE AREA: Southwest
LANGUAGE GROUP: Piman (Uto-Aztecan)
PRIMARY LOCATION: South-central Arizona
POPULATION SIZE: 14,431 (1990 U.S. Census)

Although direct evidence is inconclusive, many scholars believe that the Pimas (or Akimel O'odham) are descended from the prehistoric Hohokam people of the Southwest. The Pimas developed extensive canals and dams for their farmlands, and they were considered the best farmers of all Arizona tribes. The missionary Eusebio Kino in 1687 introduced new crops, including barley and wheat, to the Pimas and supplied them with cattle and sheep. A century later, in 1793, the Pimas numbered about four thousand and resided in seven villages near the Gila River. They grew cotton, corn, melons, and pumpkins, and they traded their spun and woven cotton cloth to the Mexicans to the south.

In the 1840's the Maricopa tribe, seeking to avoid hostilities with other tribes, took refuge among the Pima and have remained with them ever since. The Pimas came under United States jurisdiction in 1853, when the Gadsden Purchase ended Mexican rule. The United States introduced the reservation system in the 1870's. In 1990, Pima and Maricopa tribes continued to occupy the Gila River and Salt River reservations of 427,807 acres near Phoenix, Arizona.

The Gila River Farmers Association was organized in the 1930's to deal with federal government water issues. The Indian Reorganization Act of 1934 led the Pimas to exercise powers of self-government. The Gila River Pima community established a seventeen-member tribal council as its central governing body and voted for a governor and lieutenant governor every three years. A tribal constitution, adopted in 1960, dictates procedures for the election of these officers. The council members, from seven political districts based on population, are elected to serve staggered terms. The council meets twice a month. The standing committees include committees on economic development, natural resources, government and management, health and social issues, and education.

The majority of Pimas live and work in their reservation communities in schools, government agencies, a tribal hospital, and stores.

Plano

DATE: 8000-5000 B.C.E.
LOCATION: Plains
CULTURE AFFECTED: Plano

The Plano tradition, dating 8000 and 5000 B.C.E., represents the last period of the hunting of now-extinct large Pleistocene mammals, especially giant bison, in North America. It is preceded by the Clovis (9500 to 9000 B.C.E.) and the Folsom (9000 to 8200 B.C.E.) periods, although Folsom and Plano are usually discussed together. Sites of this tradition are found over a wide area of North America, ranging from Alaska to Texas.

While Clovis peoples hunted mammoth, Folsom/Plano subsistence was oriented toward the pursuit of the now-extinct giant longhorn bison (*Bison antiquus* and *Bison occidentalis*) and later the modern *Bison bison*. Folsom/Plano cultures are known from occasional campsites and a large number of kill sites marked by beds of bison bone with stone artifacts. Tool technology was characterized by a wide variety of projectile point and knife styles used for killing and butchering. Folsom points, marked by a broad channel scar that runs most of the length of the point, belong to the fluted-point tradition that begins with Clovis. Plano cultures are associated with several unfluted styles, among them Plainview/Firstview, Eden, Scottsbluff, Claypool, Milnesand, Agate Basin, San Jon, and Angostura.

Plano Lifeways. The Folsom/Plano peoples ranged across the Great Plains in small, nomadic groups that followed seasonal rounds conditioned by the migration of bison herds. On these migrations, they took advantage of several sources for fine-grained, knappable stone. This material was used to manufacture points, knives, scrapers, and other tools, many of which required a high degree of skill in pressure flaking. Bison hunting, although likely to have included single-animal kills, was made very productive through the employment of mass-kill techniques. These included driving animals over cliffs or into natural traps, such as ditches and arroyos, box canyons, stream channels, and crescent-shaped sand dunes, and then killing them with spears. These techniques would have required the participation of more than a single family and would have provided enough meat and hides for several bands. Animal resources such as skins, meat, bone, and marrow were efficiently utilized, often with very little waste.

Plano Archaeological Sites. Plano campsites tend to be situated on knolls or hills from which watering holes and bison herds could be observed. Lindenmeier is the largest known camp associated with the Folsom culture. It was located on the banks of a marshy lake in northeastern Colorado, now buried under sediments. Excavations revealed remains of hearths with broken tools and discarded bones that have been dated to approximately 9000 B.C.E. Bison bones were the most numerous, but bones of wolf, coyote, fox, hare, rabbit, turtle, deer, and antelope were also present. The large collection of stone tools included more than 250 Folsom points. The site appears to have been occupied by at least two different groups, based on differences in the size of projectile points and the fact that some were made of obsidian from a source in New Mexico, whereas others were made of material from Wyoming. The wide range of raw materials utilized by Folsom/Plano peoples suggests that they were covering vast distances in cyclical migrations.

The Olsen-Chubbuck site, in eastern Colorado near the Kansas state line, provides an example of a large-scale bison kill. At around 8200 B.C.E., almost two hundred bison (*Bison occidentalis*) were trapped when they were stampeded down a steep hillside into a narrow arroyo. The age of the animals, which included calves, yearlings, and bison of both sexes, suggests that the kill took place in the spring. The composition of piles of bones indicates that the animals were butchered in a consistent pattern, beginning with skinning and removal of hump meat and proceeding from the front to the hindquarters of the animals. Among the tools used were Firstview (Plainview) points, knives, scrapers, and cobbles to break bones for the extraction of marrow. Some of the chert used to make tools came from sources in Texas, supporting models for the seasonal migrations of Folsom/Plano peoples across a wide geographical range.

The Casper site in central Wyoming provides evidence for the slaughter of a small herd of bison around 6000 B.C.E. The animals were driven into the central concavity of a parabolic sand dune, where they were killed and butchered. The predominance of young animals in this bone bed suggests a degree of selectivity in the size of animals taken. Butchering was done efficiently, with deliberate stacking of bones. At the Hawken site in the Bighorn Basin of northeastern Wyoming, bison were killed when small herds were driven upstream into an increasingly narrow, steep-sided arroyo until they were wedged against one another and trapped at its box canyon terminus, where they were killed by hunters with spears. The Horner site, also in northeastern Wyoming, has evidence of two bison kills spaced approximately a thousand years apart. Bison may have been corralled with drive lines; excavator George Frison suggests the practice of frozen caching of partially butchered carcasses for utilization at different times.

Plano Technology. In general, Folsom/Plano populations practiced a more sophisticated use of natural resources than did their predecessors.

They covered much greater geographical ranges, probably moving with seasonal migrations of bison herds, and took advantage of several different sources of lithic materials. In addition to improvements in stone tool manufacture, there were significant technological advances in the ways that animals were slaughtered, butchered, and utilized. The wide variety of projectile point styles suggests the gradual emergence of distinct cultural groups whose identities became strengthened through periodic episodes of cooperative hunting.

The Plano tradition comes to an end with the decline of populations of giant bison, probably precipitated by climatic changes that reduced the size and range of their modern descendants for several thousand years. Patterns that evolved from Plano, however, continued for thousands of years. The hunting of bison remained one of the most important strategies for survival in the Plains until the destruction of large herds by European settlers in the nineteenth century.

John Hoopes

Bibliography

Frison, George C., ed. *The Casper Site: A Hell Gap Bison Kill on the High Plains.* New York: Academic Press, 1974.

_____. *Prehistoric Hunters of the High Plains.* New York: Academic Press, 1978.

Frison, George C., and Lawrence D. Todd, eds. *The Horner Site: The Type Site of the Cody Cultural Complex.* Orlando, Fla.: Academic Press, 1987.

Irwin, H. T., and H. M. Wormington. "Paleo-Indian Tool Types in the Great Plains." *American Antiquity* 365 (1970): 24-34.

Wheat, Joe Ben. "The Olsen-Chubbuck Site: A Paleo-Indian Bison Kill." Vol. 37 in *American Antiquity.* Washington, D.C.: Society for American Archaeology, 1972.

Wilmsen, Edwin N. *Lindenmeier: A Pleistocene Hunting Society.* New York: Harper & Row, 1974.

Pomo

CULTURE AREA: California
LANGUAGE GROUP: Hokan
PRIMARY LOCATION: Clear Lake, Northern California
POPULATION SIZE: 4,766 (1990 U.S. Census)

The Pomo Indians are one of the many California native groups who shared traits with a wide variety of hunter-gatherer tribes in the California area. In 1770, the number of Pomo was estimated at 8,000, which had dropped to 1,143 by the 1930 census. Pomo Indian traditional areas include Cleone Duncan's Point and inland as far as the Clear Lake (Stony Creek) area, north of the San Francisco Bay.

California Indians generally are not to be understood as "tribes," but rather as small "tribal groups" of a hundred persons at most. These groups, usually not permanent, surrounded a centrally recognized permanent village. The Pomo shared many common cultural traits with other village communities up and down the California coast as far south as the beginnings of the great Mexican tribal groups, where the appearance of pottery and other traditionally Mexican native arts in the region of Southern California signals a mixing of cultures on a spectrum approaching the great civilization centers of central and southern Mexico.

Pomo people are most noted for their distribution of shells as a kind of currency exchange. They also developed basketry to perhaps the highest art form among all the California tribal groupings, incorporating styles and designs that mark Pomo artistry in a manner that is clear even to those not widely familiar with California basketry. Because of their residency near Clear Lake, the Pomo also developed canoes, the use of the single-blade paddle, and the use of balsa rafts.

As with other California tribal groupings, shamanism was practiced among the Pomo as a healing and supernatural art. Pomo ceremonial life is also noted for the use of sweatlodges, heated by direct fire rather than by steam (steam was absent throughout California tribal use of sweatlodges). Of particular interest with regard to Pomo religion is the Maru Cult, a religious ceremony of ritual and dancing that is a direct descendant of the influence of the Ghost Dance of 1870 on the Pomo people. The Maru Cult rituals are still observed among many modern Pomo members.

In terms of family life, the Pomo practiced the purchase of brides as an essential aspect of matrimony. There was no recognized "chief" in Pomo tradition, but rather a leadership of recognized male leaders of the settlements.

Bibliography

Brown, Vinson, and Douglas Andrews. *The Pomo Indians of California and Their Neighbors*. Heraldsburg, Calif.: Naturegraph, 1969.

Kroeber, Alfred. "The Indians of California." In *The North American Indians: A Sourcebook*, edited by Roger Owen, James Deetz, and Anthony Fisher. New York: Macmillan, 1967.

Layton, Thomas N. *Western Pomo Prehistory: Excavations at Albion Head, Nightbirds' Retreat, and Three Chop Village, Mendocino County, California.* Los Angeles: University of California Press, 1990.

Meighan, Clement W., and Francis Riddel. *The Maru Cult of the Pomo Indians: A California Ghost Dance Survival.* Southwest Museum Papers 23. Los Angeles: Southwest Museum, 1972.

Ponca

CULTURE AREA: Plains
LANGUAGE GROUP: Siouan
PRIMARY LOCATION: Nebraska, Oklahoma
POPULATION SIZE: 2,913 (1990 U.S. Census)

The Ponca were Plains Indians who retained aspects of the culture of the woodlands from which they entered the Plains. Their closest relatives and associates were the Omaha; their relationships with the Sioux and Pawnee were always stormy. They were generally friendly with European Americans. Their chief Standing Bear forced a court ruling extending the personal liberties guaranteed by the Constitution to Indians.

Early History and Traditional Lifestyle. Sometime between 1200 and 1500, the Ponca entered the Plains from the Ohio River valley. They eventually settled along the Niobrara River in northeast Nebraska, where they lived in earthlodges and farmed the river's floodplain as they had in the eastern woodlands. In spring and early summer, and again in autumn, they moved into the Plains, where they lived in tipis and hunted buffalo as Plains Indians. The Ponca obtained horses in the mid-1700's and extended their hunting range beyond the Black Hills of South Dakota.

Ponca society and religion were much like those of other Plains Indians. Men hunted and waged war; women cooked, gardened, and made clothes and tipi covers. The women also took down the tipi before moving and put it up after the move. Unlike many Plains tribes, chief positions were hereditary. As with other Plains tribes, however, the chief had to demonstrate bravery and generosity to maintain a following. Ponca spiritual life included a sacred pipe, tribal medicine bundle, individual medicine bundles, vision quests, warrior societies, and Sun Dances.

The Ponca were always a small tribe and often united with the neighboring Omaha to defend themselves against the Sioux and Pawnee. Occasionally they joined the Sioux in disputes with the Pawnee or Omaha. Most of their conflicts occurred with the Sioux, who attacked them on their hunting grounds and in their villages. They were never at war with the United States.

Transition and Modern Life. The Ponca position on the Missouri assured them early contact with white explorers and traders. Meriwether Lewis and William Clark spent time with them on their trip to explore the Louisiana Purchase, as did Prince Maximilian zu Wied and Karl Bodmer on their trip up the Missouri. They traded early and extensively with European Americans. The Ponca were hospitable to their visitors and were respected by the explorers and traders.

Despite their friendly attitude toward the European immigrants, the Ponca ultimately were treated no better than other American Indians. In 1858 they were assigned to a reservation within their traditional homeland, but in 1868 the same land was given to the Sioux. Responding to the resultant conflict between the tribes, the government determined to move the Ponca to Indian Territory (Oklahoma), a move the Indians attempted to resist.

In 1877, the Ponca tribe, under Chief White Eagle was forcibly moved. Many died on the trip, and more died in the first years in Oklahoma. In 1879, Chief Standing Bear, determined to bury his dead son in Nebraska, suggested that the tribe return to the Niobrara. Most Poncas, including White Eagle, believed that they would only be forced back to Oklahoma and chose to stay. Nevertheless, Standing Bear and several others moved north, reaching the Omaha reservation near Omaha, Nebraska, where they were arrested by the United States Army.

An editor of an Omaha newspaper, Thomas H. Tibbles, aroused public sentiment with his accounts of the situation. Two lawyers sued the government on behalf of Standing Bear's right to go where he pleased. The government argued that Indians had no such rights. The judge ruled against the government, and government appeals (eventually to the Supreme Court) were dismissed. The ruling gave Indians the same personal liberties as white Americans. Application of the law was not that simple, but Standing Bear had forced a first legal step in the direction of Indian equality.

The Northern Ponca were eventually given a small reservation, but the General Allotment Act (Dawes Severalty Act) of 1887 gave allotments of reservation property to individual Indians and allowed the "extra" land to be sold to whites. The loss of their tribal land base was devastating to both Ponca subdivisions, but both survived because of their determination to do so. For example, when the government withdrew tribal recognition from the Northern Ponca in 1962, the Ponca returned to the courts of law. Tribal status was restored in 1990. The Ponca continue to struggle with poverty and undereducation, but their continued existence as a tribe attests their character and determination.

Carl W. Hoagstrom

Poospatuck

CULTURE AREA: Northeast
LANGUAGE GROUP: Algonquian
PRIMARY LOCATION: Long Island, New York
POPULATION SIZE: 264 (1990 U.S. Census)

The Poospatuck, also called Uncachogue, were one of thirteen tribes occupying Long Island, New York, in the seventeenth century. They, along with other Algonquian tribes, had lived in the area for thousands of years. The thirteen tribes made up the Montauk Confederacy, which controlled all of Long Island except the far western end. The chief of the Montauk tribe was considered—by both American Indians and Europeans—the head of all the thirteen tribes. Many scholars, in fact, consider the Montauk Confederacy one tribe and view the thirteen smaller units as clans.

The Poospatuck lived on the eastern half of the island's south shore. They lived in permanent villages and ate a diet of fish and seafood as well as maize, beans, and pumpkins. Food was cooked in clay pots and stirred with wooden utensils. The Poospatuck created beautiful woven fabrics and leather goods. In the early seventeenth century, the Pequots conquered the Montauk Confederacy. After the Pequots were nearly wiped out in 1637, the Narragansett began to attack the Montauk, forcing them to seek refuge with whites. In 1666, the Poospatuck were granted a reservation on the Forge River. They tried to maintain their traditional life even as their numbers dwindled. The tribe's last chief, the sachem Elizabeth Joe, died in 1832, but the Poospatuck reservation is still intact and recognized by New York State.

Potawatomi

CULTURE AREA: Northeast
LANGUAGE GROUP: Algonquian
PRIMARY LOCATION: Oklahoma, Wisconsin
POPULATION SIZE: 16,763 in U.S. (1990 U.S. Census); 85 in Canada (Statistics Canada, based on 1992 census)

The Potawatomi, a tribe of the Algonquian language group, originally came from north of Lake Superior. About 1500 C.E., they migrated south to the eastern shore of Lake Michigan, where they built a dozen villages along the St. Joseph River.

Traditional Lifeways. The Potawatomi hunted deer, elk, buffalo, and small game, fished, and gathered berries and nuts. They also planted and harvested corn and squash. Women worked the crops while the men hunted. The Potawatomi moved their villages every ten to twelve years, when the soil became exhausted. The name of the tribe resulted from a misunderstanding by Jean Nicolet, the French fur trapper and explorer who first made contact with the Potawatomi in 1634. He asked his Huron guide, "Who are these people?" The guide misunderstood and answered, "They are making fire," which sounded like "pota wa tomi" to the Frenchman. They actually called themselves Neshnabek, meaning "the true people," but the other name stuck.

Traditional Potawatomi religion stressed the power of Wiske, the Master of All Life. Wiske had a twin brother, Chipiyapos, the Destroyer, but the gods looked so much alike people could tell the difference between them only with great difficulty. Potawatomi children began being taught about the difference between good and evil at age twelve, when they went on "vision quests" in the wilderness. Here they walked alone, naked, and without food or drink, praying and meditating. If they were purified by their suffering, a guardian spirit (*manitou*) would appear to them and lead them to safety. The manitou would protect the youth for the rest of his life.

Post-contact Life. In 1641, the first Roman Catholic missionaries appeared and set up a mission at St. Joseph, Michigan, though they met with little success in converting Indians to Christianity. In the 1650's, the Iroquois of New York attacked all other tribes in Ohio, Michigan, and Indiana, seeking to expand their control of the fur trade. They defeated the Potawatomi, and the "true people" ended up in northern Wisconsin, along Green Bay.

From their new homeland, the Potawatomi became involved again in the fur trade, mainly with the French. Many French traders married Indian women, but the Potawatomi considered children of mixed marriages (called Brules—burned ones—by the natives and Metis—mixed people—by the French) aliens, and refused to let them live in their villages. Full-bloods lived in clans, which included the living, the dead, and the not-yet-born family members.

In the French and Indian War (1754-1763), the Potawatomi attacked British forces as far east as New York and Virginia. In 1755, they acquired horses for the first time, and the horse quickly replaced birchbark canoes as their major mode of transportation. In 1763, Potawatomi warriors joined in Pontiac's war against the British, but the Ottawa chief's rebellion failed and he signed a humiliating peace treaty.

In 1794, the American army defeated another Potawatomi force at the Battle of Fallen Timbers, and the Indians gave up a large amount of land in Ohio and Indiana. In 1807, the "true people" joined Tecumseh in his war to unite all Indians and expel whites from their old homelands, but this fight also ended in failure. As the fur trade declined, tribal leaders found the sale of land to whites at very low prices one method of avoiding absolute poverty. In 1831, under the terms of the Indian Removal Act, the Potawatomi agreed to resettle in Kansas, though only about a half of the tribe's twenty-seven hundred members actually moved. The others remained in the East and came under state authority, chiefly in Michigan and, later, Wisconsin.

After the Civil War, the "strolling Potawatomis" of northern Wisconsin, so called because they were landless and frequently moved from place to place, moved onto the Menominee reservation. Here they became involved with the Strange Woman religion led by a Dakota who claimed she had had a vision of Christ, who would soon return and restore his people to power and respect. If her followers would beat a giant drum and dance steadily for four days, the whites would fall dead to the earth. This "Dream Dance" is still performed four times a year, but mainly as a tourist attraction. In the twentieth century, the Potawatomi received their own reservation in Wisconsin, and they worked as migrant agricultural workers and basketmakers. The result was increasing poverty and despair. Only the legalization of bingo on tribal land offered any opportunity for economic growth; otherwise jobs and opportunity proved very scarce.

Leslie V. Tischauser

Powhatan Confederacy

Tribes affected: Chickahominy, Gingaskin, Mattaponi, Nansemond, Nottoway, Pamunkey, Patawomeck (Potomac), Rappahannock, Weyanoke, Wiccocomicos, about twenty others
Culture area: Southeast
Language group: Algonquian
Primary location: Virginia

The American Indians who encountered the first permanent English colonists at Jamestown, Virginia, in 1607 were Powhatans. This was the society to which the famous Pocahontas belonged. The name of the Powhatan can be a source of confusion because it has at least four related but distinct meanings. First, it is applied collectively to those early seventeenth century Virginia tribes that acknowledged the leadership of a paramount chief. After 1607 this chief was generally called Powhatan by the English (though his personal name was Wahunsonacock). Powhatan was also the name of the chief's native village at the falls of the James River. (The term literally meant "at the falls.") Finally, the name is applied to the Algonquian dialects spoken by Powhatan's subjects.

The Powhatan tribes lived in eastern Virginia, between the Potomac River and the south bank of the James River. There were approximately thirty tribes or groups that acknowledged Powhatan's supremacy. Some of these (such as the Mattaponi, Pamunkey, and Rappahannock) survived into later centuries; most of the others (such as the Patawomecks, Weyanokes, and Wiccocomicos) did not.

Traditional Lifestyle. By the time of contact with the English, the Powhatans had evolved a settled way of life based on a mixed economy of agriculture and foraging. Powhatan tribes lived in villages located on the many creeks and rivers that fed into Chesapeake Bay. The men hunted and foraged for food, while the women were responsible for planting and harvesting corn and vegetables. The sexes enjoyed greater equality than existed in modern European society. Powhatan society was relatively stratified, with recognized ruling families in each village, as well as priests and military leaders, all ranking above the commoners. The political organization that had evolved by the time of contact was relatively elaborate. Each group had its own chief (or *weroance*), though all swore allegiance to Powhatan. Individual village chiefs were the lowest tier of authority. Though often styled a confederacy, Powhatan's polity is more accurately termed a paramount chiefdom because it was based on the sub-

Powhatan was the leader of a powerful confederacy at the time English colonists first arrived in Virginia. (Library of Congress)

ordination of its member tribes rather than their voluntary association. Powhatan was not an absolute ruler, however, and his power was greater over some tribes than others.

Contact with the English. Powhatan's life was changed forever by the arrival of the English in Virginia in 1607. While Indian assistance in the form of food and knowledge was essential to the colony's survival, a clash of cultures almost immediately ensued, and conflict became the dominant pattern. Wars were fought with the English in 1610-1613 under Powhatan's leadership and in 1622-1632 and 1644-1646 under Opechancanough, Powhatan's younger brother and successor as paramount chief. The second of the wars began with a surprise uprising that killed a quarter of Virginia's white population. Opechancanough was killed during the last of the wars, and thereafter the paramount chiefdom disintegrated.

An attempt was made, with English encouragement, to resurrect it in the 1670's under Cockacoeske, queen of the Pamunkeys. By this time, however, the Powhatan tribes that survived preferred dealing with the English on an individual basis. In 1677, treaties were made with the colony of Virginia in which several of the tribes accepted reservations. The Powhatans were clearly a civilization in decline. The combination of wars and disease had reduced their numbers from twelve thousand in 1607 to one thousand in 1700. Over time the Indians became increasingly acculturated. By the mid-eighteenth century, the Powhatan language had died out.

Modern Struggles. Despite a decimated population and social disorganization, the Virginia tribes that survived managed to maintain a strong sense of Indian identity. During the nineteenth and early twentieth centuries, they faced an uphill struggle to preserve it. To many white Virginians, the descendants of the Powhatans did not seem very "Indian": They spoke English, farmed, and dressed like other Virginians. Moreover, many had intermarried—with blacks as well as whites—in an era of increasing racial consciousness.

The Gingaskin and Nottaway tribes (the latter a non-Algonquian group) agreed to termination in the early nineteenth century, and their reservation lands were divided among themselves. The Pamunkeys and Mattaponis maintained control of their reservation lands, though at times with difficulty. The nonreservation tribes (such as the Rappahannocks, Nansemonds, and Chickahominies) had more problems maintaining separate identities and were not recognized by the state government as Indians. (Since the treaties governing Virginia's Indians were made long before American independence, the Virginia tribes never entered into a formal relationship with the United States government and lacked federal recognition as Indians.)

Probably the greatest difficulties for Virginia's Indians came during the era of racial segregation, when state authorities sought to treat Indians as they treated African Americans. Indians resisted, however, often wearing their straight hair long to display their physical distinctiveness. During World Wars I and II, reservation Indians were able to establish their claim to Indian status and thus served in white, rather than black, units.

The twentieth century witnessed a revival among Virginia tribes of Powhatan ancestry. The Pamunkey and Mattaponi continue to maintain their reservations, and nonreservation groups organized and sought formal recognition from the state. By 1990, five such groups had obtained state recognition: the Upper Mattaponi, the United Rappahanock, the Nansemond, the Chickahominy, and the Eastern Chickahominy. Organized legally as corporations, the nonreservation tribes adopted democratic governments that elected councils and chiefs. The reservation tribes by this time also had elected governments, though they limited participation in them to male reservation residents.

William C. Lowe

Bibliography

Craven, Wesley Frank. *Red, White, and Black*. Charlottesville: University Press of Virginia, 1971.

Lemay, J. A. Leo. *Did Pocahantas Save Captain John Smith?* Athens: University of Georgia Press, 1992.

Paredes, J. Anthony, ed. *Indians of the Southeastern United States in the Late Twentieth Century*. Tuscaloosa: University of Alabama Press, 1992.

Rountree, Helen C. *Pocahontas's People: The Powhatan Indians of Virginia Through Four Centuries*. Norman: University of Oklahoma Press, 1990.

_____. *The Powhatan Indians of Virginia: Their Traditional Culture*. Norman: University of Oklahoma Press, 1989.

_____, ed. *Powhatan Foreign Relations, 1500-1722*. Charlottesville: University Press of Virginia, 1993.

Williams, Walter L., ed. *Southeastern Indians Since the Removal Era*. Athens: University of Georgia Press, 1979.

Pueblo tribes, Eastern

TRIBES AFFECTED: Cochiti, Hano, Isleta, Jemez, Nambe, Pecos, Picuris, Pojoaque, San Felipe, San Ildefonso, San Juan, Sandia, Santa Ana, Santa Clara, Santo Domingo, Taos, Tesuque, Tigua, Zia

Culture area: Southwest
Language groups: Keresan, Tanoan
Primary location: Hopi First Mesa, Rio Grande Valley
Population size: 24,055 (1990 U.S. Census)

The Puebloans say that they have occupied the Southwest from "time immemorial"; indeed, archaeological investigation has proved that they are descended from the prehistoric Anasazi, "the Ancient Ones." As the Anasazi abandoned their great population centers at Mesa Verde, Chaco Canyon, and Kayenta around the year 1300, they migrated into three main areas, one of which was the Rio Grande Valley in New Mexico. There they built new settlements, which were still occupied at the time of the Spanish entry into the Southwest around 1540; most of these continued to be occupied into the twentieth century.

The indigenous peoples whom the Spaniards encountered were, for the most part, agriculturists with a sedentary, settled lifestyle. They lived in villages consisting of terraced, flat-roofed, communal dwellings of stone and adobe built around a central plaza. The Spaniards called these villages "pueblos" and their occupants "Pueblo Indians," as distinguished from the nomadic Apache. With more than 25 percent of their yearly food supply provided by their own crops, the Puebloans had been able to develop a stable and organized way of life, with ample time to devote to art and religion.

Contact with the Spanish. The Spaniards came into the Southwest looking for gold but, finding none, settled for declaring it a missionary domain for the Franciscans. They divided the area into districts, each of which was assigned to a Roman Catholic priest. All the pueblos were given Spanish saint names, and the Puebloans were forced to swear allegiance and vassalage to the Spanish crown and the Church. Some Puebloans were driven from their homes so that the Spanish soldiers, priests, and settlers could be housed.

Spanish oppression became more and more unbearable until finally, in 1680, the Puebloans revolted, driving the conquerors back to El Paso del Norte. In 1692, however, General Don Diego de Vargas led his armies back into the territory, successfully recapturing it.

The Mexican Revolution of 1821 put an end to Spanish rule in the Southwest, but little changed for the Puebloans except that they were now designated citizens of the Mexican Republic. In 1846, war broke out between the United States and Mexico, ending in 1848 with the Treaty of Guadalupe Hidalgo, which ceded New Mexico and upper California to the United States. The treaty also obligated the United States to recognize

Indian rights previously established under Spanish and Mexican rule. In 1849, the Bureau of Indian Affairs sent the first Indian agent to the New Mexico Territory. In the Gadsden Purchase of 1853, the United States acquired more land in the Southwest from Mexico; in 1861, parts of the New Mexico Territory were designated as the Territories of Arizona and Colorado. For decades afterward, titles to Indian lands in these new territories were in question. Most of the pueblos had no documents confirming their Spanish land grants, and land-hungry settlers coming into the area took what they wanted. Beginning in 1856, federal government surveys were made and were later confirmed by the Supreme Court, with the result that many Puebloans were given official title to their lands in 1864. When both New Mexico and Arizona joined the Union in 1912, the Indians became United States citizens but were not granted citizenship by either state until 1948.

New Mexico's Taos Pueblo in 1927; the circular areas are the roofs of underground kivas in which special ceremonies were held. (Library of Congress)

Tiwa-Speaking Pueblos. The Tanoan language, one of the two major language groups of the Eastern Pueblos, contains three subfamilies or dialects: Tiwa, Tewa, and Towa. The northern Tiwa are the pueblos of Taos and

Picuris, while the southern Tiwa are located to the north and south of Albuquerque in the pueblos of Sandia and Isleta. A fifth Tiwa group, the Tigua, lives at El Paso, Texas.

Taos Pueblo, the northernmost of all those in the Rio Grande Valley, was built around 1700 after the original pueblo, dating several hundred years earlier, was destroyed by fire in the 1690's. The pueblo consists of two communal structures, Hlauuma (North House) and Hlaukwima (South House), which are located on either side of Taos Creek. The first Spanish contact was made by Pedro de Alvarado in 1540, followed by Juan de Oñate in 1598, who named the pueblo "San Miguel." The Spaniards built two churches in the pueblo, one in the early seventeenth century and one in the early eighteenth century, both of which were subsequently destroyed (the present church dates from 1847). In 1639, harsh Spanish rule forced the people of Taos to flee to the north, where they built a new pueblo in what is now Scott County, Kansas. Two years later, however, the Spaniards forced them to return to Taos. Their two-year residency among the Plains Indians influenced the dress, the customs, and even the physical makeup of the people of Taos, and for many years Taos was a trading center for the Ute, Apache, and Comanche.

The original pueblo of Picuris dates from around 1250 and was named San Lorenzo by the Spaniards, who built a mission there in 1621. Like Taos, Picuris had its problems with Spanish authority; the governor of Picuris was one of the leaders of the Pueblo Revolt, and after the Spanish reconquest in 1692, the people of Picuris escaped to western Kansas, where they lived until 1706. At that time, weakened by disease and warfare, they returned to their pueblo.

The pueblo of Sandia dates from about 1300. The Spaniards built a mission there in the early seventeenth century (San Francisco), but it was destroyed in the Pueblo Revolt. After the Spaniards destroyed Sandia Pueblo in their attempts at reconquest, the people of Sandia took refuge with the Hopi, building the village of Payupki on the Second Mesa. In 1742, about five hundred people returned to Sandia and built a new pueblo on the site of the old one.

Isleta, with its 210,445 acres, is the largest of all Rio Grande pueblos in terms of area. In the 1600's, many people from other Tiwa villages came to Isleta to escape Apache raids. At the time of the Pueblo Revolt, Isleta's population numbered about two thousand people, many of whom were forced to accompany the Spaniards as they fled south to El Paso del Norte. Their descendants, the Tiguas, still live at Ysleta del Sur, about twelve miles south of El Paso, where they built a pueblo arranged around a rectangular plaza. As several scholars have established, the northern Puebloans virtually disowned the Tiguas because they did not fight the Spaniards in the Pueblo Revolt. As a consequence, the Tiguas have never been allowed to join the Pueblo Conference, although Texas recognized their tribal status by creating the Tigua Indian Reservation in 1967.

Tewa-Speaking Pueblos. There are seven Tewa pueblos: San Juan, Santa Clara, San Ildefonso, Nambe, Tesuque, and Pojoaque in the Rio Grande Valley, and Hano in Hopi country. The pueblo of San Juan is the largest of the Tewa-speaking pueblos and has been continuously inhabited since 1300. Juan de Oñate designated San Juan as his first capital in 1598 but appropriated the pueblo of Yunqueyunque the following year, sending its inhabitants to live in San Juan. In 1675, when Spanish repression of Pueblo religion reached the point where forty-seven Pueblo leaders were convicted of witchcraft and whipped, Popé, a San Juan medicine man, was among them. It was he who later planned and led the Pueblo Revolt.

The pueblos of Santa Clara and San Ildefonso date from the early fourteenth century. The Spaniards built missions in both pueblos; both were destroyed in the Pueblo Revolt. As the Spaniards attempted to reconquer the area, people from both pueblos took refuge atop nearby Black Mesa but surrendered after a nine-month siege. Most of the Santa Clarans abandoned their pueblo again around 1696 and moved west to the Hopi villages, where they built the pueblo of Hano on First Mesa. By 1702, the Spaniards had repopulated San Ildefonso with other Tewa-speaking people, but the pueblo continued to have serious troubles throughout the eighteenth century: A smallpox epidemic decimated half the population, Spanish repression of Puebloan religion continued, and many witchcraft trials occurred at the pueblo.

The pueblos of Tesuque, Nambe, and Pojoaque, which all date from around 1300, also took part in the Pueblo Revolt after destroying the Spanish mission in each. They joined the other Tewas at Black Mesa but, by the early 1700's, had returned to their own pueblos. While Tesuque has continued to follow the traditional Puebloan way of life, both Nambe and Pojoaque have more or less ceased to exist as Pueblo communities. Only the kiva at Nambe distinguishes it from any other rural Rio Grande village.

Jemez Pueblo. The only Towa-speaking pueblo still in existence is Jemez, located on the Rio Jemez in the Jemez Mountains west of Santa Fe. Hostile toward the Spanish from the outset, the Jemez fostered two rebellions against them even before the Pueblo Revolt of 1680. After the reconquest, the Jemez, retreating to a mesa-top fortress, continued to raid the Spaniards but were defeated in the late 1690's. Those who escaped Spanish retribution took refuge with the Hopi and the Navajo. By 1703, most of the people had returned to the Jemez Valley and rebuilt their pueblo. In 1838, when Pecos Pueblo, another Towa-speaking village in the Galisteo Basin, was abandoned, its seventeen residents moved to Jemez Pueblo. Pecos, like all the other Tanoans, originated early in the fourteenth century and had continued as an important center until the early nineteenth century.

The Keresan-Speaking Pueblos. The five extant Keresan-speaking pueblos in the Rio Grande Valley are Cochiti, Santo Domingo, San Felipe, Santa Ana, and Zia. All the original pueblos dated from the late thirteenth or early fourteenth century; in the late sixteenth century, all were visited by the Spaniards, who built missions in each pueblo in the seventeenth century. All the Keres took part in the Pueblo Revolt and in resisting Spanish reconquest in the 1690's. When Zia Pueblo was attacked and destroyed, six hundred people were killed, and the others were sold into slavery. Some who escaped fled to Jemez but were induced to return a few years later to rebuild at Zia.

The Santo Domingans resisted reconquest by destroying their pueblo in 1692 and joining forces with Jemez Pueblo. When attacked by the Spaniards there in 1694, many fled to Hopi while others, accompanied by some refugees from Cochiti, moved into Acoma territory, where they built the new pueblo of Laguna. Later, some Santo Domingans returned to rebuild on the original site of their own pueblo. All the eastern Keres pueblos are still occupied, with the exception of Santa Ana. A lack of agricultural land and water for irrigation forced most of the people to move to a farming community near Bernalillo, with only a few caretakers remaining in the pueblo. In the late eighteenth and early nineteenth centuries, Cochiti Pueblo served as a refuge for Spanish and Mexican settlers from Apache and Navajo raids.

Pueblo Culture. Pueblo society is communal, with emphasis placed upon the welfare of the entire group, as opposed to that of any one individual. As many scholars have observed, the Puebloans had two highly desirable culture-forming assets: time and space. With time to think matters through carefully and space to see things clearly, they developed a culture that allowed them to enjoy the pleasures of each day to the fullest, without pressure for constant and immediate change. When change was called for, they reflected carefully, discussed it as a group, and then decided on a course of action.

The Puebloans had no written language; they maintained their culture orally, passing down knowledge from one generation to the next, often narrating it through ritual dances and other ceremonies. They have a great reverence for tradition and for truth and would never change or embellish their history for any reason, political or otherwise. As events have had an impact on Pueblo life through the centuries, they have been included in the history; thus, the Spaniards appear in the ritual stories still being told. The Puebloans, who always relate their history "from the beginning," share a similar creation belief in which humankind originated in the center of the earth, finally emerging onto the surface through a ceremonial opening known as the *sipapu*. As they came up into the light, they were divided into different groups that spoke different dialects, and they were sent to make their homes in different regions.

Religion is integrated with all other aspects of Pueblo life; it influences art, crafts, all industries, and the social structure. The fundamental belief underlying the Pueblo religion is that a person must live so that he or she is always in harmony with nature, with nature's basic rhythm. Other facets of existence have significance only in terms of how they relate to this principal belief. There are ceremonies and rites that are appropriate to each of the seasons—planting, growing, harvesting, and hunting. Many of the motifs that appear in their art are derived from their ceremonial beliefs, and even such mundane activities as the gathering of salt and clay are accompanied by special prayers. Lack of success in any endeavor is not blamed on the spirits but on the person who failed to observe the rituals properly.

The various pueblos have developed some similarities in their social and cultural patterns as they have interacted with one another through the centuries, yet each one is a closely united and distinct entity. Their ceremonials, for example, are similar, but important variations exist.

In each pueblo, authority is divided between religious and secular leaders, and the distinction between the two is carefully maintained. The slate of secular officers that resulted from a decree issued by the Spanish king in 1620 is still in effect: a governor, two lieutenant governors, a sheriff, and the *fiscales*, positions derived from the office of prosecutor. These officials serve for one year at all but four pueblos, where they serve for two years. The Spanish presented the first secular officers with metal-topped canes inscribed with the Spanish cross as emblems of their authority. When Mexican rule began in 1821, the system was maintained, and the officers were given new canes with silver tops as additional badges of office.

In 1863, Abraham Lincoln rewarded the Puebloans for their neutrality during the Civil War by giving silver-crowned ebony canes inscribed with his signature to all the secular officials, who now had three emblems of office. These canes are still displayed on important ceremonial occasions in most of the pueblos, along with the silver medals decorated with profiles of Lincoln and President Dwight D. Eisenhower made to commemorate the "Republican Centennial, 1863-1960" and the small cherrywood canes with white bronze tops presented to the Puebloans in 1980 in celebration of the Tricentennial of the Pueblo Revolt of 1680.

Division into Moieties. Another major cultural characteristic of the Rio Grande Pueblos is their division into dual ceremonial groups known as moieties. For example, in the pueblos of Cochiti, Jemez, Sandia, San Felipe, Santa Ana, Santo Domingo, and Zia, the moieties are divided into the Turquoise and the Squash. At San Juan, Santa Clara, San Ildefonso, Nambe, Pojoaque, Tesuque, and Hano, they are Winter People and Summer People, and at Taos Pueblo they are North and South. A moiety can also be a political division; many pueblos alternate the position of governor annually between the two moieties. A moiety is often mistaken for a clan by outsiders who do not realize that in Pueblo tradition a clan is a group of related persons who trace their matrilineal descent from a common ancestor.

In the dual system of the Tanoan Pueblos, each moiety has its own priest, or *cacique*—a term of Caribbean origin which was first used by the Spaniards to designate Pueblo religious leaders and was eventually adopted by the Puebloans themselves. In the Tanoan dichotomy, the caciques, who hold office for life, are an important part of the hierarchical form of government of each pueblo. The Keres Pueblos have a somewhat more complicated social structure involving clans, kiva groups, and medicine societies as well as moieties. In these pueblos, a single cacique is responsible for the spiritual well-being of all the people and also appoints those who hold secular offices.

While adhering to their own traditional beliefs, many Puebloans also practice Roman Catholicism; they find no inconsistencies in this, since they are able to keep the two religions separate. Each pueblo still observes the ancient ceremonies and rites, encouraging its young people to participate fully.

Puebloans in the latter half of the twentieth century found themselves plagued by the same economic problems that beset many people in the United States as a whole—such as inadequate land resources, dwindling revenues from agriculture, unemployment, and lack of adequate funding for education and health care—but they must also contend with increasing pressures from the non-Indian world. In spite of this, they continue to retain most of their native culture, being bound together by love of tradition, by common languages, and by their strong religious beliefs.

LouAnn Faris Culley

Bibliography

Baldwin, Gordon C. *Indians of the Southwest*. New York: Capricorn Books, 1970. After an excellent introduction to the prehistoric ancestors of the Puebloans, the author details the relationships between natives and the Spanish, Mexicans, and European Americans who immigrated into their lands. Illustrated with black-and-white photographs of the land and the people.

Dutton, Bertha P. *The Pueblos: Indians of the American Southwest*. Englewood Cliffs, N.J.: Prentice Hall, 1976. A brief general history of each of the Puebloan groups, with an explanation of the mythology, religion, secret societies, and cults that play such an important role in Indian life.

Parsons, Elsie W.C. *Pueblo Indian Religion*. 2 vols. Lincoln: University of Nebraska Press, 1996.

Sando, Joe S. *The Pueblo Indians*. San Francisco: Indian Historian Press, 1976. The author, himself a Puebloan from Jemez, has written the traditional Pueblo history as the Pueblo Indians themselves know it, pointing out all the ways in which their viewpoint differs from the formalized narratives, dominated by European ideology, found in most history texts.

Tanner, Clara Lee. *Southwest Indian Craft Arts*. Tucson: University of Arizona Press, 1968. A discussion of Southwest Indian arts which includes detailed information about materials, techniques, forms, styles, designs, and design elements. An in-depth exploration of intertribal contacts; Spanish, Mexican, and Anglo-American influences; and commercialization, which have all affected the styles, designs, and functions of each of the art forms.

Underhill, Ruth. *Pueblo Crafts*. Washington, D.C.: U.S. Bureau of Indian Affairs, 1944. Reprint. Palmer Lake, Colo.: Filter Press, 1979. An extremely detailed account of the materials and techniques which produced the arts and crafts of the Southwest Pueblos, from the ancient period to modern times. Illustrated throughout with diagrams and photographs.

Wormington, H. M. *Prehistoric Indians of the Southwest*. Denver, Colo.: Denver Museum of Natural History, 1970. A very readable account of the prehistoric cultures in the Southwest, intended for the layperson rather than the scientist. Illustrated throughout with helpful maps, diagrams, and photographs.

Pueblo tribes, Western

TRIBES AFFECTED: Acoma, Hopi, Laguna, Zuni
CULTURE AREA: Southwest
LANGUAGE GROUPS: Keresan, Tewa, Uto-Aztecan, Zuni
PRIMARY LOCATION: Southwest
POPULATION SIZE: 28,884 (1990 U.S. Census)

The Western Pueblos are considered to be a part of the cultural pattern known as the Desert culture, a migration that extended southward from the Great Basin and covered most of the Southwest, dating the earliest human inhabitants of this region some ten thousand years ago. During this long history, most changes in Pueblo culture have occurred since the time of contact with Europeans, specifically with the Spanish. The Pueblos have managed to control these changes, especially in their ceremonial life, through persistence and protection.

The Pueblo Revolt of 1680. As did most Indians of the Southwest, Pueblo peoples experienced the impact of three Western European cultures: Spanish, Mexican, and Anglo-American. One of the most disruptive qualities of contact for the Pueblos was Western European religion, which was intolerant of competing beliefs and ceremonies. By the middle of the seventeenth century, after almost a hundred years of forced labor and European religion, the Pueblos planned to put an end to the suffering that resulted from Spanish oppression. Aware of the strengths and weaknesses of their adversary, the Pueblo communities decided that a united resistance would be the most successful. Careful planning produced what is generally called the Pueblo Revolt of 1680. Although the Pueblos outnumbered the Spanish, the Spanish had an advantage because of their weaponry.

The Northern Pueblos laid siege to the Spanish capital of Santa Fe, where more than a thousand colonists and missionaries had taken refuge. Other Pueblos, including Acoma, Hopi, and Zuni, contributed to the revolt by killing the Spaniards and missionaries living in or near these pueblos. Spanish houses, churches, church records, and furniture were burned or destroyed. Through the later testimony of captured Indians, it became clear that the leaders of the revolt (Popé among them) wanted to obliterate all representations of Spanish culture and religion. Success of this objective was realized but was short-lived. Don Diego de Vargas reconquered the area in the winter of 1691-1692; all of New Mexico was reconquered by 1696. Faced with a conquer-and-destroy attitude for hundreds of years, it is a testimony to the strength of the people of the Western Pueblos that they survived and retained many of their customs and beliefs.

Although the Acoma, Hopi, Laguna, and Zuni tribes share many similar customs and beliefs, they should be viewed as separate, independent societies.

Acoma. The Pueblos of Acoma and Laguna share the same language, Keresan, and are closely related. Laguna lies about 40 miles west of Albuquerque. Fifteen miles west-southwest of Laguna is Acoma. The word Acoma means "place that always was." Archaeologists have generally agreed that Acoma has been inhabited at least from 1200 c.e. to the present.

447

Little is known about the origins of the Acomas, but they claim to have always lived on their mesa.

Acoma, as are most pueblos, is structured by clans that are always matrilinear in descent. A clan comprises all the descendants of a traditional maternal ancestor. Males go to live with the clan of their wife at marriage. The difference between clans and families is that clans are a ceremonial institution of membership. Acoma society is matriarchal; Acoma women own the houses and everything in them, even if an item is brought there by their husbands. Women also have claim to all domestic animals, such as sheep and chickens. Certain ceremonial rights, however, such as entrance into a kiva (ceremonial chamber), are open only to men.

Elections for officials at Acoma are held yearly during the winter solstice. The government consists of a cacique (governor), who nominates those who will run for office. To assist the governor are two lieutenant governors, three war chiefs and their two cooks, and ten *principales*. Aside from the cacique and the *principales*, who serve life terms, offices are held for one year.

The cacique sets the date for ceremonies that may vary chronologically—for example, those ceremonies held on the solstices. Rabbit hunts are held before almost all important occasions. Some dances, such as the corn dance, are recreational rather than sacred or ceremonial. Anyone can observe or participate in these dances. The most important communal ceremony is that of the K'atsina (Kachina) dancers. K'atsinas are spirit rainmakers. It is said that in the old days, the K'atsina used to come to the village bringing the people gifts and cheering them when they were sad. There was a great fight between the spirits and the people, however; the spirits refused to come to the village anymore, but they told the people they could wear masks and pretend they were K'atsinas and all would be well; rain would come.

Pottery is the main form of art pursued by the Acomas. It is less durable than Zuni pottery but more various in its designs, which include trees, leaves, birds, flowers, and geometrical patterns. Pottery serves both utilitarian and ceremonial functions and has historically been a cultural indicator of what was acceptable or fashionable.

Potters hold a special place of respect at both Acoma and Laguna. Often, because of the commercial value of Acoma pottery, a potter may be the primary wage earner of the family. Pottery produced for simple household means maintains a special significance because it was made from materials of the earth to support some type of life activity. Observers of Acoma have remarked that a pot has a "conscious existence," and Wanda Aragon, an Acoma potter, has said that "when you're finished with a pot you flow life into it and it is given life."

Regardless of culture, potters produce interpretations that reflect changing values and cultural demands. This may explain the emphasis on pottery
at Acoma, a village that has emphasized pottery in its economy more than
Laguna. Laguna has three times the population of Acoma, but Acoma has
many more potters.

Laguna. The Laguna migration to their present village is even more
mysterious than that of the Acoma. Tribal traditions and pottery found in
ruins can trace Laguna culture back to the last decade of the seventeenth
century, but no one can say where they lived before that. There is no
reference to the tribe by Spanish historians, who confused them with the
Acomas, a tribe having one central village and who spoke the same language as the Lagunas. Many historians date the founding of Laguna between 1697 and 1699 by a combination of settlers from various groups,
including Jemez, Santo Domingo, Zia, and a few disgruntled Acoma.

The Lagunas also have a matriarchal, clan-based social structure. They
have their own calendar, recognizing twenty-eight days to a moon, but there
are no year designations. Events or phenomena are used to keep track of
time. According to this calendar, the winter solstice begins the yearly ceremonies. Migration and the journey from the north are recounted in songs.
The Keres words for winter solstice are *Kú wa mi Shu ko* (*Kú wa mi*, "south";
Shu ko, "corner") meaning "the south corner time." There are also K'atsina
(Kachina) dances during planting and harvesting seasons, the importance
of rain having a significant role at Laguna.

Hopi. Rain is of major importance for the Hopis as well. Two general
characteristics appear repeatedly in pottery motifs: a respect and desire for
rain and a belief in the unity of all life. Pottery making for Hopis, as with
most Pueblo communities, is an art that exists in the mind of the potter.
There are no permanent patterns set down for design layouts. Sand paintings made on the floors of kivas are derived from clan traditions and, like
pottery, the designs are carried only in the memory of the artists.

Hopi society is complex, consisting of thousands of people, each of whom
is affiliated with one of thirteen villages. Oraibi, once the largest Hopi village,
was one of the most determined to reject religious and political imposition
during the time of the Pueblo Revolt. Much later, at the beginning of the
nineteenth century, the Oraibi split occurred. The village divided into two
factions, termed "hostiles" and "friendlies" by the United States government.
The hostiles resented policies that would forcibly educate their children. The
friendlies saw advantages to American education. The disagreement escalated,
and the hostiles were forced from the village in September of 1906. Other
theories emphasize the importance of internal, social instability in causing the
split. Whatever the case, a well-established society had fragmented.

Hopi girl preparing corn meal, around 1909. (Library of Congress)

Hopi villages are matrilineal; women own the houses and, therefore, the economy, if they distribute items such as produce from their homes. For ceremonies and politics, men have the most influence, with the major focus of rituals being concentrated in the kiva. These tendencies are generalized, however, and many exceptions occur.

There are several clans among the Hopi, serving as a source of social identity and performing what has become the most important modern function, regulating marriage. The modern government has for the most part become secularized, although some religious overtones still emerge. The board of directors' meetings can be open or closed and can discuss everything from land disputes to the writing of village history.

Zuni. Tribal traditions and history are also a major concern for the Zuni Pueblo. During the 1980's, the Zunis established their own public school system, which promoted and emphasized Zuni culture. A staff of experts frequently visit classes to explain tribal traditions. Every August there is a tribal fair, including a rodeo, a parade complete with floats, and social dances. The crowning of Miss Zuni takes place during this event; the young woman is not chosen for her beauty, but rather for her knowledge of Zuni culture. She must be fluent in the Zuni language, and she is tested on the history of the tribe, ensuring that the culture will be passed on.

Prior to 1934, members of the government, the Zuni Tribal Council, had been appointed by the Council of High Priests. Since 1934, elections of officers have been open to the tribe, but, ironically, it was not until 1965 that women were able to vote in this matriarchal society.

The present-day Zuni pueblo is settled at the location of the village of Halona wa, one of six villages existing before the eighteenth century. The other five villages were abandoned, probably because of Apache and Navajo raids, diseases introduced at the time of contact, and the Spanish reconquest. The legend of the "Seven Cities of Cíbola," reported to be large, rich cities, may have been based on the six Zuni villages. Hearing of the legend prompted Francisco Vásquez de Coronado to explore the area in 1540. He was disappointed to find some rather poor farmers supplementing their agricultural base with hunting. Spanish chroniclers would later write of the Zuni that "what they worshiped most was water."

The Zuni language is still the language of social discourse, with most Zunis also being fluent in English. The social structure is similar to that of the other Western Pueblos; it is a matriarchal, clan-based culture. Clan divisions and names of clans at Zuni are reflected among other Pueblos—Eagle, Sun, Badger, Turkey, and so on—with each clan having a specific religious function. Zuni priests act as mediators between the people and the Kachinas, the spirits who bring rain.

Most tribes in the Southwest make and use fetishes, but of all the Pueblos the Zuni have the reputation for being the most skillful at carving them. The purposes for which a fetish may be used varies. There are fetishes for hunting, curing diseases, war, gambling, and initiations. Hunting fetishes are the kind most often seen for sale. The fetish most highly prized by a Zuni is one of the natural concretion bearing resemblance to an animal. Shell, stone, wood, plant, or animal material may be used to carve a fetish; their purpose in assisting humans remains the same, regardless of the material. Fetishes are regarded as living things and must be carefully attended.

Kimberly Manning

Bibliography

Cordell, Linda S. *Ancient Pueblo Peoples*. Washington, D.C.: Smithsonian Institution Press, 1994.

Cushing, Frank. *Zuni Fetishes*. Facsimile ed. Flagstaff, Ariz.: KC Publications, 1966. A description of Zuni fetishes, their significance, and the shapes and materials used. Accompanied by some black-and-white photographs.

Dillingham, Rick. *Acoma and Laguna Pottery*. Santa Fe, N.Mex.: School of American Research Press, 1992. An excellent source of photographs and sensitive descriptions of both Acoma and Laguna pottery. A detailed account of the function, form, and design of the pottery.

Dozier, Edward P. *The Pueblo Indians of North America*. New York: Holt, Rinehart and Winston, 1970. A mostly historical accounting of the Western and Rio Grande Pueblos, with an overview of culture and ceremonies.

Dutton, Bertha P., and Miriam A. Marmon. *The Laguna Calendar*. Albuquerque: University of New Mexico Press, 1936. Dutton gives some insights into the Laguna system of time, noting when special ceremonies are held and translating Keresan words into English.

Keegan, Marcia. *Pueblo People: Ancient Traditions Modern Lives*. Santa Fe, N.Mex.: Clear Light Publishers, 1999.

Minge, Ward A. *Acoma: Pueblo in the Sky*. 2d ed. Albuquerque: University of New Mexico Press, 1991. Minge follows the Acoma people from prehistory to the modern day. Includes some information on Laguna, illustrations of Acoma, and tables covering population, livestock, and land holdings.

Sando, Joe S. *Pueblo Nations: Eight Centuries of Pueblo Indian History*. Sante Fe, N.Mex.: Clear Light, 1992.

_____. *Pueblo Profiles: Cultural Identity Through Centuries of Change*. Sante Fe, N.Mex.: Clear Light, 1998.

Scully, Vincent. *Pueblo: Mountain, Village, Dance*. 2d ed. Chicago: University of Chicago Press, 1989. Scully provides numerous photographs and descriptions of various pueblos, their plazas, structures, surrounding terrain, and dances.

Sedgwick, Mary K. *Acoma, the Sky City: A Study in Pueblo Indian History and Civilization*. Cambridge, Mass.: Harvard University Press, 1926. An examination of both the Acoma and Laguna tribes that covers history, ceremonies, social structure, and Spanish influence.

Warburg, Aby, and Michael P. Steinberg. *Images from the Region of the Pueblo Indians of North America*. Ithaca, N.Y.: Cornell University Press, 1995.

Whiteley, Peter M. *Deliberate Acts: Changing Hopi Culture Through the Oraibi Split*. Tucson: University of Arizona Press, 1988. An exploration of the Oraibi split, its history, and its effects on modern Hopi society. Whiteley also examines ritual, politics, and anthropological data.

Wood, Nancy C., ed. *The Serpent's Tongue: Prose, Poetry, and Art of the New Mexico Pueblos*. New York: E. P. Dutton, 1998.

Young, M. Jane. *Signs from the Ancestors: Zuni Cultural Symbolism and Perceptions of Rock Art*. Albuquerque: University of New Mexico Press, 1988. Young gives commentary on Zuni culture in her discussion of Zuni rock art. Drawings and illustrations are provided.

Puyallup

CULTURE AREA: Northwest Coast
LANGUAGE GROUP: Salishan
PRIMARY LOCATION: Puget Sound basin
POPULATION SIZE: 1,281 (1990 U.S. Census)

The name Puyallup comes from the Indian name for the Puyallup River, sometimes written *pwiya'lap*. The Puyallup were one of several tribes collectively called the Southern Coast Salish, living in the Puget Sound basin. The Puyallup lived at the mouth of the Puyallup River and along the neighboring Washington coastline. There were twelve subdivisions and villages; the Steilacoom, for example, lived on Steilacoom Creek and the adjacent beach. The Puyallup were hunters, fishers, and gatherers.

The Puyallup lived in villages in the winter and camps in the summer. A village consisted of large wooden houses occupied by several families. Puyallup society was divided into three social classes: upper-class freeman, lower-class freeman, and slaves. Upper-class Puyallup were from good families, possessed wealth, and had the means to participate in certain ceremonies. The wealthiest male was usually the village headman. The lower class lacked these requisites, and slaves and their descendants were captives of war who were kept by wealthy masters. Each village was closely tied to neighboring villages by means of marriages between prominent families, kinship, mutual use of the same land, and joint participation in various ceremonies. In addition, individual status was determined in part by how well an individual was known in other villages. Within the freeman class was a group of professional warriors. They occasionally led raiding parties for slaves but were primarily called upon to defend their village from attack by outside tribes, primarily the Lekwiltok.

Guardian spirits were a central part of Puyallup life. Every individual ability and accomplishment (such as wealth, war, gambling, and hunting) was facilitated by the appropriate spirit. Training began in childhood so that by age eight a child was able to seek out the appropriate guardian spirit, which came in a vision.

By the 1850's whites had established settlements on Puyallup land, and in 1854 and 1855 treaties set aside land for the Puyallup near Tacoma, Washington. Their involvement in the white economy (selling furs, fishing and logging commercially, and working in hopyards) became extensive. Attempts to Christianize the Puyallup and minimize the influence of tribal customs were only partially successful. More critically, the Puyallup were economically exploited by whites. Families sold their allotted reservation land, and by the late 1970's, the entire Puyallup reservation occupied only 33 acres. This occurred on top of epidemics of smallpox and malaria in the 1850's which significantly reduced the population.

Puyallup fortunes were reversed, however, beginning in the mid-1960's. The population had increased significantly, and they were permitted greater control over their own affairs. The Boldt Decision in 1974 reaffirmed the early treaties guaranteeing fishing rights. Tribal members became adept in business management; some established and learned to manage fisheries. They also formed a tribal government with a strong business orientation, which developed a network of stores, marinas, and restaurants on the reservation.

Quapaw

CULTURE AREA: Southeast
LANGUAGE GROUP: Siouan
PRIMARY LOCATION: Oklahoma
POPULATION SIZE: 1,538 (1990 U.S. Census)

Unlike many other American Indian tribes, the Quapaws (or Arkansas) have not preserved elaborate traditions explaining their origins. They say only that their Ancient Ones came forth from the water. Because of this, the history of the tribe is difficult to uncover. The Quapaws, or "Downstream People," migrated from the Ohio Valley to the Arkansas River near where it joins the Mississippi River in the mid-1600's. Since the Quapaws went downstream, their kindred tribes called them Ugaxpa, or "drifted downstream." Their principal villages were on the west bank of the Mississippi River in what is now Arkansas. The forests and rivers supplied plenty of berries, game, and other food. They had large, well-tilled fields and cultivated gourds, pumpkins, sunflowers, beans, squash, and corn. Corn was considered the most important agricultural product. They hunted buffalo, which was a substantial part of their diet, and preserved what was not needed immediately for winter.

The focus of Quapaw life was the permanent village, which was actually a cluster of multiple-family dwellings. Their faith played a role in every aspect of tribal life; the central force of the universe was Wah-kon-tah, who was all and in all. They believed in life after death and in a judgment that would lead to a life of joy or perpetual torment. They often traded with the

Caddoes on the Red River and had established a trade route between the two settlements. The manufactured goods of white society, which the people wanted, brought about establishment of trade with eastern tribes who had contact with the Europeans. The first Europeans to encounter the Quapaws were the French explorers Jacques Marquette and Louis Jolliet in 1673. The trading done with whites was ultimately detrimental to the Downstream People; by 1699 smallpox had killed so many that only three hundred warriors remained.

Only a thousand Quapaws were left in 1818 when they ceded 30 million acres to the United States for $4,000 and annuities. A remaining million acres were ceded in 1824. In 1925 the Quapaws moved to the Caddo Reservation in Louisiana, where they were plagued by disease and floods. Most of the tribe left and returned to Arkansas. A treaty in 1833 gave these people land in northwest Oklahoma (then Indian Territory). They scattered during the Civil War, but in the late 1800's survivors gathered on the reservation in Indian Territory to reestablish tribal life. The Downstream People remained a poor tribe until nickel and zinc were discovered on the reservation in the 1920's; then they prospered. The population dropped to 236 in 1895 but had risen to 929 in 1980 and 1,538 in 1990. Of those listed in the census as Quapaw, probably no more than 20 percent are more than one-fourth Quapaw, yet the tribe maintains its unique identity.

Quechan

CULTURE AREA: Southwest
LANGUAGE GROUP: Yuman
PRIMARY LOCATION: Southwestern Arizona, southeastern California
POPULATION SIZE: 1,972 (1990 U.S. Census)

The Quechan, or Yuma, tribe is one of the few that have never been relocated away from their ancestral land. Quechan territory lies around the confluence of the Gila and Colorado rivers. The Quechan came to this area between 1540 and 1700. (Although "Yuma" is essentially synonymous with Quechan, the term "Yuman" applies to a language group and to a number of tribes, including the Quechan, Maricopa, and Cocopa.)

The Quechan derived their subsistence from cultivating the rivers' floodplains and from gathering wild fruits, nuts, and seeds. A popular wild food was mesquite, which they ground into flour for cakes or fermented to make an intoxicating beverage.

455

Apart from shamans, the spiritual leaders, there was a *kwaxot*, or civil leader, and a *kwanami*, or war leader. The primary leader was probably the *paipataxan*, or "real person," who made the majority of decisions about issues that affected the tribe.

The Quechan were occasionally in conflicts with the Cocopa, Maricopa, and Pima. Sometimes the Quechan would ally themselves with the Mojave and Sand Papago (Tohono O'odham) tribes. Attacks were initiated to steal supplies and obtain captives that could be traded for horses and other necessities. In the 1770's, Europeans and Mexicans attempted to control the area where the Gila and Colorado rivers join by trying to "civilize" the Quechan. Eventually, the Quechan tired of their new allies' cultural impositions and destroyed the Mexican and European settlements.

In 1852, the United States was able to establish a garrison on a cliff overlooking the rivers. Fort Yuma's dealings with the Quechan were relatively peaceful. This peace was further ensured when the commander of the fort had a Quechan named Pasqual made "tribal chief."

Between the 1850's and the 1900's, the U.S. government tried to bargain land away from the group, but in 1912, the Fort Yuma Reservation was established, temporarily stabilizing Quechan landholdings. By the 1960's, however, the Quechans had sold much of their land because of economic stress. They ceased most of their farming activities and became wage earners. They were forced to adopt the federally accepted form of local government called the "tribal council." After several nonviolent protests in the 1960's and 1970's, the U.S. government finally restored 25,000 acres to the Quechan in 1978.

As of 1990, the majority of Quechans lived on this land, working as farmers, laborers, artisans, and craftspeople. They remained closely tied to their land and continued to celebrate many of their traditions.

Quileute

CULTURE AREA: Northwest Coast
LANGUAGE GROUP: Chimakuan
PRIMARY LOCATION: Western Washington
POPULATION SIZE: 580 (1990 U.S. Census)

The Quileute, a maritime people, dwelled in permanent split-cedar-roofed longhouses that accommodated several extended families or even a lineage. They were dependent primarily upon fishing, which was reflected in their ceremonies, settlement patterns, technology, and mythology. Quileute society was internally stratified with hereditary chiefs, commoners, and slaves. Status was gained through oratory, warfare, birth, and accumulation and redistribution of traditional forms of wealth (usually in the forms of copper, slaves, obsidian blades, pileated red woodpecker scalp capes, and dentalium shells). Kinship was bilateral. Residence tended to be patrilocal. They had a shamanistic religion; polygyny; complex ceremonies, including the potlatch; house and totem pole-raising; rites of passage; and the launching of hollowed red cedar canoes for trading. Raven was a cultural hero, and art was typified by geometric and representational thunderbird-whale motifs.

First European American contact was with the Spanish in 1775 and with the British in 1787. The Quileute signed a reservation treaty in 1855 with Governor Isaac I. Stevens, but through a misunderstanding the Quileute remained in their territory until 252 were removed in 1889 to a one-mile-square reservation at La Push, on the western coast of Washington. In 1893, the remaining 71 inhabitants moved to the Hoh River. In 1882, a school was established at La Push. The syncretic Indian Shaker Church was introduced to the Quileute in 1895.

In 1936, the Quileute adopted a constitution and bylaws, and in 1937 they became an independent and self-governing sovereign people governed by a five-member elected council. Their main sources of income are a fish-buying company, a tourists' trailer park, a cooperative store, and a fishing gear store that supplies local fishermen and tourists. Many Quileute are self-employed in logging and fishing. There are numerous successful efforts at revitalizing certain aspects of Quileute traditional culture, particularly with the teaching of woodworking skills.

Quinault

CULTURE AREA: Northwest Coast
LANGUAGE GROUP: Salishan
PRIMARY LOCATION: Mouth of the Quinault River, Washington
POPULATION SIZE: 967 (Quinault Reservation, per 1990 U.S. Census);
    2,491 (Quinault Nation office at Taholah, Washington, 1994)

The name Quinault (sometimes spelled Quinaielt) is derived from *kwi' nail*, the name of their largest settlement, located at the site of the present-day village of Taholah at the mouth of the Quinault River. The

Quinault are one of several tribes referred to as Southwestern Coast Salish. Traditionally, the Quinault were primarily fishers and hunters and, to a lesser extent, gatherers. Salmon was the basic staple. The Quinault were excellent canoemen, and in their large oceangoing canoes, they were the southernmost coastal tribe to hunt whales.

The Quinault lived in large houses, holding from two to ten families, in about twenty villages. Social class was divided into slave and free, with free divided into nobility and commoners. Nobility consisted of those with inherited status and wealth. The Quinault extensively traded and intermarried with neighboring tribes, and these regional networks also contributed to status. Commoners lacked these perquisites. Slaves were obtained in raids or in trades.

The village leader or chief was chosen by village members from among those males with enough wealth to ensure that some of that wealth could be distributed to others at potlatches. The potlatch in turn served to enhance the leader's prestige. The leader advised and mediated disputes but otherwise had no prescribed powers.

Religion focused on acquisition of guardian spirits, which were necessary for a successful life. Particular spirits conveyed particular powers to their recipient (such as wealth or success at gambling, curing illness, or whaling). Other important mythical spirits were Misp, creator and caretaker of the world, and Xwoni Xwoni, the trickster buffoon. Salmon were the focus of several taboos and ceremonies.

Whites had established trading settlements in the area by the early 1800's. In the early 1830's a malaria epidemic reduced the population from 1,250 (in 1805) to 158 by 1857. In 1855 the Quinault signed the Treaty of Olympia with the United States. They kept a large reservation on the mouth of the Quinault River, where they were subject to the machinations of whites to Christianize them and make them give up their traditional lifestyle and customs.

The reservation economy centered on fishing and government jobs but never provided sufficient employment. It was estimated in 1985 that 30 percent of the adults living there were unemployed. As a result, many have left the reservation permanently to seek employment in urban locations. Beginning in 1907, and over the opposition of the Quinault, Congress authorized allotment of Quinault land to other tribes. By the 1980's the Quinault Indian Nation was composed of the Quinault and six affiliated tribes. About a third of the 190,000-acre Quinault reservation is owned by non-Indians.

Salinan

CULTURE AREA: California
LANGUAGE GROUP: Salinan
PRIMARY LOCATION: Monterey and San Luis Obispo counties, California
POPULATION SIZE: 301 (1990 U.S. Census)

Like many other California Indians, the Salinan are not distinguished by political or social organization but rather by language. The term Salinan has been adopted by modern scholars from the Salinas (Spanish for "salty") River, although others claim that the people's own name was Ennesen. Three subdivisions have been identified: Antoniaño, after Mission San Antonio (founded 1771), or Kahtritram; Migueleño, after Mission San Miguel (founded 1797), or Tepotrahl; and Playano, after the *playa* (Spanish for beach), or Lahmkahtrahm.

Europeans first encountered the Salinan, who numbered about three thousand, when Gaspar de Portolá led a Spanish expedition from San Diego in search of Monterey Bay. Based on several records of that expedition that described the Salinan as "docile," "friendly," and otherwise amenable, Franciscan missionaries established San Antonio and began the work of replacing native culture with Christianity and other aspects of Spanish culture. The effort was not wholly successful, as a report by the padres in 1814 indicated that many features of Salinan culture (language, diet, even religion) still persisted.

Despite the evidence of cultural survival, the numbers of Salinan at San Antonio and later at San Miguel underwent a steady downward progression. By the time of secularization, around 1834, the approximate population at San Antonio was less than 550 and at San Miguel around 600. Subsequent numbers are difficult to define because enumerators did not always identify Salinans clearly, but they almost certainly show a continued decline. A special survey in 1904 showed only 105 Salinans living in Monterey County and another ten in San Luis Obispo County. The federal roll of 1928 located eleven full Salinans of the San Antonio branch and four from San Miguel, as well as other combinations for a total of thirty-five people with varying degrees of Salinan ancestry. According to an informant in 1987, all pure Salinans had since died. Although some three hundred individuals who claimed to trace partial Salinan origin resided in the area at the time of the 1990 census, no recognized tribal organization has ever existed.

Even in the early twentieth century, when some pure Salinans were still alive to impart sketches of their language to linguists and recollections of their culture to anthropologists, most scholars conceded that Salinan culture was essentially extinct. Available evidence indicates that the Salinans differed little from other Indians of California. As hunter-gatherers, they consumed a wide variety of animals and plants, especially acorns. While some religious mythology has been recorded—shamans clearly played an important role in Salinan society—their religion seems to have regarded no animal as sacred and thus immune to hunting. The fur of some animals was used for winter blankets, but normal dress was nonexistent for men; women wore a simple apron. Pottery, metallurgy, masonry, and complex religious or political organizations were all unknown. The simplicity of Salinan culture made it highly vulnerable to white cultural conquest and contributed to its early elimination.

Salish

CULTURE AREA: Northwest Coast
LANGUAGE GROUP: Salishan
PRIMARY LOCATION: Northwest Washington State, southwest British Columbia
POPULATION SIZE: 4,455 in U.S. (1990 U.S. Census); 1,900 in Canada ("Straits Salish," Statistics Canada, based on 1991 census)

The term "Salish" refers to a category of Native American languages that are spoken by native peoples based largely in northwestern Washington and southwestern British Columbia, although extending into northern Idaho and Montana with the Flathead (or Inland Salish) tribes, who also speak a Salishan language, and as far north on the Canadian coast as the Bella Coola villages around Dean and Burke channels. The Salish-speaking peoples (whose various dialects have been extensively mapped and studied by Wayne Suttles of Portland State University) extend as far south as the Chinook at the mouth of the Columbia River in Oregon and Washington. There is a major dialect division between the Coastal Salish and the Inland Salish. It is presumed that Salish-speaking people first traveled from inland, down the Fraser River, before spreading out along the coast, where their traditional lands now overlap major urban areas such as the Seattle-Tacoma area of Washington State and Vancouver in British Columbia.

While it is difficult to generalize about a large number of unique groups who share a general linguistic family, it is possible to say that the Coastal Salish developed a strong maritime culture, based on the extensive supplies of salmon, halibut, cod, and sea mammals, all of which they harpooned or netted in a variety of ingenious ways. The vast forests of the Pacific Northwest also allowed the Salish (as well as other coastal peoples of the Northwest such as the Tlingit and Haida) to develop artwork in wood and to build large plank-house dwellings. Cedar bark was even developed into a kind of textile, used for clothing. Canoes were another specialty, although the Northwest Coast peoples generally were not seafarers as were the Polynesians or the Scandinavian peoples.

Salish society was typically highly stratified, divided into elite, common, and slavery classes—classes that were maintained by elaborate social rituals and observance of a strict etiquette of behavior, such as marrying within one's level of society. Salish religious traditions were elaborate, placing particular emphasis on the importance of dreams.

Bibliography

Arlee, Johnny, and Robert Bigart. *Over a Century of Moving to the Drum: The Salish Powwow Tradition on the Flathead Indian Reservation*. Helena: Montana Historical Society Press, 1998.

Barnet, Homer. "The Coast Salish of Canada." In *The North American Indians: A Sourcebook*, edited by Roger Owen, James Deetz, and Anthony Fisher. New York: Macmillan, 1967.

Bierwert, Crisca. *Brushed by Cedar, Living by the River: Coast Salish Figures of Power*. Tucson: University of Arizona Press, 1999.

Bigart, Robert, and Clarence Woodcock. *In the Name of the Salish and Kootenai Nation: The 1855 Hell Gate Treaty and the Origin of the Flathead Indian Reservation*. Pablo, Mont.: Salish Kootenai College Press, 1996.

Drucker, Philip. "Indians of the Northwest Coast." In *The North American Indians: A Sourcebook*, edited by Roger Owen, James Deetz, and Anthony Fisher. New York: Macmillan, 1967.

Hill-Tout, Charles. *The Salish People*. Edited by Ralph Maud, 1978. Reprint. Seattle: University of Washington Press, 1987.

Miller, Jay. *Lushootseed Culture and the Shamanic Odyssey: An Anchored Radiance*. Lincoln: University of Nebraska Press, 1999.

Suttles, Wayne, and Ralph Maud, eds. *Coast Salish Essays*. Seattle: University of Washington Press, 1987.

Turner, Dolby, and Delmar J. Seletze. *When the Rains Came and Other Legends of the Salish People*. Victoria, B.C.: Orca, 1992.

Samish

CULTURE AREA: Northwest Coast
LANGUAGE GROUP: Salishan
PRIMARY LOCATION: Puget Sound, Washington
POPULATION SIZE: 173 (1990 U.S. Census)

The Samish tribe is linguistically and culturally grouped with the Straits Salish, speaking the Straits dialect of the Coastal Salishan language. They are respected for their skillful carving of canoes, construction of longhouses, gift-giving potlatches, and strong spirituality based on the teachings of the Winter Spirit Dance Ceremony, having preserved their customs and implements during the years of repression by the federal government.

The Samish historically occupied land and maritime sites adjacent to Haro and Rosario Straits, with a sphere of influence extending from the crest of the Cascades down Puget Sound and out to the Pacific Ocean. There are about five hundred tribally enrolled Samish living mainly in the Puget Sound area. Tribal headquarters are located in Anacortes, Washington.

Although documentation shows that more than a hundred Samish men, women, and children were at the Point Elliott treaty grounds in 1854 and that they were included in the initial draft of the treaty, the Samish (and Lummis) were omitted from the final draft. They were therefore denied the land promised in pretreaty talks. Since 1859, the Samish have struggled to correct this injustice and to obtain federal recognition. In 1979 the Bureau of Indian Affairs declared the tribe extinct; however, in 1992, federal judge Thomas Zilly reversed the bureau's findings and remanded the issue to an administrative law judge on grounds of denial of Fifth Amendment due process rights.

Sanpoil-Nespelem tribes

CULTURE AREA: Plateau
LANGUAGE GROUP: Salishan
PRIMARY LOCATION: Northeastern Washington

The term Sanpoil is a French corruption of the native name *snpui'lux*, a riverine people who lived at the confluence of the Columbia and Sanpoil rivers and who have been ethnographically included with the Nespelem. They maintained close social and economic ties with the contiguous Nespelem and Lower Spokane peoples and spoke an Interior Salish dialect that was shared with the Colville, Okanagan, Lake, Nespelem, and Sinkaietk.

Traditional Lifeways. The dominant culture features were an annual subsistence round with an emphasis on fishing and root gathering that regulated socioeconomic life and certain religious behaviors. The Sanpoil had specialized fishing technology, mutual exploitation of root grounds and fishing stations, extended trade, leadership through inherited chieftainship and consensus of opinion, a sweathouse complex, vision quest for power and a tutelary (guardian) spirit, animism, shamanism, a midwinter rite of intensification ceremony and world renewal rites, bilateral descent, polygyny, and politically decentralized neolocal residence.

Though the Sanpoil used clay for medicines, cleaning buckskin, and making toys, they had no pottery, using bark and woven fiber burden and storage baskets. Food was cooked in earth ovens, by spit-broiling, or by stone-boiling. Status was gained by oratory abilities, generosity, hunting and utilitarian skills, storytelling, and curing. Social control was achieved through peer pressure, gossip, sorcery, and a well-defined supernatural hierarchy.

Historic Period. The estimated aboriginal Sanpoil population of 1,650 (including the Nespelem) was reduced by half in the smallpox epidemic of 1782-1783. Numbers were further reduced in 1846 and again in 1852-1853, from direct contact with European Americans. Major changes to Sanpoil culture were wrought by the introduction of Christianity, European American trade, settler conflict, and the Yakima War of 1855-1858. The Sanpoil, under the spiritual leader Kolaskin, adopted the Dreamer Religion or Prophet Dance, a syncretic nativistic movement that taught a distrust of white teachings and religion. A minority of the Sanpoil remained Roman Catholic, following the devout Chief Barnaby, thereby causing further factionalism.

The Sanpoil population was estimated at 538 with the establishment of the Colville Indian Reservation by executive order of July 2, 1872, when they and twelve other ethnic groups were forced onto the reservation in an area that encompassed some of their aboriginal land. With intrusion by white settlers and gold miners, the northern half of the reservation was reduced by one-half (1,500,000 acres) in 1891.

Modern Period. The construction of Grand Coulee Dam in 1935 destroyed salmon fishing and its value as a trade item, thereby destroying the last of their traditional subsistence economy. There are no remaining full-blooded Sanpoil, and those few of diminished blood degree are members of the Confederated Colville Tribe, with tribal headquarters and a Bureau of Indian Affairs agency south of Nespelem. Main sources of income include tourism, logging, cattle raising, government and tribal employment, and to a lesser extent annual per capita payments and litigation settlements for the loss of aboriginal resource areas and water rights.

Bibliography

Cox, Ross. *Adventures on the Columbia, Including the Narrative of a Residence of Six Years on the Western Side of the Rocky Mountains.* 2 vols. London: Henry Colburn and Richard Bentley, 1831.

Lewis, Albert Buell. *Tribes of the Columbia Valley and the Coast of Washington and Oregon.* Reprint. Millwood, N.Y.: Kraus Reprint, 1983.

Ray, Verne F. *The Sanpoil and Nespelem: Salishan Peoples of Northeastern Washington.* Seattle: University of Washington Press, 1933.

Ross, John Alan. "Political Factionalism on the Colville Reservation." *Northwest Anthropological Research Notes* 2, no. 1 (1968).

Ruby, Robert H., and John A. Brown. *Dreamer-Prophets of the Columbia Plateau: Smohalla and Skolaskin.* Norman: University of Oklahoma Press, 1989.

Sarsi

CULTURE AREA: Plains
LANGUAGE GROUP: Athapaskan
PRIMARY LOCATION: Alberta
POPULATION SIZE: 810 (Statistics Canada, based on 1991 census)

The Sarsi (or Sarcee), a branch of the Athapaskan family, lived along the upper Saskatchewan and Athabaska rivers. Their name is from the Blackfoot *sa arsi*, meaning "not good." At one time, they lived farther north as part of the Beaver tribe, migrating southward by the early eighteenth century. They lived in bands of related families who traveled and hunted together. There was no tribal government; each loosely connected band was headed by a man whose counsel was respected but not necessarily heeded.

They obtained most of their food by hunting, especially for buffalo, which were typically driven over a cliff or into corrals by large groups of men gathered together for that purpose. The buffalo were used for food, clothing, skin tipis, bow strings, bone tools, and other necessities of life.

Women were responsible for making and erecting the buffalo-skin tipis. Most medical care was provided by women, who lacked the knowledge of healing herbs that some other tribes had. Instead, they relied on cauterization for most treatments. Sarsi families consisted of a man and two to four wives, plus several children. Girls were members of their mother's band, while boys joined their father's band. Bands came together for ritual events, including Sun Dances.

The Sarsis' first contact with whites came in the late eighteenth century, when the Hudson's Bay Company set up trading posts nearby. Contact introduced firearms and horses to the Indians, which in turn escalated

Late nineteenth century Sarsi woman preparing a meal, combining traditional techniques with European American kitchen implements. (Library of Congress)

their fighting. By the nineteenth century, the Blackfoot and the Sarsi had formed an alliance to defend themselves against the Cree and Assiniboine. The Sarsi suffered great losses from these attacks, and their population was diminished further by smallpox in 1836 and 1870 and by scarlet fever in 1856.

In 1877, the Sarsi signed a treaty with the Canadian government, giving up their lands. They were placed on a reservation near Calgary, Alberta, along with other members of their alliance. In the second half of the twentieth century, they made their living by farming, stock raising, and logging.

Sauk

Culture area: Northeast
Language group: Algonquian
Primary location: Kansas, Oklahoma
Population size: 4,517 ("Sac and Fox," 1990 U.S. Census)

A t the time they first encountered Europeans, the Sauk (also spelled "Sac") lived in present-day Wisconsin. By the late 1700's, they were settled in the Mississippi and Rock River valleys of modern Illinois. They are closely related by culture and language to the Kickapoo and Mesquakie (Fox); a formal alliance with the latter lasted from 1733 to 1850 and led the United States government to regard the two as a single "Sac and Fox" tribe.

Engraving of Sauk leader Black Hawk made in 1836. (Library of Congress)

In the early nineteenth century, the Sauk became divided over attitudes toward the United States. One group, led by Black Hawk, supported the British in the War of 1812 while another party, led by Keokuk, cultivated the Americans. An 1804 treaty sold Sauk lands in Illinois to the United States and led to the tribe's movement west of the Mississippi. An attempt by some to return to their old lands led to the disastrous Black Hawk War (1832).

After the war, the Sauk people moved increasingly southward. Iowa lands were ceded, and the tribe settled in Kansas. Pressured there by settlers, in 1867 the tribe accepted a reservation in Indian Territory (present-day Oklahoma). In 1891, tribal lands were allotted to individual members and tribal government was effectively dissolved. In the 1930's, the tribe reorganized as the Sac and Fox tribe of Oklahoma, with an elected chief.

Sekani

Culture area: Subarctic
Language group: Athapaskan
Primary location: Mackenzie (Arctic) drainage, British Columbia
Population size: 630 (Statistics Canada, based on 1991 census)

The four bands of Sekani were primarily hunters of caribou, moose, mountain sheep, and goats and trappers of all fur-bearing animals. Sekani waters were devoid of salmon, but whitefish, trout, and sucker were caught. Winter shelters were conical lodges covered with spruce bark. Summer structures were conical moosehide tents, or windbreaks of hide, bark, or firboughs. Transportation was primarily by foot, but spruce bark canoes were used for spring and summer hunting and—after the Sekani had established contact with whites—for transporting trade furs.

In 1793, Alexander Mackenzie became the first white person to contact the Sekani. Fort Connelly was built in 1826 for trading of furs and other items with the Sekani and other more westerly groups. The Iroquois and other Indians helped the spread of Christianity, which later developed into messianic cults. In 1870, Roman Catholicism was introduced; by 1924, most Sekani were Roman Catholic. The 1861 Omineca gold rush nearly destroyed the Sekani, reducing their population through disease and conflict. The construction of the W. A. C. Bennett Dam in the 1960's flooded great tracts of Sekani land and necessitated the removal of several intact Sekani groups.

Semiahmoo

CULTURE AREA: Northwest Coast
LANGUAGE GROUP: Salishan
PRIMARY LOCATION: Washington, British Columbia

The sea-oriented Semiahmoo lived in permanent winter dwellings. They maintained close socioeconomic relations with the contiguous Nooksack, Downriver Halkomelem, and other Central Coast Salish tribes. Fish were the main provider of subsistence, especially salmon, which stored well for winter. All methods of fishing were employed. Sea mammals, including the whale, were also taken, usually by harpooning. Land hunting and gathering provided a wide variety of foods and by-products. The Semiahmoo, like all Central Coast Salish, were noted weavers, using down, dog wool, and mountain-goat wool.

The Strait of Juan de Fuca was first discovered in 1787 by the fur trader Charles Barkley, and by 1827 the Hudson's Bay Company established Fort Langley on the Fraser River, which became a major trade center for the region. The Lummi Reservation was established on Semiahmoo territory in 1855 with the signing of the Treaty of Point Elliott. Many thousands of miners and gold-seekers entered the area when gold was discovered in 1858, creating further deculturation and conflict for the indigenous peoples.

Seminole

CULTURE AREA: Southeast
LANGUAGE GROUP: Muskogean
PRIMARY LOCATION: Florida, Oklahoma
POPULATION SIZE: 13,797 (1990 U.S. Census)

The Seminoles were the last of the major southeastern tribes to evolve. During the eighteenth century, Oconees, Sawoklis and other groups from the Lower Creek (Muskogee) towns in modern Georgia and Alabama moved into northern Florida. The name Seminole, in fact, derived from the Muskogee word *seminola* (which in turn was borrowed from the Spanish *cimarron*), meaning "wild," and carried the sense of one going to live in an untamed area. The Creeks themselves were a diverse group, and many of those whose descendants became Seminoles sought to escape control by the dominant Muskogees and spoke Hitchiti and other non-Muskogee languages. Others hoped to distance themselves from the growing presence of English colonists in Georgia. The Seminoles also absorbed the remnants of earlier Florida tribes such as the Apalachees and Tocobogas. Lacking a central tribal government, the Seminoles did generally acknowledge a principal chief from the line established by Cowkeeper. Only gradually did the Seminoles acquire a sense of separate identity from their Creek relatives.

Nineteenth Century. After the American Revolution, friction developed between the Seminoles and the United States. Many Seminoles continued to look to Britain for protection, and American settlers complained that Seminoles raided their lands and provided a refuge for runaway slaves. There was some truth in the latter charge, for there came to be a substantial black presence among the Seminoles. Some black Seminoles were slaves, while others lived in their own communities. Many Seminoles supported the Red Sticks faction of Creeks in the Creek War (1813-1814). After their defeat by General Andrew Jackson, many Red Sticks joined the Seminoles in Florida. In 1818 Jackson launched an invasion of Florida (the First Seminole War). The Seminoles were defeated and saw their towns in northern Florida destroyed.

After Florida was ceded to the United States in 1819, the Seminoles found themselves on land claimed by their old enemies. In 1823, they agreed to give up their claim to northern Florida. Soon the government began to pressure the tribe to leave Florida altogether. Federal commissioners obtained the agreement of a few Seminoles to the Treaty of Payne's Landing in 1832, in which the tribe agreed to remove to Indian Territory (present-day Oklahoma). Seminole leaders, however, regarded the treaty as a fraud. When attempts were made to begin removal in 1835, the Second Seminole War erupted. A protracted guerrilla struggle concluded in 1842, though about five hundred Seminoles evaded removal by taking refuge in the Everglades. Their numbers were halved by the Third Seminole War (1855-1858), which marked the last government attempt at forced removal.

Engraving of Seminole leader Billy Bowlegs that appeared in Harper's Weekly *in 1858.*
(Library of Congress)

Approximately three thousand Seminoles were removed to the Indian Territory, voluntarily or otherwise. Originally assigned to Creek lands, the Seminoles were reluctant to acknowledge Creek authority. Tension between the two groups also arose over black Seminoles (whom the Creeks regarded as escaped slaves). Eventually, in 1855, the Seminoles were given their own lands farther west. During the Civil War, most of the Oklahoma Seminoles desired to remain neutral. A minority signed an alliance with the Confederacy, however, and at the end of the war, the tribe was forced to give up all of its former land and was given a smaller area purchased from the Creeks (now Seminole County). Seminole slaves were freed and incorporated into the tribe. A new tribal government was organized, with its capital at Wewoka.

Twentieth Century. In 1906 the Seminole government was ended, along with those of other tribes in Indian Territory, and the tribe's land was allotted among its members, each one receiving 120 acres. A few Seminoles became wealthy when oil was discovered in Seminole County in the 1920's. Tribal government was reorganized in 1969.

Two hundred or so Seminoles had remained behind in Florida, surviving in small groups and adapting their lifestyle to the Everglades. In the 1890's, the federal government began to acquire reservation land for them, though it was not until the 1930's that a majority of Florida Seminoles lived on reservations. In 1957 the tribe organized as the Seminole Tribe of Florida, uniting both Muskogee and Hitchiti speakers. Some of the more traditionalist Hitchiti speakers, however, decided to preserve a separate identity and in 1961 organized as the Miccosukee Tribe of Indians of Florida.

William C. Lowe

Bibliography

Britten, Thomas A. *A Brief History of the Seminole-Negro Indian Scouts.* Lewiston, N.Y.: Edwin Mellen Press, 1999.

Covington, James W. *The Seminoles of Florida.* Gainesville: University Press of Florida, 1993.

Downs, Dorothy. *Art of the Florida Seminole and Miccosukee Indians.* Gainesville:'University Press of Florida, 1995.

Howard, James H., with Willie Lena. *Oklahoma Seminoles.* Norman: University of Oklahoma Press, 1984.

Kersey, Harry A., Jr. *An Assumption of Sovereignty: Social and Political Transformation Among the Florida Seminoles, 1953-1979.* Lincoln: University of Nebraska Press, 1996.

Lancaster, Jane F. *Removal Aftershock: The Seminoles' Struggles to Survive in the West, 1836-1866.* Knoxville: University of Tennessee Press, 1994.

Lantz, Raymond C. *Seminole Indians of Florida, 1875-1879.* Bowie, Md.: Heritage Books, 1995.

Littlefield, Daniel F. *Africans and Seminoles: From Removal to Emancipation.* Westport, Conn.: Greenwood Press, 1977.

_____. *Seminole Burning: A Story of Racial Vengeance.* Jackson: University of Mississippi Press, 1996.

McReynolds, Edwin C. *The Seminoles.* Norman: University of Oklahoma Press, 1957.

Paredes, J. Anthony, ed. *Indians of the Southeastern United States in the Late Twentieth Century.* Tuscaloosa: University of Alabama Press, 1992.

Porter, Kenneth W., Alcione M. Amos, and Thomas P. Senter. *The Black Seminoles.* Gainesville: University Press of Florida, 1996.

Schultz, Jack M. *The Seminole Baptist Churches of Oklahoma: Maintaining a Traditional Community.* Norman: University of Oklahoma Press, 1999.

Weisman, Brent R. *Like Beads on a String: A Culture History of the Seminole Indians in Northern Peninsular Florida.* Tuscaloosa: University of Alabama Press, 1989.

_____. *Unconquered People: Florida's Seminole and Miccosukee Indians*. Gainesville: University of Florida Press, 1999.

West, Patsy. *The Enduring Seminoles: From Alligator Wrestling to Ecotourism*. Gainesville: University Press of Florida, 1998.

Wickman, Patricia R. *Osceola's Legacy*. Tuscaloosa: University of Alabama Press, 1991.

Wright, James Leitch, Jr. *Creeks and Seminoles: The Destruction and Regeneration of the Muscogulge People*. Lincoln: University of Nebraska Press, 1986.

Seneca

CULTURE AREA: Northeast
LANGUAGE GROUP: Iroquoian
PRIMARY LOCATION: New York State
POPULATION SIZE: 9,167 in U.S. (1990 U.S. Census); estimated 1,000 in Canada; 6,469 enrolled members of Seneca Nation

The Senecas, members of the Iroquois Confederacy, have resided in western New York from at least the sixteenth century. Traditionally they lived in bark longhouses and traced descent through women. The women owned land, appointed chiefs, and raised maize, beans, and squash. Men were hunters, warriors, traders, and diplomats.

The fur trade and dependence on European goods resulted in competition with the French and other Indians. In 1687 the French destroyed Seneca fields and villages in retaliation for attacks. Afterward, one group of Senecas remained along the Genesee River and another moved west to the Allegany. The Senecas joined the British in the American Revolution and at war's end found themselves abandoned. Some fled to Canada with other pro-British Iroquois, but most remained in New York. The Fort Stanwix Treaty (1784) imposed conquest conditions, and the Pickering Treaty (1794) defined Seneca boundaries. By 1797 the Senecas retained only 310 square miles in New York.

Demoralized by land speculators and whiskey, the tribe was revitalized in 1799 by the teachings of Handsome Lake, to whom representatives of the Creator had revealed a new way of life combining retention of traditional rituals with a new social structure based on nuclear households and male agriculture. Alcohol and witchcraft were forbidden. Reports of the movement's success came from Quakers residing with the Senecas.

Cornplanter became a major Seneca leader after the American Revolution, advising peace with whites. (Library of Congress)

Fraudulent land deals culminated in the 1838 sale of all remaining Seneca land in New York. With Quaker aid, a compromise treaty was adopted in 1842 by which the Senecas surrendered the reservations at Buffalo Creek and Tonawanda but retained those at Allegany and Cattaraugus. Disputes over annuity distributions led to the abolition of government by chiefs and withdrawal from the confederacy by Allegany and Cattaraugus. They jointly created the Seneca Nation of Indians (SNI) in 1848, adopting a written constitution which established an elected council and executive. The Tonawanda Senecas were able to repurchase part of their reservation in 1857, retaining government by hereditary chiefs and becoming the Tonawanda Band of Senecas.

Railroads crossed Seneca territory, and white villages developed within reservation boundaries, particularly at Allegany. The illegal villages were given congressional sanction in 1875 and reauthorized in 1892 for another century. Extremely low rents caused long-standing resentment among Senecas until the leases were renegotiated in 1992 at fair rates. The construction of Kinzua Dam in the 1960's flooded an additional 10,000 acres at Allegany, leaving only 10,000 for the Senecas and forcing the removal of nearly eight hundred people to two new communities of tract houses. Congressional compensation was used to provide college scholarships and to build government offices, medical clinics, and libraries on each SNI reservation as well as a museum, bowling alley, and sports complex.

By the end of the century many Senecas were Christian, but the Longhouse religion of Handsome Lake remained a strong force. Successful SNI enterprises such as gas stations, mini-marts, and bingo provided employment for many, but conditions at Tonawanda were less favorable. Debates over the advisability of casino gambling polarized the reservations as leaders attempted to address unemployment and financial security issues.

Seri

CULTURE AREA: Mesoamerica
LANGUAGE GROUP: Sonoran
PRIMARY LOCATION: Sonora, Mexico

The Seris are one of the smallest Indian groups in Mexico, numbering about five hundred people, a 90 percent drop from a 1600 estimate of the population. Their homeland was the southern part of the Arizona-Sonora desert along the Gulf of California and on Tiburón Island, where they hunted and fished. They call themselves the Kunkaahac ("Our Great Mother Race"), and six bands constitute the ethnic group.

The Spanish encountered the Seris in the seventeenth century and established missions for them. Given their nomadic lifestyle, however, most refused to join the Jesuit and Franciscan missions and continued raiding Spanish settlements. The seizure of Seri lands after 1748 saw raids continue intermittently through the century.

After Mexican independence, the government sought to resettle the Seris outside of Hermosillo, but trouble continued. In the 1920's the Seris remained on the margins of society, and the 1930's saw an economic revival when there was a demand for shark livers. When American sport fishermen discovered the area in the 1950's, many Seris found jobs as guides for fishermen and anthropologists. Protestant missionaries worked with them. Although the Seris resisted, they are an example of a largely non-Hispanized group that was finally incorporated into Mexican society.

Serrano

CULTURE AREA: California
LANGUAGE GROUP: Takic
PRIMARY LOCATION: Southern California
POPULATION SIZE: 265 (1990 U.S. Census)

The Serrano tribe occupied a portion of California east of Los Angeles. Serrano is Spanish for "mountaineer" or "highlander." The Serrano were hunters and gatherers who occasionally fished for subsistence. Women gathered acorns, piñon nuts, roots, bulbs, berries, and cacti fruit in baskets. Surplus materials were sun-dried. Periodically, gathering districts were burned over to increase plant yields. Men were in charge of hunting large animals, including deer, antelope, and sheep. Large game were trapped and/or shot with the bow and arrow. Smaller animals such as rabbits, rodents, and birds were captured in deadfalls, nets, and snares. Excess meat was dried in the sun for winter use.

Extended families lived in circular-shaped homes covered with tule thatches; village locations were determined by the proximity of water. Clothing was made of deerskin; rabbitskin blankets provided winter warmth. Ceremonial costumes were decorated with feathers.

Shamans were believed to have special psychic powers acquired through dreams. Dreams were enhanced by the use of the datura plant, which was dried and mixed with water to make a tea producing hallucinogenic effects. Serrano shamans were healers. They used herbal medicines or sucked out foreign objects that were believed to cause illness or pain. The Serrano believed in twin gods who created the world as well as various other supernatural beings.

First Indian-white contact probably occurred in the 1770's when the San Gabriel Mission was established or when Pedro Fage made an expeditionary trip through Serrano territory. These meetings had little effect on the tribe until 1819, when a small mission was built near Redlands. Between 1819 and 1834, many Serranos were forcibly taken into the missions. Not enough Serranos remained behind to retain a native way of life. In the region northeast of San Gorgonio Pass, a small group survived and preserved what little was left of Serrano culture. Throughout the remainder of the twentieth century, most Serranos lived on the Morongo and San Manuel reservations in Southern California. The Serrano continued to participate in native ceremonies and political organizations with other Indian groups.

Shasta

CULTURE AREA: California
LANGUAGE GROUP: Shastan
PRIMARY LOCATION: Base of Mt. Shasta, Northern California, southern Oregon's Rogue River valley
POPULATION SIZE: 584 (1990 U.S. Census)

The Shasta people lived around the area of Mt. Shasta in Siskiyou County, Northern California. The Shasta people recognize four groupings: the Klamath River people (Wiruwhitsu), the Scott Valley people (Irvaitsu), the

Shasta Valley people (Ahotireitsu), and the Rogue River people (from Southern Oregon, Ikirukatsu). There are headmen of each of the four groups, but the head of the Oregon group is recognized as the leader overall, and he is often sent for in matters of great urgency. The Shasta are closely related to other Northern California tribal groupings, such as the Karok, Yurok, and Hupa.

The Shasta people were noted for the use of obsidian in the making of knives and arrow points as well as in wood work. They traditionally hunted deer, and, as with many California groups, the acorn provided the main staple for their diet. Acorns were ground to a kind of flour from which various breadlike products were produced. The Shasta also gathered berries. In these cultural traits the Shasta were traditionally very similar to other Klamath River groups.

While mostly a peaceful people, the Shasta would organize war raids on occasions of great tribal importance. Of equal importance, and practiced far more frequently, were elaborate peace negotiations and rituals. The Shasta practiced a form of shamanism to drive away the evil powers of spirits. Women could be shamans as well as men in the Shasta tradition. Other than a great fear of the power of spirits, the Shasta do not have an elaborate religious ideology.

Bibliography
Kroeber, Alfred L. "The Indians of California." In *The North American Indians: A Sourcebook*, edited by Roger Owen, James Deetz, and Anthony Fisher. New York: Macmillan, 1967.

Renfro, Elizabeth. *The Shasta Indians of California and Their Neighbors*. Happy Camp, Calif.: Naturegraph Publishers, 1992.

Shawnee

CULTURE AREA: Northeast
LANGUAGE GROUP: Algonquian
PRIMARY LOCATION: Oklahoma
POPULATION SIZE: 6,179 (1990 U.S. Census)

The Shawnee were a prominent Algonquian-speaking tribe of the Northeast. Their name means "Southerner," but the tribe moved so much in historical times that the original tribal homeland is somewhat obscure. Most scholars, however, believe that they originally hailed from the Cumberland

River area of Tennessee. Through much of the eighteenth century, the Shawnee homeland was the Muskingum and Scioto River valleys in the Ohio country.

The tribe was divided into five main divisions: Chillikothe, Kispokotha, Piqua, Hathawekela, and Spitotha. There were as many as twelve clans in each division, and descent was traced through the patrilineal family line. Authority was vested in hereditary clan and division chiefs; war chiefs were also important, usually warriors of proven ability.

The basic Shawnee dwelling was the *wegiwa* (wigwam), basically a framework of bent poles covered with elm or birch bark. Women tended corn and other crops, while the men supplemented the diet by hunting and fishing.

The tribe allied themselves with the British during the American Revolution, in part because land-hungry former colonists seemed the greater threat. After the war, American westward settlement increased, and the Shawnee took up the hatchet to protect their lands. They joined a coalition of tribes that managed to inflict two stinging defeats on United States army forces, most notably when General Arthur St. Clair was crushed in 1791. The Indians were defeated at the Battle of Fallen Timbers in 1794, however, and the next year signed the Treaty of Greenville with the United States. Under the provisions of this pact, the Indians were forced to relinquish Ohio and part of Indiana to the victors.

The Shawnee chief Tecumseh led a resurgence of the tribe in the first decade of the nineteenth century. Tecumseh is generally acknowledged as one of the greatest Indians of all time. He condemned the sale of Indian lands to whites, urged abstinence from alcohol, and promoted intertribal unity. Tecumseh's forces clashed with an American army under General William Henry Harrison at Tippecanoe in 1811. The battle was a draw but was still a check on Tecumseh's prestige. He joined the British forces during the War

Shawnee leader Tecumseh was one of the earliest Native Americans to attempt to organize a pantribal alliance to resist white expansion. (Library of Congress)

of 1812; his death in battle was a great loss for all Shawnee and all Indians.

The Shawnee dispersed during the course of the nineteenth century. One group of Shawnee moved to Missouri and from there to a Kansas reservation. About 1845, scattered Shawnee from Kansas, Louisiana, Arkansas, and Texas migrated to Oklahoma, where they were collectively known as the Absentee Shawnee. Yet another group settled in Ottawa County, Oklahoma, where they were called the Eastern Shawnee. The main body of Shawnee incorporated with the Cherokee tribe in 1869.

Not all Shawnee made the trek south to Oklahoma. Small groups of Shawnee filtered back and settled in Ohio and Indiana. Their descendants make up the Midwest's Shawnee Nation United Remnant Band. A milestone was reached when the Shawnee Nation United Remnant Band purchased a 28-acre tract for a sacred ceremonial ground. For the first time, the Shawnee reclaimed a piece of original territory.

Shinnecock

CULTURE AREA: Northeast
LANGUAGE GROUP: Eastern Algonquian
PRIMARY LOCATION: Long Island
POPULATION SIZE: 1,522 (1990 U.S. Census)

The Shinnecock, Corchaug, and Montauk formed the Montauk Confederacy, living as horticulturalists in permanent villages of circular, domed, mat-covered houses. They supplemented their main diet of corn, beans, and squash by hunting moose, deer, and other animals in addition to fishing. The Shinnecock traded extensively and used wampum as a badge of office, adornment, and form of wealth.

The 400-acre Shinnecock Reservation, established in 1666, was effectively diminished by the Indians' renting land to white farmers. Disease reduced the Shinnecock population, and acculturation was enforced by a growing number of non-Indians and increased loss of land, forcing many Shinnecock into a cash economy. Most whaling crews were Indian, and Shinnecock lifeboat crews were well known for saving many lives.

The 1934 Indian Reorganization Act stimulated tribal incorporation and the establishment of various self-help organizations. Many Shinnecocks have now left the reservation for urban centers and university study.

Shoshone

CULTURE AREA: Great Basin
LANGUAGE GROUP: Uto-Aztecan
PRIMARY LOCATION: California, Idaho, Nevada, Utah, Wyoming
POPULATION SIZE: 9,215 (1990 U.S. Census)

At first European American contact, the Shoshone occupied the area around Death Valley in California, much of Nevada and northwestern Utah (Western Shoshone, including the Panamint), southern Idaho (Northern Shoshone), and western Wyoming (Eastern Shoshone). Culturally and linguistically the three groups form a single unit. The Shoshone were generally at peace with their Uto-Aztecan neighbors—the Utes, Paiutes, and Bannocks—but the Northern and Eastern Shoshone often fought the Blackfoot, Sioux, and Cheyenne when they moved onto the Plain to hunt buffalo. They resisted the invasion of their homeland by European Americans but were eventually settled on reservations and in tribal groupings scattered around their original territory.

Early History and Traditional Lifestyle. The origin of the Shoshone and their entry into the Great Basin is not well documented. Prehistoric Indians in the Basin had a lifestyle much like that of the Western Shoshone, but many students of the region believe that the Shoshone did not develop directly from Great Basin ancestors. Instead, they think the Shoshone moved into the Basin from its southwest corner between one thousand and two thousand years ago. They spread north and east, eventually reaching the Great Plains, into which they expanded north into Canada and east beyond the Black Hills. When the Blackfoot, Sioux, Cheyenne, and other tribes moved west from the eastern woodlands, the Shoshone retreated into the region they occupied at the time of contact.

The Shoshone present an excellent example of a people's versatile and efficient response to their environment. The groups occupying the Great Basin, where no single resource is available in abundance, made use of the many resources that were present in small amounts or were abundant for a time at a particular location. They used plant seeds (grasses, pines) and vegetative parts of plants (especially camas—a type of lily with edible bulbs). They hunted and trapped whatever large (bighorn sheep, deer) and small (rabbits, ground squirrels) game was available, and they fished when they had the opportunity (migrating salmon). Because the environment could not support large populations, they migrated around the Great Basin in small bands using resources as they became available. Because available forage was insufficient to support large horse herds, they traveled on foot, using dogs as beasts of burden. In winter, several bands gathered near caves from which food, collected and stored there during the summer, could be retrieved.

In contrast, the Northern and Eastern Shoshone who moved into the Plains responded to the availability of an abundant and versatile resource: the buffalo. Because an efficient buffalo hunt required large numbers of people, the buffalo hunters lived in large groups from the spring to the fall. They too used dogs to carry their belongings until the 1720's, when they obtained horses. The horse made both moving and buffalo hunting more efficient, and it may have made it possible for some Eastern and Northern Shoshone to continue buffalo hunts in the Plains despite the opposition of Blackfoot, Sioux, and Cheyenne. Smaller extended family groups

Statue of Sacagawea, a Shoshone woman who served as the guide on the great exploratory journey of Meriwether Lewis and William Clark in 1805-1805. (Library of Congress)

moved to sheltered valleys in the Rocky Mountain foothills for winter, where enough forage could be found for the horses of a small group, but not for larger herds.

The spiritual and social lives of the Plains and Great Basin groups also differed, reflecting different group sizes and environments. Both groups were deeply spiritual, but the Plains Shoshone adopted the complex of dances, warrior societies, and other social and ceremonial activities of Plains Indians. The smaller Great Basin groups had one major ceremonial dance—the round dance—and a less elaborate ceremonial and social structure.

Transition and Modern Life. Except for the Mormons, European Americans initially showed little interest in the barren lands the Shoshone occupied. The discovery of gold and other mineral deposits in the Great Basin eventually brought on the familiar scenario of broken treaties and displaced Indians as European Americans moved westward. As a result, the modern Shoshone struggle with many problems—lack of education, poverty, lack of opportunity, and threats to their culture. They have sued the federal government over water rights, land ownership, improper compensation for past treaties, and storage of nuclear waste on Shoshone land. They have not always won—the deck is somewhat stacked against any tribe arguing for ownership of a large part of a state (Nevada)—but their ability to function well in such battles is further evidence of Shoshone versatility and bodes well for the future of the tribe.

Carl W. Hoagstrom

Shuswap

CULTURE AREA: Plateau
LANGUAGE GROUP: Salishan
PRIMARY LOCATION: British Columbia
POPULATION SIZE: 4,920 (Statistics Canada, based on 1991 census)

The Shuswap, a branch of the Salishan family, lived along the Fraser, Thompson, and Columbia rivers in present-day British Columbia. They were the dominant Salishan tribe in the region, holding more land and power than their neighbors—the Lillooet, the Thompson and the Okanagon—with whom they often fought. They called themselves Sequa'pmug or Suxwa'pmux, whose meaning is not known.

The Shuswap were divided into about seven autonomous bands, with their own hereditary chiefs. They owned slaves, whom they acquired in battle or trade. Their staple food was fish, especially salmon, which they caught with spears, nets, and traps. They also hunted bear, beaver, rabbit, raccoon, squirrel, and mountain goat. They made good use of the animals they hunted, using the skins for clothing, quills for ornamentation, and wool and hair for weaving cloth. Their homes were often made of logs or wood planks, and they housed four to eight families. Other villages had rectangular earthlodges with warming earth berms for winter and circular mat houses for summer. Some bands traveled widely throughout the year to search for food. For travel they used bark canoes, snowshoes, and horses.

In the early nineteenth century, the Hudson's Bay Company established trading posts nearby. The Shuswap traded skins, furs, and food for woven goods, steel weapons and tools, and glass beads. By the middle of the century, intertribal warfare had faded, but epidemics of measles, smallpox, scarlet fever, and other diseases wiped out large numbers of Shuswap and other Interior Salish peoples. Weakened numbers led to weakened influence. In 1945, in an attempt to force the Canadian government to be more responsive to their needs, the Shuswap joined with the Chilcotin and others to form the British Columbia Interior Confederacy. In the end, the Shuswap managed to hold on to their traditional lands and ways longer than most tribes. In the late 1970's they were given about 146,000 acres of reserve land in British Columbia, where they continue to maintain some of the old ways.

Siletz

CULTURE AREA: Northwest Coast
LANGUAGE GROUP: Salishan
PRIMARY LOCATION: Oregon coast
POPULATION SIZE: 1,554 (1990 U.S. Census)

The Siletz are the band of Salish-speaking Tillamook people who traditionally lived along the river of the same name in northwestern Oregon. This band is generally thought to be the southernmost branch of Salishan peoples in the Northwest Coast culture area.

Before contact with European American peoples, the Siletz existed, as did most of the peoples of the Oregon coast, in a quiet, relatively isolated autonomy. The Siletz lived in bands and villages around the mouth of, and inland along, the Siletz River and were related by close familial and cultural bonds. Their lifestyle was based on fishing, hunting, and gathering of the abundant local maritime, estuarine, riverine, and woodland resources. They are related to the Nehalem, Tillamook Bay, Nestucca, and Neaehesna (Salmon River) peoples.

After contact with colonizing Americans, most native coastal peoples in Oregon were removed to a reservation in upriver Siletz territory around 1855. The Siletz reservation became the home for a wide variety of previously unrelated peoples for many years, and much mixing of languages and cultures occurred. Among the language groups and cultures represented on the Siletz reservation were Athapaskan, Yakonan, Kusan, Takelman, Shastan, and Sahaptian people from all over the coastal northwest. The peoples now identified as the Confederated Tribes of Siletz Indians of Oregon comprise at least twenty-two bands living together in and around what was once the traditional territory of the Siletz peoples alone.

Sinagua

DATE: 500-1400
LOCATION: Northern Arizona
CULTURES AFFECTED: Anasazi, Hohokam, Mogollon

The Sinagua culture is known from sites in central Arizona around the Sunset Crater volcano near Flagstaff, Arizona, and in the upper Verde Valley. Its interpretation is complex, and Sinagua has been variously identified as a branch of the Mogollon, Patayan, or Hakataya traditions. In general, Sinagua is representative of a blending of cultural traits through either population movements or the adoption of features from neighboring peoples. This blending is a combination of earlier local traditions with those of neighboring Anasazi, Mogollon, and Hohokam peoples.

Three phases of Sinagua culture have been identified as dating to before major eruptions of Sunset Crater in 1064. These are Cinder Park (500-700), Sunset (700-900), and Río de Flag (900-1064). Sinagua culture shows a strong continuity of styles in ceramics, architecture, settlement patterns, and subsistence strategies through these early phases. Posteruptive phases are the contemporaneous Padre, Angell, and Winona phases (1070-1120), followed by the Elden (1130-1200), Turkey Hill (1200-1300), and Clear Creek (1300-1400) foci. These are marked by increased variation in material culture, including occasional Hohokam elements. After 1400, the Sinagua population declined.

Sinagua Lifeways. Information on Sinagua culture comes from several sites, including Tuzigoot and Montezuma Castle. House types of the early phases of Sinagua culture include pit houses with circular to rectangular foundations. The earliest tend to be shallow and round, while later examples were deeper, more rectangular, and lined with timbered walls. Especially large circular pit houses may have had a ceremonial function similar to that of kivas at later sites in the Southwest. Stone-lined pit houses and aboveground masonry constructions appear in the later phases. During the pre-eruption phases of the site, dead were disposed of by cremation. In post-eruption phases, burials were made in pole-covered or recessed graves, with occasional flexed burials beneath the floors of pueblo rooms. Sinagua subsistence was based on maize farming, with evidence for cultivation using both rainfall and irrigation. This was supplemented with hunting and gathering.

The characteristic ceramic ware throughout the Sinagua culture sequence is Alameda Brown, made with crushed stone temper and finished with a paddle-and-anvil technique. Earlier phases have yielded evidence for occasional Hohokam and Kayenta Anasazi vessels that were probably obtained through trade. Circular ball courts of stone masonry have been identified at a number of later Sinagua sites, and the playing of a ritual ball game is often interpreted as evidence of influence from northern Mesoamerica.

Volcanic Eruptions and Migrations. Major eruptions of the Sunset Crater volcano have been documented for the years 1064-1065 and 1066-1067, with evidence for continued episodes of volcanic eruptions for two centuries afterward. Archaeologists had initially argued that the weathering of tephra from these eruptions provided a moisture-conserving mineral mulch and added nutrients to the soil, resulting in a local area of high agricultural fertility. Rainfall farmers who recognized the benefits of rich soils were believed to have colonized the region, resulting in a multicultural occupation that combined Sinagua, Hohokam, Mogollon, and Anasazi peoples. The abandonment of the region after 1400 was attributed to the erosion of volcanic soils, resulting in a decrease in agricultural productivity.

This interpretation has been modified by more recent research that finds little support for either a substantial population increase or significant numbers of non-Sinagua migrants to the area. Hohokam presence in the Sinagua region is limited to a single pit house and associated trash midden at Winona Village that has been interpreted as the residence of a Hohokam trader. While thirteen ball courts in the Sinagua area may represent Hohokam influence, it is possible that these were erected without direct participation by Hohokam peoples. Although the introduction of stone masonry to the Sinagua has been attributed to the Kayenta Anasazi, there is evidence that this was present prior to the period of supposed migrations. Later Sinagua prehistory is now interpreted as a predominantly local process, affected by more extensive contacts with the Hohokam and Anasazi cultures.

Spanish explorers who arrived in the Verde Valley in the sixteenth century encountered the Yuman-speaking Yavapai tribe. Their specific relationship with earlier Sinagua culture remains poorly understood.

John Hoopes

Bibliography
Breternitz, David A. "The Eruption(s) of Sunset Crater: Dating and Effects." *Plateau* 40, no. 2 (1967): 72-76.

_____. "Excavations at Three Sites in the Verde Valley, Arizona." *Museum of Northern Arizona Bulletin* 34 (1960).

Cheek, Larry. *A.D. 1250: Ancient Peoples of the Southwest.* Phoenix, Ariz.: Arizona Highways, 1994.

Colton, Harold S. "Prehistoric Culture Units and Their Relationships in Northern Arizona." *Museum of Northern Arizona Bulletin* 17 (1939).

_____. "The Sinagua: A Summary of the Archaeology of the Region of Flagstaff, Arizona." *Museum of Northern Arizona Bulletin* 22 (1946).

Kamp, Kathryn Ann, and John C. Whittaker. *Surviving Adversity: The Sinagua of Lizard Man Village.* Salt Lake City: University of Utah Press, 1999.

McGregor, John C. "Winona and Ridge Ruin. Part 1, Architecture and Material Culture." *Museum of Northern Arizona Bulletin* 18 (1941).

_____. "Winona Village." *Museum of Northern Arizona Bulletin* 12 (1937).

Pilles, Peter J., Jr. "Sunset Crater and the Sinagua: A New Interpretation." In *Volcanic Activity and Human Ecology*, edited by Payson D. Sheets and Donald K. Grayson. New York: Academic Press, 1979.

Sioux tribal group

CULTURE AREA: Plains

LANGUAGE GROUP: Siouan

PRIMARY LOCATION: Montana, South Dakota, North Dakota, Minnesota, Nebraska, Manitoba, Saskatchewan

POPULATION SIZE: 103,255 in U.S. (1990 U.S. Census); 10,040 in Canada ("Dakota," Statistics Canada, based on 1991 census)

Sioux is the term popularly used to refer to a northern Plains Indian group most often considered in relation to their material culture—tipis, war bonnets, buffalo hunting, and an equestrian lifestyle. Among the Sioux the people call themselves Dakota or Lakota, terms which mean "friends" or "allies." Use of the term "Sioux" dates to the seventeenth century, when the Dakota were living in the Great Lakes area. Fur traders, explorers, and Jesuit missionaries heard from the Ojibwa (Chippewa) and Huron of the Nadouwesou tribe, which was much feared. Nadouwesou comes from the Ojibwa term meaning "adders." This term, shortened and corrupted by French traders, resulted in retention of the last syllable as Sioux. There are three major subgroups of Sioux—the Santee, Yankton, and Teton.

Origins and Westward Migrations. The term "Sioux" did not designate a single tribe or national entity but a complex web of bands or tribes that were spread across forested regions of the upper Mississippi, across the prairies of Minnesota and Dakota Territory, and beyond the Missouri River on the high plains of Nebraska, North and South Dakota, Wyoming, Montana, Manitoba, and Saskatchewan. A common language was important in defining the Sioux as a nation. Those who spoke a dialect of Dakota considered themselves allies, while all who spoke any other language were considered enemies unless a peace was negotiated. The Sioux did not form a political unit that acted in concert to control tribal areas or enforce tribal laws, but they did share a common language and common philosophy that molded their national culture and shaped their political and social life. By the 1700's, while still located in the Great Lakes or Woodlands area, the Sioux formed a relatively loose alliance known as the Seven Fireplaces or Oceti Sakowin, consisting of the Mdewakanton (Spirit Lake Village), Wah pekute (Leaf Shooters), Wahpetunwan (Leaf Village), Sisituwan (meaning unknown), Ihanktunwan (End Village), Ihanktunwanna (Little End Village), and Tintatuwan (Prairie Village). These subdivisions were not culturally distinct from one another in their Woodlands home but became more distinct as the people moved westward.

The first four were collectively called Isanti (knife), because these people once lived near a large body of water known to them as Knife Lake. The French later changed "Isanti" to "Santee." The Santee are the easternmost Sioux and were the last to leave the lake region. They speak the Dakota dialect in which there are no *l*'s and the *d* is used.

The Ihanktunwan and Ihanktunwanna have come to be called Yankton and Yanktonais in English, and as a group they are sometimes called the Wiciyela, or "middle people," because they lived between the Santee and Teton. The Yankton were originally one tribe, but economic factors forced them to divide into two groups as they became more populous. They originally spoke the Nakota dialect, which uses the *n* in place of the *d*, although they most commonly speak the Dakota dialect.

The Tintatuwan, or Teton, were the first to move westward onto the prairie. After the move the Teton became so numerous that by the late eighteenth century they in turn divided into seven tribes. This subdivision is also referred to as the Seven Fireplaces, because the Teton's social and political order replicated the national alliance. By the 1860's the Teton were most commonly known by the seven tribal names: Sicangu (Burnt Thigh), also known by the French name Brule; Oglala (Scatters Their Own); Sihasapa (Blackfeet, not to be confused with the Algonquian-speaking Blackfeet Indians of Montana and Alberta); Oohenunpa (Two Kettle); Itazipco (Without Bows), also known by the French name Sans Arc; Minneconjou (Planters by the Water); and Hunkpapa (Campers at the End of the Horn). These people collectively refer to themselves as the Lakota, using the *l* in place of the *d*.

In the Great Lakes setting the Sioux were semisedentary and had a Woodlands economy based on fishing, hunting and gathering, and some cultivation of corn. By the mid-seventeenth century the Sioux had been pushed westward by enemy tribes, principally the Ojibwa, who obtained guns through the French fur trade. The Teton and middle divisions moved westward to the Great Plains, where they acquired horses and a dependence on the buffalo for food and many material needs such as housing, clothing, and implements. The Middle Sioux settled along the Missouri River, while the Tetons pushed farther west into the Black Hills and beyond to the present-day states and provinces of Nebraska, Wyoming, Montana, North and South Dakota, Manitoba, and Saskatchewan. Although they too were pushed westward, the Eastern or Santee Sioux remained essentially Woodland people in territory and culture, settling in the area of southwestern Minnesota and eastern North and South Dakota. By the early nineteenth century, political and cultural differences among the Sioux groups became pronounced, and true Eastern, Middle, and Teton (Western) divisions emerged.

Political and Social Organization. The core of traditional Sioux society was the smallest unit, the extended family, which was a group of relatives living together cooperatively. The next level of organization was the tiyospaye, or "lodge groups." These were social units often referred to as bands, collections of lodges of related people who were usually guided by a respected elder known as itancan, or headman. The itancan was recognized as a leader by fully living a spiritual existence and demonstrating the values of his people—bravery, fortitude, generosity, and wisdom. The itancan's was not a permanent position; he served at the will of the people and could be replaced. Groups composed of several tiyospaye, and usually interrelated, were called oyate, meaning "people"; this is commonly understood as a "tribe." The oyate corresponded to the "fireplaces" of the Seven Fireplaces.

The model of tiyospaye provided the mechanism for maintaining social and political order when the various oyate came together in the large summer encampments during the time of the Sun Dance and buffalo hunts. Councils of adult men represented the will of the people and met to deliberate on all matters pertaining to group welfare. The headmen acted as symbolic fathers to their various tiyospaye and helped provide direction and guidance to the council, composed of younger men. All decision making was by consensus, ensuring that all the people had a voice. No formal voting took place, and those who disagreed with council decisions were free to move and begin their own tiyospaye. Council decisions and social order were enforced by the akicita, or "soldiers lodge," which saw to it that all people cooperated for the common good. Membership in the akicita changed with each new encampment, so responsibility and authority for the people's well-being eventually fell to each male.

This sociopolitical structure of headman, council, and soldier lodge was replicated in every Sioux camp and served to create and maintain social order and cohesion as a people. In this system, group well-being was dominant over individual needs, and at all levels, group harmony was ensured by a government run by consensus.

When European nations, and later the United States, needed to conduct business with Indians, they looked for a single individual or a centralized government rather than dealing with the whole tribal group. Traditional tribal governments that operated by consensus incorporated guards against concentration of power to preserve values of freedom, respect, and harmony. Consensus building is a slow process and simply did not fit the European Americans' needs or ways of conducting business. Since the time of initial contact, Europeans sought out or appointed one individual with whom to deal—a "chief." As relations with the tribes changed over the years, both the United States and Canadian governments continued to look for ways to centralize Indian governments, and this tension between centralizing and maintaining tribalism still exists in relations between tribal groups and federal governments.

When Indian people were forced onto reservations in Canada and the United States, the federal governments of both countries attempted to dissolve the traditional governments and to extinguish the languages and spiritual beliefs and practices of the people. It was expected that the people would become Christian, farm, and eventually assimilate into the general population. Still, many of the people continued conducting their business according to more traditional patterns.

Early in the reservation era the various Sioux tribes banded together in councils to work on issues related to illegal seizure of lands and treaty violations. These councils followed traditional patterns; however, they had little success in dealing with the government agents who enforced assimilation policies. These early councils met to discuss matters of importance among the people, to plan social events, and to represent the concerns of their reservation to the federally appointed Indian agents. At all levels council meetings were open, and input from the people was solicited.

Wars, Treaties, and Reservations. The Sioux in both Canada and the United States negotiated treaties and later agreements with the governments beginning in the early 1800's. Constant broken promises, unresolved issues, and encroachment on tribal lands brought various Sioux divisions into direct conflict with the United States between 1862 and 1877. These encounters, famous in American history, are known collectively as the Sioux Wars and include such events as the Minnesota Uprising (1862), the war for the Bozeman Trail (1866-1868), the Wagon Box Fight (1867), and the Battle of the Little Bighorn (1876). The Sioux, especially the Teton, who placed greater emphasis on warfare than other Sioux, were the most active in opposing American expansion into their lands. Eventually the depletion of the buffalo herds, relentless attacks by the United States military, and growing numbers of settlers on their land caused many of the Sioux to seek refuge in Canada or settle on reservations in the Dakotas and Nebraska.

Sioux boys arriving at the Carlisle Indian School in 1879; there teachers would attempt to suppress their Indian identity. (National Archives)

Most Sioux in the United States were settled on reservations by 1877, and life was miserable for the people. Prior to the 1870's, the Sioux had been living well on the basis of a buffalo hunting and trade economy, were rich in horses, had kept numerous tribal enemies in check, and lived in a vast territory. After confinement to the reservation, the Sioux were destitute, stripped of power, and forced to bend to the will of reservation authorities. Government policies were strict and sought to force assimilation by allotment of lands, encouragement in farming, Christianization, and establishment of educational institutions which sought to replace traditional values with mainstream American values; schools for Indian children often removed children from their homes. In order to hasten assimilation, laws were passed restricting traditional religious and social practices. By 1889 the Sioux as a whole were in poor health, starving, and embittered over the loss of millions of acres of the Great Sioux Reservation. In this atmosphere, word of a revitalization movement known as the Ghost Dance passed among the people. Some Sioux participated in the movement. Although many did not, much government and military attention focused on Sioux involvement with the Ghost Dance. The resulting atmosphere of fear and mistrust culminated in the massacre at Wounded Knee (1890), where more than three hundred Sioux men, women, and children were killed by the Seventh Cavalry.

After Wounded Knee, government policies aimed at assimilation pressed relentlessly forward, and Sioux relations with the federal governments in both Canada and the United States have been marked by tensions involving efforts to end the reservation system and terminate the special legal status of Indians. The Sioux have struggled to maintain their cultural identity, define their reservations as homelands, exercise their sovereignty, and regain illegally seized land, particularly the Black Hills.

Politics in the Twentieth Century. In 1920 the Canadian government passed legislation intended to end the reserve system as a way to force assimilation and bow to public demands to acquire Indian lands. Tribal governments were weakened, but some patterns of traditional governance remained and councils were active in opposing government policy.

In 1934, with the passage of the Indian Reorganization Act (IRA), the U.S. government sought to shift its relationship with tribes throughout the country. By 1934 the Bureau of Indian Affairs was directing much of the day-to-day business on the reservations as well as influencing national policy in Indian affairs. The federal government sought to get out of micromanagement of reservation affairs by proposing that tribes establish constitutional forms of government and elect officials who would then govern their reservation and make some of the decisions that affected reservation residents on a local level. In actuality, the Bureau of Indian Affairs maintained a strong presence on the reservations. The IRA gave the tribes greater voice in stating opinions, but it did not give them much real power because the Bureau of Indian Affairs reserved the right to approve most tribal decisions, to certify elections, and so on.

The Sioux people living in both Canada and the United States seek to preserve their inherent tribal sovereignty and to preserve the heritage of the Dakota/Lakota/Nakota peoples. The tribes exert sovereignty by pursuing legislation in Congress and Parliament on behalf of tribal members, manage a variety of programs formerly run by the federal governments, establish laws and rules of conduct on the reservation, and invest tribal capital in business ventures. In their governing system, the Sioux tribal nations seek to maintain continuity with the past as they work to preserve and protect the best interests of all the people.

The Sioux population continues to increase, with the largest concentration living in six reservations in South Dakota. Large off-reservation populations of Sioux exist in Rapid City (South Dakota), Denver, Los Angeles, and the San Francisco Bay area. The Sioux are leaders in implementing social and educational reforms and are particularly prominent in their Indian community colleges. Sioux reservations in Canada and the United States actively promote expressions of traditional Sioux culture and values through a wide range of events, arts, and ceremonies.

Carole A. Barrett

Bibliography

Anderson, Gary C. *Sitting Bull and the Paradox of Lakota Nationhood.* New York: HarperCollins, 1995.

Beasley, Conger. *We Are a People in This World: The Lakota Sioux and the Massacre at Wounded Knee.* Fayetteville: University of Arkansas Press, 1995.

Biolsi, Thomas. *Organizing the Lakota: The Political Economy of the New Deal on the Pine Ridge and Rosebud Reservations.* Tucson: University of Arizona Press, 1992. An insightful case study of the impact of the Indian Reorganization Act on two Lakota reservations. It focuses on the ways tribal organization ultimately failed to transfer power from the federal government to the newly organized tribal governments.

Black Elk, with John Neihardt. *Black Elk Speaks.* Lincoln: University of Nebraska Press, 1979. An important as-told-to narrative of a Lakota holy man who, though a convert to Christianity, remained committed to his enduring vision of the traditional Sioux way. This narrative also contains interesting eyewitness accounts of the Fetterman Fight, the Battle of the Little Bighorn, and the Wounded Knee Massacre.

Brown, Joseph Epes, ed. *The Sacred Pipe: Black Elk's Account of the Seven Rites of the Oglala Sioux.* Norman: University of Oklahoma Press, 1953. A seminal work in understanding the spiritual teachings as well as rituals of the Sioux people as told by a sometime practitioner.

Bucko, Raymond A. *The Lakota Ritual of the Sweat Lodge: History and Contemporary Practice.* Lincoln: University of Nebraska Press, 1998.

Clodfelter, Michael. *The Dakota War: The United States Army Versus the Sioux, 1862-1865.* Jefferson, N.C.: McFarland, 1998.

Densmore, Frances. *Teton Sioux Music and Culture.* Lincoln: University of Nebraska Press, 1992. Songs and ethnohistorical data gathered in 1918 provide important information on the social and religious beliefs of the Lakota. Most information was gathered on the Standing Rock Reservation in North and South Dakota.

Doll, Don. *Vision Quest: Men, Women, and Sacred Sites of the Sioux Nation.* New York: Crown, 1994.

Frazier, Ian. *On the Rez.* New York: Farrar, Straus & Giroux, 2000.

Hassrick, Royal B. *The Sioux: Life and Customs of a Warrior Society.* Norman: University of Oklahoma Press, 1964. This book is often regarded as a standard resource in study of Sioux society in the period between 1830 and 1870. Focus is on the male role, structure of society, and psychological aspects of the culture.

Hedren, Paul L. *Traveler's Guide to the Great Sioux War: The Battlefields, Forts, and Related Sites of America's Greatest Indian War.* Helena: Montana Historical Society Press, 1996.

Hoover, Herbert T., Karen P. Zimmerman, and Christopher J. Hoover. *The Sioux and Other Native American Cultures of the Dakotas: An Annotated Bibliography.* Westport, Conn.: Greenwood Press, 1993.

Hyde, George E. Red Cloud's Folk: *A History of the Oglala Sioux Indians.* Norman: University of Oklahoma Press, 1937. A tribal history of the Oglala Sioux. The book recounts in detail all the major episodes in the Sioux tribe's relationship with the United States. It explores divisions within the tribe and sheds light on contemporary reservation situations.

_____. *A Sioux Chronicle.* Norman: University of Oklahoma Press, 1956. A compilation of historical information from intertribal warfare, battles with the United States, and an exploration of the vagaries of federal Indian policy in the early reservation era.

_____. *Spotted Tail's Folk: A History of the Brule Sioux.* Norman: University of Oklahoma Press, 1961. Focuses on the history of the Rosebud Reservation in South Dakota, exploring internal divisions within the tribe, aspects of the Sioux Wars, and tribal history. Somewhat cynical in tone but a solid reference.

Laviolette, Gontran. *The Dakota Sioux in Canada.* Winnipeg, Man.: DLM Publications, 1991.

Lawson, Michael L. *Dammed Indians: The Pick-Sloan Plan and the Missouri River Sioux, 1944-1980.* Norman: University of Oklahoma Press, 1994.

Lazarus, Edward. *Black Hills/White Justice: The Sioux Nation Versus the United States: 1775 to the Present.* New York: HarperCollins, 1991.

Manzione, Joseph. *"I Am Looking to the North for My Life"—Sitting Bull, 1876-1881.* Salt Lake City: University of Utah Press, 1991.

Meyer, Roy. *History of the Santee Sioux.* Lincoln: University of Nebraska Press, 1967. A good exploration of the eastern or Santee Sioux. The book is thorough and contains an extensive bibliography.

Mooney, James. *The Ghost Dance Religion and the Sioux Outbreak of 1890.* Annual Report of the Bureau of American Ethnology 14. Washington,

D.C.: Government Printing Office, 1896. The seminal work in exploring the Ghost Dance and its aftermath. First published by the Bureau of American Ethnology in 1896, this book remains the key source for understanding the Ghost Dance.

Oehler, C. M. *The Great Sioux Uprising*. New York: Da Capo Press, 1997.

Rice, Julian. *Before the Great Spirit: The Many Faces of Sioux Spirituality*. Albuquerque: University of New Mexico Press, 1998.

Robinson, Charles M. *A Good Year to Die: The Story of the Great Sioux War*. New York: Random House, 1995.

Robinson, Doane. *History of Dakota or Sioux Indians*. 1904. Reprint. Minneapolis: Ross and Haines, 1956. Originally published in 1904. Although now dated, Robinson's work contains many interesting details not found elsewhere and is regarded as an important contribution to the literature on the Sioux.

Schultz, Duane P. *Over the Earth I Come: The Great Sioux Uprising of 1862*. New York: St. Martin's Press, 1992.

Utley, Robert M. *The Lance and the Shield: The Life and Times of Sitting Bull*. New York: Henry Holt, 1993.

Walker, James R. *Lakota Belief and Ritual*. Edited by Raymond J. DeMallie and Elaine Jahner. Lincoln: University of Nebraska Press, 1983. This volume explores the theological underpinnings of Lakota spiritual belief and provides explanation of some rituals, particularly the rites connected with the Sun Dance. Walker gathered this information from Lakota informants between 1896 and 1914.

_____. *Lakota Society*. Edited by Raymond J. DeMallie. Lincoln: University of Nebraska Press, 1982. This book contributes important information to the understanding of Lakota social structure. Walker, a physician on the Pine Ridge Reservation from 1896 to 1914, gathered and recorded the material from informants.

Young Bear, Severt, and R. D. Theisz. *Standing in the Light: A Lakota Way of Seeing*. Lincoln: University of Nebraska Press, 1994.

Siuslaw

CULTURE AREA: Northwest Coast
LANGUAGE GROUP: Yakonan
PRIMARY LOCATION: Southwestern Oregon
POPULATION SIZE: 44 (1990 U.S. Census)

The Siuslaw people live in the creek and river bottoms draining into the Siuslaw River along the southern Oregon coast. The temperate maritime rain forest is mild in climate and rich in resources. They are classified as Penutian speakers of Yakonan genetic stock, though such classifications are disputed by some tribal members.

Prior to white contact the Siuslaw lived a relatively isolated lifestyle focused on hunting, gathering, and fishing. Salmon was a primary food source. Large and small game, migratory waterfowl, many kinds of fish, shellfish, and marine mammals, as well as an abundance of plant life, provided them with many other foods. There was no need for farming. Life was relatively simple.

After contact the Siuslaw were rapidly forced to the margins of their environment as white settlers poured into the coastal river valleys in the middle and late 1800's in search of gold and farmland. They entered into a political confederation with their neighbors to the south, the Lower Umpqua and the Coos, in 1855. In spite of this the Siuslaw were forced to move onto a reservation on the Siletz River.

Their numbers declined, and they became federal wards. They attempted to make treaties in good faith, but their lands were taken over by settlers and their property looted or burned. They lost their property, their way of life, and much of their unique tribal cultural heritage and political legacy. They still endure, though there are only a few families left.

Skagit

CULTURE AREA: Northwest Coast
LANGUAGE GROUP: Salishan
PRIMARY LOCATION: Washington State
POPULATION SIZE: 1,362 (Skagit, Stillaguamish, Swinomish, 1990 U.S. Census)

The Skagit tribe has always lived along the Skagit River in northwestern Washington State, traditionally in a marine-oriented culture. The tribe was divided into two groups, the Upper and Lower Skagit. The Upper Skagit lived further east, toward the Cascade Mountains, and were more heavily influenced by the culture of Plateau Indians to their east. The Lower Skagit lived near the mouth of the Skagit River at Puget Sound.

The Swinomish people were often grouped together with the Lower Skagit since they lived nearby and spoke very similar dialects of the Southern Coast Salish language. They are, however, a separate group. The Kikial-lus people are a subdivision of the Lower Skagits and once inhabited two villages south of present-day Mount Vernon, Washington, and adjacent Camano Island. (The Skagit River was formerly named the Kikiallus; the meaning of the word "Skagit" is unknown.) The Stillaguamish people, a related tribe, centuries ago lived in twenty-nine villages along the Stil-laguamish, slightly south of the Skagit River. The Stillaguamish had close ties with the Kikiallus people.

All these groups based their economies on salmon and cedar. Living in permanent villages of large cedar plank longhouses and highly organized according to clans, they moved seasonally to follow sources of seafood, living in temporary shelters made of cattail mats. Cedar was used to make canoes, clothing, and baskets as well as tools and ceremonial items. Weav-ing, berry gathering, clam digging, camas root digging, and (after European contact) potato cultivation were women's activities. Men hunted for game.

Contact with the English and Spanish changed life for these groups, especially after the establishment of a Hudson's Bay Company trading post north of Skagit territory in 1827. American settlers started disrupting Skagit lands and lifestyle in the 1850's and 1860's, and the Treaty of Point Elliott (signed by the Puget Sound tribes and the U.S. government in 1855) meant the end of tribal recognition for some groups and the loss of much land. Several tribal groups were forced to live on reservations dominated by larger tribes, and as of 1990, the federal government still had not recognized the Kikiallus as a tribe. In 1976, the federal government did recognize the Stillaguamish as a tribe but did not provide for trust land or a land base. The Swinomish reservation is home to the Swinomish proper, along with some Lower Skagits (others of whom live on the Lummi reservation) and Samishes. The Samish tribe is closely related to the Skagit.

Slave

CULTURE AREA: Subarctic
LANGUAGE GROUP: Athapaskan
PRIMARY LOCATION: Alberta, British Columbia, Yukon Territory
POPULATION SIZE: 5,120 (Statistics Canada, based on 1991 census)

Related to other Athapaskan tribes, the Etchaottine (possibly meaning "people dwelling in the shelter") were given the name Awokanak, or "Slave," by their Cree neighbors, and this designation was adopted by explorers and traders. (The spelling "Slavey" is also used.) Their location may once have extended as far south as Lake Athabasca, but in more recent times they have been located in reserves in the Yukon Territory, British Columbia, and Alberta in Canada.

Tribal governance was informal, with effective organization in independent bands. War leaders were chosen when necessary, and a council of hunters provided direction at other times. The Etchaottine diet consisted primarily of fish and game. Fish were caught with hooks and nets, while snares were used to catch beaver and other game animals. Their food was cooked in vessels of spruce bark or woven spruce roots. Clothing for men and women included shirts, leggings, and moccasins made of skins. Spruce roots were woven into caps for women, and babies were transported in bags made of rabbit fur. Canoes of birch or spruce bark (and, less frequently, of moose hide) enabled the Etchaottine to travel over water; snowshoes and toboggans facilitated overland travel.

Two families might share a fireplace in their summer lodges, although winter cabins were usually large enough only for one family. Etchaottine men were known for showing respect to women and for taking especially good care of the elderly and ill. Burial customs were typical of Subarctic Athapaskans; bodies of the dead were either placed on scaffolds or covered with leaves and snow. The unusually contemptuous name "Slave" derives from the relationship of the Etchaottine with the powerful Cree, who early received weapons from Europeans and used them to encroach on Etchaottine land, dominate the tribe, and turn many of them into captives, either for labor or for sale to other tribes. The name, also used by Europeans, reflects the subservient position of the tribe in its locality. Eventually the Etchaottine found refuge on the islands of the Great Slave Lake. Contact with traders, explorers, and others began in 1789 with the visit of Alexander Mackenzie.

Snohomish

Culture area: Northwest Coast
Language group: Salishan
Primary location: Lower Snohomish River and south end of Whidbey Island, Washington
Population size: 402 (1990 U.S. Census)

The socioeconomically stratified Snohomish were dependent upon the sea for much of their food. The basic residential group was the permanent winter village. Though warfare was essentially defensive, one could gain status as a warrior. Numerous intergroup socioeconomic ties were sustained by intermarriage.

The first European American contact was in 1792 with George Vancouver, who explored Hood Canal and Puget Sound. Sustained contact commenced in 1827 when Hudson's Bay Company established Fort Langley on the Fraser River. Introduced ideas and technology brought major changes to the traditional cultures of the area, which had already experienced numerous devastating epidemics. Christian missionary work began in 1839 when Jesuit priests used Chinook jargon to deliver prayers and teach doctrine. During the 1950's, termination of Indian land and status was successfully opposed by the Inter-Tribal Council of Western Washington.

Snoqualmie

CULTURE AREA: Northwest Coast
LANGUAGE GROUP: Salishan
PRIMARY LOCATION: Snoqualmie River, Washington
POPULATION SIZE: 345 (1990 U.S. Census)

The inland Snoqualmie (including the Skykomish) depended to a large extent upon hunting and gathering, despite their access to saltwater and freshwater fish. Cattails, tules, and shredded cedarbark were used by women to make a variety of utilitarian products. The Snoqualmie lived in permanent winter gable-roofed and shed-roof dwellings, and in temporary structures at other times. The politically autonomous villages had permanent membership. Young men practiced vision quests to acquire a tutelary spirit.

After the arrival of European Americans, little ethnographic information about the Snoqualmie was systematically gathered, and what documentation was done occurred long after depopulation by disease and conflict with settlers. The Treaty of Point Elliott of 1855 called for the cession of land annuity provisions, antislavery, fishing rights, and the eventual removal of Indians living west of the Cascade Mountains.

The nonreservation and unrecognized Snoqualmie, along with the Duwamish, Samish, Snohomish, and Steilacoom, petitioned to be recognized in the 1974 fishery treaty, but Judge George Boldt denied their motion in

1979. Boldt's decision maintains that the traditional fisheries are protected by the 1854 and 1855 negotiated treaties.

Sooke

Culture area: Northwest Coast
Language group: Salishan
Primary location: Washington

The Central Coast Salish Sooke (or Sunghees) were a maritime people with bilateral kinship. They lived in large, rectangular split, hand-hewn cedar dwellings in permanent winter villages that cooperated in defense. The Sooke intermarried with adjacent people, particularly the Nitinaht. Their principal food source was the sea; they fished and harpooned sea mammals. During the summer and fall they hunted and gathered numerous types of animals and plants for food and utilitarian products. The major ceremonies were the Spirit Dances, the Secret Society, First Salmon Ceremony, and the Cleansing Ceremonies. Potlatching was staged for certain rites of passage, house erection, canoe launching, and change of status. Young men trained for a vision quest to become shamans and to attain a tutelary spirit. Little is recorded of these people; after 1850 their population was greatly reduced by the influx of gold miners and settlers, who brought disease.

Spokane

Culture area: Plateau
Language group: Salishan
Primary location: Northeastern Washington State
Population size: 2,118 (1990 U.S. Census)

The Spokane of northeastern Washington spoke a Salishan language shared, in different dialects, with the Coeur d'Alene, Flathead, and Kalispel. They called themselves Spoqe'ind (round head). The subsistence orientation of the three bands of Spokane was culturally reflected by permanent winter villages, specialized fishing technology, a sweathouse complex, shamanism, vision quest, tutelary spirits, the Blue Jay and Midwinter

497

Ceremonies, leadership through consensus of opinion, modified bilateral descent, and extensive utilization of fish and vegetal products gathered during spring, summer, and fall for winter consumption.

Exploitation of resource areas was further facilitated by intergroup marriage through exogamy, polyglottalism, and established trade relations. Even prior to the introduction of the horse, in the early 1800's, the Spokane ventured annually onto the Plains to trade and hunt for buffalo.

First mention of the Spokane by white travelers was by Captains Meriwether Lewis and William Clark in 1805 and David Thompson of the Northwest Fur Company, who surveyed the area from 1808 to 1811. Cultural change, however, had already commenced in the early 1700's with diffusion of European American trade items. The devastating epidemics of 1846 and 1852-1853 created severe population decline. Consequently, the rise of religious nativistic revitalization movements, particularly the Dreamer Cult, modified traditional belief systems. Protestant missionization commenced in 1839 with the establishment of the Tshimakin Mission.

Uncontrolled encroachment by white miners and other settlers ultimately led to warfare with the U.S. Army and to the 1858 military defeat of the Spokane at the battle of Four Lakes by Colonel George Wright, who destroyed Spokane livestock, horses, farms, and crops. As a consequence, a January 18, 1881, executive order set aside 154,898 acres of public land for the establishment of the Spokane Indian Reservation. The Spokane experienced severe deculturation as a result of tribalization, confinement to a reservation, government schooling, a dramatic shift to non-indigenous foods, and the introduction of religious and political factionalism.

A major event that disrupted Spokane access to fish as a primary food source was the 1911 construction of Little Falls Dam. The later construction of Grand Coulee Dam, under the August 30, 1935, New Deal authorization, effectively stopped the annual migration of all salmon to their spawning areas.

The Spokane reservation is organized around an elected tribal council with headquarters, museum, community center, and tribal store located at Wellpinit. Both Protestant and Roman Catholic churches are on the reservation, but not the Indian Shaker or Pentacostal churches. Factions are based on religious affiliation and geographical areas. Dominant modern concerns are issues of legalizing gaming, high unemployment, and ongoing litigation over loss of fishing sites and resource areas. Small per capita payments are generated by land leases and timber sales. In 1989 the Spokane tribe established a successful fish hatchery staffed by enrolled members. Approximately 50 percent of the 2,100 enrolled Spokane live on the reservation.

Bibliography

Chalfant, Stuart A. *Ethnohistorical Reports on Aboriginal Land Use and Occupancy.* Vol. 4 in *Interior Salish and Eastern Washington Indians.* New York: Garland, 1972.

Ross, John Alan. *An Ethnoarchaeological Survey of the Spokane Indian Reservation.* 17 vols. Wellpinit, Wash.: U.S. Bureau of Indian Affairs and U.S. Department of Forestry, Spokane Tribal Council, 1993.

_____. "The Spokan." In *Indians of the Plateau*, edited by Deward E. Walker, Jr. Vol. 12 in *Handbook of North American Indians*, edited by William Sturtevant. Washington, D.C.: Smithsonian Institution Press, 1994.

Stratton, David H., ed. *Spokane and the Inland Empire: An Interior Pacific Northwest Anthology.* Pullman: Washington State University Pres, 1991.

Squamish

CULTURE AREA: Northwest Coast
LANGUAGE GROUP: Salishan
PRIMARY LOCATION: British Columbia
POPULATION SIZE: 2,030 (Statistics Canada, based on 1991 census)

The Squamish were both maritime and river-oriented, living in politically autonomous permanent winter villages with rectangular dwellings of split and hewn cedar. Hunting of land animals and gathering of food plants supplemented a diet of many different fish and sea mammals. Kinship was bilateral with patripotestal authority. Intervillage socioeconomic relations were maintained by trade and marriage. Life was regulated by an annual round of moving to areas, in search of food, according to the season. Concurrently, there were ceremonies of redistribution of resources, known as potlatches.

Charles Barkley probably established contact with the Squamish in 1787; he was followed by land-based fur traders. Fort Langley on the Fraser River was established as a trading post in 1827. Consequently, the drastic effects of introduced disease and forced deculturation demoralized and greatly reduced indigenous populations. By the 1880's the Indian Shaker Church helped, and continues to help in some cases, to ameliorate cultural deprivation and aid in the curing of some diseases. Modern Squamish work as fishermen, as loggers, and in various skilled labor positions. There have been numerous efforts to revitalize traditional language, myth, and crafts.

499

Suquamish

CULTURE AREA: Northwest Coast
LANGUAGE GROUP: Salishan
PRIMARY LOCATION: West side of Puget Sound, Washington
POPULATION SIZE: 726 (1990 U.S. Census)

The Suquamish were typical of Northwest Coast peoples, relying mostly upon marine resources, occupying permanent winter villages, practicing extensive trade and intermarriage, and performing elaborate ceremonies.

The first European American contact was probably in 1792 when George Vancouver explored the region. In 1824 John Work of the Hudson's Bay Company traversed the area, and in 1827 he established Fort Langley on the Fraser River, which commenced sustained trade within the region. Roman Catholics were the first missionaries, teaching their doctrine in Chinook jargon. The 1846 Treaty of Washington gave the area to the United States, and the 1850 Donation Land Act of Oregon opened the region to settlers. Eventually, most Suquamish settled on the Suquamish Reservation.

The Suquamish Museum was established in 1985; it depicts their history and houses a museum store for selling traditional crafts, mostly cedar boxes, Salish weaving, and basketry. There has been a revival of winter spirit dancing, bone games, and other traditional activities. Tourism and other economic ventures are a significant means of income for the tribe.

Susquehannock

CULTURE AREA: Northeast
LANGUAGE GROUP: Iroquoian
PRIMARY LOCATION: Pennsylvania
POPULATION SIZE: 125 (1990 U.S. Census)

The Susquehannocks, a member of the Iroquoian language group, are known primarily from seventeenth century historical records and twentieth century archaeological excavations. First mentioned by Captain John Smith in 1608, the Susquehannocks at the time of European contact lived in the lower Susquehanna River valley in southeastern Pennsylvania and northern Maryland. Archaeological evidence suggests that their original homeland was on the North Branch of the Susquehanna River, in an area north of the Wyoming Valley and south of Binghamton, New York.

Throughout the historical period, the Susquehannocks were in conflict with the Iroquois over questions of trade and hunting rights. In the early seventeenth century the Susquehannocks served as middlemen between European traders and other Indian groups to the north and west, including the Iroquois; when the Iroquois, particularly the Senecas, wanted more direct access to European trade goods, they waged war on the Susquehannocks, forcing them out of their homeland and into the lower Susquehanna River valley. The Susquehannocks were militarily defeated by the Iroquois in 1676 and were forced to resettle near the Oneidas in New York. Later, allowed to return to southeastern Pennsylvania, they settled near Lancaster, where they became known as the Conestogas.

In December, 1763, white settlers in Lancaster, Pennsylvania, made several unprovoked attacks on Conestoga Indians in an episode known as the "Paxton riots." (Library of Congress)

Throughout the historic period, the Susquehannocks' numbers diminished from warfare and disease introduced by Europeans. An estimated population of five thousand in 1600 had been reduced to only twenty persons in 1763 when the last full-blood Susquehannocks were massacred by whites angered by the failure of the Pennsylvania Assembly to make reprisals for attacks by Indians on the western Pennsylvania frontier.

Very little is known about the Susquehannocks other than their role as traders. During the historic period, they lived in palisaded towns along the Susquehanna River, but these towns were probably a response to warfare. Archaeological research suggests that originally the Susquehannocks lived in widely scattered hamlets comprising only a few families. They practiced a mixed economy based on hunting wild animals, gathering wild plants, and shifting cultivation of corn and a few other agricultural products.

Thought to be closely related to the Cayugas, the Susquehannocks are believed to have been quite similar socially to the Iroquois, with a similar division of labor; women did the farming, and men hunted and engaged in war. The Susquehannocks apparently practiced matrilineal kinship, as did other Iroquoian cultures; descent and inheritance were passed through the mother's line, and women were socially influential. Archaeologically, the Susquehannocks are best known from their burials and their distinctive pottery. In the prehistoric period, the Susquehannocks buried their dead without grave goods in a flexed position in previously dug cache pits. In the seventeenth century, town-dwelling Susquehannocks buried their dead in cemeteries outside the town in specially dug graves; the dead were accompanied by pottery vessels and personal belongings. Susquehannock pottery was made using a paddle-and-anvil (rather than coiled) method; starting with a circular lump of clay, the potter shaped the bowl against the fist with a cord-wrapped paddle. The resulting pottery was incised with patterns around the lip; occasionally human faces were modeled into the lip.

Throughout the historic period, the Susquehannocks were known by a variety of names, including the Conestoga, the Andaste, the Meherrin, and the Minquaas. This variety has led some researchers to speculate that the Susquehannocks were not a distinct tribe but a confederacy of tribes formed in opposition to the Iroquois. There is no evidence to support the confederacy theory, however. It is more likely that the various names arose out of European confusion and the similarities between the Susquehannocks and their Iroquoian neighbors.

Swallah

CULTURE AREA: Northwest Coast
LANGUAGE GROUP: Salishan
PRIMARY LOCATION: Washington

The maritime Swallah had bilateral kinship and lived in permanent winter villages located near water. Some villages were palisaded for protection, as conflict was common between villages. Different types of dugout canoes were used for travel, fishing, and warfare. Major rites were the Spirit Dance, First Salmon Ceremony, Secret Society, and Cleansing Ceremonies. The Swallah potlatch served to recognize status change, redistribution of wealth, house-raising or canoe launching, and hereditary naming. The Swallah had a complex mythology in which Raven and Mink were tricksters. The Swallah maintained considerable social and economic ties with other Central Coast Salish tribes.

The Strait of Juan de Fuca was discovered by Europeans in 1787 by Charles Barkley. British and Spanish explorers visited the area, and by 1811 fur traders had established themselves at the mouth of the Columbia. The 1846 Treaty of Washington divided the Central Coast Salish into British and American regions. Because of disease, indigenous populations had greatly declined since the late 1700's.

Tahltan

CULTURE AREA: Subarctic
LANGUAGE GROUP: Athapaskan
PRIMARY LOCATION: Subarctic Cordillera, British Columbia
POPULATION SIZE: 1,330 (Statistics Canada, based on 1991 census)

The Tahltan had four named matrilineal clans based on moiety structure. Their society was stratified, with rankings indicated by titles and economic privileges. Winter dwellings were rectangular, roofed with vertical stripped saplings. Subsistence was based on hunting caribou, black and grizzly bear, moose, mountain sheep and goat, and wood buffalo, and on trapping fur-bearing animals. Both men and women joined in fishing. They traded cured hides, leather goods, and babiche for coastal dentalia, copper plates, eulachon oil, slaves, and blankets. Divorce and polygyny were equally rare.

First European American contact with the Tahltan was in 1799 by fur traders, and later gold miners, who introduced numerous changes in land-use patterns, trade relations, and goods. Approximately three-fourths of the Tahltan population died from disease during the nineteenth century. By 1874, white traders had effectively disrupted the previous Tlingit-Tahltan trade relationship, forcing many people to adopt a wage economy. During

World War II, many Tahltan men worked on the Alaskan Highway. Currently, the main sources of income are guiding, packing for outfitters and sportsmen, and government employment.

Tanaina

CULTURE AREA: Subarctic
LANGUAGE GROUP: Athapaskan
PRIMARY LOCATION: Southwestern Alaska
POPULATION SIZE: 490 (1990 U.S. Census)

Tanaina Indians occupied the south-central region of Alaska. Five species of salmon, which made up the basis of Tanaina subsistence, inhabited local lakes. In summer, men used nets, spears, and basket traps to catch fish, which the women split and dried. In autumn, hunters used bows and arrows as well as harpoons to hunt harbor seals. Arrows tipped with copper, antler, or stone were used to kill caribou, sheep, moose, or goats. After entering the fur trade, the Tanaina trapped during the spring and fall.

The Tanaina traveled extensively on lakes and rivers, using birchbark canoes and mooseskin boats. Snowshoes aided winter travel. Tanaina Indians lived in large, multifamily dwellings that housed ten or more families. Both men and women wore long caribou-skin tunics with animal-skin shirts on top. Clothing was decorated with porcupine quills, shells, and ermine tails.

The Tanainan Indians placed great importance on the accumulation and display of wealth. The richest tribesman acted as headman, in charge of the health and welfare of others. He accumulated animal skins, manufactured items, wives, and slaves. Rich men were noted for their generosity. They gave lavish parties, called potlatches, which included large gift-giving ceremonies.

Tanainan religion revolved around shamans, men or women who acted as doctors and priests for the tribe. They were believed to receive their powers—sometimes unwillingly—through dreams and could cast spells both good and bad. The Tanaina also believed in spirits and animals with supernatural powers.

Russian fur traders searching for otter first entered Tanaina territory after 1741. Though they traded with Russian posts, Tanainans were very opposed to the establishment of any permanent settlements. During the first half of the nineteenth century, the Tanaina were struck by a number of epidemics. Smallpox, tuberculosis, and syphilis killed more than four thousand.

In 1845, Russian Orthodox missionaries arrived and slowly converted the Tanainans. Fur prices fell at the turn of the century, and salmon canneries prevented the Indians from fishing in the most productive streams. Fish and fur-bearing animal populations dwindled. Some natives found jobs in the canneries, and gradually tribesmen became involved in commercial fishing.

Tanana

CULTURE AREA: Subarctic
LANGUAGE GROUP: Athapaskan
PRIMARY LOCATION: Alaska
POPULATION SIZE: 349 (1990 U.S. Census)

The Tanana inhabited the southeastern portion of Alaska around the Tanana River, hunting and fishing for their subsistence. The Tananas' most important food source was caribou—in the fall, tribesmen trapped them against fences, then killed them with lances and arrows. Surplus meat was dried for winter use. In the spring, the Tanana hunted moose, muskrat, and beaver. Beginning in June, whitefish and salmon were caught in nets and cylindrical fishtraps. Women gathered berries and roots and snared marmots and squirrels.

Tanana shelters varied with the seasonal activity. Dome-shaped lodges covered with skins were used in winter camps. Log lean-tos which held two families were used in more temporary camps. Bark-covered huts were constructed in fishing camps. Tanana Indians used birchbark or skin canoes for water transportation. Snowshoes and toboggans pulled by women were used for land travel. Tanana made clothing of tanned caribou decorated with shells and porcupine quills.

Each band had a chief and a "second chief" who, together, owned the caribou fences. The Tanana believed that shamans possessed supernatural powers. Illnesses were attributed to evil spirits which entered the body, and shamans possessed the power to remove them.

The first documented Tanana-white contact occurred around 1875 and was with trader-prospector A. C. Harper. Although non-Indian trade goods had already found their way into the area through Russian trading posts, Tanana Indians primarily traded through intermediaries. Participation in the fur trade changed annual migration patterns for the Tanana. When this occurred, economic importance shifted from the entire group to the family.

In 1886, the discovery of gold brought thousands of non-Indians into Tanana territory. Roads transformed little villages into large towns. Many natives hunted food for miners. The tribe suffered epidemics of measles, influenza, and tuberculosis, which devastated a number of villages. In the 1880's, Anglican ministers established missions and mission schools, which brought Tanana Indians into more permanent settlements. In 1958, when Alaska became a state, fish and game laws had the net effect of essentially ending old patterns of life and forcing the Tanana into wage-labor jobs.

Tenino

CULTURE AREA: Plateau
LANGUAGE GROUP: Sahaptian
PRIMARY LOCATION: Oregon

The Tenino (also known as the Warm Springs tribe), a branch of the Sahaptian family, originally occupied the valley of the Des Chutes River in Oregon. As is generally true for the Sahaptian tribes, there is no ethnographic evidence or traditional lore to show where the Tenino lived earlier than their first encounter with white explorers and traders in the early 1800's. Sahaptian tribes lived in village communities of varying size. Because they relied on hunting and fishing—salmon was a chief staple of their diet—as well as on gathering roots and berries, they were forced to move throughout the year to find food in different seasons. This necessity prevented the villages from growing and developing as political or social centers over time.

Sahaptian tribes do not seem to have relied on agriculture. They were skilled with horses and used them in their travels seeking food. For the most part, Sahaptian tribes dealt peacefully with their neighbors and with white settlers—largely because of the refusal of the Sahaptian to engage in violent retaliation for ill treatment. There is no record of any major battles between the Tenino and whites. Under the terms of the Wasco Treaty of 1855, the Tenino were placed on the Warm Springs Reservation in Oregon, along with the Tyigh and other tribes. Their population as a separate group has not been counted since.

Thompson

CULTURE AREA: Plateau
LANGUAGE GROUP: Salishan
PRIMARY LOCATION: Southwestern British Columbia
POPULATION SIZE: 3,925 ("Ntlakapamux," Statistics Canada, based on
1991 census)

The Thompson, a large branch of the Salishan, lived along the Fraser,
Thompson, and Nicola rivers in southwestern British Columbia. They
called themselves Ntlakyapamuk, whose meaning is unknown. They lived
in scattered villages along the rivers. The Lower Thompson, who lived at
the lower end of the Fraser, were divided into several small bands. The
Upper Thompson were divided into four bands, the largest of which was
the Nicola. These bands, made up of related families, lived mostly independently. Each had a hereditary chief, who had little authority. A central
council of older men made decisions for the tribe. The Thompsons' primary
food was fish, especially salmon, which they caught with spears, nets, and
traps. Men hunted bear, deer, elk, beaver, and caribou, while women
worked to preserve the meat and to gather berries and roots. The Thompson
were skilled at making and using birchbark canoes and snowshoes. They
also made beautiful juniper bows and birchbark and cedar root baskets.
Their homes in winter were circular pole frame lodges. These were half-
buried in the ground for warmth and were entered through the roof. In
summer, the Thompson lived in circular mat houses. They also had sweathouses for ritual use.

Their first contact with whites was probably with Simon Fraser in 1809.
Within a decade, the Hudson's Bay Company established trading posts in
the area. The contact and trading was at first beneficial to both sides. When
gold miners arrived in 1858, however, tension led to fighting and death. In
1863, the Thompson lost many people to a smallpox epidemic. These pressures caused a decline in population from about five thousand in 1780 to
about eighteen hundred in 1906. During the twentieth century, conditions
improved, and numbers increased. In the late twentieth century, many were
still living in their traditional territory on several reserves. They continued
to hunt, fish, and trap but added to their income with new pursuits: farming, the sale of crafts, and wage labor.

Thule

DATE: c. 900-1450

LOCATION: Bering Sea, northwestern Alaska, northern Canada, islands of the Beaufort Sea, Labrador, Greenland

CULTURES AFFECTED: Aleut (Atka, Aleut, Unalaska Aleut), Inuit (Eskimo)

A rchaeological evidence on the Thule tradition was assembled initially by Therkel Mathiassen, Knud Rasmussen, Henry Collins, Diamond Jenness, and James Ford between 1900 and the mid-1950's. Their studies, along with later contributions by James L. Giddings, Jr., among others, identified the principal cultural characteristics of the pre-Eskimo Thule tradition and provided it with an accurate historical context. These same archaeologists loosely borrowed the name Thule from the ancient Greek's designation of the world's northernmost lands to depict the climactic phase of late prehistoric Inuit development in the subarctic.

Excavations of sites along the Bering Strait have made possible the construction of an eight-stage chronology beginning before 2000 B.C.E. with Okvik and Old Bering Sea cultures—the Arctic small tool tradition—which were superseded by the Birnik, Punuk, and then Thule cultures. From these, in turn, arose both the Prehistoric Recent and Modern Eskimo cultures. Certainly by 900 C.E. a Thule tradition had emerged from Birnik culture in northern Alaska. Composed of an Inuit people originally living along the Bering Strait, the Thule culture was marked by a sophisticated adaptation to Arctic whaling (particularly of the bowhead whale), fishing, and seal, walrus, and caribou hunting.

Artifacts yielded by the excavation of Thule sites across thousands of miles of the subarctic include skillfully crafted, often elegant, harpoon heads, umiaks (skin boats), cutting tools, snow goggles, eating utensils, fishhooks, throwing sticks, bow drills, saws, female fetishes, and the remains of elaborate pit houses, sustaining Robert McGhee's conclusion that the Thule enjoyed an abundant, secure economy and a quality of life as rich as any other in the nonagricultural and nonindustrial world.

An extended period of climatic warming from the tenth through the fifteenth century presumably allowed Thule culture to spread rapidly eastward (during the same centuries when sustained warming allowed the Norse to move westward into Iceland and then Greenland), doubtless following whales and seals among the relatively ice-free islands and straits of the Beaufort Sea. By the eleventh century, the Thule tradition had extended itself 2,600 miles east from its origins in northern Alaska and the Bering Sea islands across subarctic Canada and into Labrador and northwestern Greenland, perhaps overlapping or displacing the indigenous Dorset culture, but more likely filling in areas vacated by the earlier collapse of the Dorset tradition. There is ample archaeological evidence that by the fifteenth century, the Thule had firmly established their culture throughout these eastern coastal regions, where some evidence indicates they encountered the Norse. There, in the east, Thule culture subsequently underwent regional adaptations or tribal specializations, from which sprang the Inuit or Eskimo culture known to historic times.

Tillamook

CULTURE AREA: Northwest Coast
LANGUAGE GROUP: Salishan
PRIMARY LOCATION: Oregon coast
POPULATION SIZE: 65 (1990 U.S. Census)

Tillamook is a Chinook name which means "people of Nekelim." It was more often spelled and pronounced "Killamook." The Tillamook were the principal and probably most powerful tribe on the Oregon coast in the early nineteenth century. They lived along a long coastal strip extending from Tillamook Head (near Seaside) to the Siletz River in Lincoln County.

Their population in the early nineteenth century has been estimated at about twenty-two hundred. The Tillamook lived primarily in numerous small villages built near the mouths of the main rivers that flow into the Pacific. Their economy was one of hunting, fishing, and gathering. Salmon, a variety of plants, shellfish, and both land and water mammals were consumed.

The Tillamook apparently developed an extensive regional trading network. Hides, canoes, and baskets were taken to the Columbia River to trade for or purchase shells, buffalo hides, wapato roots, and other items. Transportation, as well as gathering of seafood, was accomplished primarily by rivergoing and seagoing canoes which could hold from twelve to thirty people.

In addition to traveling between villages and trading, the Tillamook ventured forth to capture slaves. They raided neighboring tribes to the south and sold captured slaves mainly to the northern Clatsop and Chehalis tribes in Washington.

Individual villages were presided over by a chief, a position based on wealth and possession of supernatural powers. Additionally, task leaders occupied an important role in planning and performing various tribal activities. These shamans, headmen, and warriors each had particular areas of expertise (medicine, accumulation of wealth, hunting, war, and slave raiding). These individuals, generally male (although some powerful and important shamans were women), were the high class and elite of the village. Unlike tribal members of lesser status, the elite were polygynous. Women's status was based on the status of their family, husband, or guardian. Each shaman sponsored a winter ceremonial dance in order to revitalize his or her powers. Singing, dancing, and the generous proffering of food and gifts over a five- to ten-day period characterized the most elaborate of Tillamook ceremonies.

The Tillamook apparently did not worship any deities. The earth was viewed as all-powerful and judgmental of Tillamook behavior. Much of an individual's status and prestige was determined by that individual's ability to form a lifelong relationship with a guardian spirit.

Primarily as a result of disease epidemics in the 1830's, the population declined precipitously, with populations of twenty-five and ten being reported in the 1910 and 1930 censuses, respectively.

Timucua

CULTURE AREA: Southeast
LANGUAGE GROUP: Possibly Muskogean or Chibchen-Paezan
PRIMARY LOCATION: Northern Florida

The Timucua (or Utina, which means "earth") is a collective name for early tribes living in northern Florida. The Timucua may have been connected to the Muskogee group, which dominated the southeastern quarter of what would become the United States. First European contact with the Timucua tribes occurred about 1513, when the Spanish explorer Ponce de Leon entered the area, followed by Panfilo de Narvaez in 1528 and Hernando de Soto in 1539. At that time, the Timucua numbered between thirteen thousand and fifteen thousand and lived in large houses in permanent, well-fortified villages. They depended heavily on agriculture and surrounded their villages with extensive cornfields. De Soto was soon followed by French settlers, who gave way again to the Spanish. The Timucua were gradually conquered and converted, although a rebellion is documented in 1656. Disease and war reduced their numbers severely, so that by 1736 only a few Timucua remained in Volusia County. Those few were probably absorbed by the Seminoles, refugees from other tribes who entered north Florida in the late 1700's to escape the encroachment of white settlers. No Timucua Indians still remain.

The Timucuas were highly organized, building permanent homes and cultivating large tracts of land. They were most easily distinguished for their practice of tattooing their bodies—the men extensively, the women less so. Like most Southeastern Woodlands tribes, the Timucua women were responsible for planting, cultivating, and preserving the crops, primarily corn, beans, and squash. Although the men helped with major tasks such as clearing land and harvesting, they spent most of their time hunting, fishing, and warring.

Women were also important in the social structure of these tribes. Most southeastern Indians followed a clan system, a loose organization of family groups. Membership followed the mother's line, and status in a clan depended on the mother's connections. Women were responsible for the corn crop, important not only as a dietary staple but also as part of the religious symbolism of the tribe. The most significant and universally observed communal celebration, the Green Corn Dance, was a ceremony of forgiveness, purification, and thanksgiving that usually involved the entire tribe.

Tiou

CULTURE AREA: Southeast
LANGUAGE GROUP: Tunica
PRIMARY LOCATION: Yazoo River, Mississippi

Nothing is known of the traditional culture of the Tiou except that they lived in several permanent villages and had established peaceful relations with neighboring groups. Being horticulturalists, they were largely dependent upon their maize, beans, squash, and other cultivated plants. These foods were supplemented by hunting and trapping. When not farming, women gathered roots, nuts, and a variety of seeds.

First mention of the Tiou was probably made in 1697. The Tiou were described as living in two large villages, one above the Tunica and one below. Their population was greatly reduced by introduced diseases, and by 1699 some of the survivors settled among the Natchez after having been driven from their homes by the Chickasaw. The Tiou became fragmented.

Some remained on the Yazoo River, while later some were absorbed by the Bayogoula and some by the Acolapissa. By 1731 they probably had been destroyed by the Quapaw.

Tlingit

CULTURE AREA: Northwest Coast
LANGUAGE GROUP: Na-Dene
PRIMARY LOCATION: Northern California to southern Alaska coast
POPULATION SIZE: 13,925 in U.S. (1990 U.S. Census); 1,170 in Canada (Statistics Canada, based on 1991 census)

Tlingit literally means "the people." Among the Tlingit people themselves, there is a growing use of the spelling "Lingit" in order to avoid the use of the initial t sound, which is a European attempt to render a somewhat difficult initial sound in the Tlingit language (for the purpose of this article, the traditional spelling will be maintained).

It is probable that the Tlingit people began to occupy roughly their present southeastern coastal Alaska locale soon after the last Ice Age, or roughly 6000-5000 b.c.e. In this area, where the modern Alaskan city of Sitka also celebrates its Tlingit heritage, the weather is much more moderate than inland because of the prevailing currents from Asia which bring milder temperatures. Population estimates for 1740 were roughly 10,000 Tlingit. In 1992, population estimates for the Tlingit people, including those who live in urban areas throughout the Northwest, ranged close to 18,900. This represents an impressive endurance, particularly given the devastation of smallpox in 1836, brought by (vaccinated) Russian settlers and tradespersons.

In 1741, Russian ships first made contact with the Tlingit peoples. The Russians were attracted by the mild temperatures and the presence of otter and seals. Quickly following the Russian tradesmen were Russian missionaries, and Russian Orthodoxy remains a widely professed form of Christianity among the Tlingit as well as among other Alaska and Northwest Coastal native peoples.

Kinship and Social Status. There are two important kinship divisions ("moieties") of the Tlingit, the Raven (sometimes called Crow), and the Eagle (sometimes called Wolf). Each of these divisions are divided into a number of clans or sibs. In Tlingit tradition, an Eagle should marry a Raven, although in modern practice, this is not always observed scrupulously. The political organization of the Tlingit people is based not on the larger moieties but rather on the clans. Sib identity is permanent, and there is a recognized sib/clan leader; there is no recognized leader for the two main groupings of Raven and Eagle. The clans, in turn, are divided into "house groups." Identity is passed through the mother rather than the father, so children must spend time with the mother's male relatives in order to learn about their identity.

Wealth and social status are singularly important in Tlingit society, but status is determined as much by distribution and generosity in distribution as it is by one's inherent wealth. The most widely known example of this is the ceremony of the potlatch (based on the Chinook/Salish term *patshatl*), forms of which are found among many Northwest Coastal Indians along the Alaskan, Washington, and Canadian coasts. The potlatch ceremony takes careful preparation and is not merely and crudely to be understood as a massive "giveaway." There are important spiritual and social elements to the ceremony in Tlingit life.

Tlingits, as did other Northwest Coast peoples, maintained slaves, who were normally prisoners of war or their descendants. It was possible for a slave to become a free person and even to marry into the lower levels of Tlingit society, but mixing too widely across the castelike status boundaries was not encouraged.

Religion and Expressive Culture. Tlingit spirituality is evident in an elaborate mythology of the powers of animal spirits in the maintenance of life. All animals have spirits that can communicate to humans, and there is an element of reincarnation to some Tlingit spirituality. Shamanism is an important practice among the Tlingit, as protection from "Kushtaka" (evil spirits) is an important consideration for families and individuals. While elaborate, Tlingit religion is largely non-ideological in content and is concerned primarily with the maintenance of order, nature, and life. One of the most important aspects of Tlingit spirituality is the great significance attached to the interpretation of dreams and the communication with animal spirits that takes place during dreams. In Tlingit mythology, there is an elaborate cycle of stories about Raven, the most important character in Tlingit mythology, who is also considered the progenitor of the people themselves.

Tlingit culture is perhaps most notable for its elaborate and strikingly beautiful artwork, which can be found both in the wood carvings that decorated boats and homes and in woven clothing such as the famous "Chilkat" blankets. Basketry is also a well-developed art form among the Tlingit. Elements of Tlingit art motifs can be found with variations in other coastal peoples such as the Haida.

Daniel L. Smith-Christopher

Bibliography

Dauenhauer, Nora, and Richard D. Davenhauer, eds. *Haa Kusteeyi, Our Culture: Tlingit Life Stories.* Seattle: University of Washington Press, 1994.

_____. *Haa Shuka, Our Ancestors: Tlingit Oral Narratives.* Seattle: University of Washington Press, 1987.

_____. *Haa Tuwunaagu Yis, for Healing Our Spirit: Tlingit Oratory.* Seattle: University of Washington Press, 1990.

Emmons, George T., and Frederica De Laguna. *The Tlingit Indians.* Seattle: University of Washington Press, 1991.

Hinckley, Ted C. *The Canoe Rocks: Alaska's Tlingit and the Euramerican Frontier, 1800-1912.* Lanham, Md.: University Press of America, 1996.

Kan, Sergei. *Memory Eternal: Tlingit Culture and Russian Orthodox Christianity Through Two Centuries.* Seattle: University of Washington Press, 1999.

_____. *Symbolic Immortality: The Tlingit Potlatch of the Nineteenth Century.* Washington, D.C.: Smithsonian Institution Press, 1989.

Krause, Aurel. *The Tlingit Indians.* Translated by Erna Gunther. Seattle: University of Washington Press, 1956.

Olson, Wallace M. *The Tlingit: An Introduction to Their Culture and History.* Auke Bay, Ak.: Alaska Heritage Research, 1997.

Pelton, Mary Helen, and Jacqueline DiGennaro. *Images of a People: Tlingit Myths and Legends.* Englewood, Colo.: Libraries Unlimited, 1992.

Tohome

CULTURE AREA: Southeast
LANGUAGE GROUP: Muskogean
PRIMARY LOCATION: West bank of Tombigbee River

There may have been two major divisions of the Tohome: the Big and the Little Tohome. The Tohome were, like their neighbors, horticulturalists, dependent on cultivated maize, squash, beans, and other field plants. Men supplemented the diet with the hunting of buffalo, deer, and other animals. Women gathered food and medicinal plants. Prior to European American incursion, the Tohome maintained socioeconomic liaisons with other groups, particularly the Mobile.

The Tohome were probably first visited by the Spanish in 1559, and later by Pierre le Moyne Iberville in 1702. The pressures created by European American settlers and introduced disease greatly reduced their population. It is believed the Tohome and Mobile eventually united with the Choctaw.

Tohono O'odham

CULTURE AREA: Southwest
LANGUAGE GROUP: Piman (Uto-Aztecan)
PRIMARY LOCATION: South-central Arizona
POPULATION SIZE: 16,041 (1990 U.S. Census); 17,704 (1990, Arizona Commission of Indian Affairs)

The Tohono O'odham, as this tribe has always called itself, means "desert people." They are also known as the Papago, but the tribe prefers their own ancient name of Tohono O'odham. A cave called Ventana Cave has produced evidence of eleven thousand years of human existence. Some have considered the Tohono O'odham to be descendants of the ancient Hohokam, an extinct agricultural people who had learned to irrigate the desert by a series of canals.

The Spanish conquistadors and padres, in their contacts with the Tohono O'odham in the late seventeenth, eighteenth, and early nineteenth centuries, considered them peaceful farmers who were quick to accept the ways of the newcomers. By 1762 Spanish missions had started the process of breaking down the culture of the desert people. The United States continued the process when in 1848 it acquired from Mexico the territory in which the Tohono O'odham lived. In the 1870's the United States introduced the reservation system to the Tohono O'odham. They began to live on the reservations of Sells, San Xavier, Ak-Chin, and Gila Bend. Sells is their largest reservation.

The Indian Reorganization Act of 1934 set the terms for the Tohono O'odham organization of their reservation into eleven political districts. Each district has its own council from which two members are elected to represent it on the Tohono O'odham Tribal Council. In addition to the twenty-two council members, there are elected at large by the tribe a chair, vice-chair, secretary, and treasurer.

Many Tohono O'odham live and work outside the reservations in towns and cities. The majority, however, choose to live on the reservations and continue to farm, work in the mines, or work at schools, stores, or other facilities.

Tolowa

CULTURE AREA: California
LANGUAGE GROUP: Athapaskan
PRIMARY LOCATION: Northwest California
POPULATION SIZE: 504 (1990 U.S. Census)

Though the patrilineal Tolowa acquired wealth in order to gain prestige, their society lacked social stratification. They lived in eight permanent river villages with houses of square horizontal-set split redwood planks with sloping roofs. They exploited sea mammals, fish, land mammals, and numerous plant foods, particularly acorns. Each village controlled clamming beaches, sea stacks, berry patches, and adjacent wooded areas.

Tolowa woman wearing an apron decorated with shells in 1923. (Library of Congress)

The first documented European American contact with the Tolowa was in 1828 by Jedediah Smith, though disease had been introduced earlier. By 1850, white settlement had increased through gold mining, logging, and farming, resulting in a drastic reduction of the Indian population. In 1908, a tract of land on the mouth of the Klamath was acquired by the government for displaced California Indians; it became the Smith River Rancheria. The Tolowa were influenced by the Ghost Dance of 1870 and the Indian Shaker movement in 1929. Some modern Tolowa pursue traditional woodworking skills. On a cash basis, many Tolowa work in local lumber businesses as well as in clerical and administrative jobs.

Toltec

CULTURE AREA: Mesoamerica
LANGUAGE GROUP: Nahuatl
PRIMARY LOCATION: Northwestern Mexico

The Toltecs became a prominent tribe in central Mexico in the Post-Classic era after the fall of Teotihuacán. They were originally one of the Chichimec or barbarian tribes from the north of Mexico before moving toward the central valley and establishing themselves at Tula. The name "Tula" is a corruption by the Spanish of Tollan, or "place of rushes," and Toltec meant "one from Tollan." This site, located on a ridge overlooking the Tula River, is about thirty miles northwest of modern Mexico City, on the northern fringe of the heavily populated Valley of Mexico.

In the early tenth century, the Toltecs became the dominant tribe, and they ruled a wide area of central Mexico for about two hundred years. While not as artistic or original as the inhabitants of the nearby, but deserted and destroyed, Teotihuacán, the Toltecs were the first of the indigenous tribes to have a recorded history. This history, a mixture of epic tales and facts, is significant for two reasons. First, it describes a cleavage in society that may explain the growth of a militaristic state. Second, it presents one of the most complete depictions of the flight of the god-king Quetzalcóatl. Toltec history begins with a king, Mixcóatl (Cloud Snake), who was assassinated by his brother. The dead king's pregnant wife fled and gave birth to a son, called Tolpiltzin, who became a priest to the god Quetzalcóatl, the Feathered Serpent, most often identified as an agricultural deity. Tolpiltzin returned to Tula and avenged the death of his father by killing his uncle and taking the throne. He ruled as a priest-king, becoming so identified with the god that he became Tolpiltzin-Quetzalcóatl. One day, the story goes, Tezcatlipoca, a jealous rival god of war, tricked Tolpiltzin-Quetzalcóatl and made him drunk. When he awoke, Tolpiltzin found himself with his sister and, in shame, fled his city. The legend said he traveled over the water to the east and that he would one day return to regain his throne. This tale would haunt the Aztecs hundreds of years later when the Spaniard Hernán Cortés was believed to be this god returned.

The story may have described a challenge to the agricultural ruling class by a warrior group bent on conquest; the society did become more aggressive. Heavily armed warriors, along with fierce jaguars and eagles, were carved on stone reliefs to mark the increased importance of warfare among the Toltecs. The *chacmool*, a stone carving of a reclining figure with contorted features, held a vessel in which human hearts may have been placed. This thoroughly militaristic society dominated a wide area for nearly two hundred years, only to fall before continued onslaughts of new tribes coming from the north in the middle of the twelfth century. Among these tribes were the Mexica, who would become known as the Aztecs.

Tonkawa

CULTURE AREA: Plains
LANGUAGE GROUP: Tonkawan
PRIMARY LOCATION: Oklahoma
POPULATION SIZE: 261 (1990 U.S. Census)

The Tonkawa lived a nomadic life over vast stretches of eastern and central Texas. "Tonkawa" comes from the Waco language and means "they all stay together," although they lived in twenty or so independently wandering bands. Their name for themselves was *Titska watitch* ("the most human of people"). The Tonkawa hunted for most of their food, eating bear, deer, and buffalo as well as smaller game, including rattlesnake. When they were near the coast, they ate fish and shellfish. They also ate nuts, berries, and herbs that they gathered in their wanderings. The early Tonkawa practiced a form of peyote religion, eating the mescal "bean" from a shrub that grew in their territory. This ingestion caused a blinding red vision and vomiting. For the Tonkawa, the red symbolized success in battle and hunting; the vomiting purged the body of evil. By the 1890's they had substituted the milder and less dangerous peyote.

Judging by the traditional stories of neighboring tribes, the Tonkawa were disliked by their neighbors, who thought them warlike and dishonest. They were said to be good with bows, whether aiming at game or at enemies. They were almost always at war with the Apache and the Comanche. In 1782, some four thousand Tonkawa and Apache met to trade horses and to discuss the possibility of forming an alliance against the Spanish, who were proving an even greater threat. They could not reach an agreement, however, and hostilities soon broke out again. In 1855, they were removed with other Texas tribes to two small reservations on the Brazos River. Three hundred strong, they were moved again four years later to the Washita River in Oklahoma. In 1862 they were attacked by a large group of enemy tribes, and all but a hundred or so were massacred. After more wandering, they were finally settled on a small reservation near the Ponca River in Oklahoma.

Tsetsaut

CULTURE AREA: Subarctic
LANGUAGE GROUP: Athapaskan
PRIMARY LOCATION: British Columbia

The highly mobile Tsetsaut probably comprised five named composite bands, divided into two matrilineal clans, the Eagle and Wolf. They subsisted primarily on inland game hunting and trapping, descending only in the summer to the Portland Inlet to fish and dry salmon for winter storage. Their principal food was marmot, supplemented with porcupine, mountain goat, and bear. Winter travel was facilitated by snowshoes and the use of rare yellow cedar dugout canoes in spring and summer. The Tsetsaut had no permanent villages, only temporary camps and shelters of single or double lean-tos covered with bark.

Lean-to

The Tsetsaut were probably first contacted in 1862 by fur traders of the Hudson's Bay Company post at Port Simpson. In the same year, William Duncan established a new Christian village of Metlakatla and entered into competition for furs. Robert Tomlinson established a mission at Kincolith in 1867, and when Franz Boas visited the site in 1894 he found that the Tsetsaut population numbered only twelve, a reduction from five hundred only sixty years earlier.

Tsimshian

CULTURE AREA: Northwest Coast
LANGUAGE GROUP: Tsimshian
PRIMARY LOCATION: Northwestern British Columbia, southeastern Alaska
POPULATION SIZE: 4,550 in Canada (Statistics Canada, based on 1991 census); 2,432 in U.S. (1990 U.S. Census)

A rchaeological evidence suggests a Tsimshian residency of some five thousand years in the area. There are three major divisions: Tsimshian proper (which have been separated into the Southern Coast and Tsimshian), Niska (Nishga), and Gitksan. Each speaks a different dialect. Tsimshian derives from *emsyan* ("inside the Skeena River").

The Tsimshian subsisted on a variety of land and sea animals as well as plants that were gathered seasonally. Salmon was the most important food source. Eulachon, or candlefish, were particularly important for their oil or grease. The Tsimshian had a virtual monopoly on candlefish and the grease trade and became very wealthy as a result. The Tsimshian transported themselves between areas primarily in canoes.

The Tsimshian lived in fishing villages and camps in the spring and summer and in large houses made from red cedar in the winter. A chief's house might measure 50 by 30 feet. The chief and his family lived in several cubicles at the rear of the house. Other families of lesser status occupied the side walls. The houses were also used for dances during the winter ceremonial season.

The Tsimshian were divided into four phratries (tribal subdivisions, comprising several clans): Eagle, Wolf, Raven, and Killer Whale. Membership in a phratry was matrilineal, and marriage outside the phratry was prohibited. Each phratry controlled a defined territory. Social order and customs were maintained through elaborate ceremonial feasts and potlatches. The readily available and plentiful sources of sustenance allowed the Tsimshian time to devote to other activities. The Tsimshian became expert artisans and are especially well known for their intricate totem poles. Copper was the highest symbol of wealth, and the Tsimshian hammered native copper for their chief into beautiful ceremonial shields.

In the late eighteenth century the Tsimshian traded extensively with Europeans and Americans, and many moved to trading posts on the peninsula, where they built settlements. Contact with the outside world was intensified by the discovery of gold in 1867 and the building of a railroad. In 1871 the Canadian government assumed responsibility for the Tsimshian. Reserves were created at traditional sites, and allocations were unilaterally imposed by the government. The effects of missionization were also felt, and Tsimshian villages became a hybrid mixture of English and Indian custom and tradition. The Tsimshian have actively resisted government controls and usurpation of their aboriginal lands.

An entirely separate community of about thirteen hundred Tsimshians resides on Annette Island in Alaska in a community known as New Metlakatla. These are the descendants of the original fifty Tsimshian whom a missionary named William Duncan moved to Metlakatla in 1862. The colony moved to Alaska in 1887 after a disagreement with church authorities. A century later, it still retained much of its traditional values.

Tubatulabal

CULTURE AREA: California
LANGUAGE GROUP: Tubatulabal
PRIMARY LOCATION: Southern Sierra foothills, California
POPULATION SIZE: 29 (1990 U.S. Census)

The highly mobile Tubatulabal comprised three discrete bands speaking mutually intelligible dialects, each with their own chief. They occupied either patrilineal or matrilineal exogamous, semipermanent hamlets of several extended families, but they had no strict rules of exogamy or endogamy above the hamlet level. Chiefs were even-tempered, enunciated sound judgment, possessed oratory skills, and were generous with advice and their time. Leaders had limited authority, but they negotiated arbitration and resolved conflict. Living structures were simple but effective, made of domed, bent willow covered with brush and mud, with tule mats for beds and floor coverings. Women made coiled and twined baskets of split willow, yucca roots, and deer grass in representative and geometric designs. The most important foods were acorn and piñon nuts, collectively gathered and stored for winter consumption. All land mammals were hunted, and great amounts of various insects were dried as winter stores. Individual and communal fishing made an important contribution to their diet. Jimson weed probably was used only in curing ceremonies.

The first European American contact was in 1776, when Francisco Garcés explored the lower Kern River. By 1850, white settlers and cattlemen had established homesteads and ranches; and in 1857, the Kern River gold rush brought miners, who eventually displaced most of the Tubatulabal. After considerable conflict, the Tubatulabal located themselves on the Tule River Reservation from 1900 to 1972.

The major source of income for most modern Tubatulabal men is working as cowhands. Some tribal women are employed as secretaries. There are only a few elders who pursue certain types of traditional technology, particularly basketry and root digging. The low population and deculturation of the Tubatulabal reflects the historical 1863 massacre by whites and the devastating effects of disease and epidemics. Migration from the area and intermarriage with non-Indians have further decreased the tribe's numbers.

Tunica

CULTURE AREA: Southeast
LANGUAGE GROUP: Tunica
PRIMARY LOCATION: Louisiana
POPULATION SIZE: 33 (1990 U.S. Census)

The Tunica traditionally lived in Mississippi and Arkansas, just north of the area where the Yazoo River joins the Mississippi. They farmed, fished, and hunted, and they lived in small villages of rectangular thatched-roof houses; villages often included a temple building. They made pottery, wove cloth of mulberry fibers, and mined salt to trade with other tribes. The culture involved a high level of material security, and chiefs enjoyed nearly kinglike status.

The Tunicas were friendly with the French and were allies with them in French struggles against other tribes, notably the Natchez. In 1731 a large party of Natchez and allies attacked the Tunica, leading to heavy casualties on both sides; the principal chief of the Tunica was killed in the fight. Around the 1730's, the population began to decline, primarily because of diseases brought by the Europeans. When only a few hundred remained, the remnants of the Tunica and other Tunica-speaking tribes started to band together. In the late 1700's, the combined group moved up the Red River and settled near what is now Marksville, Louisiana. Some also migrated to the Oklahoma area with their Choctaw neighbors around that time.

Tuscarora

CULTURE AREAS: Northeast, Southeast
LANGUAGE GROUP: Iroquoian
PRIMARY LOCATION: New York, Ontario
POPULATION SIZE: 2,943 in U.S. (1990 U.S. Census); estimated 1,200 in Canada

The Tuscarora probably originated in New York and Pennsylvania and migrated southward to the coastal plain and the eastern piedmont of North Carolina after 500 B.C.E. The Tuscarora were principally farmers who produced corn, hemp, gourds, beans, peaches, and apples in great abundance. Despite their skills as farmers, the Tuscarora placed a greater reliance on hunting and gathering than neighboring Indian peoples.

The colonization of North Carolina by the English prompted the Tuscarora War of 1711-1713. The English encroached upon Tuscarora lands, enslaved the Tuscarora, and cheated them at trade. In the war, an alliance of the English and the Yamasee Indians defeated the Tuscarora. Nearly one thousand Tuscarora were killed and another seven hundred enslaved. In the peace treaty, the Tuscarora forfeited their rights to lands south of the Neuse River but received a small reservation in Bertie County, North Carolina.

Shortly after the war, about fifteen hundred Tuscarora moved to New York to seek shelter with the Iroquois Confederacy, which accepted the Tuscarora as members in 1722 or 1723. Over the next ninety years, the remaining Tuscarora moved northward, and in 1804, the North Carolina reservation closed.

During the American Revolution, most of the Tuscarora and many of the Oneida broke with other Iroquois and supported the Americans against the British. As a result, Tuscarora villages were attacked and destroyed by the British and other Iroquois, forcing the Tuscarora to find new lands to the west at Lewiston, New York. These lands became the site of the modern Tuscarora Reservation. The American Revolution also divided the Tuscarora. In the 1780's, a small pro-British faction of the Tuscarora moved to English Canada near the Grand River. These lands became the site of the modern Six Nations Reserve in Ontario.

Studies of the Tuscarora in the late twentieth century showed that they retained an unusually large portion of their traditional culture, social structure, and national identity. In the late 1950's, the Tuscarora challenged an effort by a utility company to build a reservoir on the Tuscarora Reservation. Although the U.S. Supreme Court ruled against the Tuscarora, their legal struggles helped inspire the emerging Indian rights movement of the 1960's.

Tuskegee

CULTURE AREA: Southeast
LANGUAGE GROUP: Muskogean
PRIMARY LOCATION: Between the Coosa and Tallapoosa rivers, Alabama

Little ethnographic data exist for the Tuskegee, who were horticulturalists and warriors. They possessed stone tools, practiced extensive intertribal trade, and possessed specialized predation and war technology. As did many tribes with maize economies, they had complex ceremonies, including fertility cults and planting and harvesting rituals. They gathered salt from natural sources, and they collected ash from burnt hickory, animal bones, and certain mosses. They exploited the buffalo for food and by-products.

It is known that Hernando de Soto visited these people in 1540. By the end of the seventeenth century they had probably divided into two bands, one settling on the Chattahoochee River near Columbus, the other on the upper Tennessee near Long Island. By 1717 French rule led to the removal of the Tuskegee (who had by that time been absorbed by the Creek); the Tuskegee formed a town in Oklahoma on the southwestern part of the Creek territories. Their greatly diminished population finally settled to the northwest near Beggs.

Tutchone

CULTURE AREA: Subarctic
LANGUAGE GROUP: Athapaskan
PRIMARY LOCATION: Yukon Territory
POPULATION SIZE: 1,610 (Statistics Canada, based on 1991 census)

The six bands of highly mobile matrilineal Tutchone were organized into two moieties and lived in coastal-type rectangular dwellings of logs. Subsistence was gained primarily through hunting caribou, moose, and mountain goat, and the trapping of smaller land mammals. Migratory waterfowl were taken, in addition to freshwater fish and salmon. Some gathering of vegetable foods and berries supplemented the Tutchone diet.

The first European Canadian contact with the Tutchone was made by Robert Campbell of the Hudson's Bay Company in 1842; he established Fort Selkirk in 1848. In 1874, white traders reentered the area and established Fort Reliance for fur traders. Thousands of gold prospectors arrived in 1898, but by 1900 only a few continued to mine for gold, silver, and copper. With the collapse of the fur trade in the 1930's, woodcutting became a main source of income for many Tutchone families. Surface and subsurface mining attracted non-Indian populations, and this migration was facilitated by the 1942 Alaskan Highway. Most Tutchone are involved in the wage economy, locally or through migration to urban centers. The Tutchone population was estimated to be about fifteen hundred in the mid-1970's.

Tutelo

CULTURE AREA: Northeast, Southeast
LANGUAGE GROUP: Siouan
PRIMARY LOCATION: Virginia, North Carolina

The Tutelo were a northern Siouan people who came into the present-day Virginia piedmont from the upper Ohio Valley. The meaning of the name is unknown; it was probably taken from a southern Indian language by the Iroquois. They were also known as Katteras or Shateras. In 1671, English explorers visited a Tutelo village, Shamokin, near present-day Salem, Virginia. By the beginning of the eighteenth century, the tribe had moved itself to an island in the Roanoke River, near the junction of the Stanton and Dan, and shortly thereafter to the headwaters of the Yadkin River in western North Carolina, where they were able to hunt elk and buffalo.

By 1709, the Tutelo and five other tribes (Saponi, Ocaneechi, Keyauwee, Shakiori, and Stuckanox) were estimated to total only 750 in population. For their own survival, this group of peoples gradually moved eastward, settling at Fort Christanna on the Meherrin River. Following the peace of 1722 between the Iroquois and Virginia tribes, the Tutelo, along with the Saponi, moved north, and by 1744 had settled in Pennsylvania under the protection of the Iroquois. By then the Manahoac, Monacan, and Saponi tribes had been mostly absorbed by the Tutelo. In 1753, they were admitted into full membership of the League of the Iroquois. In 1771, they settled on the east side of Cayuga Inlet and established a town, Coreorgonel, which was destroyed by General John Sullivan in 1779. Following this defeat, some of the tribe continued to live with the Cayuga and retained their own language. A remnant of the tribe located near Buffalo, New York. Others settled and intermarried with the Iroquois.

Little is known about the social organization of the Tutelo except that they gathered in clans. A tribal leader and council made political and social decisions. It is believed the leadership was not by lineage. During the nineteenth century, cultural and linguistic material was gathered on the Tutelo by the Smithsonian Institution. The last full-blooded Tutelo died in 1871, and the last person to speak the Tutelo language died in 1898.

Tututni

CULTURE AREA: Northwest Coast
LANGUAGE GROUP: Athapaskan
PRIMARY LOCATION: Lower Rogue River and southwest Oregon coast

The Tututni language group includes Upper Coquille, Tututni, Chasta Costa, and Chetco. All these tribes were typical of the Northwest Coast with stratified societies, winter plank houses, extensive overland and water trade, and traditional forms of wealth. Only the Tututni were matrilineal. The Tututni comprised seven divisions: Kwatami, Yukichetunne, Khwaishtunnetunne, Chetleshin, Mikonotunne, Chemetunne, and Tututni. Though they were oriented toward the sea and rivers, they gained most of their food from land animals, small animals, roots, tubers, seeds, berries, nuts, and insects. Differential food and utilitarian resources encouraged trade and intermarriage.

Robert Gray first contacted and traded with these people in 1792. In 1826 the botanist David Douglas visited the Upper Umpqua. The population for these groups was greatly reduced by disease, gold seekers, and the Rogue River War of 1855-1856. Some people were settled on the Siletz and Grande Ronde Reservations and became adherents to the Ghost Dance movement after its 1870 introduction.

Twana

CULTURE AREA: Northwest Coast
LANGUAGE GROUP: Salishan (Twana)
PRIMARY LOCATION: Washington
POPULATION SIZE: 714 ("Skokomish," 1990 U.S. Census)

The patrilocal and patrilineal Twana (including the Skokomish and Toanho people), like their neighbors, lived in permanent winter villages. Both maritime and land hunting were specialized in technology and associated ritual. The socially stratified Twana maintained their positions through birth, redistribution of wealth, and certain physical and religious attributes.

George Vancouver explored Puget Sound and Hood Canal in 1792. In 1827 the Hudson's Bay Company established Fort Langley on the Fraser River, which became a major trading post. The Indian Shaker Church influenced the Twana and Skokomish (a tribe of the Twana) in the early 1830's. In 1910 there were only sixty-one Twana.

The Twana Reservation at Skokomish had a population of 1,029 in 1984, which did not include all off-reservation Twana or recognize those of varying blood degrees from other groups. The Southern Coast Salish tribes have experienced considerable socioeconomic, political, and cultural revitalization because of recent changes in federal legislation and policies, particularly in sovereignty and fishing rights.

Tyigh

CULTURE AREA: Plateau
LANGUAGE GROUP: Sahaptian
PRIMARY LOCATION: Oregon

The Tyigh (also spelled "Tygh"), a branch of the Sahaptian family, were so named by white explorers and traders because they lived near the Tyigh and White rivers in what is now Wasco County, Oregon. As is generally true for the Sahaptian tribes, there is no ethnographic evidence or traditional lore to show where the Tyigh lived earlier than their first encounter with whites in the early 1800's. Sahaptian tribes lived in village communities of varying size. Because they relied on hunting and fishing (salmon being a chief staple of their diet) as well as on gathering roots and berries, they moved throughout the year to find food in different seasons. This prevented villages from growing and developing as political or social centers.

Sahaptian tribes do not seem to have relied on agriculture. They were skilled with horses and used them in their travels. Tyigh speak the Tenino language. Under the terms of the Wasco Treaty of 1855, the Tyigh were placed on the Warm Springs Reservation in Oregon, along with the Tenino and other tribes. Their population as a separate group has not been counted since.

Umatilla

CULTURE AREA: Plateau
LANGUAGE GROUP: Sahaptian
PRIMARY LOCATION: Oregon
POPULATION SIZE: 1,159 (1990 U.S. Census)

527

The Umatillas are recognized as Plateau Indians who traditionally inhabited the Mid-Columbia Plateau. They are a Sahaptian-speaking group, and their population was estimated at fifteen hundred in 1780. Their modern descendants reside on the Umatilla Reservation, which is located in northeastern Oregon.

The Umatillas, part of the larger Mid-Columbia Plateau culture, existed for ten thousand years in the Columbia Basin before the coming of European Americans. During this period, their culture remained relatively stable, with seasonal moves to winter villages; there were rich salmon fishing resources on the Columbia River as well as roots and berries that were gathered. By the time of European American contact, the horse was part of Umatilla culture. Horses changed Umatilla subsistence patterns but not to the extent that the horse changed Nez Perce culture. Perhaps because of the plenitude of their resources, particularly salmon, the Umatillas' economy still consisted primarily of fishing and gathering, whereas some Plateau tribes began to hunt buffalo with the arrival of the horse.

Although there is evidence of epidemics, such as smallpox brought by trading ships, occurring in the Mid-Columbia Plateau as early as 1775, white settlement did not directly affect the Umatillas until the 1840's. Their villages were near the Emigrant Road, or Old Oregon Trail. When the Cayuse War broke out after the Whitman Massacre in 1848, some Umatillas took part. In 1855, the Walla Walla Council, led by Washington Territorial Governor Isaac Stevens, had an immediate impact on the Umatillas in that the Umatillas ceded lands in return for the Umatilla Reservation, an area originally established with 245,699 acres. The reservation comprises 85,322 acres. The Umatilla Reservation was to be home to the Umatillas, the Walla Wallas, and the Cayuse. It came to be known as the Confederated Tribes of the Umatilla Indian Reservation after the tribe organized in 1949 under the Indian Reorganization Act (1934).

The Umatillas, similar to many other Indian tribes, lost land after the General Allotment Act of 1887. Earlier, they had lost lands under the Donation Land Act, which allowed settlers to homestead lands in Oregon before the Indians rescinded their right to the land. Beginning in 1951, the Confederated Tribes of the Umatilla Reservation began filing claims with the Indian Claims Commission to recover lost lands or a financial settlement in lieu of land. Other lawsuits concerned lost fishing rights. In the case *Maison v. The Confederated Tribes of the Umatilla Reservation* (1958), Indian fishing rights were recognized. Other suits involved lost water rights on the Umatilla River as a result of dam construction. The Confederated Tribes of the Umatilla Reservation received several monetary compensations for these claims.

The Confederated Tribes of the Umatilla Reservation rely on an economy of grazing and farming, particularly wheat, with limited industry. Some aspects of traditional life are still evident, as some members practice the Waashat religion and can speak the tribal language.

Umpqua

CULTURE AREA: Northwest Coast
LANGUAGE GROUPS: Athapaskan, Penutian
PRIMARY LOCATION: Southwestern Oregon
POPULATION SIZE: 653 (1990 U.S. Census)

The Umpqua people traditionally lived along the Umpqua River of southwestern Oregon. The river flows from the Cascade Mountain Range in eastern Oregon to the Pacific Ocean in the west. The terrain through which it flows is mostly mountainous. The environments along its shores are varied, from cool, dry, upland coniferous forests in the east to lush, temperate-zone rain forests near the sea.

There are two fairly distinct Umpqua subgroups, the upper Umpqua and lower Umpqua. The people who live along the upper Umpqua River are most probably of Athapaskan origin, whereas the people of the lower river are apparently more closely related to other Penutian speakers of Yakonan stock. These assertions are disputed by some. Many Umpqua people believe they originated in their traditional homeland. The dividing point between upper and lower areas of the river is commonly considered to be at the town of Scottsburg.

Before white contact in the early nineteenth century, the Umpqua lived relatively solitary lives, hunting, gathering, and fishing. They would join with their neighbors, the Siuslaw to the north and the Coos to the south, for common defense and occasional potlatches.

After contact with white settlers, the Umpqua were pushed toward the margins of their homeland, then placed on the Siletz reservation in the 1850's. The lower Umpqua joined in political confederation and formed the Confederated Tribes of the Coos, lower Umpqua, and Siuslaw Indians. This confederation still exists as a federally recognized Indian nation.

The upper Umpqua fought for their land and sovereignty and are now recognized as the Cow Creek Band by the U.S. government.

Ute

CULTURE AREA: Great Basin
LANGUAGE GROUP: Uto-Aztecan
PRIMARY LOCATION: Utah, Colorado
POPULATION SIZE: 7,273 (1990 U.S. Census)

The Utes (or Yutas) inhabited the eastern fringe of the Great Basin and the Colorado and northern New Mexican Rocky Mountains; some hunted buffalo as far east as the Great Plains. Utes called themselves Nutc (the people). The state of Utah is named for the Utes.

Early History. Utes were nomadic hunters and gatherers, traveling in extended family groups in established nomadic circuits. They lived in either brush huts or, when large game was available, skin-covered tipis. With the acquisition of the horse in the seventeenth century larger bands congregated, the nomadic circuit extended, and larger game became more accessible. These bands were identified by their geographic locations and were led by chiefs whose authority lay in their hunting and raiding power. Utes were regarded as warlike, and raiding became a natural extension of hunting. Ute religion was not complex, and most religious observances were related to healing ceremonies or folkloric rituals and taboos.

European Contact. The Utes' first contact with Europeans was with the Spanish in New Mexico by the seventeenth century and was based on trade, both at New Mexican settlements and with traders who penetrated into Colorado and Utah. Ute-Spanish relations were generally friendly, although conflict was not unknown. From the Spanish the Utes obtained horses and arms in return for buckskins and Indian captives. The Utes became a major link in the spread of the horse to other Indians.

Although fur trappers had operated throughout the Ute territory, extensive white penetration began in 1847 with the Mormon arrival in Utah, and in 1848 when the Mexican-American War brought an influx of U.S. citizens to New Mexico. Although relations remained generally friendly in Utah, antagonism flared briefly in 1853 under Walkara and again from 1863 to the 1870's under the direction of Black Hawk. During the 1860's Utah Utes were consolidated on the Uintah Reservation. Once there they became known as Uintah Utes. A related tribe, part Ute and part Paiute, known as the Pahvant, remained friendly to the Mormons; they converted almost en masse to that religion and successfully resisted removal to the reservation.

A preliminary treaty between the United States and Utes in Colorado and New Mexico was signed as early as 1849. As precious minerals were discovered in the Colorado Rockies, however, additional treaties were negotiated, ceding increasingly larger tracts of land in 1863, 1868, and 1873. During these negotiations a central Colorado Ute chief, Ouray, rose to prominence because of his ability to communicate with whites and his ability to convince other chiefs to conciliate with, rather than fight, the United States. As a result Ouray was appointed the spokesman and head chief of the "consolidated" Ute Nation.

With the treaties came agencies that localized Ute bands and gave rise to modern identifications: The three major northern Colorado bands (the Yampa River, Grand River, and White River Utes) became the White River Utes, the central Colorado Tabeguaches became the Uncompaghre Utes, the Mouache and Capote became the Southern Utes, and the Weeminuche became the Ute Mountain Utes.

The Meeker Massacre. In 1879 Nathan C. Meeker, a new agent at the White River Agency, antagonized northern Utes by moving the agency to, and plowing up, their prized winter horse pasturage and race track. When Meeker called for troops to protect him, troops under the command of T. T. Thornburgh were dispatched to the reservation. The Utes feared that the troops were there to remove them forcibly to Indian Territory (Oklahoma). On September 29, more than three hundred Utes under the direction of Captain Jack, Antelope, and Colorow attacked and besieged the column as they entered the reservation. Upon hearing of the attack on Thornburgh, other Utes massacred the agency personnel and took the women there captive.

As punishment for the uprising, the White River bands were forced to cede their reservation to pay reparations and were removed to the Uintah reservation in Utah. Although the other Ute bands had refused to join in the uprising and Ouray had assisted the U.S. government in quelling the violence and retrieving the captives, the remainder of the Utes were forced to negotiate another treaty in 1880. Within a year, using a technicality in the treaty, the Uncompaghres were also expelled from Colorado and given a barren reservation (called the Ouray reservation) adjoining the Uintah reservation. The Southern Utes successfully resisted attempts to remove them from their narrow, southern Colorado reservation, though conflicts involving bloodshed were not infrequent. Some Utes affiliated with the Ute Mountain Tribe also obtained southeastern Utah lands through homesteading.

In 1887 the U.S. Congress passed the General Allotment Act, under which Indian lands were to be allotted as individual homesteads and the residual opened to white settlement. By the early twentieth century most Ute land had been allotted except on the Ute Mountain Ute Reservation. Unfortunately, many of the Indian allotments were subsequently lost

Southern Ute leaders meeting with Bureau of Indian Affairs officials around 1880.
(National Archives)

through taxes, irrigation assessments, and entangled inheritance questions.

Modern Period. In 1934 the Indian Reorganization Act allowed the Utes to develop self-governing tribal entities, and three tribal organizations were formed: the Uintah-Ouray Ute Tribe, the Southern Ute Tribe, and the Ute Mountain Ute Tribe. Tribal organizations helped regain alienated lands and obtained legal counsel for court battles. Working together as the Confederated Ute Tribe, the three tribes were the first American Indians to combat the federal government successfully over reparation claims; as a result of their suit, the Indian Claims Commission was established in 1946 with the Confederated Utes as its first successful (and largest) claimant. During the 1980's and 1990's other legal battles were fought to regain jurisdictional rights over original reservation lands and water rights. Tribal governments have established tribal industries, judicial and policing services, and social services and activities.

Although many traditional Ute ways have given way to western technology, Ute values continue in modern religious manifestations such as the Ute Sun Dance, Bear Dance, and, for some, the Native American Church.

Bibliography

Chapoose, Connor, and Y. T. Witherspoon. *Conversations with Connor Chapoose: A Leader of the Ute Tribe of the Uintah and Ouray Reservation*. Eugene: University of Oregon, 1993.

Delaney, Robert. *The Southern Ute People*. Phoenix: Indian Tribal Series, 1974.
_____. *The Ute Mountain Utes*. Albuquerque: University of New Mexico Press, 1989.

Denver, Norma, and June Lyman, comps. *Ute People: An Historical Study*, edited by Floyd A. O'Neil and John D. Sylvester. Salt Lake City: University of Utah Press, 1970.

Emmitt, Robert. *The Last War Trail: The Utes and the Settlement of Colorado*. Norman: University of Oklahoma Press, 1954.

Janetski, Joel C. *The Ute of Utah Lake*. Salt Lake City: University of Utah Press, 1991.

Jorgensen, Joseph G. *The Sun Dance Religion: Power for the Powerless*. Chicago: University of Chicago Press, 1972.

Miller, Mark A. *Hollow Victory: The White River Expedition of 1879 and the Battle of Milk Creek*. Niwot: University of Colorado, 1997.

Osburn, Katherine. *Southern Ute Women: Autonomy and Assimilation on the Reservation, 1887-1934*. Albuquerque: University of New Mexico Press, 1998.

Rockwell, Wilson. *The Utes: A Forgotten People*. Denver: Sage Books, 1956.

Sapir, Edward, and William Bright. *Southern Paiute and Ute: Linguistics and Ethnography*. Berlin, N.Y.: Mouton de Gruyter, 1992.

Smith, Anna M., and Alden C. Hayes, eds. *Ute Tales*. Salt Lake City: University of Utah Press, 1992.

Young, Richard K. *The Ute Indians of Colorado in the Twentieth Century*. Norman: University of Oklahoma Press, 1997.

Veracruz

DATE: 1200-400 B.C.E

LOCATION: Southern Mexican Gulf Coast

CULTURES AFFECTED: Aztec, Maya, Olmec

In the jungles of Mexico's Gulf Coast, now the modern states of Veracruz and Tabasco, a culture emerged which set the patterns for later civilization in Mesoamerica. Nothing is known of the origin or the ultimate fate of the people who established this ancient and elaborate civilization, but they produced the pre-Columbian art known as "Olmec." Father Bernardino de Sahagún, a Jesuit monk, wrote of the Olmec ("rubber people") from Tamoanchán, a Mayan name meaning "Land of Rain or Mist"; the Mayan name suggests a linguistic relationship. Many later civilizations in Mexico traced their ancestry to the Olmec.

Three basic cultural traits of Mesoamerican civilization are believed to have originated with the Olmec; worship of a fertility and rain god, monumental architecture, and extensive trade. Southern Veracruz, the Olmec "heartland," was dense tropical forest and swampy lowland with an annual rainfall of 120 inches. Extremes of the environment brought about a religion which involved ritual and ceremony for controlling rainfall and protecting people from jungle spirits.

The cult of the jaguar was Mesoamerica's first formal religion; it was based on the legendary union of a woman and a jaguar which produced the race of infantlike monsters called "were-jaguars"—men with sacred jaguar blood. These "jaguar babies," gods of rain and fertility, evolved into the Mesoamerican image of the rain god.

In the Formative Period, between 1200 and 400 B.C.E., this complex culture flourished, first at San Lorenzo, then by 900 B.C.E. at La Venta, its most important religious center. In both centers massive architecture and huge stone carvings were the focus of daily life organized and directed by the elite class. The level of Olmec civilization is judged by the presence of major public works, the first built in North America. These included ceremonial plazas, pyramids with temples, reservoirs, and well-developed water transport systems.

Monumental sculptures, another indicator of a complex civilization, were evident throughout Veracruz. La Venta was a site of the famous colossal heads carvings, some weighing more than 20 tons, each carved from a single stone. These helmeted images combined features of a human infant and a jaguar, likely the rain god, first of the Mesoamerican deities. The same distinctive art style was also expressed in small clay figurines and finely detailed jade pendants which carried images of the infant-jaguar god.

Religious symbolism in Olmec art served as a visible common bond within the culture, linking peasants with political and royal leaders, who were intermediaries between gods and men. A balance was achieved as peasants farmed corn to provide food for royalty, while royalty organized public life in the spiritual, political, and economic realms via an intricate ritual and civic calendar.

Seasonal markets where vast amounts of food and goods were exchanged provided structure through the year. Artifacts found in locations far from Veracruz indicate that Olmec political and economic influence extended via trade routes to the central Mexican highlands and along the Pacific Coast to El Salvador. Some theories suggest that Preclassic Olmecs might have been Mayas who later moved into the Yucatán peninsula.

Waccamaw

CULTURE AREA: Southeast
LANGUAGE GROUP: Siouan
PRIMARY LOCATION: South Carolina
POPULATION SIZE: 1,023 (1990 U.S. Census)

The Waccamaw were a relatively small horticultural tribe, living in permanent villages. They relied mostly on maize, beans, squash, and other cultivated plants, and various roots, tubers, seeds, nuts, and fruit gathered by women. Little is known of their early encounters with European Americans, except that the Cheraw probably attempted to incite them to attack the British in 1715. A trading post was established in their territory in 1716, and in 1720 they staged a brief war with the colonists in which many of their people were killed. In 1775, while living in white settlements, they and some Pedee were killed by warring Natchez and Cherokee.

Waco

CULTURE AREA: Plains
LANGUAGE GROUP: Caddoan
PRIMARY LOCATION: Oklahoma

The Waco, a small group, were a part of the Caddoan family, which had inhabited the southern Great Plains for thousands of years before their first contact with European Americans. "Caddo" is a shortened form of *Kadohadacho* ("real chiefs"). The Waco were either neighbors of another Caddoan group, the Tawakoni, or a division of that tribe. Both spoke a dialect similar to that of the Wichita, the dominant tribe in the area. Not much is known about the early history of the Waco. Tradition tells that they moved about with other Caddoans through Oklahoma and Texas.

The name "Waco" does not appear in records until after 1824, when white people encountered them living in a village where Waco, Texas, now stands. "Waco" may be a derivative of *Wehiko* ("Mexico"), given because they were continually fighting the Mexicans. The Waco lived in round thatched houses and in 1824 had some 200 fenced acres under cultivation. They were involved in no major skirmishes with whites, but they suffered greatly at the hands of northern Great Plains tribes. A smallpox epidemic in 1801 further decimated their numbers. They joined with the Wichita in treaties made with the United States and in 1872 were given a reservation in Oklahoma. In the 1990's the Waco experienced a renewed interest in tribal heritage. They made recordings of stories and songs and worked to pass traditions to their children.

Walapai

CULTURE AREA: Southwest
LANGUAGE GROUP: Yuman
PRIMARY LOCATION: Colorado
POPULATION SIZE: 1,207 (1990 U.S. Census)

The Walapai (or Hualapai) were divided into seven autonomous divisions. Men hunted deer, elk, antelope, and bear, and women gathered seeds, nuts, berries, tubers, and roots. Acorns were an important food, storing well in winter granaries. A wide range of insects, particularly grasshoppers and locusts, were gathered in communal hunts. Their technology, partially specialized for leaching tannic acid from acorns, had other applications as well. A variety of types of baskets were used daily for stoneboiling, storage, burden, and other utilitarian purposes. The Walapai had a high degree of mobility and were intimately aware of their territory and where to find plant resources within it.

The area inhabited by the Walapai was probably visited in 1540 by Spanish explorer Hernando de Alarcón, and later in 1598 by Marcos Farfan de los Godos. In 1776, Francisco Garcés made contact with the Walapai but recorded scant ethnographic data. Population decline is attributed mostly to introduced disease; from an estimated 700 in 1680, population fell to around 450 in 1937. The Walapai Reservation was established in northwest Arizona. Walapai income is gained from wage labor, cattle raising, government employment, and urban jobs.

Walla Walla

CULTURE AREA: Plateau
LANGUAGE GROUP: Sahaptian
PRIMARY LOCATION: Umatilla Reservation, Oregon
POPULATION SIZE: 228 (1990 U.S. Census)

The Walla Walla, a branch of the Sahaptian family, lived along the lower Walla Walla, Columbia, and Snake rivers in Washington and Oregon. Their name means "little river." As is generally true for the Sahaptian tribes, there is little or no ethnographic evidence or traditional lore to show where the Walla Walla lived in prehistoric times. Their first encounter with white people occurred in 1805, when the explorers Meriwether Lewis and William Clark passed through their territory. Like other Sahaptian tribes, the Walla Walla lived in village communities of varying size.

Because they relied on hunting, fishing, and gathering roots and berries, they moved throughout the year to find food in different seasons. They were skilled with horses. For the most part, they dwelt peacefully with whites, largely because of their refusal to engage in violent retaliation for ill treatment. The middle of the nineteenth century proved devastating for the Walla Walla. Epidemics of smallpox and measles, probably brought by traders, trappers, and miners, killed many of their people. When gold was discovered in the area in 1855, miners flooded onto Walla Walla lands. The fighting that eventually resulted ended with the shooting or hanging of several chiefs. Under the terms of an 1855 treaty signed at the Walla Walla Council, the Walla Walla, Cayuse, Nez Perce, and other tribes were forced to give up 60,000 square miles of their lands and were placed on the Umatilla Reservation in Oregon. They were given three cents per acre for their land, and they were assured the right to fish using traditional methods off reservation land. In actuality, these fishing rights were not protected, and this remained a source of strife for more than one hundred years afterward. By the end of the twentieth century, the Confederated Tribes of the Umatilla Reservation had lived and worked together for decades. They present an annual rodeo and pageant, the Pendleton Roundup, to demonstrate and pass on traditional culture and skills.

Wampanoag

CULTURE AREA: Northeast
LANGUAGE GROUP: Algonquian
PRIMARY LOCATION: Southeastern Massachusetts, eastern Rhode Island
POPULATION SIZE: 2,175 (1990 U.S. Census)

The Wampanoag, also known as the Pokanoket, spoke the Massachusetts language, one of the five Eastern Algonquian languages spoken in southern New England. The Wampanoag, like all southern New England groups, have deep historical roots. Archaeologists point to the evolution of prehistoric cultures from the Paleo-Indian cultural time period of some twelve thousand years ago up through the historic cultural time period of 1500 C.E. and the beginning of European exploration and trade along the Atlantic coast. The Wampanoag are best known for this latter contact period when Europeans began to document their visits to the native peoples via diaries, letters, and books. In 1620, the English colonists known as the Pilgrims landed in present-day Plymouth, Massachusetts. There began the now famous relationship between the Indians and colonists and there occurred the celebration of the first Thanksgiving.

The most important seventeenth century Wampanoag figures included the supreme sachem Massasoit and his sons and successors Wamsutta (Alexander) and Metacomet (King Philip). These sachems signed treaties, and they traded and bartered lands with the Pilgrims. Toward the end of the

Early nineteenth century illustration of a skirmish in King Philip's War of 1675.
(Library of Congress)

century, they were also fighting with the Pilgrims. The supreme sachems were supported by sachems of several territorial subdivisions. All sachems were skillful and generous leaders who governed their people not through absolute power but through consensus and charisma. Sachems worked with councils of "esteemed men," and together they maintained balance between the spirit world and the people.

The Wampanoag lived in various locations and in various family groups depending on the season. During the summer, they lived in farming hamlets near their cornfields. These hamlets consisted of a few wigwams (bark and mat-covered houses) which housed several related nuclear families or an extended family. These hamlets were also near the fishing resources of the coast. During the winter, families moved to the warmer inland areas and set up larger "longhouses" to house up to fifty or more people. This settlement pattern alludes to the Wampanoags's rich and eclectic diet: From their fields they harvested northern flint corn along with a variety of beans and squashes, Jerusalem artichokes, gourds (for storage containers), and tobacco (for smoking). From the sea they harvested shellfish, a variety of ocean fish, and beached whales. From the inland areas they took deer, beaver, squirrel, fox, and other small game.

Wampanoag cosmology taught the people how to use these resources. Resources were never to be wasted but were to be used in their entirety. For example, from the deer came meat, the hide for clothing, the organs for pouches and sinew, and the brain for tanning agents. The pow-wow was the religious leader who oversaw resource use. He also conducted rites such as the Green Corn Ceremony, in which the Creator was thanked for the corn.

The relationship between the Pilgrims and the Indians came to a head in 1675 with the outbreak of King Philip's war. The Wampanoag sachem King Philip attempted to confederate Indian tribes throughout New England in the hope that Indians would be able to take back their lands from the colonists. His war failed, and Philip was killed.

During the eighteenth and nineteenth centuries, surviving Wampanoag lived in small Indian enclaves or in white communities throughout southeastern Massachusetts and on Cape Cod. Some of the best known of these Indian communities included Mashpee on Cape Cod and Gay Head on Martha's Vineyard.

Bibliography

Bourne, Russell. *The Red King's Rebellion: Racial Politics in New England, 1675-1678*. New York: Athenuem, 1990.

Campisi, Jack. *The Mashpee Indians: Tribe on Trial*. Syracuse, N.Y.: Syracuse University Press, 1991.

Moondancer. *Wampanoag Cultural History: Voices from Past and Present*. Newport, R.I.: Aquidneck Indian Council, 1999.

Peters, Russell M. *The Wampanoags of Mashpee: An Indian Perspective on American History*. Somerville, Mass.: Media Action, 1987.

Weinstein, Laurie. "We're Still Living on Our Traditional Homeland: The Wampanoag Legacy in New England." In *Strategies for Survival*, edited by Frank W. Porter III. New York: Greenwood Press, 1986.

Weinstein-Farson, Laurie. *The Wampanoag*. New York: Chelsea House, 1989.

Wanapam

CULTURE AREA: Plateau
LANGUAGE GROUP: Sahaptian
PRIMARY LOCATION: Washington State

The Wanapam, a branch of the Sahaptian family, lived in northwestern Oregon and southwestern Washington. The significance of their name is unknown. They were closely related to the Palouse. As is generally true for the Sahaptian tribes, there is no ethnographic evidence or traditional lore to show where the Wanapam lived earlier than their first encounter with whites in the early 1800's. At this time, their population numbered approximately eighteen hundred. Sahaptian tribes lived in village communities of varying size. Because they relied on hunting, fishing (salmon was a chief staple), and gathering roots and berries, they moved throughout the year to find food in different seasons. This prevented the villages from developing into political or social centers.

Sahaptian tribes do not seem to have relied at all on agriculture. They were skilled with horses and used them in their search for food. There is no record of any major battles between the Wanapam and white settlers. No official enumerations of Wanapam have been made since the eighteenth century. The tribe was probably absorbed by the Palouse.

Wappinger

CULTURE AREA: Northeast
LANGUAGE GROUP: Algonquian
PRIMARY LOCATION: Connecticut, New York

The Wappinger are often considered to have comprised two main sub-groups, the Western Wappinger (who lived in what is now New York State, along the lower Hudson River) and Eastern Wappinger (who lived eastward to the lower Connecticut River valley). It is estimated that at the first encounter with the Dutch, in the early 1600's, the Western Wappinger numbered about 3,000 and the Eastern Wappinger about 1,750.

The Wappinger were closely related in customs and organization to the Delaware (Lenni Lenape) and to Indians of southern New England. They hunted, fished, and grew crops, primarily corn. They were noted for their manufacture of wampum beads. Their totem was the wolf. The tribe was headed by a sachem (male or female) and a council of lesser chiefs.

With the arrival of Dutch settlers and traders, the Wappinger were thrown into close proximity with whites. Indians and whites coexisted peacefully for a number of years, and the Western Wappinger became involved in fur trading. In 1640 a number of sources of friction led to a five-year war between whites and Indians, including the Western Wappinger. Destruction and casualties were inflicted by both sides, with the Indians losing half their population, the Western Wappinger bearing the brunt. Disease further reduced their population. Nevertheless, the tribe remained intact until 1756, when they joined the Nanticoke; both tribes were later absorbed into the Delaware. Their last public appearance was at the Easton Conference in 1758.

In contrast, the Eastern Wappinger never warred with whites. They gradually sold off their land to settlers and merged with other tribes, including the Scaticook and Stockbridge. At this point, the Wappinger tribe ceased to exist as a separate entity.

Wappo

CULTURE AREA: California
LANGUAGE GROUP: Wappo
PRIMARY LOCATION: Napa River, Clear Lake, and Alexander Valley, California
POPULATION SIZE: 125 (1990 U.S. Census)

The Wappo, contiguous with the Southern Pomo, Central Pomo, Patwin, and Lake and Coast Miwok, were territorially divided into the Clear Lake and the Southern Wappo. They located their oval, grass houses in permanent villages on stream systems, acquiring subsistence by fishing, hunting, trapping, and gathering food plants including acorns, tubers, roots, and numerous grasses. They tended to be monogamous and discouraged divorce. The Wappo excelled in manufacturing baskets.

There are indications that the Wappo fought against the Spanish in the Napa Valley; some Wappo were apparently held at the Sonoma Mission. The reservation at Mendocino was established in 1856, closing in 1867. Disease, displacement of groups, degradation of the environment and its resources by European Americans, and ensuing conflict all served to reduce the Wappo population and traditional lifeways. By 1910, only twenty Wappo had any knowledge of their language and traditional ways. By 1960, only five Wappo speakers remained.

Wasco

CULTURE AREA: Plateau
LANGUAGE GROUP: Upper Chinookan
PRIMARY LOCATION: The Dalles and lower Columbia River, Oregon

The Wasco and Wishram were contiguous tribes, sharing linguistic and cultural characteristics. The stronger Wasco ultimately absorbed the other group. Both groups maintained themselves through trading and exploiting the resources of the Columbia River and gathering various roots, particularly lomatium. They were noted for their weaving techniques and design in making soft cylindrical blankets.

After the Meriwether Lewis and William Clark expedition of 1805-1806, the first sustained European American contacts were with land-based traders desiring sea otter, beaver, fox, and other furs. The acquiring of European trade goods enhanced the Wasco-Wishram position on the Columbia River, which was the main trade route. The combined population of the Wasco-Wishram in 1937 was 351. Some Wasco live on the Warm Springs and Yakima reservations, employed both on and off the reservations.

Washoe

CULTURE AREA: Great Basin and California
LANGUAGE GROUP: Hokan
PRIMARY LOCATION: West central Nevada
POPULATION SIZE: 1,520 (1990 U.S. Census)

A rchaeological evidence and oral tradition suggest that the homogene-ous Washoe (also spelled "Washo") culture had origins along the west-ern foothills of the Sierra Nevada slope. Their annual subsistence round successfully exploited plant and animal resources in specialized vegeta-tional zones within a 10,000-square-mile region, ranging from lowland valleys of abundant game, vegetation, and water to high mountain mead-

Datsolalee, an early twentieth century Washoe woman who lifted basketmaking to its highest level of art. (Library of Congress)

ows that provided berries, tubers, and seeds. The northern Washoe were largely dependent on acorns, the southern Washoe on pine nuts. Because they used different resources, the Washoe enjoyed peaceful relations with neighboring groups, intermarrying and trading freely.

Sustained contact with European Americans began in 1825 with trappers and explorers; in the 1840's, immigrant parties began to arrive in Washoe territory. Conflict with settlers reached a climax in the 1857 "Potato War" and continued with settlers confiscating traditional resource areas. Under the General Allotment Act of 1887, small parcels of barren and nearly waterless land were allotted. In 1917 the government provided funds for purchasing additional small tracts of land near Carson City. Later, 40 acres were donated by a white rancher near Gardnerville, and an additional 20 acres near Reno became the Reno-Sparks Indian Colony.

Some Washoe practiced the peyote religion (Native American Church) in the early 1920's; by 1938 factionalism had developed, partly caused by disagreements over church rituals. The Indian Reorganization Act of 1934 recognized the Washoe as a legally constituted tribe, and they were authorized to live on 795 acres on the Carson River.

Efforts at farming and raising livestock were hindered in the 1950's by poor management, factionalism, and poor relations with the Bureau of Indian Affairs. Ongoing litigation with the government over the loss of 9,872 square miles of aboriginal lands resulted in the 1970 Indian Claims Commission award of approximately $5 million. A Washoe tribal council headquarters and Indian crafts enterprise is located near Gardnerville, where there is a park with camping facilities on the Carson River, and in Dresslerville the tribe operates a Health Center and Senior Citizens' Center. The tribe also supports an aquaculture and construction company.

Wenatchi

CULTURE AREA: Plateau
LANGUAGE GROUP: Salishan
PRIMARY LOCATION: Washington State
POPULATION SIZE: 26 (1990 U.S. Census)

The Wenatchi (also spelled "Wenatchee"), a part of the Salishan family, lived along the Wenatchee River, a tributary of the Columbia River in Washington. Their earliest known homeland was farther inland, perhaps as far east as western Montana. Their name, and the name of the river that was their home, is from the Yakima word *winätshi* ("river issuing from a canyon"). The Wenatchi were probably closely related to the Pisquow. Another, smaller group, the Chelans, spoke the same dialect as the Wenatchi and may have once been a part of the tribe. The Wenatchi lived in villages of varying size. Because they relied on hunting and fishing—salmon was a chief staple of their diet—as well as on gathering roots and berries, they moved throughout the year to find food in different seasons. The Wenatchi were involved in no protracted struggles with their neighbors. The Wenatchi had no continuous contact with whites until the eighteenth century, when they started to feel pressure to vacate their lands. In 1850, a group of fifty Wenatchi were living on the Yakima reservation. By the end of the twentieth century, the Wenatchi were part of the Colville agency.

Wichita tribal group

CULTURE AREA: Plains
LANGUAGE GROUP: Caddoan
PRIMARY LOCATION: Oklahoma
POPULATION SIZE: 1,275 (1990 U.S. Census)

The Wichita people were a confederacy of six or seven subtribes including the Wichita proper, the Tayovaya, Yscani, Tawakoni, Waco, and Kichai. Only the Kichai group spoke a separate Caddoan language; the rest spoke similar dialects of their Caddoan language. The name Wichita is of unknown origin; they refer to themselves as *Kitikiti'sh*, meaning "the people" or "the preeminent people." French traders referred to them as *Pani Piqué*, meaning "Tattooed Pawnee." (They were closely related to the Pawnees.) Other tribes had names for the Wichitas which referred to their distinctive tattooing.

The Wichitas were the fabled people of Quivira whom the Spanish explorer Francisco Vásquez de Coronado encountered in 1541. Their ancestral homeland seems to have been the region of the great bend of the Arkansas River in south-central Kansas. In Coronado's time, this confederacy probably numbered around fifteen thousand; the number was reduced to about four thousand in the eighteenth century. By 1902, there were only 340 members of the Wichita tribe; they have rebounded since.

From the 1600's to the 1800's, the Wichitas lived in a number of villages located along rivers, each village having about eight hundred to a thousand grass lodges. These were conical in shape, 15 to 30 feet in diameter, and had the appearance of a haystack. Wichita society was matrilocal—a married couple lived with the wife's family, whose head of household was a grandmother or great-grandmother. The Wichitas were also matrilineal, although no clan system operated in the tribe.

Women farmed to produce corn, beans, squash, pumpkins, and tobacco, while men hunted buffalo, deer, antelope, and bear. There was a seasonal rhythm to Wichita life, with permanent villages occupied in the spring and summer during the planting and harvesting season. In the fall, many left on

545

extended hunting trips, living in portable skin tipis while traveling. Gathered fruits and nuts rounded out the diet. The Wichitas often farmed a surplus and sold it to neighboring tribes that did not engage in agriculture.

By around 1700, the Wichitas had acquired horses, which made buffalo hunting and warfare easier. The Wichitas remained essentially a peaceful people, however, going to war only when provoked. They also retained much of their sedentary farming-oriented culture, rather than becoming solely reliant on buffalo hunting as some other Plains groups did.

In the early 1600's the Osage tribe began to press into Wichita territory, so the Wichitas began moving south into Oklahoma and Texas. By about 1720, the Wichitas began trading with the French, who assisted in establishing peaceful relations between the Wichitas and the Comanche tribe in 1746. The two tribes traded peacefully after 1746 and sometimes allied against Apache invaders in their region. The Wichitas' relationship with the Spanish was much more troubled than their relationship with the French. In the middle-to-late eighteenth century, they were often at war with the Spanish. From that time until the 1900's, warfare with other groups such as the Osage, as well as smallpox and other disease epidemics, took their tool on the Wichita confederacy, and its numbers dwindled. By the 1820's there were also conflicts with American settlers.

In the 1830's, other eastern tribes were being resettled in or near Wichita territory (now called "Indian Territory") by the U.S. federal government. This caused conflicts as well, despite various peace treaties and settlements. During the American Civil War, the Wichitas fled to Kansas but returned to what is now Oklahoma after the war. They were assigned a reservation in Caddo County. The reservation was allotted to individual families and therefore dissolved in 1901. In the late twentieth century, Wichita interest in maintaining their heritage increased as more tribal members learned their songs, dances, and language once more.

Winnebago

Culture area: Plains
Language group: Siouan
Primary location: Nebraska
Population size: 6,920 (1990 U.S. Census)

The Winnebago tribe is of Siouan origin. Although the date of its migration westward with other Siouans is unknown, it is believed that the

Winnebagos entered what would become Wisconsin during the second of four main Siouan migrations. Their most closely related kin, therefore, would be the Iowas, Otos, and Missouris. More distant relations include the Crows, Omahas, Osage, and Dakotas. Tribal tradition regarding Siouan ties is vague. Modern Winnebagos, now widely dispersed from the land of their adoption, generally claim that their tribe was originally from Wisconsin, specifically the region around Green Bay, where they were first encountered by Europeans.

Early History and Treaties. It was the Frenchman Jean Nicolet, agent for Quebec governor Champlain, who first reported contacts with the Winnebagos in 1634 in the Green Bay area. Nicolet called them by the name they used for themselves, which was variously translated as "People of the Parent Speech" or "Big Fish people." Winnebago was a name given to them by the central Algonquians (including Miamis, Sauk, and Fox), who inhabited most of the area surrounding them. Fifty years after Nicolet, the Winnebagos had expanded both westward and southward from the Lake Michigan coast, claiming major portions of central and southern Wisconsin.

These claims pitted them against their Algonquian neighbors, and a number of local eighteenth century Indian wars occurred. Sometimes, the French used the Winnebagos as their allies against other Indian groupings, the most notable example being the Fox Wars. This potential source of support for Winnebago predominance disappeared suddenly in 1763, when the French lost their hold on Canada and Britain became the main European power to contend with (at least for the next twenty years, until United States independence). After several decades of relative isolation, clashes with representatives of the American government would begin, ushering in the first stages of Winnebago political and territorial decline.

Winnebago resistance to the presence of white settlers and army forces in their traditional lands peaked during the Black Hawk War of 1832. Their defeat was followed by a thirty-year period of U.S.-imposed treaties that effectively put an end to Winnebago claims over land in Wisconsin and, by removing them in stages farther west into Nebraska Territory, reduced them to full dependence on the government for their very existence.

The evolution of Winnebago treaties with the U.S. government reveals the extent of their territorial losses in less than fifty years. In the first peace treaty of 1816, the Winnebagos were invited to accept the sole protection of the U.S. government and to confirm that any land they had previously given up to the British, French, or Spanish governments was to be considered U.S. public domain. At this time, Winnebago lands still covered most of south-central Wisconsin and portions of northeastern Illinois. By 1828, President John Quincy Adams committed to pay the Winnebagos (and neighboring

Studio portrait of late nineteenth century Winnebago man named Young Eagle.
(Library of Congress)

tribes) some twenty thousand dollars in goods to compensate for "injuries sustained . . . in the consequence of occupation" of land for mining by white settlers.

Within four years, in 1832, President Andrew Jackson agreed to pay the Winnebagos a fixed sum over twenty-seven years for what was considered the fair difference between the value of lands ceded by the Indians (running from Lake Winnebago southward to the Rock River at the Wisconsin-Illinois border) and lands west of the Mississippi (in Iowa) "traded" by the U.S. government. By 1837, the rest of Winnebago land running to the Mississippi in western Wisconsin was ceded by another treaty.

A Winnebago Agency was created in the northeast corner of Iowa in 1848. By the Treaty of 1846, some 800,000 acres of former Chippewa land in central Minnesota had been granted as additional Winnebago territory, hundreds of miles away from the Iowa Agency. Within nine years, the central Minnesota land was taken back, and a much smaller (18-square-mile) Winnebago Reservation was established on Blue Earth River in southern Minnesota.

The reservation founded in 1857 functioned for only two years before half of it was sold to private settlers for cash "held in trust [by the Government] for Winnebago benefits." An act of Congress in February, 1863, called for the sale of the remainder of the Blue Earth River Reservation.

The crowning acts of U.S. government displacement of the Winnebagos occurred during the Abraham Lincoln presidency. In 1865, the tribe was obliged to cede its reservation in Dakota Territory (which later became part of the Great Sioux Reserve). In return, a section of Omaha tribe land in Nebraska was set aside for the now dwindling population of the Winnebagos, it being agreed that a sawmill and gristmill and fencing be erected on the new site for them. In addition, the government was to provide guns, horses, and oxen, plus some agricultural implements to assist the Winnebagos in their final exile westward to Nebraska Territory.

Archaeology and Traditional Cultural Values. A unique feature of Winnebago archaeology in their homeland in Wisconsin is what is called the effigy mound, first studied in the 1850's by I. A. Lapham. More common conical burial mounds associated with other Siouans are found throughout Wisconsin, but effigy mounds are limited to Winnebago areas. Archaeologists suppose that these structures were meant to represent animals, which were important as symbols of each clan's mythology and served to "stake out" their local territory. Only two effigy mounds portray figures that appear to be human. Their significance remains a mystery.

Despite the disappearance of many traditional social practices once observed by the Winnebagos, many elders remember that clan names not only reflected particular animals but also provided for a division of the Winnebago people into two general groups: "those who are above" (birds) and "those on earth" (land and water animals). In addition to symbolic qualities of association (eagle and hawk are birds of prey, bears represent soldiers), this name dichotomy also seems to have reflected a sort of code for regulating different functions, some practical (including marriage patterns, clan "alignments" while on the warpath) and ceremonial (relationships during feast celebrations, proper recognition of roles in ceremonial lacrosse games).

The game lacrosse combined sport and ceremony among the Winnebagos. A number of other traditional games also existed, including the friendly moccasin "guessing" game and the very rough "kicking game."

Traditional Winnebago religious practices and beliefs were all somehow tied to respect for the preservation of life. Central to their belief system was a concern for the interrelationship between supernatural spirits and the physical domain of nature. In the latter, a stark reality prevails, frequently involving the necessity to kill in order to survive. At the highest and most general level, reverence was offered to spirit deities such as the Earthmaker, the Sun, and the Moon. These gods remained, however, beyond the sphere of daily survival in nature. A distinct set of animal spirits was recognized, therefore, as symbols of the survival cycle. Winnebagos performed a variety of offerings and dance ceremonies involving these animal spirits in order to assure that the spirits of animals that might be killed would be properly appeased, thus allowing for continuity in the necessary life-death cycle.

Certain clans bore the names of the animals who represented these spirits on earth; moreover, key ceremonies throughout the year were dedicated to observance of the animals' importance. The chief feast, accounts of which are less detailed than those covering lesser spirits, was organized around the Thunderbird, usually the symbol of the dominant clan. The Thunderbird chieftain received the food offerings of all other clans, not as a sign of submission to his clan but as a general act of thankfulness for Thunderbird's overriding importance in the sphere of nature.

Lesser feasts (or fasts) were meant to propitiate the spirits of other key animals. These included (among others) the Bear clan feast in the winter (involving offerings of the favorite berries enjoyed by bears) and the Snake clan feast in the fall (involving four chickens offered to the symbol of the first four snakes created by Earthmaker).

Effects of Dispersal and Population Depletion. Because of the multiple displacements of the Winnebago and the fact that some tribal members stayed behind and were deleted from official records of their whereabouts, it is nearly impossible to reconstitute surviving numbers. Most Winnebagos live in Wisconsin and Nebraska. Since 1972, representatives of the tribe have published a small newspaper focusing mainly on Winnebago community issues on the Nebraska reservation.

Byron D. Cannon

Bibliography

Blowsnake, Sam. *The Autobiography of a Winnebago Indian*. Berkeley: University of California Press, 1920.

Fay, George E., comp. *Treaties Between the Winnebago Indians and the United States of America, 1817-1856*. Greeley: Colorado State College Museum of Anthropology, 1967.

Jones, John Alan. *Winnebago Ethnology*. New York: Garland, 1974.

Radin, Paul. *The Culture of the Winnebago*. Baltimore: Waverly Press, 1949.

_____. *The Winnebago Tribe*. 2d ed. Lincoln: University of Nebraska Press, 1990.

Smith, David L. *Folklore of the Winnebago Tribe*. Norman: University of Oklahoma Press, 1997.

Wintun

CULTURE AREA: California
LANGUAGE GROUP: Wintun (Penutian)
PRIMARY LOCATION: Trinity River, northwestern California
POPULATION SIZE: 2,244 (1990 U.S. Census)

For the patrilineal Wintun, the family was the basic economic and sociopolitical unit. They lived in riverine villages with subterranean lodges. They hunted all large land mammals as well as trapping birds, rodents, and insects. Fishing was an important source of food, in addition to seeds and acorns. Numerous plants, roots, and tubers were dug and stored for winter.

The Wintuns' first contact with European Americans occurred in 1826, as recorded by Jedediah Smith and Peter Ogden. From 1830 to 1833, trapper-introduced malaria reduced the Wintun population by approximately 75 percent. The discovery of gold exacerbated white-Indian tensions, resulting in violent incidents, particularly a "friendship feast" given by local whites who poisoned the food and killed a hundred Wintun. Violence against the Indians continued in the form of arson and massacres. In 1859, approximately one hundred Wintun were sent to the Mendocino Reservation. Throughout the 1860's, the Wintun were hunted down, captured, and sent to reservations. By 1871, they had adopted the Earthlodge cult. In the twentieth century, the construction of various dams further dispersed the Wintun, with the Clear Creek Reservation being removed from trust status.

Wishram

CULTURE AREA: Northwest Coast
LANGUAGE GROUP: Chinookan (Penutian)
PRIMARY LOCATION: Columbia River, Oregon/Washington coast

The Wishram, a small southern tribe of Northwest Coast Indians, originally lived on the eastern slopes of the Cascade Mountains along the Deschutes River, due south of the confluence of the Deschutes with the Columbia River at The Dalles. Archaeological evidence suggests that Wishram culture was present in the Hood River area toward the Willamette Valley at least nine thousand years ago.

Historic village sites and traditional fishing areas were flooded by the Bonneville, The Dalles, and John Day dams. Many rimrock petroglyphs are now underwater and visible only to scuba divers, though excellent examples are on display at the Winquatt Museum in The Dalles. Tsagigla'lal, an elaborate and impressive petroglyph on the north side of the Columbia River, also remains visible. The site is commonly known simply as "Wishram" and is at the head of Five-Mile Rapids.

In addition to rock carving, Wishram culture was articulated through storytelling. The Wishram tell a full complement of Coyote tales, including the cycle of Coyote tales going east up the Columbia River. Linguist Edward Sapir's notable *Wishram Texts* (1909) collected many Wishram Coyote tales; more recently, Jarold Ramsey has added to the storehouse of Wishram texts.

Wishram culture was diluted in the nineteenth century by the location of the tribe at the western terminus of the Oregon Trail. It was the poor luck of the Wishram to be situated in superior and coveted farmland. Wishram culture was diluted further in the twentieth century by the federal policy of creating multitribal reservations in areas where tribal bands were small and varied. The Wishram, with nine other tribes, share the Confederated Warm Springs Reservation in north-central Oregon near the southern banks of the Columbia River.

Wiyot

CULTURE AREA: California
LANGUAGE GROUP: Algonquian
PRIMARY LOCATION: Northern California
POPULATION SIZE: 450 (1990 U.S. Census)

The patrilineal, socially stratified Wiyot located their villages of split redwood planked, rectangular dwellings on major streams flowing into the Pacific Ocean. Like many central California people, they excelled at basketry. Their redwood canoes permitted effective exploitation of sea mammals and other tidewater resources. When fishing inland waters, they utilized various fish poisons. The Wiyot had numerous complex rites of intensification, particularly the World Renewal, Big Time, Jumping Dance, and White Deerskin ceremonies, whose collective intent was resource renewal, the prevention of natural catastrophe, and a reiteration of the mythical and moral order among the people.

By the time of the initial ethnographic research on Wiyot culture, they had suffered considerable deprivation stemming from contact with European Americans. Whites had slaughtered them in small groups, and a massacre at Gunther Island in 1860 killed approximately 250 Wiyot. Survivors were forced onto the Klamath and Smith reservations.

Woodland

DATE: 1000 B.C.E.-700 C.E.
LOCATION: Eastern North America
CULTURES AFFECTED: Adena, Hopewell

Copper tools, pearl beads, carved stone tablets, and mica ornaments excavated from burial sites tell the story of ancient moundbuilding peoples, known as the Adena, who lived in eastern North America as early as 1000 B.C.E. The Adena were named for an estate near Chilicothe in southern Ohio, heartland of their culture and site of a large burial mound excavated in 1902. Adena culture ranged through the woodlands of present Kentucky, Ohio, West Virginia, Pennsylvania, and New York. These mound builders maintained their way of life for about 1,200 years, coexisting with the Hopewell from around 300 B.C.E. Hopewell culture radiated from its Ohio center throughout the Midwest to the Gulf of Mexico and the Great Lakes. It existed until around 700 C.E. The name Hopewell was used by archaeologists during the 1893 Chicago World's Fair to identify an exhibit of artifacts from thirty mounds on the Ohio farm of M. C. Hopewell.

The Woodland tradition is an archaeological term for these forest-based cultures supported by hunting, gathering, and some agriculture. Pumpkins and sunflowers were a major food source for the Adena, and tobacco was grown for ceremonial use. The Hopewell expanded this agricultural base to include corn. Plentiful food permitted a sedentary lifestyle which allowed the development of large ceremonial centers. There is evidence of a complex, multilevel social organization. Highest status belonged to the priest-chiefs, who guided daily life through ceremonies; then came merchants, warriors, and finally the common people who hunted and farmed to support the community of thousands.

During the many centuries of their existence, mound builders created massive earthworks to honor their deceased leaders, who were buried in ceremonial outfits with bone masks and sacred objects they had used in rituals. Decorated in the unique Woodlands art style, these finely crafted artifacts indicate a preoccupation with death among the Adena and Hopewell. This prevalent theme suggests a possible relationship to the Southern Cult (Southern death cult) found in many cultures in the region of the Gulf of Mexico.

Adena earthworks of geometric shapes often surrounded the burial mounds. The most well known of these is the Great Serpent Mound in southern Ohio. A low, rounded construction in the form of an undulating snake, it is 20 feet wide and 1,330 feet long and was created by workers carrying thousands of basketfuls of earth under the direction of the priest-chiefs. Hopewell burial and effigy mounds, usually within geometric enclosures, were larger than Adena mounds. Some stood 40 feet high and contained several layers added over long periods of time. Artifacts found at these burial sites were made by skilled artisans who used raw materials from as far away as Canada, Florida, the Rockies, and the Atlantic Coast.

Neither the origin nor the ultimate fate of the Adena and Hopewell is known, although it is thought they may have descended from eastern Archaic or Mesoamerican cultures. Theories about their cultural demise include epidemics, war, or climate changes affecting the food source. At their zenith these cultures represented a complex lifestyle organized around a unifying religious belief. Religion and trade, rather than warfare, linked the Adena and Hopewell network of ceremonial centers across a wide sphere of influence.

Yahi

CULTURE AREA: California
LANGUAGE GROUP: Hokan
PRIMARY LOCATION: Upper Sacramento Valley

The Northern, Central, and Southern Yahi had numerous tribelets, each constituting a major village located on an east-west stream. A village had a major chief who inherited his position. Deer was the most important animal for food and by-products, but all other land mammals were hunted and trapped. Women were responsible for gathering and collecting a wide variety of plant products for food and utilitarian use. Many of these subsistence-getting activities were collective, particularly the acquiring of smaller animals and insects.

Ishi, the last survivor of the Yahi tribe of California, in 1913. (Museum of Natural History)

In 1821, Captain Luis Arguell and approximately fifty-five soldiers became the first Europeans to contact the Yahi. The Hudson's Bay Company, from 1828 to 1846, occupied much of the Yahi territory. In 1837 cattlemen entered the region, and by 1845 the first permanent white settlement was established. The Mexican government granted leases to settlers and cattlemen.

The whites introduced new diseases to the Yahi, whose population of 1,800 was reduced to 35 by 1884. Numerous massacres of Yahi continued until the late 1800's. Ishi, a Yahi Yana, was the last survivor in 1911.

Yakima

CULTURE AREA: Plateau
LANGUAGE GROUP: Sahaptian
PRIMARY LOCATION: Washington State
POPULATION SIZE: 7,850 (1990 U.S. Census)

The Yakimas originally inhabited the Columbia Basin Plateau in Washington state. They are identified as Plateau Indians and belong to the Sahaptian language group. Many scholars believe that evidence of human settlement in the Columbia Basin dates back fifteen thousand years. The Yakimas first were exposed to European Americans with the arrival of the Lewis and Clark expedition in 1805.

Although this was the first direct contact the Yakimas had with white people, European American culture had already touched Yakima society, as they were already using horses, and other trade goods were evident. Scholars estimate the introduction of the horse at about 1730. The tribe that would be referred to as the Yakimas was probably composed of other Plateau Indians, such as the Nez Perce and the Palouse (Palus).

The land that they inhabited was arid. Subsistence patterns consisted of hunting, fishing, and gathering berries and roots, particularly camas. Fishing continues to be pursued, and in the early 1990's the Yakimas were involved in a lawsuit with various irrigators along the Yakima River over water rights.

After the first contact with whites, fur traders and missionaries crossed the Columbia Basin. Finally in 1855, the Yakimas were subjected to treaty negotiations with Washington Territorial Governor Isaac Stevens in which they conceded their claim of approximately ten million acres in the Columbia Basin. The Yakimas, who were one of the few tribes to be ascribed the status of a sovereign nation (hence their title Yakima Nation), were granted 1,250,000 acres on what would be the Yakima Reservation. By the early twentieth century, almost half a million acres had been lost through the provisions of the General Allotment Act, although the Yakima Nation recovered part of this acreage later in the century. The reservation included traditional lands. In addition to the Yakimas, members of the Klikitat tribe moved to the reservation. Dissatisfaction with the treaty grew, however, fueled by the continued traffic of whites across reservation lands, resulting in the Yakima War of 1855.

Although the Yakimas fared well in the initial fighting, internal dissension erupted, caused in part by hostility toward the Yakima leader, Kamiakin, whose father was a Palouse. American troops succeeded in winning the war in 1856, and the Yakimas were forced to accept the terms of the Yakima Treaty, which had been signed by the fourteen confederated tribes of the Yakima Nation on June 9, 1855. The treaty was ratified in 1859. Life on the reservation was difficult for the confederated tribes throughout the nineteenth century. The Yakimas were subjected to Indian agent James Wilbur, a Methodist minister who believed that the future of the Indians lay in their

Yakima Indians picking the hops used to make beer during the early twentieth century.
(Library of Congress)

ability to convert to Christianity and learn farming. The Yakimas also sustained land losses through allotment. Yet traditional practices continued.

The modern tribal government was organized in 1935 and includes a tribal council with fourteen members. During the last half of the twentieth century, the Yakimas pursued claims filed with the Indian Claims Commission for either the return of traditional lands or, in lieu of land, a financial settlement. They have been successful with some of the claims and have received awards in both land and money. Other legal matters include water rights claims on the Yakima River for fishing and irrigation interests.

In the late twentieth century, the reservation's economy relied on farming, grazing, and limited industry. Traditional Yakima culture is still valued and maintained, as evidenced in the persistence of Yakima religious practices and cultural celebrations.

Yamasee

CULTURE AREA: Southeast
LANGUAGE GROUP: Muskogean
PRIMARY LOCATION: Georgia, Florida, South Carolina

Little is known regarding the language and culture of the Yamasee tribe, which no longer exists as a distinct entity. The Yamasee spoke a Muskogean language, probably a dialect of Hitchiti. It is assumed by scholars that the Yamasee were culturally similar to the Creeks, another Muskogean people with whom the Yamasee had close relations. The Yamasee may have been the friendly Indians encountered by Hernando de Soto along the Altamaha river in eastern Georgia in 1540. Spanish expeditions to the same area one-half century later made contact with the Yamasee, who were reported as friendly to the Spanish.

In the 1680's, the Yamasee became disenchanted with Spanish efforts to enslave some of the Yamasee. The Yamasee moved north to the English colony of South Carolina; they became trading partners and military allies of the English. In the 1680's, South Carolina induced the Yamasee to attack the Spanish at Santa Catalina. The Yamasee assisted the South Carolinians in a war against the Apalachees of Florida in 1705. In the Tuscarora War of 1711-1713, the Yamasee provided most of the soldiers in the Carolinians' successful war against the Tuscarora.

Following the Tuscarora War, relations between the Yamasee and Carolinians worsened. The Yamasee were angered by their growing dependence upon English trade goods, their indebtedness to English traders, English penetration of Indian lands, and the enslavement of some Yamasee by the English. Deteriorating English-Yamasee relations led to the Yamasee War of 1715-1728, in which the Yamasee were defeated by an army of colonial militia, black slaves, and Cherokee warriors.

The Yamasee were virtually annihilated by the war and subsequently lost their identity as a distinct people. Scattered remnants of the Yamasee settled with the Apalachees, Choctaws, Creeks, and Seminoles in Georgia and Florida. For a time, some Yamasee maintained their tribal identity under Spanish protection in villages near St. Augustine and Pensacola, Florida. These Yamasee continued to act as allies of the Spanish, helping to defeat an invasion of Florida by Governor James Oglethorpe of Georgia in 1740. By 1761, Yamasee villages in Florida were reduced to fewer than fifty families. By 1773, many Yamasee had been enslaved by the Seminoles.

Yana

CULTURE AREA: California
LANGUAGE GROUP: Yanan
PRIMARY LOCATION: Between the Sacramento River and Sierra Nevada, bounded by Rock Creek and the Pit River

The Yana were a tribe of Native Americans living in California between the Sacramento River on the west and Lassen Peak and the Sierra Nevada on the east. Rock Creek marked the traditional southern boundary of Yana territory, while the Pit River served as the northern limit of the Yanas' land. This area would correspond roughly to the triangle of land between Lake Shasta, Mount Lassen (which the Yana called Waganupa), and the city of Chico, about 2,400 square miles. They were bordered on the west by the Wintun tribe, on the north by the Wintun and Achumawi, on the east by the Atsugewi, and on the south by the Maidu.

Most anthropologists agree that there are few if any Yana alive today, and even at their zenith they numbered only fifteen hundred to three thousand. In the Yana language the word "Yana" meant person. There were four distinct divisions among the Yana peoples. The Northern Yana were by far the smallest group. The others were the Central Yana, Southern Yana, and Yahi. The Yahi were the southernmost group. The linguistic anthropologist Edward Sapir made a detailed study of the Yana in the first decades of the twentieth century and found the Yana to belong to the Hokan linguistic family. Each of the four subgroups had its own dialect and usage of the Yana tongue, and communication among the various groups was possible but difficult. Each used two forms of oral communication; one was for women and one was for men.

The Yana/Yahi were hunter-gatherers. They lived on acorns, deer, salmon, rabbit, squirrel, bulbs, and roots. Since they had to move periodically to obtain food, their dwellings consisted of small huts in small villages. Agriculture was not practiced by the Yana. The Yana usually had small families and sometimes were polygamous. All members of the tribes worked according to age, gender, and ability. Both children and the elderly were cherished, and with the exception of the Yahi, who cremated their dead, the Yana buried the deceased in cemeteries near their villages. While raids were not uncommon, true weapons of war were never developed; tools and other everyday implements were used to defend the people.

Following hundreds of years of relatively peaceful and prosperous existence, the Yana were suddenly devastated because of their proximity to the California Trail, the gold rush of 1849, and European diseases. The game and food supply of the Yana dwindled as competition from European Americans increased. More significantly, whites, acting from ignorant self-interest, did not recognize the value of Yana culture and considered the Yana nothing more than an obstacle to eliminate. In 1864, for example, a group of miners surrounded a large Yana village and massacred all but about fifty Indians.

Numbers dwindled from that time until 1911, when a fifty-four-year-old Yahi man walked into Oroville, California, in search of food. He called himself Ishi, meaning "man" (his true name was never known, since it was too private for Ishi to tell). He was the last living member of his tribe. From 1911 until his death in 1916, Ishi lived and worked at the University of California Museum of Anthropology in Berkeley. While he was there, Alfred Kroeber worked closely with Ishi to salvage a portion of Yahi and Yana culture and language. It is through Alfred and Theodora Kroeber's writings that some aspects of Yana life are known.

Yaqui

CULTURE AREA: Southwest
LANGUAGE GROUP: Uto-Aztecan
PRIMARY LOCATION: Sonora, Mexico
POPULATION SIZE: 9,931 in U.S. (1990 U.S. Census), estimated 24,000 in Mexico

After being forced from their lands at the end of the nineteenth century, some Yaquis found their way into present-day Arizona and settled in the environs of Tucson and other parts of the southwestern United States. They were, and continue to be, a fiercely independent tribe. In 1533, Diego de Guzmán suffered defeat at the hands of the Yaqui when he attempted to enter their territory, and the Spaniards were faced with numerous Yaqui uprisings throughout their three-hundred-year tenure in New Spain.

The fundamental issue for these confrontations was the fact that the Yaqui held communally owned village lands that were a potential source of material wealth and power for the Spaniards and, later, the Mexicans. To the Yaquis, land always meant an ancient, divinely given heritage to be held in sacred trust. This sacredness of the land, the *yo aniya* (enchanted world), had become intricately bound with every aspect of Yaqui life. From 1886 to 1910, General Porfirio Díaz, the last dictator before the Mexican Revolution, sold millions of Yaqui-occupied acres to foreigners at bargain prices. The Yaquis, led by Cajeme, drove back government expeditions sent out to take possession of their land. The resistance was declared an intolerable crime, and the Yaquis were forced to surrender by being starved into submission. Yacqui lands became private landholdings, Cajeme was "tried" and shot in 1887, and thousands of Yaquis were sold like cattle for seventy-five pesos each to rich plantation owners in Yucatán and Quintana Roo. There, unaccustomed to the hot tropical sun, they were worked as slaves in brutal conditions, and, with no hope for the future, died in large numbers. By the 1990's, however, the restless Yaqui spirit had been rekindled in its ancestral homeland and other areas. Timeless rituals were revived to coalesce into ceremonies reflective of the *yo aniya*, the land where all sources of divine power lie.

Yaquina

CULTURE AREA: Northwest Coast
LANGUAGE GROUP: Salishan
PRIMARY LOCATION: Yaquina River and Yaquina Bay, Oregon

The patrilineal Yaquina were oriented toward the sea and rivers, but they were also dependent upon land animals and plants for food and needed by-products. Their environment provided numerous tidal foods, birds, and waterfowl. They lived in rectangular, multifamily, cedar plank winter houses in autonomous permanent villages. Yaquina society was stratified, and wealthy men were often polygamous. Marriage reinforced trading relationships, established status, and redistributed wealth. Slaves, one form of traditional wealth, were usually acquired by raids. They excelled, as did their southern neighbors, the Alsea, in woodworking skills.

The first European American contact in the area was by the American ship *Columbia* in 1788. Unfortunately, little is known of the Yaquina or Alsea people, whose numbers were greatly reduced by early epidemics, particularly smallpox. By 1856 the remaining Alsea and Yaquina had been placed on the Coast Reservation, a small portion of their original territory. The Coast Reservation was split in 1865, and in 1910 only nineteen people who identified themselves as Yaquina remained.

Yavapai

CULTURE AREA: Southwest
LANGUAGE GROUP: Yuman
PRIMARY LOCATION: Western and central Arizona
POPULATION SIZE: 579 (1990 U.S. Census)

The Yavapai have lived in central and western Arizona since about 1100 C.E., when they arrived from the West. Primarily hunters and gatherers, the Yavapai followed the cycles of nature, moving from one area to another harvesting wild plants. Animals were captured either by hand or by a throwing stick or bow and arrow.

As they migrated, the Yavapai made their shelters in caves and in domed stone or timber huts. Occasionally, hostilities erupted between the Yavapai and the Walapai, Havasupai, Tohono O'odham, Pima, and Maricopa. The Yavapai were most friendly with the Navajo, Hopi, Mojave, Quichan (Yuma), and especially the Apaches, whom they sometimes married.

The first European incursion occurred in the late fourteenth and early fifteenth centuries, when Spanish explorers passed through Yavapai territory. When the Arizona gold rush hit in the 1860's, contact with outsiders, especially European Americans, increased greatly. The Yavapai usually sought peace with these invaders. The Yavapais' numbers dwindled because of various hardships, and in 1865, the two thousand remaining Yavapai were moved to the Colorado River Reservation, the first of many reservations they would be relocated to; others included Fort McDowell, Rio Verde, San Carlos, Camp Verde, Middle Verde, Clarkdale, and Prescott. With the exceptions of River Verde and San Carlos, the Yavapai continue to inhabit these reservations.

Prior to U.S. government intervention, the Yavapai were led by articulate members of the tribe and by shamans notable for their powerful dreams and their healing skills. Past influential Yavapai leaders include Chief Yuma Frank, Chief Viola Jimulla, and Carlos Montezuma.

Modern Yavapais make their living primarily from farming, working for wages, and making and selling traditional crafts. The tribe is governed by an elected board. Modern Yavapai spirituality is expressed in a variety of forms, including Christian denominations and the Holy Ground Church, which emphasizes the sacred relationship between humanity and the earth that supports it.

Yazoo

CULTURE AREA: Southeast
LANGUAGE GROUP: Muskogean
PRIMARY LOCATION: Mississippi

In 1682 Henri de Tonti found this small tribe living on the Yazoo River, close to the Mississippi River, north of present-day Natchez, Mississippi. The Yazoo tribe was closely associated with the Koroa tribe, resembling them in speech patterns. Both tribes used an "r" sound in speaking, which other tribes in the area did not.

As European trade increased in the lower Mississippi Valley, many of the tribes eagerly sought the goods that could be obtained by trading fur pelts and widely increased their hunting range. The Yazoos took captives, especially the Chawashas, and sold them as slaves to British traders; at times they were made captives themselves (particularly by the Chickasaws), sold into slavery, and sent to Charleston markets. Some were purchased by local planters, but the rest were shipped to the West Indies.

The houses of the Yazoos were round and constructed of poles plastered with a clay-moss mixture. This structure was then covered with cypress bark or palmetto. There was one door, approximately five feet high, but no windows or chimneys. Little is known about tribal customs. After a death, the corpse was carried into the woods, escorted by relatives carrying lighted pine torches that were thrown into the grave before it was covered. Relatives and friends went to cry nightly at the burial site for six months. A post, carved with the figure he painted on his body, marked the head of a chief's grave.

The Yazoos joined with the Natchez Indians in an uprising against the French, who controlled the area along the Mississippi. In 1729 they, along with the Koroas, attacked and destroyed the entire French garrison of Fort Rosalie, a fort not far from the mouth of the Yazoo River, and murdered the French missionary Father Souel, who had settled among them in 1727. Shortly after this event, the Yazoos were attacked and nearly destroyed by the Quapaws; only fifteen Yazoo men were left. The few remaining Yazoos apparently joined with the Chickasaws and Choctaws, and the Yazoos disappeared as a separate tribe.

Yellowknife

CULTURE AREA: Subarctic
LANGUAGE GROUP: Athapaskan
PRIMARY LOCATION: Western Canada

This highly mobile hunting-and-trapping culture was dependent upon the movements of the barren-ground caribou, which involved them in sustained socioeconomic relations with the contiguous Chipewyan and Dogrib groups. Little is known of these people because of a general decline in population caused by introduced communicable diseases and intergroup conflict. At the time of their first contact with whites, the Yellowknife were in constant conflict with the Dogrib, Hare, and Slave; they were even fighting with the Chipewyan. Their winter dwellings were covered with stitched, tanned caribou hides. By the end of the nineteenth century, the Dogrib had expanded their aboriginal territory by defeating the Yellowknife.

The European first contact with the Yellowknife was effected in 1770 by Samuel Hearne. Later, after Arctic explorer Sir John Franklin's 1819-1822 account, most ethnographic data was provided by the Hudson's Bay Company. In 1913, ethnologist J. Alden Mason provided brief descriptions of the Yellowknife whom he met; they were then living in canvas-covered conical lodges at Fort Resolution. By 1914 the Yellowknife had essentially lost their tribal identity, preferring to be known as Chipewyan.

Yokuts

CULTURE AREA: California
LANGUAGE GROUP: Yokutsan
PRIMARY LOCATION: Central California
POPULATION SIZE: 2,802 (1990 U.S. Census)

The Yokuts inhabited a south-central portion of California. They hunted, fished, and gathered for subsistence. Yokuts Indians fished throughout the year using nets, spears, and basket traps to catch trout, perch, and chub. Fish not eaten immediately were sun-dried. Men used nets, snares, and wood-tipped arrows to capture deer, rabbit, squirrel, and pigeons. Nets and snares were utilized to capture geese, ducks, and other waterfowl. Seeds, turtles, roots, and shellfish were gathered.

The Yokuts lived in permanent single-family, oval-shaped dwellings covered with tule mats or in long mat-covered structures that housed ten or more families. Water transportation was accomplished with the use of canoe-shaped balsa or tule rafts. Men wore deerskin breechclouts, and women wore aprons of the same material. Mudhen or rabbit cloaks were worn in cooler weather.

Tribe members observed a number of superstitions and taboos to preserve health and good luck. Shamans were generally men. They were thought to receive their powers through dreams. Shamans cured the ill and led rituals. Healing methods included sucking out diseases or draining portions of blood. Several shamans used the datura plant, processed into a hallucinogenic drug, to arrive at a diagnosis.

In 1772, Pedro Fages explored Yokuts territory. Other explorers followed but had little direct effect on tribal life. Indians from other tribes fleeing the missions reached Yokuts tribes. Some stayed and introduced their own tribal ways to their Yokuts hosts. Through these visitors the Yokuts learned of the horse, and they wished to join the equestrian ranks. They raided local ranches and missions for horses and soon became known as the "horsethief Indians." Ranchers organized campaigns to recover their livestock and punish the Yokuts.

In 1833, a malaria epidemic devastated the tribe, killing 75 percent of its members. Though the Yokuts avoided the infiltration of gold miners suffered by other Californian tribes, numerous whites settlers came into their territory. These settlers met with little resistance from a shrinking Indian population. In the late 1800's, the Yokuts were forced onto reservation lands. They found work on local ranches and in the logging industry, but social problems—including poor education, alcoholism, and poverty—persisted throughout the twentieth century.

Yuchi

CULTURE AREA: Southeast
LANGUAGE GROUP: Yuchi
PRIMARY LOCATION: Oklahoma
POPULATION SIZE: 430 (1990 U.S. Census)

In the 1540's, Hernando de Soto encountered the Yuchis (also known as the Westos) in present-day eastern Tennessee; by the eighteenth century, the tribe had migrated southward, with the majority of Yuchis settling on the lower Chattahoochee River. Here, the tribe lived as part of the Creek Confederacy.

Though they were similar to other Creek peoples in many aspects of their culture, the Yuchis retained a strong sense of separate identity. They regarded themselves as descendants of the sun and as the original human inhabitants of what is now the southeastern United States. Their language reinforced their sense of distinctiveness—unrelated to any of the languages spoken by other southeastern tribes, Yuchi was difficult for other Indians to master.

From the late eighteenth century, the Yuchis functioned within the context of Creek and Seminole history. Among the most conservative and traditionalist of Creeks, the Yuchis resented the attempt of Muskogee-speakers to dominate Creek affairs. Some Yuchis joined the migration to Florida that eventually gave birth to a distinctive Seminole identity. During the Creek War (1813-1814), the majority of Yuchis supported the traditionalist Red Sticks faction against American forces and their Indian allies. After the Red Sticks defeat, more Yuchis joined their Seminole kinsmen in Florida. Almost all Yuchis were eventually removed to Indian Territory (modern Oklahoma) either with the Creeks in the 1830's or with the Seminoles in the 1840's. In Indian Territory, the Yuchis settled primarily in the area around Sepulpa in the Creek Nation. Like other traditionalists, they were often opposed to the policies pursued by the more acculturated leaders of the tribal government. During the American Civil War, for example, the Yuchis were predominantly unionist despite the Creek Nation's formal alliance with the confederacy.

The acculturating influences of the twentieth century eventually weakened Yuchi traditionalism. By the 1970's, it was estimated that fewer than fifty speakers of the Yuchi language remained. A small core persisted, however, and in the 1980's an organization of Yuchis petitioned the federal government for formal recognition as a separate tribe.

Yuki

CULTURE AREA: California
LANGUAGE GROUP: Yuki
PRIMARY LOCATION: Upper Eel River, northwestern California
POPULATION SIZE: 265 (1990 U.S. Census)

The Yuki, Huchnom, and Coast Yuki each spoke a dialect of the Yuki language. They all had tribelets, with the village constituting the main socioeconomic unit, presided over by a chief. They lived in conical dwellings of bark, banked with earth. Subsistence was acquired through hunting, gathering, and fishing; salmon and acorns were their main foods. Trade was primarily with the Pomo and Huchnom, and it involved the exporting of food products in exchange for seafood and various types of shell beads. Dress was minimal, though the women wore a fringed leather apron. Deerskin caps were worn in winter.

The Yukis' first contact with settlers was in 1856, when the Nome Cult Indian Farm, essentially a reservation, was established in Round Valley. Settlers attempted to exterminate the Yuki, who resisted white encroachment and depredation. They recognized and participated in the two waves of the early 1870's Ghost Dance. The Yuki continued to live in the Round Valley area into the twentieth century. By the 1960's, all Round Valley Indians were leading a rural life; problems included sanitation, water supplies, and health care.

Yurok

CULTURE AREA: California
LANGUAGE GROUP: Algonquian
PRIMARY LOCATION: Northeastern California and Oregon
POPULATION SIZE: 4,296 (1990 U.S. Census)

Fishing played a major role in the Yurok economy. This Yurok fisherman was photographed in 1923 by Edward S. Curtis. (Library of Congress)

The sedentary Yurok were a marine-oriented people living in permanent villages of split-plank redwood houses in coastal northwestern Oregon and on the lower forty-five miles of the Klamath River in southwestern Oregon and northwestern California. Close socioeconomic ties were maintained between villages. The major sociopolitical and descent group was the "house," which was neither matrilineal nor patrilineal. Villages owned communal property with exploitation rights to major fishing sites, clamming beaches, berry patches, felled redwood trees, acorn groves, deer-hunting areas, and beached whales. The Yurok excelled at woodworking and basketweaving and had a complex fishing technology. Their society was stratified, with nobles, commoners, and slaves, the latter being established by incurred debt. Traditional forms of wealth and heirlooms were paired obsidian blades, albino deerskins, and dentalium necklaces. Social control was maintained by threats of sorcery, destruction of an accused person's property, liability for injuries, and consensus of opinion.

The Yurok were probably first sighted by Spanish galleons in 1565. The first known contact was in 1828 by Hudson's Bay Company fur traders. Sustained European American contact and incursion commenced in 1850 with gold miners and land developers, usually with considerable violence and killing. Despite numerous attempts by several whites to protect Yurok sovereignty, much of the aboriginal territory was confiscated. By 1939, many of the traditional dances and ceremonies had stopped, particularly the traditional Jumping, Boat, Kick, and Deerskin dances, and the First Salmon Rite. In World War II, during the Battle of the Bulge, a Yurok taught the Brush Dance to his non-Indian unit as a form of exercise. Indian Shakerism was introduced in 1927 and continues to be their most popular religion.

Revivals of the Brush Dance started in 1972, as well as a revitalization of certain traditional skills such as weaving and woodworking. By the 1960's, some young males reinstated the traditional regime of training by using the sweathouse, swimming, and running. Competitive sports, particularly playing shinny or field hockey, are conducted between certain villages. Wage earning primarily involves fishing and logging.

Zapotec

CULTURE AREA: Mesomaerica
LANGUAGE GROUP: Oto-Manguean
PRIMARY LOCATION: Oaxaca, Mexico

The pre-Hispanic Zapotec kingdom was centered in the Valley of Oaxaca, at the mountaintop site of Monte Albán (estimated population ten thousand). From there, the Zapotec extended their rule over the entire valley and over much of the present-day Mexican state of Oaxaca. The Zapotec were participants in many general Mesoamerican cultural institutions such as the ball game, ceremonial bloodletting, human and animal sacrifice, formal religious art, a hieroglyphic writing system, and the 260-day calendar. Zapotec script is incompletely deciphered.

The origins of Zapotec society can be seen at the Valley of Oaxaca site of San José Mogote. By 1500 B.C.E., small farming hamlets were ubiquitous, but San José Mogote emerged as a unique settlement, as evidenced by a nonresidential public building and by social stratification within the community. Evidence suggests that coercion may have been involved in the rising importance of San José Mogote. By 500 B.C.E., the mountaintop settlement of Monte Albán had been founded, and San José Mogote ceased to grow. Zapotec society expanded rapidly in social, political, and economic complexity throughout the succeeding centuries.

Like most Mesoamerican civilizations, the Zapotec were a highly stratified society. Divine kings topped the social hierarchy, followed by lesser hereditary nobility and priests; craftsworkers occupied an intermediate position. Maize, beans, and squash farmers formed the bulk of the population and were spread throughout the valley, practicing irrigation agriculture. Tribute was paid to the Zapotec kings. Professional warriors controlled Zapotec society and expanded its borders to capture new territory.

The Zapotec portrayed their military conquests on stone slabs at Monte Albán. Conquest slabs depict some thirty specific places that were conquered by Monte Albán from around 300 to 500 C.E. Another set of carved tablets, of a type known as Danzantes, are most commonly interpreted as tortured and slain captives, also attesting the militaristic nature of Zapotec society.

The Zapotec kings had a political relationship, which remains poorly understood, with Teotihuacán, a large and powerful kingdom in central Mexico. As depicted on stone monuments at Monte Albán, Teotihuacán kings paid official visits to the Zapotec kings. There is also a residential area of Teotihuacán known as the Oaxaca Barrio. It appears that Zapotec lived there but retained their identity over hundreds of years—they continued to bury their dead in traditional Zapotec custom and to make their pottery in traditional styles. The Zapotec do not appear to have been ambassadors to Teotihuacán, as their dwellings are modest and are far removed from the central precincts.

For a variety of reasons, Monte Albán declined in power, and by 900 C.E. its population was dispersed throughout the valley. A series of small, independent kingdoms emerged to replace the centralized power of Monte Albán. Beginning in the late 1400's, most Zapotec kingdoms successively fell prey to the expanding Aztec empire. Less than twenty-five years later, the Zapotec kingdoms again fell prey to the Spanish. An estimated 472,000 people still spoke the Zapotec language during the 1990's.

Appendixes

FESTIVALS AND POW-WOWS

Select calendar of annual American Indian gatherings.

JANUARY

Annual Native American Film Festival
Southwest Museum
Los Angeles, California
Kachina Dances
Hopi Cultural Center
Second Mesa, Arizona
San Ildefonso Feast Day
San Ildefonso Pueblo
Santa Fe, New Mexico

FEBRUARY

Lincoln's Birthday Celebration Pow-wow
Warm Springs Tribal Council
Warm Springs, Oregon
O'odham Tash Celebration
Tohono O'odham Nation
Sells, Arizona
Seminole Tribal Fair and Rodeo
Hollywood Reservation
Hollywood, Florida

MARCH

Agua Caliente Indian Market
Palm Springs, California
Epethes Pow-wow
Nez Perce Tribe
Lapwai, Idaho
Mul-Chu-Tha Community Fair
Gila River Indian Community
Sacaton, Arizona
San Jose Feast Day
Laguna Pueblo
Laguna, New Mexico

APRIL

All-Indian Days Pow-wow
Scottsdale Community College
Scottsdale, Arizona
Annual American Indian Days
Chico State University
Chico, California
Annual Pow-wow
Western Washington University
Bellingham, Washington
Annual South Umpqua Pow-wow
Myrtle Creek, Oregon
Annual Spring Pow-wow
University of Wyoming
Laramie, Wyoming
Cocopah Festivities Day
Somerton, Arizona
Institute of American Indian Arts Pow-wow
Santa Fe, New Mexico
Spring Roundup All-Indian Rodeo
White Mountain Apache Tribal Council
Whiteriver, Arizona
University of California, Berkeley, Pow-wow
Berkeley, California
University of Washington Pow-wow
Sandpoint Naval Air Station
Seattle, Washington

MAY

Annual First Peoples Cultural Festival
Capilano Longhouse
North Vancouver, British Columbia
Annual Intertribal Pow-wow
Trout Lake Community Centre
Victoria, British Columbia

Annual Pow-wow
  Montana State University
  Bozeman, Montana
Annual Pow-wow
  Stanford University
  Palo Alto, California
Chehalis Tribal Day Celebration
  Oakville, Washington
Choctaw Annual Rodeo
  Jones Academy
  Hartshorn, Oklahoma
**Louisiana Indian Heritage
Association Pow-wow**
  Folsom, Louisiana
San Carlos Tribal Fair
  San Carlos Apache Tribe
  San Carlos, Arizona
Spring Pow-wow
  Portland State University
  Portland, Oregon
Tse-Ho-Tso Intertribal Pow-wow
  Window Rick High School
  Fort Defiance, Arizona
**Tuscarora Nation of North Carolina
Pow-wow**
  Tribal Grounds
  Maxton, North Carolina
University of Washington Pow-wow
  Seattle, Washington

JUNE

Bear Dance
  Ute Mountain Ute Tribe
  Towaoc, Colorado
Big Wind Pow-wow
  Shoshone and Arapaho Tribes
  Fort Washakie, Wyoming
Cherokee Pow-wow
  Eastern Band of Cherokee Indians
  Cherokee, North Carolina
Cheyenne-Arapaho Pow-wow
  Concho, Oklahoma
Osage Tribal Ceremonial Dances
  Pawhuska, Oklahoma
Potawatomi Pow-wow
  Shawnee, Oklahoma

San Juan Feast Day
  Taos Pueblo
  Taos, New Mexico
**Shoshone Indian Days Pow-wow and
Rodeo**
  Fort Washakie, Wyoming
Stommish Festival
  Lummi Indian Tribe
  Bellingham, Washington
Warriors Memorial Pow-wow
  Nez Perce Tribe
  Lapwai, Idaho

JULY

**Annual Chumash Intertribal
Pow-wow**
  Santa Ynez, California
Annual Homecoming Celebration
  Winnebago, Nebraska
**Annual Northern Cheyenne Fourth of
July Pow-wow**
  Lame Deer, Montana
**Annual Northern Ute Pow-wow and
Rodeo**
  Fort Duchesne, Utah
Annual Taos Pueblo Pow-wow
  Pow-wow Grounds
  Taos, New Mexico
Arikara Celebration and Pow-wow
  White Shield, North Dakota
Arlee Fourth of July Pow-wow
  Pablo, Montana
Coeur d'Alene Pow-wow
  Plummer, Idaho
**July Fourth Celebration Pow-wow
and Rodeo**
  Window Rock, Arizona
Mescalero Festival
  Mescalero, New Mexico
North American Indian Days
  Blackfeet Tribal Council
  Browning, Montana
Onion Lake Pow-wow
  Onion Lake Reserve
  Saskatchewan/Alberta, British
  Columbia

Poundmaker-Nechi Pow-wow
St. Albert, Alberta
Santa Ana Feast Day
Santa Ana Pueblo
Bernalillo, New Mexico
Shoshone-Paiute Annual Pow-wow
Owyhee, Nevada
Sisseton-Wahpeton Pow-wow
Sisseton, South Dakota
White Earth Pow-wow
White Earth, Minnesota

AUGUST

American Indian Exposition
Anadarko, Oklahoma
Annual Indian Fair Days and Pow-wow
Sierra Mono, California
Annual Intertribal Indian Ceremonial
Church Rock, New Mexico
Annual Piegan Indian Days
Brocket, Alberta
Chief Seattle Days
Suquamish, Washington
Crow Fair
Crow Agency, Montana
Kalispel Pow-wow
Usk, Washington
Land of the Menominee Pow-wow
Kenesha, Wisconsin
Little Shell Pow-wow
New Town, North Dakota
Looking Glass Pow-wow
Lapwai, Idaho
Lower Brule Pow-wow
Lower Brule, South Dakota
Ni-Mi-Win Celebration
Duluth, Minnesota
Northern Arapaho Pow-wow
Arapaho, Wyoming
Oglala Nation Pow-wow and Rodeo
Pine Ridge, South Dakota
Ottawa Pow-wow
Miami, Oklahoma
Ponca Indian Fair and Pow-wow
Ponca City, Oklahoma

Rocky Boys Pow-wow
Box Elder, Montana
Rosebud Fair and Rodeo
Rosebud, South Dakota
Shoshone-Bannock Indian Festival and Rodeo
Fort Hall, Idaho
Snake Dance
Hopi Cultural Center
Second Mesa, Arizona
Standing Rock Pow-wow
Fort Yates, North Dakota
Wichita Tribal Pow-wow
Anadarko, Oklahoma

SEPTEMBER

Cherokee Nation Pow-wow
Tahlequah, Oklahoma
Cheyenne and Arapaho Labor Day Pow-wow
Colony Indian Park
Colony, Oklahoma
Cheyenne River Labor Day Pow-wow
Eagle Butte, South Dakota
Choctaw Annual Pow-wow
Arrowhead State Park
Canadian, Oklahoma
Navajo Nation Fair
Window Rock, Arizona
Shoshone Indian Fair
Fort Washakie, Wyoming
Spokane Tribal Fair and Pow-wow
Wellpinit, Washington
Turtle Mountain Labor Day Pow-wow
Belcourt, North Dakota
United Tribes International Pow-wow
Bismarck, North Dakota

OCTOBER

Annual Canadian Thanksgiving Pow-wow
Mt. Currie, British Columbia
Apache Days
Globe, Arizona
Cherokee Fall Festival
Cherokee Nation of Oklahoma
Tahlequah, Oklahoma

Cherokees of Georgia Gathering and Pow-wow
Tribal Grounds
St. George, Georgia
Chickasaw Nation Annual Day
Chickasaw Nation of Oklahoma,
Oklahoma
Four Nations Pow-wow
Nez Perce Tribe
Lapwai, Idaho
Northern Navajo Fair
Shiprock, Arizona
Pow-wow and Fall Festival
Nashville, Tennesee

NOVEMBER

American Indian Film Festival
Palace of Fine Arts
San Francisco, California
Poarch Band of Creeks Pow-wow
Atmore, Alabama
San Diego Feast Day
Jemez Pueblo
Jemez, New Mexico

San Diego Feast Day
Tesuque Pueblo
Santa Fe, New Mexico
Veteran's Day Pow-wow
Nespelem Community Center
Nespelem, Washington
Veteran's Day Pow-wow
Owyhee, Nevada
Veteran's Day Rodeo
San Carlos, Arizona

DECEMBER

Annual All-Indian Rodeo
Colorado River Reservation
Parker, Arizona
Christmas Pow-wow
Portland State University
Portland, Oregon
Christmas Pow-wow
Umatilla Reservation
Pendleton, Oregon
Shalako
Zuni Pueblo
Zuni, New Mexico

MUSEUMS, ARCHIVES, AND LIBRARIES

Select list of museums, archives, and libraries in four parts: museums in the United States; museums in Canada; libraries and archives in the United States; libraries and archives in Canada. Each part is arranged alphabetically, first by state, territory, or province, then by city.

MUSEUMS IN THE UNITED STATES

ALABAMA

Alabama Museum of Natural History
Smith Hall, University of Alabama
Tuscaloosa, 35487-0340
Resource center of Southeastern
Indians; ties with Moundville
Archaeological Park.

ALASKA

Alaska State Museum
395 Whittier Street
Juneau, 99801-1718
Alaskan Native Gallery; Subarctic
and Northwest Coast items.

Totem Heritage Center
601 Deermount
(mailing address: 629 Dock Street)
Ketchikan, 99901
Programs and artifacts in Northwest
Coast arts; index to all Alaska totem
poles.

ARIZONA

Museum of Northern Arizona
Fort Valley Road
(mailing address: Route 4, P.O. Box
720)
Flagstaff, 86001
Southwest Anglo and Indian art,
with Hopi and Navajo emphasis.
Harold S. Colton Memorial Library
of 24,000 volumes.

**Colorado River Indian Tribes
Museum**
Route 1, Box 23B
Parker, 85344
Artifacts from Mojave, Chemehuevi,
Hopi, and Navajo as well as
prehistoric cultures.

Heard Museum
22 E. Monte Vista Road
Phoenix, 85004-1480
Southwest emphasis; inventory of
8,200 Native American artists.
Library of 40,000 volumes includes
Fred Harvey Company documents
and photo archives.

Gila River Arts and Crafts Center
P.O. Box 457
Sacaton, 85247
Museum and crafts reflect all tribes
of the area.

Arizona State Museum
University of Arizona
Tucson, 85721
Extensive collections from the
historic and prehistoric peoples of
the area.

Navajo Tribal Museum
Highway 264
(mailing address: P.O. Box 308)
Window Rock, 86515
Four Corners archaeology and
ethnography, including re-creation
of 1870-1930 era trading post.

ARKANSAS
Arkansas State Museum
P.O. Box 490
State University, 72467
Emphasizes northeastern Arkansas
tribes such as the Osage, Caddo,
Chickasaw, and others.

CALIFORNIA
Fowler Museum of Cultural History
University of California, Los Angeles
405 Hilgard Avenue
Los Angeles, 90024-1549
Extensive archaeological and
ethnographic collections include
Native American materials.
**Natural History Museum of Los
Angeles County**
Times-Mirror Hall of Native
American Cultures; Hall of
Pre-Columbian Cultures
900 Exposition Boulevard
Los Angeles, 90007
Excellent permanent displays, with
changing exhibitions on
contemporary issues in art and
culture. The Pre-Columbian Hall
covers cultures form Mexico to Peru.
Southwest Museum
234 Museum Drive
(mailing address: P.O. Box 558)
Los Angeles, 90065
Collections range from Alaska to
South America, with permanent
displays focusing on the Southwest,
Great Plains, California, and
Northwest Coast. Braun Research
Library contains 50,000 volumes,
100,000 photos, 900 recordings, and
archival material.
Maturango Museum
100 E. Las Flores
(mailing address: P.O. Box 1776)
Ridgecrest, 93556
A small regional museum focusing
on one of the richest petroglyph ar-
eas in the United States at China
Lake.

Bowers Museum of Cultural Art
2002 North Main Street
Santa Ana, 92706
Collection of 85,000 items focuses
on the fine arts of indigenous
peoples, including pre-Columbian
and Native American.

COLORADO
Denver Art Museum
100 W. 14th Avenue Parkway
Denver, 80204
Art collection includes Indian
clothing, Southwest pottery and
kachinas, and Northwest Coast
carvings. Frederick H. Douglas
Library includes 6,000 volumes.
Denver Museum of Natural History
2001 South Colorado Boulevard
Denver, 80205
Strong on Paleo-Indian culture,
including the original Folsom spear
point; a 24,000-volume library.
**Southern Ute Cultural Center and
Gallery**
Highway 172
(mailing address: P.O. Box 737)
Ignacio, 81137
Early history; contemporary bead
and leather work.

CONNECTICUT
Peabody Museum
Yale University
170 Whitney
New Haven, 06511-8161
Extensive holdings include both
archaeological and ethnographic
materials of the Americas.
**American Indian Archaeological
Institute (AIAI)**
38 Curtis Road
(mailing address: P.O. Box 1260)
Washington Green, 06793-0260
Continental coverage, but focus is
on Northeast Woodlands.
Reconstructed Indian village, with
Indian Habitats Trail; 250,000
artifacts and a 2,000-volume library.

DELAWARE
Delaware State Museum
    316 South Governors Avenue
    Dover, 19901
    Eastern prehistory; 1,000-volume
    library; State Archaeological
    Collection.

DISTRICT OF COLUMBIA
**U.S. National Museum of Natural
    History**
    Smithsonian Institution
    Washington, DC 20560

FLORIDA
Florida State Museum
    University of Florida
    Gainesville, 32601
    Pearsall Collection of ethnographic
    items ranges from Seminole to Inuit.
Ah-Tha-Thi-Ki Museum
    3240 North 64th Avenue
    Hollywood, 33024
    Artifacts and activities document
    and preserve Seminole traditions;
    village, burial site, nature trails.

GEORGIA
New Echota
    Route 3
    Calhoun, 30701
    Restoration of Cherokee capital of
    1825-1838. Trail of Tears material.

IDAHO
Nez Perce National Historic Park
    Highway 95
    (mailing address: P.O. 93)
    Spalding, 83551
    Prehistoric as well as historic
    regional items. Park notes sites of
    Indian-U.S. battles. A 600-volume
    library and archive of 3,000 photos.

ILLINOIS
Field Museum of Natural History
    Roosevelt Road at Lake Shore Drive
    Chicago, 60605

Extensive Native American
collections, including Pawnee earth
lodge replica. Webber Resource
Center houses books and
audio-visual materials on
indigenous cultures.

INDIANA
**Eiteljorg Museum of American
    Indian and Western Art**
    500 West Washington Street
    Indianapolis, 46204
    Extensive collection that
    emphasizes Northeast Woodlands,
    great Plains, and Southwest culture
    areas.

IOWA
**Putnam Museum of History and
    Natural Science**
    1717 West 12th Street
    Davenport, 52804
    Regional ethnographic collections
    and important Mississippian
    materials.

KANSAS
Indian Center Museum
    650 North Seneca
    Wichita, 67203
    Collection reflects Indian art and
    religion.

KENTUCKY
J. B. Speed Art Museum
    2035 South Third Street
    (mailing address: P.O. Box 2600)
    Louisville, 40201-2600
    Collection emphasizes regional
    materials and the Great Plains,
    complemented by a 14,000-volume
    art library that includes the
    Frederick Weygold Indian
    Collection.

LOUISIANA
**Tunica-Biloxi Regional Indian Center
    and Museum**

Highway 1
(mailing address: P.O. Box 331)
Marksville, 71351
Focuses on descendants of the
mound builders. The tribal museum
is built in a classic Mississippian
style. Collections include colonial
Indian-European materials returned
to the tribe under the Indian Graves
and Repatriation Act.

MAINE
Peary-MacMillan Arctic Museum and
  Studies Center
Hubbard Hall, Bowdoin College
Brunswick, 04011
MacMillan collection of Inuit and
Subarctic material culture.

MASSACHUSETTS
Peabody Museum of Archaeology
  and Ethnology
11 Divinity Avenue
Harvard University
Cambridge, 02138
Worldwide collection of 2,000,000
artifacts has a North and South
American focus; 180,000-volume
library.

MICHIGAN
Cranbrook Institute of Science
500 Lone Pine Road
(mailing address: P.O. Box 801)
Bloomfield Hills, 48303-0801
Collection reflects all North
American culture areas.

MINNESOTA
Minnesota Historical Society's Grand
  Mound and Interpretive Center
Route 7
(mailing address: P. O. Box 453)
International Falls, 56649
Burial mounds with extensive
exhibits of Woodland, Laurel, and
Blackduck cultures.

Mille Lacs Indian Museum
HCR 67
(mailing address: P.O. Box 95)
Onamia, 56359
Ojibwa and Dakota artifacts
illustrate traditional lifeways.

MISSISSIPPI
Grand Village of the Natchez Indians
400 Jefferson Davis Boulevard
Natchez, 39120
Artifacts explore the culture of the
descendants of the Mississippian
mound builders.

MISSOURI
St. Louis Science Center
5050 Oakland Avenue
St. Louis, 63110

MONTANA
Museum of the Plains Indian and
  Crafts Center
U.S. 89
(mailing address: P.O. Box 400)
Browning, 59417
Northern Plains material culture;
reconstruction of 1850's Blackfeet
camp.

NEBRASKA
Fur Trade Museum
East Highway 20, HC 74
(mailing address: P.O. Box 18)
Chadron, 69337
Museum of Nebraska History
131 Centennial Mall North
Lincoln, 68508
Anthropology and art of the central
Plains tribes.

NEVADA
Lost City Museum
721 South Highway 169
Overton, 89040
Reconstructed pueblo and kiva;
archaeological museum;
400-volume library.

NEW JERSEY
Montclair Art Museum
3 South Mountain Avenue
Montclair, 07042
Rand Collection of Native American
art. Art history library of 13,000
volumes.
New Jersey State Museum
205 West State Street
Trenton, 08625
Local material as well as Plains,
Arctic, Southwest, and Northeast
collections.

NEW MEXICO
Maxwell Museum of Anthropology
University of New Mexico
Roma and University, N.E.
Albuquerque, 87131-1201
Extensive Southwest collections.
Library of 12,500 volumes and
photo archives.
Museum of Indian Arts and Culture
708 Camino Lejo
(mailing address: P.O. Box 2087)
Santa Fe, 87504
Exhibits focus on Pueblo, Apache,
and Navajo cultures. A
20,000-volume library on the
anthropology of the southwest.
Western New Mexico University Museum
(mailing address: P.O. Box 43)
Silver City, 88061
Eisele collection of classic Mimbres
pottery.

NEW YORK
American Museum of Natural History
79th Street and Central Park West
New York, 10024-5192
Exhibitions are especially strong on
the cultures of the Arctic and Pacific
Northwest.
National Museum of the American Indian
George Gustav Heye Center
Alexander Hamilton Custom House

3753 Broadway at 155th Street
New York, 10032
The first of three planned facilities
of the National Museum of the
American Indian, part of the Smithsonian Institution, opened in New
York in 1994. The largest facility is
planned for the National Mall in
Washington, D.C., with a projected
opening in the year 2000. Much of
the extensive New York collection
will be moved to Washington.
Seneca Iroquois National Museum
Broad Street Extension
(mailing address: P.O. Box 442)
Salamanca, 14779
Special wampum belt exhibit;
typical nineteenth century elm-bark
longhouse reconstruction;
contemporary art.

NORTH CAROLINA
Indian Museum of the Carolinas
607 Turnpike Road
Laurinburg, 28352
Exhibits feature Southeast cultures
and lifeways.
Native American Resource Center
Pembroke State University
Pembroke, 28372
Eastern Woodlands materials; North
and South America.

NORTH DAKOTA
Turtle Mountain Chippewa Heritage Center
Highway 5
(mailing address: P.O. Box 257)
Belcourt, 58316
Promotes tribal history and traditions.
Contemporary art gallery.
North Dakota Heritage Center
612 East Boulevard
Bismarck, 58505
Plains cultures. A 100,000-volume
library on ethnology and history.

OHIO
Cincinnati Museum of Natural History
1301 Western Avenue
Cincinnati, 45203
Good selection of mound builder artifacts from the Ohio Valley.
Cleveland Museum of Natural History
1 Wade Oval Drive
University Circle
Cleveland, 44106-1767
Research fields include archaeology and physical anthropology. A 50,000-volume natural history library.

OKLAHOMA
Museum of the Great Plains
601 Ferris Avenue
Lawton, 73502
Artifacts, library, and photo archives relating to Plains tribes.
Cherokee Heritage Center
Willis Road
(mailing address: P.O. Box 515)
Tahlequah, 74465
Reconstructed village; contemporary arts and crafts.
The Philbrook Museum of Art, Inc.
2727 South Rockford Road
Tulsa, 74114
Clark Field Basket Collection; Lawson Collection of Indian clothing; Philbrook Collection of American Indian paintings; Lawson Indian library.
Seminole Nation Museum and Library
6th and Wewoka
(mailing address: P.O. Box 1532)
Wewoka, 74884

OREGON
High Desert Museum
59800 South Highway 97
Bend, 97702
Museum of Natural History
University of Oregon

1680 East 15th Avenue
Eugene, 97403-1224
Collection includes 13,000-year-old Fort Rock Cave artifacts.

PENNSYLVANIA
Carnegie Museum of Natural History
4400 Forbes Avenue
Pittsburgh, 15213-4080
Wide coverage, including Arctic and Northwest Coast collections.

RHODE ISLAND
Haffenreffer Museum of Anthropology
Brown University
Bristol, 02809
Arctic and Subarctic materials, including Archaic Period remains of the Red Paint People of Maine.

SOUTH CAROLINA
McKissick Museum
University of South Carolina
Columbia, 29208
Catawba pottery and baskets. Folk Art Resource Center.

SOUTH DAKOTA
Indian Museum of North America
Avenue of the Chiefs, Black Hills
Crazy Horse, 57730
Sioux Indian Museum and Crafts Center
515 West Boulevard
Rapid City, 57709
W. H. Over State Museum
414 East Clark
Vermillion, 57069-2390
Plains material culture and contemporary painting.

TENNESSEE
Frank H. McClung Museum
University of Tennessee
1327 Circle Park Drive
Knoxville, 37996-3200

Tennessee State Museum
505 Deaderick Street
Nashville, 37243-1120
Strong in prehistoric Mississippian
culture.

TEXAS
Texas Memorial Museum
University of Texas
24th and Trinity
Austin, 78705
Broad focus on the anthropology of
the American Indian.
Panhandle-Plains Historical Museum
2401 Fourth Avenue
Canyon, 79016
Hall of the Southern Plains. South
and Southwest Indian focus;
10,000-volume library.
Alabama-Coushatta Museum
U.S. Highway 190
Route 3
(mailing address: P.O. Box 540)
Livingston, 77351
Witte Memorial Museum
3801 Broadway
San Antonio, 78209
Most North American culture areas.

UTAH
**College of Eastern Utah Prehistoric
Museum**
451 East 400 North
Price, 84501
Focuses on Anasazi and Fremont
cultures.
Utah Museum of Natural History
University of Utah
Salt Lake City, 84112
Regional, Great Basin, and South-
western materials.

VIRGINIA
Pamunkey Indian Museum
(mailing address: P.O. Box 2050)
King William, 23086
Contemporary and prehistoric art
and artifacts.

Mattaponi Museum
West Point, 23181
Important collection of
archaeological materials.
Jamestown Settlement
(mailing address: P.O. Box JF)
Williamsburg, 23187
Reconstruction of Indian village and
Powhatan's lodge.

WASHINGTON
Makah Cultural and Research Center
(mailing address: P.O. Box 160)
Neah Bay, 98257
Features remains from the Ozette
site, a Late Period pre-contact
Makah village buried and preserved
in a mudslide. Magnificent
Northwest Coast Tradition
assemblage of 60,000 artifacts.
The Burke Museum
University of Washington, DB-10
Seattle, 98195
Northwest Coast and Pacific Rim
collections.
Seattle Art Museum
100 University Street
(mailing address: P.O. Box 22000)
Seattle, 98122-9700
Excellent collection of Northwest
Coast art.
**Yakima Nation Cultural Heritage
Center**
Toppenish, 98948

WEST VIRGINIA
Grave Creek Mound State Park
Moundsville, 26041
Largest mound produced by the
Adena ceremonial complex, which
flourished around 500 B.C.E. to 100 C.E.

WISCONSIN
Logan Museum of Anthropology
700 College Street
Beloit College
Beloit, 53511-5595
Physical and cultural

anthropological materials from the Great Lakes, Plains, and Southwest culture areas.

Neville Public Museum
129 South Jefferson Street
Green Bay, 54301
Archaic Period materials from the Old Copper and Red Ochre cultures.

Lac du Flambeau Chippewa Museum
(mailing address: P.O. Box 804)
Lac du Flambeau, 54538
Eighteenth century dugout canoe, artifacts, and seasonal activities displays.

Milwaukee Public Museum
800 West Wells Street
Milwaukee, 53233
Collections cover North America. A 125,000-volume library.

WYOMING
Anthropology Museum
University of Wyoming
Laramie, 82071

MUSEUMS IN CANADA

ALBERTA
Glenbow Museum
130 Ninth Avenue, S.E.
Calgary, AB T2G 0P3
Provincial Museum of Alberta
12845 102nd Avenue
Edmonton, AB T5N 0M6
Regional materials; Inuit; northern Plains.

BRITISH COLUMBIA
Campbell River Museum
1235 Island Highway
Campbell Island, BC V9W 2C7
Arts of the Indian groups of northern Vancouver Island.

'Ksan Indian Village
(mailing address: P.O. Box 326)
Hazelton, BC B0J 1Y0
A center for the display, preservation, and promotion of

Gitksan arts and crafts skills. Seven traditional buildings.

Museum of Northern British Columbia
(mailing address: P.O. Box 669)
Prince Rupert, BC V8J 3S1
Northwest Coast artifacts. Promotes contemporary carving and craft skills.

Museum of Anthropology
University of British Columbia
Vancouver, BC V6T 1Z1
Major Northwest Coast collections. Center for promotion of traditional arts and customs.

Royal British Columbia Museum
675 Belleville Street
Victoria, BC V8V 1X4
Traditional Kwakiutl dance houses; Thunderbird Park totem pole exhibits; art demonstrations.

MANITOBA
Eskimo Museum
La Verendrye Street
(mailing address: P.O. Box 10)
Churchill, MB R0B 0E0
Inuit materials include kayaks dating back 3,000 years. Also, Subarctic materials from Chippewa and Cree cultures.

Manitoba Museum of Man and Nature
190 Rupert Avenue
Winnipeg, MB R3B 0N2

NEW BRUNSWICK
New Brunswick Museum
277 Douglas Avenue
Saint John, NB F2K 1E5
Regional and pre-Algonquian artifacts.

NEWFOUNDLAND
Newfoundland Museum
285 Duckworth Street
St. John's, NF A1C 1G9
Exhibits cover the six major tribal

groups of Labrador and
Newfoundland.

NORTHWEST TERRITORIES
Northern Life Museum
  110 King Street
  (mailing address: P.O. Box 420)
  Fort Smith, NT X0E 0P0
  Arctic and Subartic tools and
  artifacts.
Dene Cultural Institute
  (mailing address: P.O. Box 207)
  Yellowknife, NT X1A 2N2

NOVA SCOTIA
Nova Scotia Museum
  1747 Summer Street
  Halifax, NS B3H 3A6
  Artifacts of the Micmac.

ONTARIO
North American Indian Travel College
  The Living Museum
  RR 3
  Cornwall Island, ON K6H 5R7
**Museum of Indian Archaeology and
  Lawson Prehistoric Village**
  1600 Attawandaron Road
  London, ON N6G 3M6
  Exhibits cover five phases of culture
  dating back to Paleo-Indian times.
  On-site excavation.
Thunder Bay Art Gallery
  1080 Keewatin Street
  (mailing address: P.O. Box 1193)
  Thunder Bay, ON P7C 4X9
  Traditional items as well as
  contemporary art.
Royal Ontario Museum
  100 Queen's Park Crescent
  Toronto, ON M5S 2C6
  Ontario prehistory.

PRINCE EDWARD ISLAND
Micmac Indian Village
  (mailing address: P.O. Box 51)
  Cornwall, PEI C0A 1H0

QUEBEC
Canadian Museum of Civilization
  100 Laurier Street
  Hull, PQ J8X 4H2
  Spectacular collection of national
  cultural materials.
McCord Museum
  McGill University
  690 Sherbrook Street W.
  Montreal, PQ H3A 1E9
Abenakis Museum
  Route 226
  Odanak, PQ J0G 1H0
  Displays reflect tribal traditions and
  lore.

SASKATCHEWAN
Regina Plains Museum
  1801 Scarth Street
  Regina, SK S4P 2G9
  Metis history and the Riel
  Rebellions are covered in addition
  to Plains material.
**Saskatchewan Museum of Natural
  History**
  Wascana Park
  Regina, SK S4P 3V7
  Native Peoples Gallery focusing on
  Subarctic tribes.

YUKON TERRITORY
MacBride Museum
  (mailing address: P.O. Box 4037)
  Whitehorse, YT Y1A 3S9
  Artifacts of the Yukon region.

LIBRARIES AND ARCHIVES
IN THE UNITED STATES

ALABAMA
**Alabama Department of Archives
  and History**
  624 Washington Avenue
  Montgomery, 36130

ARIZONA
Smoki People Library
  P.O. Box 123

American Indian Tribes

Prescott, 86302
Library of 600 volumes covers
North and South American Indian
ceremonials and dances.

Tohono Chul Park, Inc.
7366 North Paseo del Norte
Tucson, 85704
Nature center, ethnic art exhibitions,
and 800-volume library on
Southwest culture and environment.

Western Archaeological and Conservation Center
1415 North Sixth Avenue
(mailing address: P.O. Box 41058,
Tucson, 85717)
Tucson, 85705
Focus on Southwest prehistory and
ethnography: 17,000-volume library,
100 periodicals, and 160,000-item
photo archive.

Navajo Nation Library System
Drawer K
Window Rock, 86515
Collection has 23,000 books, 1,000
manuscripts, and films and tapes.
Files of the *Navajo Times*. Two
libraries in Window Rock and one
in Navajo, New Mexico.

ARKANSAS
Southwest Arkansas Regional Archives (SARA)
P.O. Box 134
Washington, 71862
History of Caddo Indians and
Southwest Arkansas.

CALIFORNIA
Malki Museum Archives
11-795 Fields Road
Banning, 92220
Oral history project tapes; field
notes of J. P. Harrington and others;
manuscript and photo archives.

Native American Studies Library
University of California at Berkeley
103 Wheeler
Berkeley, 94720

Reports of the Bureau of Indian
Affairs; Indian Claims Commission
materials; special California Indian
collection; extensive holdings.

American Indian Resource Center
Public Library of Los Angeles
County
6518 Miles Avenue
Huntington Park, 90255
Special collections on Indians of
North America; 9,000 volumes.

Rupert Costo Library
UCR Library Special Collections
University of California at Riverside
Riverside, 92517
The 15,000-volume collection is
countrywide in scope with a
California concentration. Houses the
American Indian Historical Society
Archives, donated by the Costos.
Manuscripts, field notes, and 300
books cover the customs and
medicines of the Chinantec Indians
of Oaxaca.

Scientific Library
San Diego Museum of Man
Balboa Park
1350 El Prado
San Diego, 92101
Wide coverage of the Americas, including physical anthropology, archaeology, and ethnology.

COLORADO
National Indian Law Library
Native American Rights Fund
1522 Broadway
Boulder, 80302-6296
Documents, periodicals, and books
on U.S.-Indian relations and law.

Taylor Museum Reference Library
Colorado Springs Fine Arts Center
30 West Dale Street
Colorado Springs, 80903
Art of the Southwest; Hispanic and
colonial folk art. Collection houses
30,000 volumes; extensive
biographies of folk artists.

Koshare Indian Museum, Inc.
115 West 18th Street
La Junta, 81050
The 10,000-volume Special Koshare Collection focuses on Native America and Western United States.

Ute Mountain Tribal Research Archive and Library
Tribal Compound
(mailing address: P.O. Box CC)
Towaoc, 81334
Includes 2,500 books as well as 30,000 archival items, including tribal government documents.

CONNECTICUT
Mashantucket Pequot Research Library
Indiantown Road
Ledyard, 06339

DISTRICT OF COLUMBIA
American Folklife Center
U.S. Library of Congress
Thomas Jefferson Building -G152
Washington, DC 20540
Biggest collection of early Indian recordings, including the Frances Densmore Collection of 3,600 cylinders and the Helen Heffron Roberts Collection from the Northwest Coast and California.

National Anthropological Archives
Natural History Museum MRC 152
10th and Constitution Avenue
Washington, DC 20560
Extensive collections of recordings, photographs, field notes, and manuscripts of the Bureau of Ethnology.

Natural Resources Library
U.S. Department of the Interior
Mail Stop 1151
18th and C Streets, N.W.
Washington, DC 20240
More than 600,000 volumes and extensive periodicals and archival items, including materials on American Indians.

GEORGIA
Hargrett Rare Books and Manuscript Library
University of Georgia
Athens, 30602

ILLINOIS
Newberry Library
D'Arcy McNickle Center for the History of the American Indian
60 West Walton Street
Chicago, 60610
More than 100,000 volumes, including the E. E. Ayer Collection.

INDIANA
Lilly Library
Indiana University
Bloomington, 47405
Collection includes Indian accounts of Custer's defeat at the Battle of the Little Bighorn.

Fulton County Historical Society Library
Route 3
(mailing address: P.O. Box 89)
Rochester, 46975
Collection houses 4,000 volumes, including coverage of Potawatomi removal to Kansas in 1838 (the Trail of Death).

KANSAS
Mennonite Library and Archives
Bethel College
300 East 27th Street
North Newton, 67117-9989
Includes 26,000 books. Petter Manuscript Collection on the Cheyenne; H. R. Voth Manuscript and Photo Collection on the Hopi.

Mid-America All Indian Center Library
650 North Seneca
Wichita, 67203
Includes 3,000 books and 200 bound periodical volumes on Indian art, history, and culture. Blackbear Bosin

Collection of publications and personal papers.

LOUISIANA
Grindstone Bluff Museum Library
(mailing address) P.O. Box 7965
Shreveport, 71107
Contains 6,000 books and 2,000
periodical volumes on regional
archaeology and ethnology;
emphasis on Caddo Indians.

MASSACHUSETTS
Fruitlands Museums and Library
102 Prospect Hill Road
Harvard, 01451
Mashpee Archives Building
Mashpee, 02649

MICHIGAN
Custer Collection
Monroe County Library System
Monroe, 48161
Contains 4,000 books and archival
materials on Custer and the West.

MINNESOTA
Minnesota Historical Society
Divison of Archives and
Manuscripts
345 Kellogg Boulevard West
St. Paul, 55102-1906
Materials relating to the Ojibwa and
Dakota.

MISSOURI
Missouri Historical Society Library
Jefferson Memorial Building
Forest Park
St. Louis, 63112
Northern Plains; papers of William
Clark from Lewis and Clark
expedition.

MONTANA
Dr. John Woodenlegs Memorial Library
Dull Knife Memorial College

P.O. Box 98
Lame Deer, 59043-0098
Cheyenne history; oral history collection. Contains 10,000 volumes.

NEBRASKA
Native American Public Broadcasting Consortium Library
P.O. Box 83111
Lincoln, 68501
Special Collection of Native American
video programs (171 titles). Audio
program "Spirits of the Present."
NAPBC quarterly newsletter.
Materials available by mail.

Nebraska State Historical Society Library
P.O. Box 82554
Lincoln, 68501
Anderson Collection of Brule Sioux
photographs. Library has 70,000
volumes.

Joslyn Art Museum
Art Reference Library
2200 Dodge Street
Omaha, 68102
Native American art covered in collection of 25,000 volumes, 3,000
bound periodicals, and 20,000 slides.

NEW JERSEY
Firestone Library Collections of Western Americana
Princeton University
Princeton, 08544

NEW MEXICO
Mary Cabot Wheelwright Research Library
704 Camino Lejo
Santa Fe, 87502
Contains 10,000 volumes; archives
on Navajo religion and
sandpainting.

Museum of New Mexico Photo Archives
P.O. Box 2087
Santa Fe, 87504

Millicent Rogers Museum Library
P.O. Box A
Taos, 87571
Registry of New Mexico Hispanic
artists, including a number of
Indian artists.

NEW YORK
Museum of the American Indian Library
9 Westchester Square
Bronx, 10461
Contains 40,000 volumes; archives.
Akwesasne Library
Route 37-RR 1
(mailing address: P.O. Box 14-C)
Hogansburg, 13655
Iroquois Indian Museum Library
P.O. Box 9
Bowes Cave, 12042-0009
Contains 1,500 volumes; 500
archival items; exhibition catalogs.
Seneca Nation Library
Allegany Branch
P.O. Box 231
Salamanca, 14779
Cattaraugus Branch
Irving, 14981

NORTH CAROLINA
State Archives
109 East Jones Street
Raleigh, 27601-2807

OHIO
Ohio Historical Society Archives and Library
1982 Velma Avenue
Columbus, 43211

OKLAHOMA
Chickasaw Nation Library
Arlington and Mississippi Streets
Ada, 74830
Oklahoma Historical Society Archives and Manuscript Division
2100 North Lincoln Boulevard
Oklahoma City, 73105

State Indian Agency records; Dawes
Commission papers; 125,000
photographs.
Gilcrease Library
1400 Gilcrease Museum Road
Tulsa, 74127
John Ross (Cherokee chief) and
Peter Pitchlynn (Choctaw chief)
papers; 50,000 volumes.

OREGON
Siletz Library and Archives
119 East Logsden Road, Building II
Siletz, 97380

PENNSYLVANIA
Free Library of Philadelphia
Logan Square
Philadelphia, 19103
University Museum Library
33rd and Spruce Streets
University of Pennsylvania
Philadelphia, 19104
Brinton Collection on Indian
linguistics; Delaware materials.

SOUTH DAKOTA
Center for Western Studies
Augustana College
P.O. Box 727
Sioux Falls, 57197
Great Plains history. Collection has
30,000 volumes, 1,500 linear feet of
manuscripts.

TEXAS
Fikes Hall of Special Collections
DeGolyer Library
Southern Methodist University
Dallas, 75275
National Archives
Southwest Region
501 Felix at Hemphill, Building 1
P.O. Box 6216
Fort Worth, 76115
Bureau of Indian Affairs records for
Oklahoma.

UTAH
Ute Tribal Museum, Library, and Audio-Visual Center
Fort Duchesne, 84026

WASHINGTON
Jamestown Klallam Library
Blyn, 98382
Special Collections
University of Washington
Seattle, 98195

WEST VIRGINIA
ERIC Clearinghouse on Rural Education and Small Schools (CRESS) Library
1031 Quarrier Street
(mailing address: P.O. Box 1348)
Charleston, 25325
Microfiche containing 300,000 documents. Indian/Hispanic issues.

WISCONSIN
Hoard Historical Museum Library
407 Merchant Avenue
Fort Atkinson, 53538
Rare Black Hawk War materials.
Fairlawn Historical Museum
Harvard View Parkway
Superior, 54880
George Catlin lithographs; David F. Berry Collection of Indian photographs and portraits.

WYOMING
McCracken Research Library
Buffalo Bill Historical Center
P.O. Box 1000
Cody, 82414

LIBRARIES AND ARCHIVES IN CANADA

ALBERTA
Canadian Circumpolar Library
University of Alberta
Edmonton, AB T6G 2J8

University of Lethbridge Library
Special Collections
4401 University Drive
Lethbridge, AB T1K 3M4
Native American studies; English literature; education.

BRITISH COLUMBIA
Alert Bay Library and Museum
199 Fir Street
Alert Bay, BC B0N 1A0
Kamloops Museum and Archives
207 Seymour Street
Kamloops, BC V2C 2E7
Interior Salish and Shuswap material.
University of British Columbia Library
1956 Main Hall
Vancouver, BC V6T 1Z1

MANITOBA
Department of Indian Affairs and Northern Development Regional Library
275 Portage Avenue
Winnipeg, MB R3B 3A3
People's Library
Manitoba Indian Cultural Education Centre
119 Sutherland Avenue
Winnipeg, MB R2W 3C9

NEW BRUNSWICK
Education Resource Centre
University of New Brunswick
D'Avray Hall
P.O. Box 7500
Fredericton, NB E3B 5H5

NORTHWEST TERRITORIES
Thebacha Campus Library
Arctic College
Fort Smith, NT X0E 0P0

NOVA SCOTIA
Nova Scotia Human Rights Commission Library

P.O. Box 2221
Halifax, NS B3J 3C4
Rights of indigenous peoples,
women, and others; 4,000 books.

ONTARIO
**Department of Indian Affairs and
Northern Development
Departmental Library**
Ottawa, ON K1A 0H4
**University of Sudbury Library and
Jesuit Archives**
Sudbury, ON P3E 2C6

QUEBEC
**Canadian Museum of Civilization
Library**
100 Laurier Street
Hull, PQ J8X 4H2

SASKATCHEWAN
**Gabriel Dumont Institute of Native
Studies and Applied Research
Library**
121 Broadway
Regina, SK S4N 0Z6
Indian History archives; 30,000
volumes.
Indian Federated College Library
University of Regina
Regina, SK S4S 0A2
Collection has 15,000 volumes.
Branch library of 4,000 volumes on
Saskatoon Campus.
Saskatchewan Provincial Library
1352 Winnipeg Street
Regina, SK S4P 3V7
Has a 4,000-volume Indian
collection. Strong in languages.

ORGANIZATIONS, AGENCIES, AND SOCIETIES

All Indian Pueblo Council
Founded: 1958
P.O. Box 3256
Albuquerque, NM 87190

American Indian Council of Architects and Engineers
Founded: 1976
P.O. Box 230685
Tigard, OR 97223

American Indian Culture Research Center
Founded: 1967
Box 98
Blue Cloud Abbey
Marvin, SD 57251

American Indian Graduate Center
Founded: 1969
4520 Montgomery Boulevard NE
Ste. 1-B
Albuquerque, NM 87109

American Indian Health Care Association
Founded: 1975
245 E. 6th Street
Ste. 499
St. Paul, MN 55101

American Indian Heritage Foundation
Founded: 1973
6051 Arlington Boulevard
Falls Church, VA 22044

American Indian Higher Education Consortium
Founded: 1972
513 Capitol Court NE
Ste. 100
Washington, DC 20002

American Indian Horse Registry
Founded: 1961
Route 3, Box 64
Lockhart, TX 78644

American Indian Liberation Crusade
Founded: 1952
4009 S. Halldale Avenue
Los Angeles, CA 90062

American Indian Library Association
Founded: 1979
50 E. Huron Street
Chicago, IL 60611

American Indian Lore Association
Founded: 1957
960 Walhonding Avenue
Logan, OH 43138

American Indian Movement (AIM)
Founded: 1968
710 Clayton Street
Apartment 1
San Francisco, CA 94117

American Indian Registry for the Performing Arts
Founded: 1983
1717 N. Highland Avenue
Ste. 614
Los Angeles, CA 90028

American Indian Research and Development
Founded: 1982
2424 Springer Drive
Ste. 200
Norman, OK 73069

American Indian Science and Engineering Society
Founded: 1977
1630 30th Street
Ste. 301
Boulder, CO 80301

Americans for Indian Opportunity
Founded: 1970
3508 Garfield Street NW
Washington, DC 20007

Arrow, Incorporated (Americans for Restitution and Righting of Old Wrongs)
Founded: 1949
1000 Connecticut Avenue NW
Ste. 1206
Washington, DC 20036

Associated Community of Friends on Indian Affairs
Founded: 1869
Box 1661
Richmond, IN 47375

Association of American Indian Physicians
Founded: 1971
Building D
10015 S. Pennsylvania
Oklahoma City, OK 73159

Association of Community Tribal Schools
Founded: 1982
c/o Dr. Roger Bordeaux
616 4th Avenue W
Sisseton, SD 57262-1349

Association on American Indian Affairs
Founded: 1923
245 5th Avenue
New York, NY 10016

Bureau of Catholic Indian Missions
Founded: 1874
2021 H Street NW
Washington, DC 20006

Cherokee National Historical Society
Founded: 1963
P.O. Box 515
Tahlequah, OK 74465

Coalition for Indian Education
Founded: 1987
3620 Wyoming Boulevard NE
Ste. 206
Albuquerque, NM 87111

Concerned American Indian Parents
Founded: 1987
CUHCC Clinic
2016 16th Avenue S
Minneapolis, MN 55404

Continental Confederation of Adopted Indians
Founded: 1950
960 Walhonding Avenue
Logan, OH 43138

Council for Indian Education
Founded: 1970
517 Rimrock Road
Billings, MT 59102

Council for Native American Indians
Founded: 1974
280 Broadway
Ste. 316
New York, NY 10007

Council of Energy Resource Tribes (CERT)
Founded: 1975
1999 Broadway
Ste. 2600
Denver, CO 80202

Crazy Horse Memorial Foundation
Founded: 1948
The Black Hills
Avenue of the Chiefs
Crazy Horse, SD 57730

Creek Indian Memorial Association
Founded: 1923
Creek County House Museum
Town Square
Okmulgee, OK 74447

Dakota Women of All Red Nations (DWARN)
Founded: 1978
c/o Lorelei DeCora
P.O. Box 423
Rosebud, SD 57570

First Nations Development Institute
Founded: 1980
69 Kelley Road
Falmouth, VA 22405

Gathering of Nations
Founded: 1984
P.O. Box 75102
Sta. 14
Albuquerque, NM 87120-1269

Indian Arts and Crafts Association
Founded: 1974
122 La Veta Drive NE

Ste. B
Albuquerque, NM 87108
Indian Heritage Council
Founded: 1988
Henry Street
Box 2302
Morristown, TN 37816
Indian Law Resource Center
Founded: 1978
508 Stuart Street
Helena, MT 59601
Indian Rights Association
Founded: 1882
1801 Market Street
Philadelphia, PA 19103-1675
Indian Youth of America
Founded: 1978
609 Badgerow Building
Sioux City, IA 51101
Institute for American Indian Studies
Founded: 1971
38 Curtis Road
P.O. Box 1260
Washington, CT 06793-0260
Institute for the Development of Indian Law
Founded: 1971
c/o K. Kirke Kickingbird
Oklahoma City University
School of Law
2501 Blackwelder
Oklahoma City, OK 73106
Institute for the Study of American Cultures
Founded: 1983
The Rankin
1004 Broadway
Columbus, GA 31901
Institute for the Study of Traditional American Indian Arts
Founded: 1982
P.O. Box 66124
Portland, OR 97290
Institute of American Indian Arts
Founded: 1962
P.O. Box 20007
Santa Fe, NM 87504

International Indian Treaty Council
Founded: 1974
710 Clayton Street
Number 1
San Francisco, CA 94117
Inter-Tribal Indian Ceremonial Association
Founded: 1921
Box 1
Church Rock, NM 87311
Lone Indian Fellowship and Lone Scout Alumni
Founded: 1926
1104 St. Clair Avenue
Sheboygan, WI 53081
National American Indian Court Clerks Association
Founded: 1980
1000 Connecticut Avenue NW
Ste. 1206
Washington, DC 20036
National American Indian Court Judges Association
Founded: 1968
1000 Connecticut Avenue NW
Ste. 1206
Washington, DC 20036
National Center for American Indian Enterprise Development
Founded: 1969
953 E. Juanita Avenue
Mesa, AZ 85204
National Congress of American Indians
Founded: 1944
900 Pennsylvania Avenue SE
Washington, DC 20003
National Council of BIA Educators
Founded: 1967
6001 Marble NE
Ste. 10
Albuquerque, NM 87110
National Indian Council on Aging
Founded: 1976
6400 Uptown Boulevard NE
City Centre
Ste. 510-W
Albuquerque, NM 87110

National Indian Counselors Association
Founded: 1980
Learning Research Center
Institute of American Indian Arts
P.O. Box 20007
Santa Fe, NM 87504

National Indian Education Association
Founded: 1970
1819 H Street NW
Ste. 800
Washington, DC 20006

National Indian Health Board
Founded: 1969
1385 S. Colorado Boulevard
Ste. A-708
Denver, CO 80222

National Indian Social Workers Association
Founded: 1970
410 NW 18th Street
Number 101
Portland, OR 97209

National Indian Training and Research Center
Founded: 1969
2121 S. Mill Avenue
Tempe, AZ 85282

National Indian Youth Council
Founded: 1961
318 Elm Street SE
Albuquerque, NM 87102

National Native American Cooperative
Founded: 1969
P.O. Box 1030
San Carlos, AZ 85550-1000

National Urban Indian Council
Founded: 1977
10068 University Station
Denver, CO 80210

Native American (Indian) Chamber of Commerce
Founded: 1990
c/o Native American Cooperative
P.O. Box 1000
San Carlos, AZ 85550-1000

Native American Community Board
Founded: 1984
P.O. Box 572
Lake Andes, SD 57356-0572

Native American Educational Services College
Founded: 1974
2838 West Peterson
Chicago, IL 60659

Native American Indian Housing Council
Founded: 1974
900 2nd Street NE
Ste. 220
Washington, DC 20002

Native American Policy Network
Founded: 1979
Barry University
11300 2nd Avenue NE
Miami, FL 33161

Native American Rights Fund (NARF)
Founded: 1970
1506 Broadway
Boulder, CO 80302

North American Indian Association
Founded: 1940
22720 Plymouth Road
Detroit, MI 48239

North American Indian Chamber of Commerce
Founded: 1983
P.O. Box 5000
San Carlos, AZ 85550-1000

North American Indian Museums Association
Founded: 1979
c/o George Abrams
260 Prospect Street
Number 669
Hackensack, NJ 07601-2608

North American Indian Women's Association
Founded: 1970
9602 Maestor's Lane
Gaithersburg, MD 20879

North American Native American Indian Information and Trade Center

Founded: 1991
P.O. Box 1000
San Carlos, AZ 85550-1000
Order of the Indian Wars
Founded: 1979
P.O. Box 7401
Little Rock, AR 72217
Pan-American Indian Association
Founded: 1984
P.O. Box 244
Nocatee, FL 33864
Seventh Generation Fund for Indian Development
Founded: 1977
P.O. Box 10
Forestville, CA 95436
Smoki People
Founded: 1921
P.O. Box 123
Prescott, AZ 86302
Survival of American Indians Association
Founded: 1964
7803-A Samurai Drive SE
Olympia, WA 98503

Tekakwitha Conference National Center
Founded: 1939
P.O. Box 6768
Great Falls, MT 59406-6768
Tiyospaya American Indian Student Organization
Founded: 1986
P.O. Box 1954
St. Petersburg, FL 33731
United Indians of All Tribes Foundation
Founded: 1970
Daybreak Star Arts Center
Discovery Park
P.O. Box 99100
Seattle, WA 98199
United Native Americans
Founded: 1968
2434 Faria Avenue
Pinole, CA 94564
United South and Eastern Tribes
Founded: 1969
1101 Kermit Drive
Ste. 302
Nashville, TN 37217

POPULATIONS OF U.S. RESERVATIONS

Alphabetical listing of U.S. reservations and populations; population figures are rounded off.

Reservation	Population	Reservation	Population
Absentee-Shawnee Tribe	1,500	Choctaw Indian	3,715
Acoma Pueblo	3,100	Choctaw Nation of Oklahoma	22,000
Agua Caliente	200	Citizen Band Potawatomi	
Allegheny	750	Tribe	4,500
Alturas Rancheria	15	Cochiti Pueblo	975
Apache Tribe of Oklahoma	5,500	Cocopah	550
Bad River	1,550	Coeur d'Alene	850
Barona	330	Cold Springs Rancheria	235
Benton Paiute	68	Colorado River	2,400
Berry Creek Rancheria	275	Colorado River Indian	2,800
Big Bend Rancheria	110	Colusa Rancheria	55
Big Cypress	450	Colville	3,750
Big Lagoon Rancheria	12	Comanche Indian Tribe of	
Big Pine	110	Oklahoma	4,000
Big Sandy Rancheria	55	Coquille Indian Tribe	630
Bishop Indian	1,075	Cortina Rancheria	90
Blackfeet	7,000	Coushatta	295
Blue Lake Rancheria	35	Creek Nation of Oklahoma	32,500
Bridgeport Indian Colony	90	Crow Creek	2,500
Brighton	440	Crow Indian	5,500
Burns Paiute Indian Colony	220	Cuyapaipe	30
Cabazon	27	Delaware Tribe of Western	
Caddo Indian Tribe	1,250	Oklahoma	1,150
Cahuilla	175	Devil's Lake Sioux	3,500
Camp Verde	600	Dilkon Community	1,000
Campo	225	Dry Creek Rancheria	30
Cattaraugus	5,500	Duck Valley	1,100
Cayuga Nation	110	Duckwater	150
Cedarville Rancheria	22	Eastern Shawnee	395
Chehalis	750	Ely Indian colony	350
Chemehuevi	135	Enterpise Rancheria	20
Cherokee	8,800	Fallon Reservation and Colony	700
Cherokee Nation of Oklahoma	45,000	Flandreau Santee Sioux	440
Cherokee Tribe of Virginia	150	Flathead	3,500
Cheyenne-Arapaho Tribe	75,000	Fond du Lac	1,750
Cheyenne River	5,500	Forest County Potawatomi	
Chickasaw Nation of		Community	450
Oklahoma	75,000	Fort Apache Indian	8,500
Chitimacha	310	Fort Belknap	2,500

Reservation	Population	Reservation	Population
Fort Berthold	4,000	L'Anse (Keweenaw Bay)	950
Fort Bidwell	200	Las Vegas Indian Colony	125
Fort Hall	4,000	Laytonville Rancheria	110
Fort Independence	110	Leech Lake	5,200
Fort McDermitt	710	Lone Pine	150
Fort McDowell	550	Los Coyotes	195
Fort Mojave	600	Lovelock Indian Colony	175
Fort Peck	5,500	Lower Brule	1,100
Fort Sill Apache Tribe of		Lower Elwha Klallam	470
Oklahoma	380	Lower Sioux Indian Community	230
Gila Bend	300	Lummi	3,300
Gila River	9,750	Makah	1,250
Golden Hill	5	Manchester/Point Arena	
Goshute	200	Rancheria	95
Grand Portage (Pigeon River)	325	Manzanita	25
Grande Ronde Indian		Maricopa (Ak Chin)	450
Community	640	Menominee	3,750
Hannahville Indian Community	375	Mesa Grande	70
Havasupai	500	Mescalero Apache	2,750
HOH	75	Miami Tribe of Oklahoma	1,516
Hoopa Extension	300	Miccosukee	495
Hoopa Valley	2,200	Michigan Bay Mills	395
Hopi	8,500	Mille Lacs	950
Hopland Rancheria	150	Mississippi Choctaw	4,750
Houlton (Maliseet Band)	290	Moapa River Indian	395
Houma Indian Communities	2,750	Morongo	375
Hualapai	1,200	Muckleshoot	2,500
Inaja & Cosmit	15	Nambe Pueblo	400
Indian Township	395	Navajo	185,000
Iowa	310	Nett Lake (Bois Fort)	1,250
Iowa Tribe of Oklahoma	6,000	Nez Perce	2,200
Isabella	450	Nisqually Indian	1,400
Isleta Pueblo	3,500	Nooksack	750
Jamestown S'kallam	250	Northern Cheyenne	3,300
Jemez Pueblo	2,000	Ojibwa of the Red River	850
Jicarilla Apache	2,600	Omaha	1,500
Kaibab	250	Oneida (New York)	1,100
Kalispel	250	Oneida (Wisconsin)	2,700
Kaw Tribe of Oklahoma	1,250	Onondaga	1,500
Kickapoo	625	Osage Tribe of Oklahoma	6,000
Kickapoo Tribe of Oklahoma	800	Otoe-Missouria Tribe of	
Kiowa Tribe of Oklahoma	4,500	Oklahoma	1,250
Kootenai	135	Paiute Indian Tribe of Utah	600
Lac Courte Oreilles	2,000	Pajoaque Pueblo	175
Lac du Flambeau	2,400	Pala Indian	395
Laguna Pueblo	4,250	Pamunkey Indian	90
La Jolla Band of Mission Indians	235	Pauma Band of Mission Indians	40

Reservation	Population	Reservation	Population
Pawnee Indian Tribe of		Sault Ste. Marie Tribe of	
Oklahoma	2,500	Chippewa Indians	2,500
Penobscot	1,150	Seminole	500
Picayune Rancheria	65	Seminole Nation of Oklahoma	4,000
Picuris Pueblo	200	Seneca-Cayuga Tribe of	
Pine Ridge	14,500	Oklahoma	800
Pleasant Point	800	Shakopee Sioux community	110
Ponca Tribe of Oklahoma	2,500	Shinnecock	375
Poospatuck	100	Shoalwater Bay	100
Port Gamble Indian		Siletz Reservation	800
Communtiy	450	Sisseton-Wahpeton	4,000
Port Madison	440	Skokomish Indian Reservation	550
Prairie Island	135	Skull Valley Indian	
Prairie Potawatomi	1,350	Community	85
Pyramid Lake	850	Soboba Indian	450
Quapaw Tribe of Oklahoma	1,450	Sokaogon Chippewa	
Quileute	300	Community	850
Quinault	2,200	Southern Ute	1,200
Red Cliff	1,500	Spokane	1,200
Red Lake	4,850	Squaxin Island	100
Reno-Sparks Indian Colony	630	Standing Rock	8,500
Rincon	150	Stewarts Point Rancheria	100
Rocky Boy	1,100	Stockbridge-Munsee	
Rosebud	9,900	Community	1,350
Round Valley	450	Sulphur Bank Rancheria	55
Sac and Fox	700	Susanville Rancheria	350
Sac and Fox Tribe of		Swinomish	750
Oklahoma	1,700	Sycuan	70
St. Croix	1,100	Table Bluff	218
St. Regis Mohawk Indian	6,250	Taos Pueblo	1,450
Salt River	3,500	Tesuque Pueblo	325
San Carlos Apache	6,000	Tohono O'odham (Sells)	7,700
San Felipe Pueblo	2,200	Tonawanda	675
San Ildefonso Pueblo	475	Tonkawa Tribe of Oklahoma	1,500
San Juan Pueblo	1,100	Torres-Martinez	90
San Manuel	55	Tulalip	950
San Xavier	1,000	Tule River	550
Sandia Pueblo	320	Turtle Mountain	8,950
Sanostee	550	Tuscarora	775
Santa Ana Pueblo	1,350	Uintah and Ouray	2,000
Santa Clara Pueblo	2,750	Umatilla	1,750
Santa Rosa	110	Upper Sioux Indian	
Santa Rosa Rancheria	135	Community	150
Santa Ynez	100	Upper Skagit Indian	200
Santa Ysabel	325	Ute Mountain	1,600
Santee Sioux	425	Viejas (Baron Long)	195
Sauk-Suiattle Indian	215	Walker River	1,100

Reservation	Population	Reservation	Population
Wampanoag	550	Wyandotte Tribe of Oklahoma	500
Warm Springs	2,750	Yakima	9,000
Washoe	1,020	Yankton Sioux	2,500
White Earth	3,200	Yavapai-Prescott	175
Wichita Tribe of Oklahoma	700	Yerrington Indian Colony	430
Winnebago (Nebraska/Iowa)	1,100	Yomba	135
Winnebago (Wisconsin)	1,350	Zia Pueblo	650
Winnemucca Indian Colony	110	Zuni	7,450

Source: Data are from Klein, Barry T., *Reference Encyclopedia of the American Indian.* 6th ed. West Nyack, N.Y. Todd Publications, 1993.

Note: Some reservations are not listed because they contain no "in residence" population.

RESERVATIONS: UNITED STATES

A listing by state of U.S. American Indian reservations. List represents 1991 data.

ALABAMA

Choctaw Indian
Poarch Band of Creek Indians

ARIZONA

Beclabito
Bird Springs
Blue Gap
Broadway
Cameron
Camp Verde
Chilchinbeto
Chinle
Coalmine
Cocopah
Colorado River Indian
Copper Mine
Cornfields
Coyote Canyon
Crystal
Dennehotso
Dilkon Community
Forest Lake
Fort Apache Indian
Fort Defiance
Fort McDowell
Fort Mohave
Fort Yuma
Ganado
Gila Bend
Gila River
Greasewood
Havasupai
Hopi
Houck
Hualapai
Inscription House
Jeddito

Kaibab
Kaibito
Kayenta
Kinlichee
Klagetoh
Lechee
Leupp
Low Mountain
Lukachukai
Lupton
Many Farms
Maricopa (Ak Chin)
Mexican Springs
Mexican Waters
Naschitti
Navajo
Navajo Mountain
Nazlini
Oak Springs
Oljatoh
Pascua Yaqui Indian Community
Pinon
Red Lake
Red Mesa
Red Rock
Rough Rock
Round Rock
St. Michaels
Salt River
San Carlos Apache
San Xavier
Sanotsee
Sawmill
Shonto
Steamboat
Teecnospos
Teesto
Tohatchi
Tohono O'odham (Sells)
Tolani Lake

Tonto Apache Community
Tsaile-Wheatfields
Tselani
Tuba City
Twin Lakes
White Cone
Wide Ruins
Yavapai-Prescott

CALIFORNIA

Agua Caliente
Alturas Rancheria
Augustine
Barona
Benton Paiute
Berry Creek Rancheria
Big Bend Rancheria
Big Lagoon Rancheria
Big Pine
Big Sandy Rancheria
Big Valley Rancheria
Bishop Indian
Blue Lake Rancheria
Bridgeport Indian Colony
Buena Vista Rancheria
Cabazon
Cahuilla
Campo
Capitan Grande
Cedarville Rancheria
Chemehuevi
Chicken Ranch Rancheria
Cloverdale Rancheria
Cold Springs Rancheria
Colorado River
Colusa Rancheria
Cortina Rancheria
Coyote Valley
Cuyapaipe
Dry Creek Rancheria
Elk Valley Rancheria
Enterprise Rancheria
Fort Bidwell
Fort Independence
Fort Mojave
Fort Yuma
Greenville Rancheria

Grindstone Rancheria
Guidiville Rancheria
Hoopa Extension
Hoopa Valley
Hopland Rancheria
Inaja & Cosmit
Jackson Rancheria
Jamul Indian village
Karok Tribe of California
La Jolla Band of Mission Indians
La Posta
Laytonville Rancheria
Lone Pine
Los Coyotes
Lytton Rancheria
Manchester/Point Arena Rancheria
Manzanita
Mesa Grande
Middletown Rancheria
Mooretown Rancheria
Morongo
North Fork Rancheria
Pala Indian
Pauma Band of Mission Indians
Pechanga
Picayune Rancheria
Pinolville Rancheria
Pit River
Potter Valley Rancheria
Quartz Valley Indian
Ramona Band Cahuilla Rancheria
Redding Rancheria
Redwood Valley Rancheria
Resighini Rancheria
Rincon
Robinson Rancheria
Rohnerville Rancheria
Round Valley
Rumsey Rancheria
San Manuel
San Pasqual
Santa Rosa
Santa Rosa Rancheria
Santa Ynez
Santa Ysabel
Scotts Valley
Sherwood Valley Rancheria
Shingle Springs Rancheria

Smith River Rancheria
Soboba Indian
Stewarts Point Rancheria
Sulphur Bank Rancheria
Susanville Rancheria
Sycuan
Table Bluff
Table Mountain Rancheria
Timbisha Shoshone
Torres-Martinez
Trinidad Rancheria
Tule River
Tuolumne Me-Wuk Rancheria
Twenty-Nine Palms
Upper Lake Rancheria
Viejas (Baron Long)
Winnemucca Indian Colony
Woodfords Community
Yurok Indian

COLORADO

Southern Ute
Ute Mountain

CONNECTICUT

Eastern Pequot
Golden Hill
Mashantucket Pequot
Schaghticoke Indian

FLORIDA

Big Cypress
Brighton
Miccosukee
Seminole

IDAHO

Coeur d'Alene
Duck Valley
Fort Hall
Kootenai
Nez Perce
Northwestern Band of Shoshone
  Nation
Summit Lake

IOWA

Omaha
Sac and Fox
Winnebago

KANSAS

Iowa
Kickapoo
Prairie Potawatomi
Sac and Fox Tribe of the Missouri

LOUISIANA

Chitimacha
Coushatta
Houma Indian Communities
Tunica-Biloxi Indian

MAINE

Houlton (Maliseet Band)
Indian Township
Penobscot
Pleasant Point

MASSACHUSETTS

Grand Traverse
Hannahville Indian Community
Isabella
Lac Vieux Desert Band of Chippewa
  Indians
L'Anse (Keweenaw Bay)
Michigan Bay Mills
Sault Ste. Marie Tribe of Chippewa
  Indians
Wampanoag

MINNESOTA

Fond du Lac
Grand Portage (Pigeon River)
Leech Lake
Lower Sioux Indian Community
Mille Lacs
Nett Lake (Bois Fort)
Prairie Island

Red Lake
Shakopee Sioux Community
Upper Sioux Indian Community
White Earth

MISSISSIPPI

Mississippi Choctaw

MISSOURI

Eastern Shawnee

MONTANA

Blackfeet
Crow Indian
Flathead
Fort Belknap
Fort Peck
Northern Cheyenne
Rocky Boy

NEBRASKA

Iowa
Omaha
Pine Ridge
Sac and Fox Tribe of the Missouri
Santee Sioux
Winnebago

NEVADA

Battle Mountain
Carson Indian Colony
Dresslerville Indian Colony
Duck Valley
Duckwater
Elko Indian Colony
Ely Indian Colony
Fallon Reservation and Colony
Fort McDermitt
Fort Mohave
Las Vegas Indian Colony
Lovelock Indian Colony
Moapa River Indian
Pyramid Lake
Reno-Sparks Indian Colony

Ruby Valley (Te-Moak)
South Fort Indian Colony
Summit Lake
Walker River
Washoe
Wells Indian Colony
Yerrington Indian Colony
Yomba

NEW MEXICO

Acoma Pueblo
Aneth
Baca
Becenti
Beclabito
Bread Springs
Burnham
Canoncito
Casamero Lake
Cheechilgeetho
Church Rock
Cochiti Pueblo
Crownpoint
Crystal River
Dalton Pass
Fort Defiance
Huerfano
Isleta Pueblo
Jemez Pueblo
Jicarilla Apache
Laguna Pueblo
Lake Valley
Little Water
Manuelito
Mariano
Mescalero Apache
Mexican Water
Nageezi
Nambe Pueblo
Nenahnezad
Ojo Encino
Pajoaque Pueblo
Picuris Pueblo
Pinedale
Pueblo Plaintado
Puertocito (Alamo)
Ramah Navajo

Red Lake
Red Mesa
Red Rock
Rock Point
Rock Springs
San Felipe Pueblo
San Ildefonso Pueblo
San Juan Pueblo
Sandia Pueblo
Sanostee
Santa Ana Pueblo
Santa Clara Pueblo
Santo Domingo Pueblo
Sheep Springs
Shiprock
Smith Lake
Standing Rock
Sweetwater
Taos Pueblo
Teecnospos
Tesuque Pueblo
Thoreau
Torreon and Star Lake
Tsaile-Wheatfields
Tsayatoh
Two Grey Hills
Upper Fruitland
Ute Mountain
White Rock
Whitehorse Lake
Yanbit
Zia Pueblo
Zuni

NEW YORK

Abenaki Indian Village
Allegheny
Cattaraugus
Cayuga Nation
Oil Spring
Oneida
Onondaga
Poospatuck
St. Regis Mohawk Indian
Seneca Nation
Shinnecock
Tonawanda
Tuscarora

NORTH CAROLINA

Cherokee

NORTH DAKOTA

Devil's Lake Sioux
Fort Berthold
Ojibwa of the Red River
Standing Rock
Turtle Mountain

OKLAHOMA

Absentee-Shawnee Tribe
Alabama-Quassarte Tribe Town
Apache Tribe of Oklahoma
Caddo Indian Tribe
Cherokee Nation of Oklahoma
Cheyenne-Arapaho Tribe
Chickasaw Nation of Oklahoma
Choctaw Nation of Oklahoma
Citizen Band Potawatomi Tribe
Comanche Indian Tribe of Oklahoma
Creek Nation of Oklahoma
Delaware Tribe of Western Oklahoma
Eastern Shawnee Tribe of Oklahoma
Fort Sill Apache Tribe of Oklahoma
Iowa Tribe of Oklahoma
Kaw Tribe of Oklahoma
Kialegee Tribal Town
Kickapoo Tribe of Oklahoma
Kiowa Tribe of Oklahoma
Miami Tribe of Oklahoma
Modoc Tribe of Oklahoma
Osage Tribe of Oklahoma
Otoe-Missouria Tribe of Oklahoma
Pawnee Indian Tribe of Oklahoma
Peoria Tribe of Oklahoma
Ponca Tribe of Oklahoma
Quapaw Tribe of Oklahoma
Sac and Fox Tribe of Oklahoma
Seminole Nation of Oklahoma
Seneca-Cayuga Tribe of Oklahoma
Thlopthlocco Tribe of Oklahoma
Tonkawa Tribe of Oklahoma
United Keetoowah of Oklahoma
Wichita Tribe of Oklahoma
Wyandotte Tribe of Oklahoma

OREGON

Burns Paiute Indian Colony
Confederated Tribes of Coos, Lower
   Umpqua, and Siuslaw Indians
Coquille Indian Tribe
Cow Creek Band of Umpqua Indians
Fort McDermitt Reservation
Grande Ronde Indian Community
Klamath
Siletz
Umatilla
Warm Springs

RHODE ISLAND

Narragansett Indian

SOUTH DAKOTA

Cheyenne River
Crow Creek
Flandreau Santee Sioux
Lower Brule
Pine Ridge
Rosebud
Sisseton-Wahpeton
Standing Rock
Yankton Sioux

UTAH

Chilchinbeto
Dennehotso
Goshute
Kayenta
Mexican Water
Navajo Mountain
Oljatoh
Paiute Indian Tribe of Utah
Red Mesa
Shonto
Skull Valley Indian Community
Teecnospos
Uintah and Ouray
Ute Mountain
Washakie

VIRGINIA

Cherokee Tribe of Virginia
Pamunkey Indian

WASHINGTON

Chehalis
Colville
HOH
Jamestown S'kallam
Kalispel
Lower elwha Klallam
Lummi
Makah
Muckleshoot
Nisqually Indian
Nooksack
Port Gamble Indian Community
Port Madison
Puyallup
Quileute
Quinault
Sauk-Suiattle Indian
Shoalwater Bay
Skokomish Indian
Spokane
Squaxin Island
Stillaquamish
Swinomish
Tulalip
Upper Skagit Indian
Yakima

WISCONSIN

Bad River
Forest County Potawatomi Community
Lac Courte Oreilles
Lac du Flambeau
Menominee
Oneida
Red Cliff
Sokaogon Chippewa Community
Stockbridge-Munsee Community
Winnebago

WYOMING

Wind River

RESERVES AND BANDS: CANADA

A listing by province and territory of Canadian reserves and bands. List represents 1991 data.

ALBERTA

Alexander
Alexis
Athabasca Chipewyan
Bearspaw (Stoney)
Beaver Lake
Bigstone Cree Nation
Blood
Boyer River
Chiniki (Stoney)
Cold Lake First Nations
Cree
Dene Tha' Tribe
Driftpile
Duncan's
Enoch
Ermineskin
Fort McKay First Nation
Fort McMurray First Nation
Frog Lake
Goodstoney (Stoney)
Grouard
Heart Lake
Horse Lake
Janvier
Kehewin
Little Red River Cree Nation
Louis Bull
Lubicon
Montana
O'Chiese
Paul
Piegan Nation
Saddle Lake
Samson
Sawridge
Siksika Nation
Sturgeon Lake
Sucker Creek

Sunchild Cree First Nation
Swan River First Nation
Tallcree
Tsuu T'ina Nation
Whitefish Lake
Woodland Cree

BRITISH COLUMBIA

Adams Lake
Ahousaht
Aitchelitz
Alexandria
Alexis Creek
Alkali
Anaham
Anderson Lake
Ashcroft
Beecher Bay
Bella Coola
Blueberry River
Bonaparte
Boothroyd
Boston Bar
Bridge River
Broman Lake
Burns Lake
Burrard
Campbell River
Canim Lake
Canoe Creek
Cape Mudge
Cayoose Creek
Chawathil
Cheam
Chehalis
Cremainus
Chaslatta Carrier Nation
Clayoquot
Coldwater

Columbia Lake
Comox
Cook's Ferry
Coquitlam
Cowichan
Cowichan Lake
Dease
Dease River
Ditidaht
Doig River
Douglas
Ehattesaht
Esquimalt
Fort George
Fort Nelson
Fort Ware
Fountain Indian
Gitanmaax
Gitanyow (Kitwancool)
Gitlakdamix
Gitsegukla
Gitwangak
Gitwinksihlkw
Glen Vowell
Gwa'sala-'Nakwaxda'zw
Hagwilget
Halalt
Halfway River
Hartley Bay
Heiltsuk
Hesquiaht
High Bar
Homalco
Ingenika
Iskut
Kamloops
Kanaka Bar
Katzie
Kincolith
Kispiox
Kitamaat
Kitasoo
Kitsumkalum
Kittkatla
Kittselas
Kitwancool
Klahoose
Kluskus

Kwakiutl
Kwa-Kwa-A-Pilt
Kwa-Wa-Aineuk
Kwiakah
Kwicksutaineuk-Ah-Kwaw-Ah-Mish
Kyuquot
Lakahahmen
Lakalzap
Lake Babine
Langley
Lax-Kw-Alaams
Lillooet
Little Shuswap
Lower Kootenay
Lower Nicola
Lower Similkameen
Lyackson
Lytton
McLeod Lake
Malahat
Mamaleleqala Qwe-qwa'sot'enox
Masset
Matsqui
Metlaktla
Moricetown
Mount Currie
Mowachaht
Musqueam
Nadleh Whuten
Nak'azdli
Nanaimo
Nanoose First Nation
Nazko
Nee-Tahi-Buhn
Nemaiah Valley
Neskonlith
Nicomen
Nimpkish
Nooaitch
North Thompson
Nuchatlaht
Ohamil
Ohiaht
Okanagan
Opetchesaht
Oregon Jack Creek
Osoyoos
Oweekeno

Pacheenaht
Pauquachin
Pavilion
Penelakut
Penticton
Peters
Popkum
Prophet River
Qualicum
Quatsino
Red Bluff
St. Mary's
Samahquam
Saulteau
Scowlitz
Seabird Island
Sechelt
Semiahmoo
Seton Lake
Shackan
Sheshaht
Shuswap
Siska
Skawahlook
Skeetchestn
Skidegate
Skookumchuck
Skowkale
Skuppah
Skwah
Skyway
Sliammon
Soda Creek
Songhees
Sooke
Soowahlie
Spallumcheen
Spuzzum
Squamish
Squiala
Stellaquo
Stone
Stony Creek
Sumas
Tahltan
Takla Lake
Taku River Tlingit
Tanakteuk

Tla-O-Qui-Aht First Nations
Tlatlasikwala
Tl'azt'en Nation
Tlowitsis-Mumtagila
Tobacco Plains
Toosey
Toquaht
Tsartlip
Tsawataineuk
Tsawout
Tsawwassen
Tseycum
Tzeachten
Uchucklesaht
Ucluelet
Ulkatcho
Union Bar
Upper Nicola
Upper Similkameen
West Moberly
Westbank
Whispering Pines
Williams Lake
Yakweakwioose
Yale

MANITOBA

Barren Lands
Berens River
Birdtail Sioux
Bloodvein
Brokenhead
Buffalo Point First Nation
Chemawawin First Nation
Churchill
Crane River
Cross Lake
Dakota Ojibway
Dakota Plains
Dakota Tipi
Dauphin River
Ebb and Flow
Fairford
Fisher River
Fort Alexander
Fox Lake
Gamblers

609

Garden Hill First Nation
God's Lake
God's River
Grand Rapids First Nation
Hollow Water
Indian Birch
Interlake Reserves
Jackhead
Keeseekoowenin
Lake Manitoba
Lake St. Martin
Little Black River
Little Grand Rapids
Little Sask
Long Plain
Mathias Colomb
Moose Lake
Nelson House
Northlands
Norway House
Oak Lake Sioux
Oxford House
Pauingassi First Nation
Peguis
Pine Creek
Poplar River First Nation
Red Sucker Lake
Rolling River
Rosequ River
Sagkeeng
St. Theresa Point
Sandy Bar
Shamattawa First Nation
Shoal River
Sioux Valley
Split Lake
Swan Lake
Valley River
War Lake
Wasagamack
Waterhen
Waywayseecappo First Nation
York Factory

NEW BRUNSWICK

Big Cove
Bouctouche Micmac

Burnt Church
Edmundston
Eel Ground
Eel River
Fort Folly
Indian Island
Kingsclear
Oromocto
Pabinequ
Red Bank
St. Mary's
Tobique
Woodstock

NEWFOUNDLAND

First Nation Council of Davis Inlet
First Nation Council of Northwest
    River
Maiwpukek

NORTHWEST TERRITORIES

Aklavik
Arctic Red River
Colville Lake
Dechilao'ticouncil (Snarelake) Dene
Dene Nation
Dog Rib Rae
Fitz/Smith (Alta-N.W.T.)
Fort Franklin
Fort Good Hope
Fort Liard
Fort McPherson
Fort Norman
Fort Providence
Fort Resolution
Fort Simpson
Fort Wrigley
Hay River
Inuvik
Kakisa Lake
Lac La Martre
Lutsel K'e Dene
Nahanni Butte
Pehdzeh k'i (Wrigley) Dene
Rae Lakes Dene
Rainbow Valley

Sambaa k'e (Trout Lake) Dene
Snowdrift
Yellowknives Dene

NOVA SCOTIA

Acadia
Afton
Annapolis Valley
Bear River
Chapel Island
Eskasoni
Horton
Membertou
Millbrook
Pictou Landing
Shubenacadie
Wagmatcook
Whycocomagh

ONTARIO

Albany—Sinclair Island
Albany—Village of Kashechewan
Alderville
Algonquin of Golden Lake
Aroland
Attawapiskat
Batchewana
Bearskin Lake
Beausoleil
Beaverhouse
Big Grassy
Big Island
Big Trout Lake
Brunswick House
Caldwell
Cat Lake
Chapleau Cree
Chapleau Ojibway
Chippewas of Georgina Island
Chippewas of Kettle and Stony Point
Chippewas of Nawash
Chippewas of Rama First Nation
Chippewas of Sarnia
Chippewas of Saugeen
Chippewas of the Thames
Cockburn Island

Constance Lake
Couchiching
Curve Lake
Dalles
Deer Lake
Dokis
Eabametoong First Nation
Eargle River
Flying Post
Fort Albany
Fort Severn
Fort William
Garden River First Nation
Ginoogaming First Nation
Grassy Narrows
Gull Bay
Henvey Inlet
Hornepayne
Islington
Kasabonika
Kee-Way-Win
Kingfisher Lake
Lac des Milles Lacs
Lac La Croix
Lac Seul
Lansdowne House
Long Lake No. 58
McDowell Lake
Magnetawan
Martin Falls
Matachewan
Mattagami
Michipicoten
Missanabie Cree
Mississauga
Mississaugas of New Credit
Mississaugas of Scugog
Mocrebec Indian Government
Mohawks of Akwesasne
Mohawks of Gibson
Mohawks of the Bay of Quinte
Moose Deer Point
Moose Factory
Moravian of the Thames
Munsee-Delaware Nation
Muskrat Dam
Naicatchewenin
New Post

New Slate Falls
Nibinamik
Nickikousemene
Nipigon
Nipissing First Nation
North Caribou Lake
North Spirit Lake
Northwest Angle No. 33
Northwest Angle No. 37
Ojibways of Hiawatha
Ojibways of Onegaming
Ojibways of the Pic River
Ojibways of Walpole Island
Oneidas of the Thames
Osnaburg
Pays Plat
Pic Mobert
Pikangikum
Poplar Hill
Rainy River
Rat Portage
Red Rock
Rocky Bay
Sachigo Lake
Sagamok Anishnawbek
Sand Point
Sandy Lake
Saugeen
Saugeen Nation
Seine River
Serpent River
Shawanaga
Sheguiandah
Sheshegwaning
Shoal Lake No. 39
Shoal Lake No. 40
Six Nations of the Grand River
Stangecoming
Sucker Creek
Temagami
Thessalon
Wabauskang
Wabigoon Lake Ojibway Nation
Wahgoshig
Wahnapitae
Walpole Island
Wapekeka
Wasauksing (Parry Island)

Washagmis Bay
Wauzhushik Onigum
Wawakapewin
Webequi
Weenusk
West Bay
Whitefish Bay
Whitefish Lake
Whitefish River
Whitesand
Wikwemikong
Wunnumin

PRINCE EDWARD ISLAND

Abegweit
Lennox Island

QUEBEC

Abenakis de Wolinak
Abitibiwinni (Algonquin)
Atikamekw De Manouane
Attikameks de Weymontachie
Barriere Lake (Algonquin)
Betsiamites
Chisasibi
Eastman (Cree)
Gaspe (Micmac)
Grande Lac Victoria (Algonquin)
Huronne-Wendat
Kenesatake
Kipawa (Algonquin)
Kitigan Zibi Anishinabeg
Lac Simon (Algonquin)
Long Point (Algonquin)
Micmacs of Gesgapegiag
Mingan
Mistassini
Mohawks of Kahnawake
Montagnais de la Romaine
Montagnais de les Escoumins
Montagnais de Natashquan
Montagnais de Pakua Shipi
Montagnais de Schefferville
Montagnais de Uashat Et Maliotenam
Montagnais du Lac St-Jean
Naskapis of Schefferville

Nemaska (Cree)
Obedjiwan
Odanak (Abenaquis)
Restigouche (Micmac)
Temiskaming (Algonquin)
Viger
Waskaganish
Waswanipi (Cree)
Wemindji (Cree)
Weymontachie
Whapmagoostui
Wolf Lake

SASKATCHEWAN

Antahkakoop
Beardy's
Big C
Big River
Black Lake
Buffalo River
Canoe Lake
Carry the Kettle
Cote
Cowessess
Cumberland
Cumberland House Cree Nation
Day Star
English River
Fishing Lake
Flying Dust
Fond du Lac
Gordon
Hatchet Lake
Island Lake
James Smith
John Smith
Joseph Bighead
Kahkewistahaw
Kawacatoose
Keeseekoose
Key
Kinistin
Lac La Ronge
Little Black Bear
Little Pine
Lucky Man
Makwa Sahgaiehcan

Mistawasis
Moose Woods
Mosquito Grizzly Bear's Head
Muscowpetung
Muskeg Lake
Muskowekwan
Nekaneet
Ocean Man
Ochapowace
Okanese
Okemasis
One Arrow
Onion Lake
Pasqua
Peepeekisis
Pelican Lake
Peter Ballantyne
Pheasant Rump Nakota
Piapot
Poundmaker
Red Earth
Red Pheasant
Sakimay
Sandy Lake
Saulteaux
Shoal Lake of the Cree Nation
Standing Buffalo
Star Blanket
Sturgeon Lake
Sweetgrass
Thunderchild
Turnor Lake
Wahpeton Lake
Waterhen Lake
White Bear
William Charles
Witchekan Lake
Wood Mountain
Woosomin
Yellowquill (Nutt Lake)
Young Chipewayan

YUKON TERRITORY

Carcross/Tagish
Champagne/Aishihik
Dawson
Dease River

Kluane First Nation	Little Salmon-Carmacks
Kwanlin Dun First Nation	Na-Cho Ny'a'k-Dun
Liard River	Old Crow
Liard River IndianReserve #3	

TIME LINE

Significant events in American Indian history.

Date	Event
c. 40,000-13,000 B.C.E.	Possible years of migration to the Americas by the ancestors of present-day Native Americans.
c. 27,000 B.C.E.	Estimate of when Paleo-Indians begin to migrate southward through ice-free corridors into the American interior.
c. 15,000 B.C.E.	Clovis Period begins across native North America; centers on hunting mega-fauna, especially the woolly mammoth.
c. 9,000 B.C.E.	Folsom Period emerges, centering on bison hunting.
c. 8,000 B.C.E.	Plano Period replaces Folsom, representing a transitional cultural period culminating in the Archaic.
c. 6,000 B.C.E.	Archaic Period begins, signalling a reliance on a variety of flora and fauna. Cultural innovations such as pottery, the bow and arrow, and the domestication of plants begin to appear across North America.
c. 1,000 B.C.E.	Agriculture appears in the Southwest; it gradually diffuses across North America.
	Woodland Period emerges in eastern North America.
c. 1-500 C.E.	Complex societies flourish across North America.
c. 825-900	Athapaskan people, ancestors of the Navajo and Apache, invade the Southwest from the north, altering the cultural landscape of the Puebloan people.
c. 1007	Norsemen invade native North America along the eastern seaboard and establish a short-lived colony.
1050-1250	Cahokia, near present-day St. Louis, is established as a great Mississippian trading and ceremonial center. The city may have contained as many as thirty thousand people.
1492	Christopher Columbus lands on Guanahani (the island of San Salvador), launching Europe's exploration and colonization of North America.
c. 1500	European-introduced diseases, warfare, and slavery begin to reduce native populations (from an estimated ten to eighteen million to approximately 250,000 in 1900).
1519-1521	Hernán Cortés conquers the Aztec Empire.
1582-1598	Spanish conquistadors invade and settle in the Southwest.
1585	Roanoke Colony is founded by the British (it lasts only until approximately 1607).
1599	Massacre at Acoma Pueblo. Vincente de Zaldivar attacks Acoma on January 21 because of its resistance to Spanish authority; eight hundred Acomas are killed.

Date	Event
1607	British Virginia Company establishes colony of Jamestown, affecting local indigenous populations.
1609	Henry Hudson opens the fur trade in New Netherlands.
1620	The Pilgrims colonize present-day Massachusetts.
1622-1631	Powhatan Confederacy declares war on the Jamestown colonists.
1629	The Spanish begin establishing missions among the Pueblos, leading to a 1633 revolt at Zuni.
1630	The Puritans colonize New England, carrying with them a religious belief that Native Americans are "children of the Devil."
1636-1637	Pequot War. The Pequot and their allies attempt to defend their homelands against the Puritans.
c. 1640	The Dakota (Sioux), forced in part by hostilities initiated by the fur trade, begin to migrate westward onto the Great Plains.
1642-1685	Beaver Wars. As the supply of beaver is exhausted in the Northeast, the Iroquois Confederacy launches a war against neighboring Native American nations to acquire their hunting territories.
c. 1650	Period of widespread migrations and relocations. Prompted by the diffusion of the gun and the horse, and by the increasing hostility of Europeans, many Native Americans migrate westward.
1655	Timucua Rebellion. Timucuan mission residents rebel against Spanish cruelty in Florida.
1655-1664	Peach Wars. The Dutch launch a war of extermination against the Esophus nation after an Esophus woman is killed for picking peaches.
1670	Hudson's Bay Company is chartered, launching a westward expansion of the fur trade.
1670-1710	South Carolinians in Charleston encourage the development of a Native American slave trade across the Southeast.
1675-1676	King Philip's War. In response to English maltreatment, Metacomet (King Philip) launches a war against the English.
1676-1677	Bacon's Rebellion. Native Americans in Virginia fight a war of resistance but find themselves subject to Virginia rule.
1680	Pueblo (Popé's) Revolt. After decades of Spanish oppression, a Pueblo confederacy expels the Spanish from the Rio Grande region.
1682	Assiniboine and Cree begin to trade at York Factory, initiating European mercantile penetration of the Canadian west as far as the Rocky Mountains.
1689-1763	French and Indian Wars. King William's War initiates conflicts between the French and English that involve Native Americans and disrupt traditional patterns and alliances.
1692	Spanish reconquest of the Southwest (Nueva Mexico).
1695	Pima Uprising. Pimas burn missions in response to Spanish oppression.
c. 1700-1760	The horse diffuses across the Great Plains, prompting massive migrations and a cultural revolution.

Date	Event
1715-1717	Yamasee War. The Yamasee and their allies fight against the English for trading and other abuses.
1729	Natchez Revolt. Resisting French attempts to exact tribute, the Natchez go to war; the tribe is essentially destroyed, and many are sold into slavery.
1730	Articles of Agreement signed between the Cherokee Nation and King George II.
1740	Russia explores the Alaskan coast and begins trading operations.
1755	Some Iroquois settle near the Catholic mission of St. Regis, forming the nucleus of the Akwesasne Reserve.
1763	Proclamation of 1763. The Royal Proclamation of 1763 declares that Native Americans have title to all lands outside established colonies until the Crown legally purchases further land cessions.
1763-1764	Pontiac's War. Ottawa leader Pontiac constructs a multitribal alliance to resist the British.
1765	Paxton Riots (Paxton Boys Massacre). On December 14, 1765, seventy-five Europeans from Paxton, Pennsylvania, massacre and scalp six innocent Conestoga Mission Indians.
1768	Treaty of Fort Stanwix. The Iroquois Confederacy cedes lands south of the Ohio River (a later Fort Stanwix Treaty, 1784, changes the agreement).
1769	The California mission system is established.
1771	Labrador Inuit show missionaries where to build a trading post.
1774	Lord Dunmore's War. Lord Dunmore, the governor of Virginia, leads a fight against Shawnee led by Cornstalk.
1774-1775	The first Continental Congress establishes an Indian Department.
1777-1783	The Iroquois Confederacy is dispersed by the American Revolution.
1787	Northwest Ordinance. The U.S. Congress establishes a legal mechanism to create states from territories.
1789	The Indian Department becomes part of the U.S. Department of War.
1790	First of the Trade and Intercourse Acts enacted; they attempt to regulate trade between Europeans and Native Americans.
1790-1794	Little Turtle's War. Shawnee and their allies under Little Turtle defeat Anthony St. Clair's troops in 1791 but eventually are defeated at the Battle of Fallen Timbers, 1794, by General Anthony Wayne.
1795	Treaty of Fort Greenville. Native Americans of the Old Northwest are forced to treat with the United States after Britain refuses to assist them in their resistance efforts.
1796	Trading Houses Act. On April 18, 1796, the United States establishes government-operated trading houses.
1799	Handsome Lake, the Seneca Prophet, founds the *Gaiwiio*, "the Good Word," also known as the Longhouse religion; it becomes a strong force among the Iroquois.
1803	Louisiana Purchase. The United States acquires 800,000 square miles of new territory.
1804-1806	Lewis and Clark expedition. President Jefferson launches an expedition to collect information of national interest about Louisiana.

Date	Event
Date	*Event*
1809	Treaty of Fort Wayne. The Delaware are forced to relinquish approximately 3 million acres.
1809-1811	Tecumseh's Rebellion. Shawnee leader Tecumseh leads a multitribal force to resist United States incursions into their lands.
1811	Battle of Tippecanoe. William Henry Harrison and his forces attack and defeat Tecumseh's forces in Tecumseh's absence.
1812	War of 1812. Tribes of the Old Northwest are drawn into the European conflict.
1812	In August, the Hudson's Bay Company establishes the Red River Colony.
1813-1814	Red Stick civil war. Creeks fight a bloody civil war over disagreements about what their political relations with the United States should be.
1817-1818	First Seminole War. U.S. forces under General Andrew Jackson attack and burn Seminole villages.
1821	Sequoyah creates the Cherokee syllabary, the first system for writing an Indian language.
1823	*Johnson v. M'Intosh.* On February 28, 1823, the U.S. Supreme Court rules that Native American tribes have land rights.
1823	Office of Indian Affairs is created within the War Department.
1827	Cherokee Nation adopts a constitution.
1830	Indian Removal Act. At the urging of President Andrew Jackson, Congress orders the removal of all Native Americans to lands west of the Mississippi River. Removal proceeds from the 1830's to the 1850's.
1830	Treaty of Dancing Rabbit Creek. Choctaws cede more than 10 million acres in Alabama and Mississippi.
1830	Upper Canada establishes a system of reserves for Canadian natives.
1831	*Cherokee Nation v. Georgia.* U.S. Supreme Court rules that Native American tribes are "domestic dependent nations."
1832	Black Hawk War. Black Hawk, the Sauk and Fox leader leads a war to preserve their land rights.
1832	*Worcester v. Georgia.* U.S. Supreme Court rules that only the federal government has the right to regulate Indian affairs.
1834	Department of Indian Affairs is reorganized.
1835	Texas Rangers begin raids against the Comanche.
1835-1842	Second Seminole War. The Seminole resist removal to Indian Territory.
1838-1839	Forced removal of Cherokees to Indian Territory becomes a "Trail of Tears" marked by thousands of deaths.
1839	Upper Canadian Judge James Buchanan submits a report suggesting that Canadian natives should be assimilated into larger Canadian society.
1839	Taos Revolt. Taos Pueblos struggle against U.S. domination.
1848	Treaty of Guadalupe Hidalgo. United States acquires southwestern lands from Mexico.

Date	Event

Date   *Event*
1848-1849   California Gold Rush. Emigrants cross Native American lands, resulting in ecological destruction and spread of diseases.
1849   Metis Courthouse Rebellion. Metis resist Canadian domination.
1850   Period of genocide against California Indians begins and continues for some thirty years; thousands are killed.
1851   First Treaty of Fort Laramie. Great Plains Native Americans agree to allow emigrants safe passage across their territories.
1853   Gadsden Purchase. U.S. government purchases portions of Arizona, California, and New Mexico from Mexico.
1854-1864   Teton Dakota Resistance. The Teton Dakota and their allies resist U.S. intrusions into their lands.
1855   In the Northwest, Territorial Governor Isaac Stevens holds the Walla Walla Council and negotiates a series of treaties with Native American tribes.
1855-1856   Yakima War. Led by Kamiakin, who refused to sign the 1855 treaty, Yakimas fight U.S. forces after the murder of a government Indian agent initiates hostilities.
1855-1858   Third Seminole War. Seminoles react to the surveying of their lands.
1858   British Columbia Gold Rush precipitates large-scale invasion of Indian lands.
1858   Navajo War. Manuelito leads the Navajo against U.S. forces to fight against whites' grazing their horses on Navajo lands.
1860   The British transfer full responsibility of Canadian Indian affairs to the Province of Canada.
1862   Minnesota Uprising. Little Crow carries out a war of resistance against federal authority because of ill treatment.
1863-1868   Long Walk of the Navajo. In a violent campaign, U.S. forces remove the Navajo from their homeland and take them to Bosque Redondo.
1864   Sand Creek Massacre. Colorado militiamen under John Chivington massacre a peaceful group of Cheyennes at Sand Creek.
1866-1868   Bozeman Trail wars. Teton Dakota and their allies resist the building of army forts in their lands.
1867   U.S. government purchases Alaska.
1867   Canadian Confederation. The Dominion of Canada is created.
1867   Commission Act. Legislation calls for the U.S. president to establish commissions to negotiate peace treaties with Native American nations.
1868   Second Treaty of Fort Laramie pledges the protection of Indian lands.
1868   Canadian government adopts an Indian policy aimed at the assimilation of Indians into Canadian society.
1868   Washita River Massacre. A peaceful Cheyenne camp is massacred by the U.S. Seventh Cavalry.
1869   First Riel Rebellion. Louis Riel leads the Metis in resisting Canadian domination; partly triggered by white surveying of Metis lands.

Date	Event
1870	Grant's Peace Policy. President Ulysses S. Grant assigns various Christian denominations to various Indian reservation agencies in order to Christianize and pacify the Indians.
1871	Congress passes an act on March 3 that ends treaty negotiations with Native American nations.
1871	*McKay v. Campbell*. U.S. Supreme Court holds that Indian people born with "tribal allegiance" are not U.S. citizens.
1871	Canada begins negotiating the first of eleven "numbered" treaties with Native Canadians.
1871-1890	Wholesale destruction of the bison on the Plains.
1872-1873	Modoc War. The Modoc resist removal to the Klamath Reservation.
1874	Canadian Northwest Mounted Police move to establish order in the Canadian West.
1874-1875	Red River War. Forced by starvation and Indian agent corruption, Kiowa, Plains Apache, Southern Cheyenne, and Arapaho raid European American farms and ranches to feed their families.
1876	First Indian Act of Canada. The act consolidated Canadian policies toward its indigenous people.
1876	Battle of the Little Bighorn. General Custer and the Seventh Cavalry are annihilated by the Sioux, Cheyenne, and Arapaho camped along the Little Bighorn River.
1877	The Nez Perce are exiled from their homeland and pursued by U.S. forces as they unsuccessfully attempt to escape into Canada.
1877	Battle of Wolf Mountain. The last fight between the Cheyenne and the U.S. Army.
1877-1883	The Northern Cheyenne are forcibly removed to Indian Territory but escape north to their homelands.
1878	Bannock War. Because of settler pressures, the Bannock are forced to raid for food.
1879	Carlisle Indian School, a boarding school with the goal of "civilizing" Indian youth, is founded by Captain Richard H. Pratt.
1880	Canadian officials modify the 1876 Indian Act, empowering it to impose elected councils on bands.
1885	Second Riel Rebellion. Louis Riel leads a second protest, then armed revolt, among the Canadian Metis and Cree; defeated, Riel is executed after the rebellion.
1887	General Allotment Act (Dawes Severalty Act). Provides for the dividing of reservation lands into individual parcels to expedite assimilation. (By the early twentieth century, the allotment policy is viewed as disastrous.)
1890	Wounded Knee Massacre. The Seventh Cavalry intercepts a group of Sioux Ghost Dancers being led by Big Foot to the Pine Ridge Reservation. When a Sioux warrior, perhaps accidentally, fires his rifle, the army opens fire; hundreds of Sioux, most unarmed, are massacred.
1897	Education Appropriation Act mandates funding for Indian day schools and technical schools.

Date	Event
1897	Indian Liquor Act bans the sale or distribution of liquor to Native Americans.
1903	*Lone Wolf v. Hitchcock.* U.S. Supreme Court rules that Congress has the authority to dispose of Native American lands.
1906	Burke Act. Congress amends the General Allotment Act to shorten the trust period for individual Native Americans who are proven "competent."
1906	Alaskan Allotment Act. Allows Alaska Natives to file for 160-acre parcels.
1910	Omnibus Act. Establishes procedures to determine Native American heirship of trust lands and other resources.
1912	Classification and Appraisal of Unallotted Indian Lands Act. Permits the Secretary of Interior to reappraise and reclassify unallotted Indian lands.
1924	General Citizenship Act. As a result of Native American participation in World War I, Congress grants some Native Americans citizenship.
1928	Meriam Report outlines the failure of previous Indian policies and calls for reform.
1932	Alberta Metis Organization is founded by Joseph Dion.
1934	Indian Reorganization Act. Implements the Meriam Report recommendations, reversing many previous policies.
1934	Johnson-O'Malley Act replaces the General Allotment Act.
1936	Oklahoma Indian Welfare Act. Extends many of the rights provided by the Indian Reorganization Act of 1934 to Oklahoma Indian nations.
1944	National Congress of American Indians is founded to guard Native American rights.
1946	Indian Claims Commission Act. Provides a legal forum for tribes to sue the federal government for the loss of lands.
1950	Navajo and Hopi Rehabilitation Act is passed to assist the tribes in developing their natural resources.
1951	Indian Act of 1951. A new Canadian Indian Act reduces the powers of the Indian Affairs Department but retains an assimilationist agenda.
1951	Public Law 280 allows greater state jurisdiction over criminal cases involving Native Americans from California, Wisconsin, Minnesota, and Nebraska (extended to Alaska Natives in 1959).
1953	Termination Resolution. Congress initiates a policy (which continues into the early 1960's) of severing the federal government's relationships with Native American nations.
1955	Indian Health Service is transferred from the Department of the Interior to the Department of Health, Education, and Welfare.
1961	Chicago Indian Conference, organized by anthropologist Sol Tax, mobilizes Indian leaders to reassert their rights.
1961	National Indian Youth Council is founded by Clyde Warrior and others.

Date	*Event*
1963	State of Washington rules against Native American fishing rights.
1964	American Indian Historical Society is founded to research and teach about Native Americans.
1966	Hawthorn Report examines the conditions of contemporary Canadian natives and recommends that Indians be considered "citizens plus."
1968	American Indian Civil Rights Act guarantees reservation residents many of the civil liberties other citizens have under the U.S. Constitution.
1968	American Indian Movement (AIM) is founded in Minneapolis by Dennis Banks and Russell Means.
1969	Canadian government's White Paper of 1969 rejects the Hawthorn Report's recommendations, arguing that Canadian natives' special status hinders their assimilation and urging the abolition of the Indian Affairs Department and Indian Act.
1969	Occupation of Alcatraz Island by Native American people begins (continues through 1971).
1971	Alaska Native Claims Settlement Act marks the beginning of the self-determination period for Alaska Natives.
1972	Trail of Broken Treaties Caravan proceeds to Washington, D.C., to protest treaty violations.
1972	Native American Rights Fund (NARF) is founded to carry Indian issues to court.
1972	Indian Education Act enacted; it is intended to improve the quality of education for Native Americans (the act is revised in 1978).
1973	Wounded Knee occupation. More than two hundred Native American activists occupy the historic site to demonstrate against oppressive Sioux reservation policies.
1974	Navajo-Hopi Land Settlement Act facilitates negotiation between the two nations over the disputed Joint Use Area.
1975	Indian Self-Determination and Education Assistance Act expands tribal control over tribal governments and education.
1975	Political violence increases on the Pine Ridge Reservation; two FBI agents are killed in a shootout on June 26.
1975	James Bay and Northern Quebec Agreement is signed; Quebec Cree, Inuit, Naskapi, and Montagnais groups cede tribal lands in exchange for money and specified hunting and fishing rights.
1977	American Indian Policy Review Commission Report is released by Congress, recommending that Native American nations be considered sovereign political bodies.
1978	American Indian Freedom of Religion Act protects the rights of Native Americans to follow traditional religious practices.
1978	Federal Acknowledgment Program is initiated to provide guidelines for and assist tribes seeking official recognition by the federal government.
1978	Indian Child Welfare Act proclaims tribal jurisdiction over child custody decisions.

Date	Event
1978	The Longest Walk, a march from Alcatraz Island to Washington, D.C., protests government treatment of Indians.
1980	*United States v. Sioux Nation.* U.S. Supreme Court upholds a $122 million judgment against the United States for illegally taking the Black Hills.
1981	Hopi-Navajo Joint Use Area is partitioned between the Navajo and Hopi nations.
1982	Canada's Constitution Act (Constitution and Charter of Rights and Freedoms) is passed despite the protests of Indian, Metis, and Inuit groups.
1982	Indian Claims Limitation Act limits the time period during which claims can be filed against the U.S. government.
1985	Coolican Report declares that little progress is being made to settle Canadian native land claims.
1988	Indian Gaming Regulatory Act officially legalizes certain types of gambling on reservations and establishes the National Indian Gaming Commission.
1989	U.S. Congress approves construction of the National Museum of the American Indian, to be part of the Smithsonian Institution.
1989	Violence erupts on St. Regis Mohawk Reservation in dispute over whether to allow gambling; under guard by state and federal law enforcement officers, the tribe votes to allow gambling on the reservation.
1990	The U.S. Census finds the Native American population to be 1,959,234.
1990	In *Duro v. Reina*, the U.S. Supreme Court holds that tribes cannot have criminal jurisdiction over non-Indians on reservation lands.
1990	Canada's proposed Meech Lake Accord (amendments to the 1982 Constitution Act) is sent to defeat in Canada by native legislator Elijah Harper; the accord provided no recognition of native rights.
1991	Tribal Self-Governance Act extends the number of tribes involved in the self-governance pilot project.
1992	Native Americans protest the Columbian Quincentenary.
1992	In a plebiscite, residents of Canada's Northwest Territories approve the future creation of Nunavut, a territory to be governed by the Inuit.
1993	The International Year of Indigenous People.
1994	National Museum of the American Indian opens its first facility in New York's Heye Center (a larger museum is planned for the Mall in Washington, D.C.).
1994	The National Congress of American Indians and the National Black Caucus of State Legislators ally themselves, agreeing that they face similar political and economic forces of oppression.
1998	Canadian minister of Indian Affairs formally apologizes to Indian and Inuit peoples for past government atttempts to destroy native cultures.
1999	Eastern portion of Canada's Northwest Territories becomes new territory of Nunavut.

MEDIAGRAPHY

Select films dealing with American Indians. Documentary films are listed first, followed by feature films. A selection of Web sites, sound recordings, and CD-ROMs follows the list of film and video treatments.

EDUCATIONAL AND DOCUMENTARY FILMS

Again, a Whole Person I Have Become
Color. 19 min. 16mm.
Shenandoah Film Productions (1982)
  Stresses the importance of traditional Indian customs for Indian youth. Three tribal elders speak of the wisdom of the old ways; dances and ceremonies are portrayed. Will Sampson narrates.

Age of the Buffalo
Color. 14 min. 16mm.
National Film Board of Canada (1964)
  Shows how the buffalo met the needs of the Indians for food, clothing, shelter, and adventure, and how life changed when the buffalo were gone.

The American Indian
Color. 62 min. VHS.
Library Distributors of America (1993)
  Broad view of the origin and culture of American Indians; also examines interactions between Indians and whites.

The American Indian: After the White Man Came
Color. 27 min. 16mm.
Handel Film Corporation (1972)
  Extensive examination of American Indians since European discovery of the Americas. Moves to a discussion of the problems facing modern Indians.

The American Indian: Before the White Man
Color. 19 min. 16mm.
Handel Film Corporation (1972)
  Comprehensive study of American Indians from the early migration routes to the development of the main tribes of North America. Narrated by Iron Eyes Cody.

American Indian in Transition
Color. 22 min. 16mm.
Atlantis Productions (1976)
  Presents an Indian point of view about land and heritage, narrated by an Indian mother who uses Indian chronicles and sayings. Provides a compassionate insight into Indian life and thought.

American Indian Influence on the United States
Color. 20 min. 16mm.
Robert Davis Productions (1972)
  Depicts the manner in which life in the United States has been influenced by the American Indian economically, sociologically, philosophically, and culturally. Nine dances and ceremonies are authentically portrayed. The graphics used in the film include original Indian illustrations.

The American Indian Speaks
Color. 23 min. 16mm.
Encyclopedia Britannica Educational Corporation (1973)

Members of three Indian cultures state the position and attitudes of American Indians in the twentieth century. Includes remembrances of the Trail of Tears and Wounded Knee.

The American Indian Struggle
Color. 29 min. VHS.
Kent State University (1981)
Examination of several important episodes that contributed to the long history of conflict between American Indians and white settlers. With Kent State University professors James Gidney and Philip Weeks.

American Indians: A Brief History
Color. 22 min. 16mm.
National Geographic Society (1985)
Numerous examples of diverse Indian artistic and cultural traditions. Provides a history of the roots of conflict between the Indians and European settlers. Identifies several settlements and tribes that existed before Columbus arrived in America.

American Indians as Seen by D. H. Lawrence
Color. 14 min. 16mm.
Lewin/Cort (1966)
At the D. H. Lawrence ranch near Taos, New Mexico, Lawrence's wife, Frieda, speaks about his beliefs and thoughts. Aldous Huxley presents selections from Lawrence's works.

The Americans: The Buffalo Story
Color. 28 min. 16mm.
O'Laughlin Company (1971)
The great usefulness of the buffalo to the Plains Indians is detailed; it furnished them with food, clothing, and shelter. Buffalo masks convey the spirit of the annual Spring Buffalo Dance.

The Americans: Chief Black Hawk
Color. 23 min. 16mm.
O'Laughlin Company (1971)

Chief White Eagle explains the meaning and logic of sign language and various war paint designs. The story of Black Hawk, war chief of the Sauk Indians, follows, dramatized by paintings and sound effects.

The Americans: Chief Crazy Horse
Color. 26 min. 16mm.
O'Laughlin Company (1971)
Beginning with the Bering Strait migration theory of Indian prehistory, Chief White Eagle moves into a description of Indian cultural evolution, including introduction of horses. Crazy Horse, brilliant leader and military strategist of the Sioux, is profiled.

The Americans: Chief Joseph
Color. 23 min. 16mm.
O'Laughlin Company (1971)
After describing the kinds of horses that Indians used for various purposes and how these horses were trained, Chief White Eagle tells the story of Chief Joseph and the Nez Perce.

The Americans: Geronimo
Color. 25 min. 16mm.
O'Laughlin Company (1971)
The Indians' closeness to nature and ability to forecast weather are discussed. Geronimo is profiled.

America's Great Indian Leaders
Color. 65 min. VHS.
Questar (1994)
Examines the lives and contributions of Crazy Horse, Chief Joseph, Geronimo, and Quanah Parker, who emerged to protect their people and culture.

America's Great Indian Nations
Color. 65 min. VHS.
Questar (1995)
Profiles six of the most powerful tribes in American history: the Iroquois,

Seminoles, Shawnee, Navajo, Cheyenne, and Lakota Sioux.

America's Indians
Six-part series.
Color. 13 min. each. VHS.
Films for the Humanities & Sciences
(1993)

The Indians Were There First
How North American Indians entered the Americas from Asia; various tribes and some of their characteristics.

When the White Man Came
Life among the major tribes before Europeans arrived.

The Bison Hunters
How the Indian became mythologized as the eastern United States became industrialized.

The Trail of Tears
The harm done by explorers and pioneers.

The Warpath
How pioneers moving westward ignored treaties reserving land for Indians.

The Death of the Bison
The many Native American issues that remain unresolved.

Ann of the Wolf Clan
Color. 60 min. VHS.
Rainbow TV Works; Great Plains
   Instructional TV, University of
   Nebraska (1982)
Young, middle class Indian girl receives the gift of her Cherokee heritage from her great-grandmother while spending a summer on the reservation.

Apache
Color. 30 min. VHS.
Schlessinger Video Productions (1993)
Examines the history, changing fortunes, and current situation of the Apache

tribe. Includes a discussion of their crafts. For grades 5-10.

Apache Indian
Black and white. 11 min. 16mm.
Cort (1943)
Shows the life, ceremonies, and industries of the Apaches. The beauty of their native territory forms the setting for the tribal functions and ceremonies, including a puberty ceremony and devil dance.

The Apache Indian (Revised version)
Color. 11 min. 16mm. VHS.
Cort (1975)
Acquaints young viewers with the life, culture, and traditions of the Apache of Arizona. Emphasizes the problems that modern living has caused and the Apaches' struggle for education, health care, and economic opportunity.

Arrow to the Sun
Color. 22 min. 16mm.
Texture (1973)
Animated film by Gerald McDermott that illustrates a tale from the Acoma Pueblo of the Southwest. A boy's search for his father leads him to a dazzling voyage on an arrow to the sun.

The Ballad of Crowfoot
Color/black and white. 11 min. 16mm.
   VHS.
National Film Board of
   Canada/McGraw-Hill (1968)
Documents the events and problems that characterized the relationship between whites and Indians since whites arrived in the Canadian West in the 1820's. Records Indian traditions and attitudes.

Before the White Man Came
Black and white. 50 min. Silent. 16mm
Northwestern Film Corp. (1921)

Filmed in the Bighorn Mountains of Montana and Wyoming in 1921. In an enactment by Indians, every effort was made to present life as it was before the arrival of whites.

Behind the Masks
Color. 24 min. 16mm.
National Film Board of Canada (1973)
Study of the meaning and myths behind the masks of the tribes of the Northwest Coast. Commentary and analysis by Claude Levi-Strauss, noted French anthropologist.

Black Indians of New Orleans
Color. 33 min. 16mm.
Maurice M. Martinez (1976)
Depicts the activities of highly organized groups of African Americans with mixed Indian ancestry as they prepare for Mardi Gras, with emphasis on their distinctive music, dancing, and costumes.

Bones of Contention: Native American Archaeology
Color. 49 min. VHS
Films for the Humanities & Sciences (1998)
Examines the conflict between Native American groups and scientists, historians, and museum curators concerning the issue of the remains of more than 10,000 Native Americans unearthed at archaeological sites across the United States.

Boy of the Navajos
Color. 11 min. 16mm.
Cort (1975)
Shows the living habits and activities of a Navajo family in Arizona, with emphasis on the teenage son.

Boy of the Seminoles: Indians of the Everglades
Color/black and white. 11 min. 16mm.
Cort (1956)

Shows the living habits and activities of a teenage Seminole boy and his family in Florida.

The Broken Cord: Louise Erdrich and Michael Dorris
Color. 30 min. VHS.
PBS Video (1991)
Authors Louise Erdrich and the late Michael Dorris explain how traditions of spirit and memory weave through the lives of many Native Americans, and how alcoholism and despair have shattered so many other lives. The devastating effect of fetal alcohol syndrome on their adopted son, and on the Native American community as a whole, is also discussed. Hosted by Bill Moyers.

Broken Treaty at Battle Mountain
Color. 73 min. 16mm.
Cinnamon Production (1973)
The struggle of the Western Shoshone of Nevada to retain their culture and land is dramatically portrayed. The Shoshone struggle to keep 24 million acres of Nevada land originally promised to them by the U.S. government. Narrated by Robert Redford.

Catlin and the Indians
Color. 25 min. 16mm.
National Film Board of Canada/McGraw-Hill (1967)
Presents biographical material on George Catlin, historian and painter of Plains Indians. Includes paintings from the Smithsonian's Catlin collection.

Cherokee
Color. 26 min. 16mm.
British Broadcasting Corporation (1976)
Explores the dilemma the Cherokees face in preserving their traditions and captures the beauty of the pageants and ceremonies performed today. Includes scenes from a pageant play that recounts Cherokee history.

Cherokee
Color. 30 min. VHS.
Schlessinger Video Productions (1993)

Examines the history and current situation of the Cherokee people. Includes facts about the role of the U.S. government, debunks myths about Native Americans, explores their spiritual relationship with nature, and discusses the role of women in their societies. For grades 5-10.

Cheyenne
Color. 30 min. VHS.
Schlessinger Video Productions (1993)

Examines the history, changing fortunes, and current situation of the Cheyenne tribe. Includes facts about the role of the U.S. government, debunks myths about Native Americans, explores their spiritual relationship with nature, and discusses the role of women in their societies. For grades 5-10.

Children of the Eagle: A Tribute to
    American Indian Children
Color. 28 min. 16mm.
Oklahoma State University

Describes the American Indian family and contrasts contemporary family life with traditional Indian customs. Presents prenatal concerns, parenting behavior, and funeral rituals.

Circle of the Sun
Color. 30 min. 16mm. VHS.
National Film Board of Canada (1960)

Studies the way of life and ceremonial customs of the Blood Indians circa 1960. Pictures the Sun Dance camp and analyzes the feelings of the younger generation about the old Indian customs and the influences of whites.

Columbus Didn't Discover Us
Color. 24 min. VHS.
Turning Tide Productions (1992)

In preparation for the Columbus Quincentennial, 300 Native men and women came to the highlands of Ecuador to take part in the first Continental Conference of Indigenous Peoples. Features interviews with participants representing a wide spectrum of Indian nations from North, South, and Central America.

Comanche
Color. 30 min. VHS.
Schlessinger Video Productions (1993)

Portrayal of the Comanche tribe including their history, culture and way of life today. Challenges many prevalent myths and stereotypes. Examines the issue of the role of the U.S. government, debunks myths about Native Americans, explores their spiritual relationship with nature, and discusses the role of women in their societies. For grades 5-10.

Contrary Warriors
Color. 60 min. 16mm. VHS.
Rattlesnake Productions (1987)

The Crazy Dogs, one of the original Crow warrior societies, declared themselves "contrary warriors" and pledged to risk death when challenged by outsiders.

Corn Is Life
Color. 11 min. 16mm. VHS.
University of California Extension
    Media Center (1983)

Shows and explains traditional activities associated with corn that are still an important part of Hopi family and community life. Corn, a major cultural symbol, plays a central role in the life of every Hopi.

The Creek
Color. 30 min. VHS.
Schlessinger Video Productions (1993)

Examines the history and current situation of the Creek. Includes a discussion of their language, traditions, and crafts. For grades 5-10.

The Crow
Color. 30 min. VHS.
Schlessinger Video Productions (1993)

Examines the history and current situation of the Crow, a mobile group of hunters who developed a strict code of conduct and a deeply spiritual religion. For grades 5-10.

Crow Dog
Color. 57 min. 16mm.
Cinema Guild (1979)

Focuses on Leonard Crow Dog, spiritual leader of eighty-nine American Indian tribes and a spokesman for many Indians who wish to retain the beliefs and way of life of their forefathers. Documents the politics and spiritual power of the American Indian Movement.

Cry of the Yurok
Color. 58 min. VHS.
Films for the Humanities & Sciences (1991)

Details the many problems of the Yurok tribe of California as they struggle to survive encroachment of their lands. Some remain on the reservation, others have moved to cities. All are caught in a many-sided battle between the dominant white world and the world of the Indian.

Custer at the Washita
Color. 26 min. 16mm. VHS.
McGraw-Hill (1966)

Account of the Battle of the Washita River, one of the few decisive battles of the American Indian wars. It signaled the end of freedom for the Cheyenne and planted the seeds of Custer's defeat at the Little Bighorn.

Dineh Nation: The Navajo Story
Color. 26 min. VHS.
Filmmakers Library (1991)

Focuses on the Navajo people who inhabit the Sovereign Dineh Indian Reservation which occupies parts of Arizona, New Mexico and Utah—an area rich in oil, coal, and uranium. The Navajo seek to preserve the land but outside forces are at work, strip mining the coal and polluting the water. Film emphasizes the spiritual essence of the Navajo people who consider Mother Earth to be sacred and forbid exploitation of her resources.

Discovering American Indian Music
Color. 24 min. 16mm. VHS.
Inform (1971)

Introduces the traditional customs, costumes, and dances associated with the music of eleven representative North American tribes, principally of the Plains and Southwest.

The Drummaker
Color. 37 min. 16mm.
Pennsylvania State University Psych Cinema Register (1978)

Presents William Bineshi Baker, Sr., an Ojibwa, one of the last of his people to perfect the art of drummaking. He discusses tradition and his frustration with those who will not take the time to follow it.

End of the Trail: The American Plains Indian
Black and white. 53 min. 16mm. VHS.
McGraw-Hill (1967)

Documents the growth and development of the Plains Indian culture, which culminate with the advent of whites. Illustrates many of the hostile acts inflicted by both sides.

Family Life of the Navajo Indians
Black and white. 31 min. Silent. 16mm.
New York University (1943)

Highlights some of the ways the Navajo child becomes an adult.

500 Nations
Eight-part series.
Color. 376 min. VHS.
Warner Home Video (1995)

An 8-part CBS television documentary exploring the history and culture of Native Americans. Episodes are:

The Ancestors: Early Cultures of North America

Mexico: The Rise and Fall of the Aztecs

Clash of Cultures: The People Who Met Columbus

Invasion of the Coast: The First English Settlements

Cauldron of War: Iroquois Democracy and the American Revolution

Removal: War and Exile in the East

Roads Across the Plains: Struggle for the West

Attack on Culture: I Will Fight No More Forever

Gatecliff: American Indian Rock Shelter
Color. 21 min. 16mm.
National Geographic Society (1973)

Team of amateur archaeologists led by Dr. David Hurst Thomas of the American Museum of Natural History dig in Gatecliff Rock Shelter in Nevada. Layer-by-layer examination reveals information on inhabitants of 5,000 years ago.

Geronimo and the Apache Resistance
Color. 60 min. VHS.
PBS Home Video (1990)

In 1886, the U.S. government mobilized five thousand men, one quarter of the entire U.S. Army, to capture Geronimo. This profile of Geronimo, believed by his people to have magical powers, highlights the clash of cultures and the legacy of the battles of a century ago. (Part of the PBS series *The American Experience*.)

Girl of the Navajos
Color. 15 min. 16mm.
Inform/Cort (1977)

Young Navajo girl recalls her feelings of fear and loneliness the first time she had to herd her family's sheep into the canyon alone. Returning to the canyon the following day, she becomes friends with another girl. Filmed on a Navajo reservation.

Giving Thanks: A Native American Good Morning Message
Color. 30 min. VHS.
Great Plains National TV Library (1996)

Based on the book by Chief Jake Swamp. Presents a Mohawk prayer celebrating the beauty, bounty and resources of the Earth. Part of the Reading Rainbow series hosted by LeVar Burton.

The Great Movie Massacre
Color. 28 min. 16mm.
United Indians of All Tribes Foundation (1979)

Explores the beginning of the "savage Indian" myth in popular American literature and entertainment, including wild west shows and early motion pictures. Will Sampson narrates. (Images of Indians Series.)

The Great Plains Experience: The Lakota—One Nation on the Plains
Color. 30 min. 16mm. VHS.
University of Mid-America (1976)

Describes the movement of Indians onto the Great Plains and their adaptation to the new environment, focusing on the Lakota in the eighteenth century.

A History of Native Americans
Color. 30 min. VHS.
Schlessinger Video Productions (1993)

Examines the impact of European colonization on Native American tribes, including co-existence and trade, the struggles over land ownership and the effects of European imports like guns, horses, alcohol, religion and disease. Covers the policies of the U.S. government, the forced removal of Indians in the Trail of Tears, the Indian Removal Act and Indian boarding schools that diluted tribal cultures and shared beliefs. For grades 5-10.

Home of the Brave
Color. 4 min. 16mm.
Pyramid Film and Video (1969)
    The five-hundred-year story of a people is documented with great precision in this four-minute encapsulation.

Hopi: Songs of the Fourth World
Color. 58 min. 16mm. VHS.
Newday (no date given)
    Study of the Hopi that captures their spirituality and reveals their integration of art and daily life. A farmer, religious elder, grandmother, painter, potter, and weaver speak about the preservation of the Hopi way.

Hopi Indian Arts and Crafts (Revised version)
Color. 10 min. 16mm.
Cort (1975)
    Hopis are shown using their ancient tools and knowledge in basketweaving, potterymaking, silverworking, and weaving. Shows how methods of working are changing.

Hopi Indian Village Life
Color/Black and White. 11 min. 16mm.
Cort (1956)
    Pictures the Hopi and their mode of living as it existed in the 1950's, emphasizing the changing character of Hopi life and work.

Hopi Kachinas
Color. 9 min. 16mm.
Inform (1961)

    The Hopi kachina doll is intended primarily to teach Hopi children to see meaning in religious rituals and dances. Shows an artisan carving, assembling, and painting a doll; also shows Hopi life and dances.

Hopi Snake Dance
Black and White. 10 min. 16mm.
Inform (1951)
    Presents the preparations of the dancers, handling of snakes, costumes, and part of a snake dance.

Hopis: Guardians of the Land
Color. 10 min. 16mm.
Inform (1972)
    Hopi living on an Arizona reservation explains the tribal philosophy of seeking peace, brotherhood, and everlasting life by caring for all that is on the land. A nearby power plant and strip-mining operations threaten the union of people and land.

How Hollywood Wins the West
Color. 29 min. 16mm.
United Indians of All Tribes
    Foundation (1979)
    Explores the concept of Manifest Destiny, which encouraged the taking of Indian lands that "nobody owned" by whites in the early nineteenth century.

How the West Was Lost
Color. 300 min. VHS.
Discovery Enterprises Group (1993)
    Three-part Discovery Channel series exploring the history and culture of Native Americans. Documents the devastating effects of westward expansion on five Native American nations: the Navajo, Nez Perce, Apache, Cheyenne, and Lakota, through the recollection of their descendants, archival photographs, and historical documents.

How the West Was Lost II
Discovery Enterprises Group (1995)
Color. 350 min. VHS.

Four additional episodes of *How the West Was Lost* explore the Native American experience during the eighteenth and nineteenth centuries. Chronicles the history of the Iroquois, Cherokee, Seminole, Dakota, Modoc, Ute, and the Indian Territory.

How to Trace Your Native American Heritage
Color. 30 min. VHS.
Rich-Heape Films (1998)

Guide to discovering one's Native American roots. Explains how to obtain tribal membership and official Native American status.

The Huron
Color. 30 min. VHS.
Schlessinger Video Productions (1993)

Profiles the Huron, who flourished in southern Ontario, Canada. Originally farmers and craftsmen, a small Huron community still survives in Canada, manufacturing goods for sale or trade while maintaining the Huron heritage. For grades 5-10.

I Will Fight No More Forever: The Story of Chief Joseph
Color. 106 min. 16mm. VHS.
Wolper Productions (1975)

How Chief Joseph led three hundred Nez Perce braves along with their women and children in the historic running battle against ten separate commands of the army in 1877.

Incident at Oglala
Color. 90 min. VHS.
Miramax (1992)

Reexamines the evidence in the 1975 murder case of two FBI agents on the Pine Ridge Reservation. The conviction of Leonard Peltier for the murders appears to be a travesty of justice. Directed by Michael Apted; narrated by Robert Redford.

Indians Among Us
Color. 46 min. VHS.
Discovery Communications (1992)

Focuses on the Indians of the American Southwest and how they try to maintain their old traditions within a modern lifestyle. Originally part of the television program *Roger Kennedy's Rediscovering America*.

Indian Art of the Pueblo
Color. 13 min. 16mm.
Encyclopedia Britannica Educational Corporation (1976)

Introduces the arts and crafts of the Pueblo.

Indian Ceremonial Dances of the Southwest
Color. 11 min. 16mm.
Harold Ambrosch Film Productions (1954)

Presents a number of Southwest dances, accompanied by songs and chants. Includes the Apache crown or devil dance, the Laguna shield dance, and the Taos war dance.

Indian Crafts: Hopi, Navajo, and Iroquois
Color. 12 min. 16mm.
BFA Educational Media (1980)

Basketmaking, weaving, potterymaking, kachina carving, jewelrymaking, and mask carving.

Indian Heroes of America
Color. 17 min. 16mm.
Altana Films (1979)

Seven Indian personages are profiled, each representing an aspect of history from the coming of whites to the final confrontations in the late nineteenth century.

Indian Hunters
Black and white. 10 min. 16mm.
Inform (1948)

Shows two Indians seeking new hunting grounds for their band in the wilds of northern Canada.

Indian Musical Instruments
Color. 14 min. 16mm.
University of Oklahoma

Shows big dance drums, rawhide drums, ring and straight beaters, and other Indian musical instruments in the University of Oklahoma museum.

The Indian Speaks
Color. 41 min. 16mm.
National Film Board of Canada (1970)

Presents Indians in parts of Canada who are concerned about preserving what is left of their culture and restoring what is gone.

Indians: The Navajos
Color. 14 min. 16mm.
Hearst Metrotone News (1975)

Examines the winds of change that have been affecting the lives of 140,000 Navajos on the largest Indian reservation in the world.

In the White Man's Image
Color. 58 min. VHS.
PBS Video (1991)

Examines the experiment of federal government boarding schools for Indian children. Tells the story of the attempt to assimilate American Indians into white culture by educating them at special schools such as the Carlisle School for Indians. Founded by Richard Henry Pratt, this school and others like it attempted to wipe out all remnants of Indian culture. Narrated by Stacy Keach. Originally broadcast as an episode of the PBS television series *The American Experience*.

Into the Circle: An Introduction to Native American Powwows.
Color. 58 min. VHS.
Full Circle Communications (1992)

An introduction to Oklahoma powwows through excerpts of dances, songs and drumming sequences, interviews with tribal elders and participants, and historical photographs showing the ongoing evolution of the powwow. Narrated by J. R. Mathews.

In Whose Honor?: American Indian Mascots in Sports
Color. 47 min. VHS.
New Day Films (1997)

Discussion of Chief Illinewek as the University of Illinois mascot and the effect the mascot has on Native American peoples. Examines the practice of using American Indian mascots and nicknames in sports.

Iroquois
Color. 30 min. VHS.
Schlessinger Video Productions (1993)

Portrayal of the Iroquois including their history, culture and way of life today. Challenges many still-prevalent myths and stereotypes. Examines the issue of the role of the U.S. government, debunks myths about Native Americans, explores their spiritual relationship with nature, and discusses the role of women in their societies. For grades 5-10.

Ishi, the Last Yahi
Color. 58 min. VHS.
Rattlesnake Productions (1993)
Distributed by Center for Media and
    Independent Learning, Berkeley,
    Calif.; Shanachie Entertainment,
    Newton, N.J.

Award-winning profile of Ishi, a California Indian who came out of hiding in 1911 and lived at the anthropology museum of the University of California at Berkeley until his death in 1916.

Late Woodland Village
Color. 20 min. 16mm.
University of Iowa AV Center (1974)
    Excavations of the late Woodland Hartley Fort revealed details of life in a stockaded village of about 900 C.E.

Legend of Corn
Color. 26 min. 16mm.
Films for the Humanities & Sciences (1985)
    An Ojibwa legend, dramatized by tribespeople, about how the Great Manitou saved the tribe from starvation.

The Lenape
Color. 30 min. VHS.
Schlessinger Video Productions (1993)
    Examines the history of the Lenape, who settled in the mid-Atlantic region over 5,000 years ago. Today, the largest population of the tribe now lives on part of the Cherokee Nation reservation. For grades 5-10.

Life in the Woodlands Before the White Man Came
Color. 12 min. 16mm.
ACI Media (1976)
    Dramatizes the daily life, ceremonies, and rituals of Woodlands Indians before whites arrived.

The Maya
Color. 30 min. VHS.
Schlessinger Video Productions (1993)
    Examines the ancient civilization of the Maya, their temples, palaces, and immense cities in Mexico's Yucatan Peninsula and Guatemala. For grades 5-10.

The Maya: Temples, Tombs, and Time
Color. 53 min. VHS.
Questar (1995)
    Breakthroughs in deciphering Maya glyphs and new archeological discoveries help to provide a fresh look at the Maya, considered to be one of the most advanced of the indigenous peoples of the Americas.

Meet the Sioux Indian
Color. 11 min. 16mm.
Associated Film Artists (1949)
    Portrays the nomadic life of the Sioux and shows how they obtained, prepared, and preserved food, and made clothing.

The Menominee
Color. 30 min. VHS.
Schlessinger Video Productions (1993)
    Examines the history of the Menominee, hunters and fishermen, who lived in lodges along the upper peninsula of present day Michigan. For grades 5-10.

Mesa Verde: Mystery of the Silent Cities
Color. 14 min. 16mm.
Encyclopedia Britannica Educational Corporation (1975)
    Extensive aerial photography of the ruined cities and multiple-family cliff dwellings of a thirteenth-century civilization. Narrated by Jack Palance.

Mino-Bimadiziwin: The Good Life
Color. 60 min. VHS.
Deb Wallwork Productions (1998)
    Examines the ancient Ojibwe tradition of wild rice harvesting still practiced on Minnesota's White Earth Indian Reservation. An in-depth portrait of a community whose people continue to live off the land. Explores the themes of continuity and change in Native American society at large.

Modern Chippewa Indians
Color. 11 min. 16mm.
Simmel-Miservey (1946)
    Shows the life and work of the Chippewa Indians on the Red Lake Reservation in Minnesota.

Momaday: Voice of the West
Color. 30 min. VHS.
PBS Home Video (1992)
　Profiles Pulitzer prize-winning author, painter, poet and teacher, N. Scott Momaday, who reads from his memoirs and published works.

More Than Bows and Arrows
Color. 56 min. VHS.
Camera One Productions (1992)
　Documents the contributions of American Indians to the development of the United States and Canada. Deals with the role of the American Indian in shaping various aspects of American culture, ranging from food and housing to our view of life. Narrated by N. Scott Momaday.

Myths and Moundbuilders
Color. 60 min. VHS.
PBS Home Video (1990)
　Examines the ancient Native American practice of mound building. Features archaeological excavations of mounds and examines pottery, jewelry, and other artifacts unearthed.

Nanook of the North
Black and white. Silent. VHS.
Pathé Exchange (1922)
　This landmark of documentary filmmaking caused a sensation when it was released. Robert Flaherty spent sixteen months in the Arctic filming an Inuit family. Some events were enacted specifically for the camera, but the portrait of Arctic life is generally realistic.

The Narragansett
Color. 30 min. VHS.
Schlessinger Video Productions (1993)
　Profiles the southern Rhode Island tribe which was once the largest and most powerful of the Northeast, with ancestry dating back 11,000 years. For grades 5-10.

The Native Americans
Color. 264 min. VHS.
Turner Home Entertainment, (1994)
　Six-part TBS television documentary exploring the history and culture of Native Americans. Series takes a regional look at Indians of the Northeast, Far West, Southeast, Southwest, and Plains. Examines the historical intrusion on Indian lands and the current effort by Native Americans to preserve their heritage. Features traditional as well as original music composed and performed for the series by Robbie Robertson and other Native American musicians. Narrated by Joy Harjo.

Native American Heritage
Color. 25 min. VHS.
Schlessinger Video Productions (1997)
　Children are introduced to the history and culture of the diverse groups of Native Americans who first inhabited North America.

The Native Americans: How the West Was Lost
Color. 26 min. 16mm.
British Broadcasting Corporation (1976)
　Highlights the life of the Plains Indians as it changed with the westward movement of whites. Historical photographs and drawings illustrate the Battle of Little Bighorn and the Wounded Knee Massacre.

Native American Life
Color. 25 min. VHS.
Schlessinger Video Productions (1996)
　Highlights of Native American history through the use of graphics and animations, live-action portrayals of historic figures, and stories told from a child's point of view. Narrated by Irene Bedard.

*Natives of the Narrowland: The
   Unwritten History of the First Cape
   Codders*
Color. 35 min. VHS.
Documentary Educational Resources
   (1994)
   Examines the history of the Wampanoag tribe of Cape Cod, Massachusetts.

Navajo
Color. 30 min. VHS.
Schlessinger Video Productions (1993)
   Examines the history, changing fortunes, and current situation of the Navajo tribe. For grades 5-10.

Navajo: A People Between Two Worlds
Color. 20 min. 16mm.
Line Films (1958)
   Study of the largest Indian tribe in the United States, including life on the land and tribal government.

Navajo Night Dances
Color. 12 min. 16mm.
Lewin (1957)
   Shows a Navajo family going to the Nine Day Healing Chant, feasting, and watching the Arrow, Feather, and Fire Dance.

Navajo Talking Picture
Color. 40 min. VHS.
Women Make Movies (1986)
   Documents the life of a grandmother on the Navajo Reservation in Lower Greasewood, Arizona.

Nez Perce: Portrait of a People
Color. 23 min. 16mm.
National Audio Visual Center (No date
   given)
   Tells of the cultural heritage of the Nez Perce and shows how the Nez Perce National Historical Park has influenced and preserved this culture.

North American Indian Legends
Color. 21 min. 16mm.
CBS (1973)
   Dramatizes several Indian legends with special-effects photography to emphasize their mythical quality.

Northwest Indian Art
Color. 10 min. 16mm.
Lewin (1966)
   Examples of the highly sophisticated art of Northwest Coast Indians collected from six museums.

Now That the Buffalo's Gone
Color. 7 min. 16mm.
Pyramid Film and Video (1969)
   Uses group and individual still-photograph portraits, combined with footage from old films, to emphasize the dignity of Indian culture.

Oneota Longhouse People
Color. 14 min. 16mm.
University of Iowa Audio Visual
   Center (1973)
   Archaeological discoveries of longhouses in northwest Iowa. Including a reconstruction of a village and views of how life might have been lived at this site a thousand years ago.

Oren Lyons, the Faithkeeper
Color. 58 min. VHS.
Films for the Humanities & Sciences
   (1997)
   Native American Chief Oren Lyons, a leader in the international environmental movement, talks with Bill Moyers about the ancient legends, prophecies, and wisdom that guide the Onondaga tribe. Lyons shares the spiritual basis of his environmentalism—a vision of the degradation of the earth that was revealed to the Onondaga nation in 1799.

Paddle to the Sea
Color. 25 min. 16mm.
National Film Board of Canada (1967)
   The story of a small, hand-carved Indian and a canoe, both called "paddle to the sea." From a book of the same name by Holling C. Holling.

Painting with Sand: A Navajo Ceremony
Color. 11 min. 16mm.
Encyclopedia Britannica Educational
   Corporation (1949)
   Portrays the traditional sand painting and healing rite as performed by a Navajo medicine man for his ailing son.

People of the Buffalo
Color. 14 min. 16mm.
National Film Board of Canada (1969)
   Depicts the dependence of western Indians on the buffalo for food, shelter, and clothing. Shows how the coming of whites and subsequent slaughter of the buffalo herds changed the lifestyle of the Indians.

Pocahontas: Her True Story
Color. 50 min. VHS.
A&E Home Video (1995)
   Portrait of a remarkable native American princess, ambassador, stateswoman, and peacemaker whose brief life left an indelible mark on a fledgling nation. Interviews with Pocahontas's descendants provide a perspective on her life and times.

The Place of the Falling Waters
Color. 90 min. VHS.
Montana Public Television (1991)
   Relates the complex and volatile relationship between the people of the Confederated Salish and Koontenai Tribes and a major hydroelectric dam situated within the Flathead Indian Reservation. Covers history of tribal society and culture before the dam's construction, the construction of the Kerr Dam in the

1930's and its impact on the reservation, and the hopes and dilemmas of the Salish and Kootenai people as they prepare to take over the dam during the next three decades.

The Potawatomi
Color. 30 min. VHS.
Schlessinger Video Productions (1993)
   Examines the history and current situation of the Potawatomi of the Great Lakes region. Only a few hundred tribe members survive. Some still speak the language and practice the ways of their ancestors. For grades 5-10.

Potlatch People
Color. 26 min. 16mm.
Document Associates (1976)
   With an economy based on the abundant fish of the ocean and rivers, Northwest Coast Indians lived in communal longhouses based on a rigid class system.

The Pueblo
Color. 30 min. VHS.
Schlessinger Video Productions (1993)
   Examines the history of the Pueblo Indians of New Mexico, one of the first tribes to make contact with European explorers. Includes a discussion of their ancient ancestors, the Anasazi. For grades 5-10.

Pueblo of Laguna: Elders of the Tribe
Color. 20 min. 16mm.
National Audio Visual Center (No date
   given)
   Describes the dynamic program for taking care of elders on a reservation in Laguna, New Mexico.

The Pueblo Peoples: First Contact.
Color. 60 min. VHS.
PBS Video (1990)
   Describes the history of the Pueblo tribe at the time of their first contact

with Spanish conquistadors in the mid-1500's. Briefly discusses Pueblo philosophy and legends.

Red Sunday: The Story of the Battle of the Little Bighorn
Color. 28 min. 16mm.
Pyramid Film and Video (1975)
   An objective account of America's most famous U.S. Cavalry-Indian confrontation. Still photographs, original drawings, paintings, and live action are skillfully blended.

Report from Wounded Knee
Color. 10 min. 16mm.
Sterling Educational Films (1971)
   Details the historical events at Wounded Knee using photographic stills.

Sacajawea
Color. 24 min. VHS.
Southerby Productions (1984)
   The true story of the young Indian woman who guided the Lewis and Clark expedition.

Sacred Buffalo People
Color. 56 min. VHS.
Deb Wallwork Productions (1992)
   Explores the powerful bond between Native Americans and the buffalo, viewed by Indians as the sacred provider of life. Traditional beliefs, history, and modern reservation humor are woven together in the stories told today as buffalo return to the plains. Features Indian park rangers, wildlife managers, and dancers, along with photography of buffalo herds and examples of Indian art.

Sacred Ground
Color. 60 min. VHS.
Freewheelin' Films Ltd. (1991)
   Tour of American Indian spiritual places such as Devil's Tower and Bear Butte, and a discussion of myths and legends associated them.

Searching for a Native American Identity
Color. 30 min. VHS.
Films for the Humanities & Sciences (1994)
   Bill Moyers interviews husband and wife writing team Louise Erdrich and the late Michael Dorris who discuss their literary collaboration, their shared thinking based upon their like backgrounds as mixed-blood Native Americans, and the Native American characters who people their novels. Originally broadcast as a program in the PBS series, *A World of Ideas*.

The Search for Ancient Americans: Ancient Beginnings of Native American Culture
Color. 58 min. VHS.
Intellimation (1988)
   Demonstrates how new technologies are changing the way archaeologists work as they examine evidence of the first peoples to reach America. Examined in detail are the Mayan, Anasazi, and Florida tribal cultures. Part of *The Infinite Voyage* series.

Seminole
Color. 30 min. VHS.
Schlessinger Video Productions (1993)
   Examines the history, changing fortunes, and current situation of the Seminole people. Includes facts about the role of the U.S. government, debunks myths about Native Americans, explores their spiritual relationship with nature, and discusses the role of women in their societies. For grades 5-10.

Seminole Indians
Color. 11 min. 16mm.
University of Minnesota (1951)
   Seminole life on the hummocks of the Florida Everglades.

The Shadow Catcher: Edward S. Curtis and the North American Indian
Color. 89 min. VHS.
Mystic Fire Video (1993)

Video release of a motion picture originally produced in 1974. Profiles photographer, anthropologist and filmmaker Curtis, who spent 34 years recording the American Indian tradition. Between 1896 and 1930 Curtis collected interviews and original Indian stories, recorded some 10,000 songs and took 40,000 pictures many of which are used in the production. Retraces his journeys from the Pueblo regions of the Southwest, north to British Columbia and Alaska.

Silent Enemy
Black and white. 88 min. 16mm. VHS.
Blackhawk Films (1930)

Study of the Ojibwas' struggle for food before the arrival of European Americans. Filmed on location near Lake Superior.

Sioux Indians: Live and Remember
Color. 29 min. VHS.
Barr Films (1987)

Focuses on the struggle of the Dakota Sioux to preserve their heritage. Shows the Dakota people living in squalid camps in the midst of natural beauty.

Sitting Bull: Chief of the Lakota Nation
Color. 50 min. VHS.
A&E Home Entertainment (1995)

Portrait of the legendary chief who led the Lakota Sioux to victory over General Custer at Little Big Horn.

Sitting Bull: A Profile in Power
Color. 20 min. 16mm.
Learning Corporation of America (1976)

The heroic but sad saga of relations between the United States and the Indians unfolds through an imaginary dialogue between an interviewer and the charismatic Sioux chief.

Songs of Indian Territory Native American Music Traditions of Oklahoma
Color. 38 min. VHS.
Full Circle Communications (1990)

Features music from the workshops and concert of "The Songs of Indian Territory" held at the Kirkpatrick Center in Oklahoma City, October 14, 1988, and includes on-location highlights.

Spirit: A Journey in Dance, Drums and Song
Color. 75 min. VHS.
USA Films (1998)

Stage performance of modern and traditional Native American music, dance, and mythology. Native American flutes, percussion, chants, and keyboards provide evocative music. Narration by Chief Hawk Pope interweaves tribal legends.

The Spirit of Crazy Horse
Color. 60 min. VHS.
PBS Home Video (1990)

Milo Yellow Hair recounts the story of the Sioux tribe's struggle to reclaim their ancestral homeland. Investigates the simmering conflict of recent decades and offers a perspective on the choices that lie ahead. Originally shown as part of the PBS television series, *Frontline*.

The Spirit of the Mask
Color. 50 min. VHS.
Atlas Video (1993)

Explores the spiritual and psychological powers of masks used by Northwest Coast native peoples. Features rarely-seen ceremonies, commentary by spiritual leaders and relates how these traditions were repressed by Christian Europeans.

Storytellers of the Pacific
Color. 120 minutes. VHS.
Vision Maker Video (1996)

Two-part series focusing on the identity crisis of various Pacific cultures which, many years after colonization, slavery, and oppression, are attempting to reconstruct and live according to their true culture. Areas highlighted include northern Mexico, California, the Pacific Northwest, Alaska, Hawaii, Australia, Samoa, and Guam. Narrated by Joy Harjo.

Strangers in Their Own Land
Color. 50 min. VHS.
Strangers in Their Own Land (1993)

Records Native American ceremonies, including an emotional Kiowa wedding ceremony and the initiation of a young brave into an ancient warrior society.

The Sun Dagger (Edited version)
Color. 28 min. 16mm. VHS.
Bullfrog Films (1982)

The "dagger," an ancient Indian celestial calendar rediscovered in 1977, is presently the only known archaeological site in the world that marks the extreme positions of both the sun and the moon.

Sweating Indian Style: Conflicts Over Native American Ritual
Color. 57 min. VHS.
Women Make Movies (1994)

Presents opposing views on non-Native Americans' participation in traditional American Indian rites.

Tales of Wonder: Traditional Native American Fireside Stories
Color. 60 min. VHS.
Rich-Heape Films (1998)

Collection of traditional stories of creation and myth accompanied by music and illustrations. Appropriate for children.

Teaching Indians to Be White
Color. 28 min. VHS.
Films for the Humanities & Sciences (1993)

Shows how schools try to integrate American Indian children into mainstream society and notes problems with turning children away from their families and traditional values.

To Find Our Life: The Peyote Hunt of the Huichols of Mexico
Color. 65 min. 16mm.
University of California Extension Media Center (1968)

Filmed and recorded in the field in December, 1966, by anthropologist Peter T. Furst, this is the first documentary of the annual peyote hunt and ceremonies of the Huichol Indians of Western Mexico.

The Totem Pole
Color. 28 min. 16mm. VHS.
Educational Materials Corporation (1961)

The Kwakiutl and Haida are the Northwest Indians best known for their totem poles. Shows the several types of poles and how they are decorated.

Tribal Legacies: The Incas, the Mayas, the Sioux, the Pueblos
Color. 296 min. VHS.
Pacific Arts (1993)

Collection of four videos that depict the history and civilizations of four different native peoples of the Americas: the Incas, Mayas, Sioux, and Pueblo Indians.

Valley of the Standing Rocks
Color. 24 in. 16mm.
Thomas J. Barbre Productions (1957)

Vividly portrays the life of the Navajos on their reservation in Arizona and Utah.

Walking in a Sacred Manner
Color. 23 min. 16mm.
Stephen Cross (1982)

Using the photographs of Edward S. Curtis, shows how traditional Indian life was centered on the natural world.

Winds of Change: A Matter of Promises
Color/black and white. 58 min. VHS.
PBS Video (1990)

Navajos of Arizona and adjacent states and Lummis of Washington State focus on sovereignty, internal politics, the administration of justice, and relations with the U.S. government. Hosted by N. Scott Momaday.

Winter on an Indian Reservation
Color. 11 min. 16mm.
Inform (1973)

Shows children on a forest reservation in the Great Lakes area; provides an intimate look at both the hardships and joys of Indian life.

Wiping the Tears of Seven Generations
Color. 57 min. VHS.
Film Ideas (1992)

History of the Lakota people, culminating in the Bigfoot Memorial Ride, December 1990, intended to end the century of grieving since the Wounded Knee Massacre.

Woodland Indians of Early America
Color/black and white. 11 min. 16mm.
Cort (1958)

Depicts a family of hunter-culture Indians, illustrating the migratory nature of such cultures and showing many techniques of hunting, dress, cooking, and home building.

Yankton Sioux
Color. 30 min. VHS.
Schlessinger Video Productions (1993)

Extensive location filming takes the viewer to reservations where children and elders discuss what it means to be a Native American today. Includes photographs, film footage, tribal music, crafts and ceremonies. For grades 5-10.

FEATURE FILMS

The depictions of Indians in feature films (often by white actors) have historically been misguided and have engendered considerable outrage. What follows is a select list of films that provide relatively accurate portrayals of Indian life, past and present. In some of the films all Indians are portrayed by Indian actors; in others, white actors fill at least some Indian roles.

Black Robe
Color. 100 min. VHS.
Samuel Goldwyn (1991)

Seventeenth century Jesuit priest is led by a party of Algonquins to a distant mission. Generally accurate depiction of early Indian-white relations as well as intertribal Algonquin, Iroquois, and Huron relations and warfare. From Brian Moore's novel. Lothaire Bluteau, Aden Young, Sandrine Holt.

Cheyenne Autumn
Color. 159 min. VHS.
Warner Bros. (1964)

Renowned director of Westerns John Ford filmed this story of Cheyennes fleeing their reservation to return to their homeland. Not without its flaws, this is an early but sympathetic look at the situation of western Indians in the late nineteenth century. Richard Widmark, Carroll Baker, Ricardo Montalban, Gilbert Roland.

Crazy Horse
Color. 94 min. VHS.
Turner Home Entertainment (1994)

Made-for-cable look at the life of the Sioux and their warrior-leader, Crazy

Horse, who led his people to victory at the Battle of Little Big Horn in 1876. Michael Greyeyes, Irene Bedard, August Schellenberg, Wes Studi, Peter Horton.

Dances with Wolves
Color. 181 min. VHS.
Orion Pictures (1990)

Troubled Civil War veteran goes West and finds in the lifestyle and hunting grounds of the Lakota Sioux what he has been missing. Generally hailed by critics for its faithful depiction of Indian life and customs. Spoken Lakota is dubbed in English. Kevin Costner, Mary McDonnell, Graham Greene.

Dance Me Outside
Color. 91 min. VHS.
Una-Pix Entertainment (1995)

The story of the passage into manhood of an 18-year-old Indian on the Kidabanesee Reserve in Ontario. Adapted from a novel by W. P. Kinsella. Ryan Black, Adam Beach, Jennifer Podemski, Lisa LaCroix, Michael Greyeyes.

Geronimo
Color. 102 min. VHS.
Turner Home Entertainment (1993)

Made-for-cable look at the life of the Chiricahua Apaches and their warrior-leader, Geronimo. Joseph Runningfox, Nick Ramus, Michael Greyeyes, Tailinh Forest Flower.

Geronimo: An American Legend
Color. 115 min. VHS.
Columbia Pictures (1993)

The exploits of the Apache leader during the years 1885 and 1886 are effectively dramatized. Geronimo ultimately becomes a larger-than-life hero and an expression of Apache cultural values. Wes Studi, Jason Patric, Gene Hackman.

House Made of Dawn
Color 90 min. VHS.
New Line Studios (1996)

Tells the story of a young American Indian named Abel, home from a foreign war and caught between two worlds: the traditional one of his father and the other of industrial America. An adaptation of the Pulitzer Prize winning novel by N. Scott Momaday. Larry Littlebird, Judith Doty, Jay Varela, Mesa Bird.

The Indian in the Cupboard
Color. 98 min. VHS.
Columbia/Tristar (1995)

Fantasy based on Lynne Reid Banks's popular children's book. A young boy discovers that a toy Indian comes to life when it is locked in a cupboard. The boy also discovers that the toy is actually a historical Iroquois warrior who lived in the nineteenth century. A bond eventually develops between the boy and the warrior. Hal Scardino, Litefoot, Lindsay Crouse, David Keith.

Lakota Woman: Siege at Wounded Knee
Color. 113 min. VHS.
Turner Home Entertainment (1994)

Based on the biography of Mary Crow Dog, who went from an abused childhood and intra-tribal politics to become an eyewitness to the 1973 siege at Wounded Knee. Features an all Native American cast. Irene Bedard, Lawrence Bayne, Michael Horse, Joseph Runningfox, Floyd "Red Crow" Westerman.

The Last of the Mohicans
Color. 110 min. VHS.
20th Century Fox (1992)

Sweeping adaptation of the James Fenimore Cooper tale of colonial America during the French and Indian War. Hawkeye (Natty Bumppo) and his Indian brother Chingachgook must rescue colonists who have been captured by Indians. Daniel Day-Lewis, Madeleine Stowe, Russell Means, Eric Schweig.

Little Big Man
Color. 147 min. VHS.
CBS/Fox Video/Hiller Productions, Ltd. (1970)

Jack Crabb, 121-year-old veteran of the Old West and survivor of the Battle of the Little Bighorn, tells his story and stimulates sympathy for Indians along the way. Arthur Penn directed this off-beat epic starring Dustin Hoffman, Faye Dunaway, and Chief Dan George.

A Man Called Horse
Color. 114 min. VHS.
Cinema Center (1970)

In 1825 an English aristocrat is captured by a group of Sioux and eventually becomes their leader. A relatively realistic, even graphic, portrayal of Indian life and customs, including tribal initiations. Richard Harris, Judith Anderson, Manu Tupou.

Medicine River
Color. 96 min. VHS.
United American Video (1994)

Romantic comedy about a world-renowned photojournalist who returns home to Medicine River after a twenty-year absence to attend his mother's funeral and is conned into staying to help with a community project. Based on the 1990 Thomas King novel. Graham Greene, Byron Chief-Moon, Tom Jackson, Sheila Tousey.

Powwow Highway
Color. 89 min. VHS.
Anchor Bay Entertainment (1989)

An over-sized Cheyenne man-child goes on a spiritual quest to New Mexico while giving a ride to a lifelong Indian activist friend. Gary Farmer, A. Martinez, Graham Greene, Wes Studi, John Trudell.

Running Brave
Color. 105 min. VHS
Buena Vista (1983)

Sentimental profile of half-Sioux athlete Billy Mills from his childhood on the Pine Ridge Reservation to his victory at the 1964 Tokyo Olympics. (The casting of a white actor in the lead Indian role caused considerable protest when the film was made.) Robbie Benson, Pat Hingle.

Shadow of the Wolf
Color. 108 min. VHS.
Triumph (1993)

Young Inuit hunter sets out to live in isolation in the Arctic wilderness. After killing a white trader, he is pursued by a Canadian mountie. Lou Diamond Phillips, Jennifer Tilly.

Smoke Signals
Color. 89 minutes. VHS.
Miramax Home Entertainment (1998)

Road movie that bills itself as the first feature film written and directed by Native Americans. Screenwriter Sherman Alexie and director Chris Eyre follow two young Indians, Victor and Thomas, as they journey from Idaho's Coeur d'Alene Indian Reservation to Arizona to collect the ashes and pickup truck of Victor's dead father. Adam Beach, Evan Adams, Gary Farmer, Cody Lightning, Irene Bedard, John Trudell.

Son of the Morning Star
Color. 186 min. VHS.
Republic Pictures Home Video (1991)

Thoughtful look at the life and times of General George Armstrong Custer. Emphasis is on the ill-conceived and disastrous battle against the Sioux at Little Bighorn. Rosanna Arquette, Dean Stockwell, and Rodney A. Grant.

Squanto: A Warrior's Tale
Color. 102 min. VHS.
Disney (1994)

Based on the life of a seventeenth-century American Indian who is abducted and brought to England by British traders. Squanto is befriended by a sympathetic monk who urges him to return to America on a peace-making mission. Adam Beach, Mandy Patinkin, Michael Gambon, Irene Bedard.

Thunderheart
Color. 118 min. VHS.
Tristar Pictures (1992)
An FBI agent who is part Sioux is sent to investigate a murder on a Sioux reservation and undergoes a personal transformation. The film is noteworthy for its portrayal of contemporary reservation life. Val Kilmer, Sam Shepard, Graham Greene.

Windwalker
Color. 108 min. VHS.
United American Video (1980)
Newly dead Cheyenne patriarch returns to life to save his family from his son, an evil twin who was stolen at birth and raised by the enemy Crow. In Cheyenne and Crow languages, and subtitled in English. Trevor Howard, Nick Ramus, James Remar, Serene Hedin.

WEB SITES

Bureau of Indian Affairs
http://www.doi.gov/bureau-indian
-affairs.html
The Bureau of Indian Affairs On-Line. Provides a directory of information on law, legislation, education, tribal services, reports, and statistics concerning American Indians.

Guide to Native American Studies
Programs in the United States and
Canada. Ed. Robert M. Nelson.
University of Richmond.
http://www.richmond.edu/faculty/
ASAIL/guide/guide.html

Comprehensive survey of U.S. and Canadian Native American Studies programs being offered as majors, minors, and certifications at the baccalaureate level or above.

Internet Public Library
http://www.ipl.org/ref/native/
Provides information on primarily contemporary Native North American authors with bibliographies of their published works, biographical information, and links to online resources including interviews, online texts, and tribal Web sites.

Labriola National American Indian Data
Center
Tempe: Arizona State University.
http://www.asu.edu/lib/archives/
labriola.htm
The Labriola National American Indian Data Center's research collection brings together current and historic information on government, culture, religion and world view, social life and customs, tribal history, and information on individuals from the United States, Canada, Sonora, and Chihuahua, Mexico.

Mashantucket Pequot Museum and
Research Center
Mashantucket, Conn.
http://www.mashantucket.com/
Tribally owned-and-operated complex brings to life the story of the Mashantucket Pequot Tribal Nation, and serves as a major resource on the history of the tribe, the histories and cultures of other tribes, and the region's natural history. Information about the museum's collections, research library, exhibits, and events is available through the Web site.

Native American Book Resources on the
World Wide Web
http://www.hanksville.org/
NAresources/indices/NAbooks.htm

Includes links to Web sites on Native American authors, books available on-line, organizations, journals, book lists with Native American content, libraries, presses, book reviews, and book stores online that specialize in Native American material.

Native American Sites. Ed. Lisa A. Mitten. University of Pittsburgh. http://www.pitt.edu/~lmitten/indians.html

Provides access to home pages of individual Native Americans and nations, and to other sites that provide solid information about American Indians. Links are provided to information on individual Native nations, organizations, businesses, Indian education, languages, powwows and festivals, Native music, and contemporary Native American issues.

Smithsonian Institution National Museum of the American Indian http://www.si.edu/cgi-bin/nav.cgi

Home page of the Smithsonian Institution's National Museum of the American Indian in New York City. Provides information about the museum's collections, exhibitions, publications, recordings, and education resources. Includes research information and links to other Native American sites.

Smithsonian Institution National Museum of Natural History http://nmnhwww.si.edu/anthro/outreach/Indbibl/

Bibliography for educators and parents of children K-12, compiled by the Anthropology Outreach Office of the Smithsonian's National Museum of Natural History. Produced in response to concerns about choosing culturally sensitive and historically accurate books for children about American Indians and Alaska Natives.

SOUND RECORDINGS

Creation's Journey: Native American Music
Compact Disc
Smithsonian/Folkways (1994)

Ceremonial, social, and contemporary music of Native Americans from the United States, Canada, Mexico, and Bolivia. Music by Comanche, Navajo, Seneca, Micmac, Cherokee, Kwakiutl, Zapotec, and other native performers.

500 Nations: A Musical Journey
Compact Disc
Epic Soundtrax (1994)

Sound track from the CBS television miniseries, *500 Nations*. Music by Peter Buffett.

Honor the Earth Powwow: Songs of the Great Lakes Indians
Compact Disc
Ryko (1991)

Songs of the Ojibwa, the Menominee and Winnebago. Recorded July, 1990, at a powwow at the Lac Court Oreilles Reservation, Wisconsin.

Music for the Native Americans
Compact Disc.
Capitol Records (1994)

Soundtrack for the Turner Broadcasting Systems mini-series, *The Native Americans*. Songs composed and performed by Robbie Robertson and the Red Road Ensemble and other Native American musicians.

Music of New Mexico: Native American Traditions
Compact Disc. 68 min.
Smithsonian Folkways (1992)

Traditional and contemporary music by Pueblo, Navajo, and Apache musicians from New Mexico.

*Proud Heritage A Celebration of
Traditional American Indian Music*
Compact Disc.
Indian House (1996)

An anthology of American Indian music sung in various Indian languages including Navajo, Pueblo, Ponca, Kiowa, Creek, and Sioux.

*Songs of Earth, Water, Fire, and Sky:
Music of the American Indian.*
Compact Disc.
New World Records (1991)

An anthology of music recorded on various Indian reservations and at pow-wows. Includes traditional songs of Pueblo, Seneca, Arapaho, Plains, Creek, Yurok, Navajo, and Cherokee tribes.

*Talking Spirits: Music from the Hopi,
Zuni, Laguna & San Juan Pueblos.*
Compact Disc.
Music of the World (1992)

Tribal songs and dances recorded on location in New Mexico and Arizona by James Lascelles during the 1980s. Sung in a variety of Native American languages.

CD-ROMS

Exploring the Lost Maya
Sumeria (1996)

Contains historical material written by leading Maya scholar Robert Sharer, interactive maps of major Maya sites, nineteenth century lithographs and historical photos, an interactive multimedia time line of Maya history, movies on several facets of Maya culture, and travel information for those planning to visit the sites.

*500 Nations: Stories of the North
American Indian Experience*
Microsoft Home (1995)

Based on a Jack Leustig film of the same title. Hosted by Kevin Costner. Multimedia presentation of the history of North American Indians. Includes over 2,000 images, three-dimensional video, computer-generated recreations, animated sequences, spoken segments, and music.

Maya
Hull, Quebec: The Museum (1995)

Depicts Maya architecture, art, and lifestyle primarily through photographs. Includes a section on the making of the IMAX film, *Mystery of the Maya*. Published in collaboration with the National Film Board of Canada and the Instituto Mexicano de Cinematografia. Narrated by Geoff Winter.

Pomo Indians
Compiled by Jeannine Davis-Kimball
and Randal S. Brandt.
Berkeley: California Indian Library
Collections, University of
California, Berkeley (1994)

Interactive, multimedia collection divided into ten searchable categories, each containing photographs, sound recordings, and textual material. The exhaustive Pomo bibliography is searchable by author, title, periodical, series, keyword, and holdings.

BIBLIOGRAPHY

The following select bibliography of works on American Indians is organized into four categories: General Studies and Reference, History, Culture Areas (with eight subsections), and Contemporary Life.

GENERAL STUDIES AND REFERENCE

Allen, Paula Gunn. *Off the Reservation: Reflections on Boundary-Busting, Border-Crossing Loose Canons.* Boston: Beacon Press, 1998.

Anderson, Vicki. *Native Americans in Fiction: A Guide to 765 Books for Librarians and Teachers, K-9.* Jefferson, N.C.: McFarland, 1994.

Bancroft-Hunt, Norman. *Native American Tribes.* Edison, N.J.: Chartwell Books, 1997.

Bataille, Gretchen M., ed. *Native American Women: A Biographical Dictionary.* New York: Garland, 1993.

Bataille, Gretchen M., and Kathleen M. Sands. *American Indian Women Telling Their Lives.* Lincoln: University of Nebraska Press, 1984.

Bierhorst, John. *The Mythology of North America.* New York: William Morrow, 1985.

Baughman, Mike. *Mohawk Blood: A Native American Quest.* New York: Lyons & Burford, 1995.

Bear Heart, with Molly Larkin. *The Wind is My Mother: The Life and Teachings of a Native American Shaman.* New York: Clarkson N. Potter, 1996.

Beidler, Peter G., and Marion F. Egge, comps. *Native Americans in the Saturday Evening Post.* Lanham, Md.: Scarecrow Press, 2000.

Berlo, Janet C., and Ruth B. Phillips. *Native North American Art.* New York: Oxford University Press, 1998.

Bicklis, Robert A. *Karankawa Indians of Texas: An Ecological Study of Cultural Tradition and Change.* Austin: University of Texas Press, 1996.

Biolsi, Thomas, ed. *Indians and Anthropologists: Vine Deloria, Jr. and the Critique of Anthropology.* Tucson: University of Arizona Press, 1997.

Birchfield, D.L., ed. *Encyclopedia of North American Indians.* 11 vols. New York: Marshall Cavendish, 1997.

Bloom, Harold, ed. *Native American Women Writers.* Philadelphia: Chelsea House, 1998.

———. *Native American Writers.* Philadelphia: Chelsea House, 1998.

Boas, Franz. *Handbook for American Indian Languages.* 3 parts. Bureau of American Ethnology, Bulletin 40. Washington, D.C.: U.S. Government Printing Office, 1911.

Bonvillain, Nancy. *Native American Medicine.* Philadelphia: Chelsea House, 1997.

Bowden, Henry Warner. *American Indians and Christian Missions.* Chicago: University of Chicago Press, 1981.

Brumble, H. David. *An Annotated Bibliography of American Indian and Eskimo Autobiographies.* Lincoln: University of Nebraska Press, 1981.

Byers, Paula K. *Native American Genealogical Sourcebook.* New York: Gale Research, 1995.

Campbell, Lyle, and Marianne Mithune, eds. *The Languages of Native America: Historical and*

Comparative Assessment. Austin: University of Texas Press, 1979.

Canby, William C. *American Indian Law in a Nutshell*. 3d ed. St. Paul, Minn.: West, 1998.

Cantor, George. *North American Indian Landmarks: A Traveler's Guide*. Detroit: Visible Ink Press, 1993.

Carney, Cary M. *Native American Higher Education in the United States*. New Brunswick, N.J.: Transaction, 1999.

Castile, George P. *To Show Heart: Native American Self-determination and Federal Indian Policy, 1960-1975*. Tucson: University of Arizona Press, 1998.

Champagne, Duane, ed. *The Native North American Almanac: A Reference Work on Native North Americans in the United States and Canada*. Detroit: Gale Research, 1994.

Coe, Michael, et al. *Atlas of Ancient America*. New York: Facts on File, 1986.

Cohen, Felix. *Felix Cohen's Handbook of Federal Indian Law*. 2d ed. Charlottesville, Va.: Michie/Bobbs-Merrill, 1982.

Crow, John, Martha Crow, and Jack Sharp. *1997-1998 Indian Country Address Book*. Nyack, N.Y.: Todd Publications, 1997.

Culin, Stewart. *Games of the North American Indians*. Bureau of American Ethnology, Annual Report 24 (1902-1903). Washington, D.C.: U.S. Government Printing Office, 1907.

Curtis, Natalie. *The Indians' Book*. New York: Harper and Brothers, 1923.

Cutler, Charles L. *O Brave New Words!: Native American Loanwords in Current English*. Norman: University of Oklahoma Press, 1994.

Davis, Mary B. *Native America in the Twentieth Century: An Encyclopedia*. New York: Garland, 1994.

Davis-Kimball, Jeannine. *Finding Guide to the California Indian Library Collections: California State Library*. 8 vols. Berkeley: University of California Press, 1993.

Dawdy, Doris O., comp. *Annotated Bibliography of American Indian Painting*. Contributions from the Museum of the American Indian, Heye Foundation, vol. 21, pt. 2. New York: Museum of the American Indian, Heye Foundation, 1968.

Day, Gordon M., Michael K. Foster, and William Cowan, eds. *In Search of New England's Native Past: Selected Essays*. Amherst: University of Massachusetts Press, 1998.

Deloria, Ella C., and Vine Deloria. *Speaking of Indians*. Lincoln: University of Nebraska Press, 1998.

Deloria, Vine. *Red Earth, White Lies: Native Americans and the Myth of Scientific Fact*. New York: Charles Scribner's Sons, 1995.

Deloria, Vine, and Clifford M. Lytle. *The Nations Within: The Past and Future of American Indian Sovereignty*. Austin: University of Texas Press, 1998.

Deloria, Vine, and David E. Wilkins. *Tribes, Treaties, and Constitutional Tribulation*. Austin: University of Texas Press, 1999.

Dobyns, Henry F. *Native American Historical Demography: A Critical Bibliography*. Newberry Library Center for the History of the American Indian Bibliographical Series. Bloomington: Indiana University Press, 1976.

Dockstader, Frederick J. *Indian Art in America: The Arts and Crafts of the North American Indians*. Greenwich, Conn.: New York Graphics Society, 1961.

Driver, Harold. *Indians of North America*. Chicago: University of Chicago Press, 1975.

Dubin, Lois S. *North American Indian Jewelry and Adornment: From Prehistory to the Present.* New York: Harry N. Abrams, 1999.

Dudley, William. *Native Americans: Opposing Viewpoints.* San Diego, Calif.: Greenhaven Press, 1998.

Eagle, Adam Fortunate. *Alcatraz! Alcatraz!: The Indian Occupation of 1969-1971.* Berkeley, Calif.: Heyday Books, 1992.

Eggan, Fred, ed. *Social Anthropology of North American Tribes.* Chicago: University of Chicago Press, 1966.

Erdoes, Richard, and Alfonso Ortiz, eds. *American Indian Myths and Legends.* New York: Pantheon Books, 1984.

Estell, Kenneth. *Native Americans Information Directory.* 2d ed. Detroit: Gale Research, 1998.

Feest, Christian F. *Native Arts of North America.* New York: Oxford University Press, 1980.

Frazier, Patrick, ed. *The Many Nations: A Library of Congress Resource Guide for the Study of Indian and Alaska Native Peoples.* 6 vols. 6th ed. Washington, D.C.: Library of Congress, 1996.

Getches, David H., Charles F. Wilkinson, and Robert Williams. *Cases and Materials on Federal Indian Law.* 4th ed. St. Paul, Minn.: West, 1998.

Gibbon, Guy E., and Kenneth M. Ames, eds. *Archaeology of Prehistoric Native America: An Encyclopedia.* New York: Garland, 1998.

Gidley, M. Edward. *Edward S. Curtis and the North American Indian, Incorporated.* New York: Cambridge University Press, 1998.

Gill, Sam D. *Native American Religions: An Introduction.* Belmont, Calif.: Wadsworth, 1982.

Gill, Sam D., and Irene F. Sullivan, comps. *Dictionary of Native American Mythology.* Santa Barbara, Calif.: ABC-CLIO, 1992.

Gille, Frank H., ed. *Encyclopedia of Massachusetts Indians.* 2 vols. St. Clair Shores, Mich.: Somerset, 1999.

Gombert, Greg, comp. *Guide to Native American Music Recordings.* Fort Collins, Colo.: MultiCultural Publishing, 1994.

Gourse, Leslie. *Native American Courtship and Marriage Traditions.* New York: Hippocrene Books, 1999.

Gray, Sharon A. *Health of Native People of North America: A Bibliography and Guide to Resources.* Lanham, Md.: Scarecrow Press, 1996.

Green, Rayna. *Native American Women: A Contextual Bibliography.* Bloomington: Indiana University Press, 1983.

Grossman, Mark. *The ABC-CLIO Companion to the Native American Rights Movement.* Santa Barbara, Calif.: ABC-CLIO, 1996.

Haas, Marilyn L. *Indians of North America: Sources for Library Research.* Hamden, Conn.: Library Professional Publications, 1983.

_____. *The Seneca and Tuscarora Indians: An Annotated Bibliography.* Metuchen, N.J.: Scarecrow Press, 1994.

Hamilton, Charles, ed. *Cry of the Thunderbird.* Norman: University of Oklahoma Press, 1972.

Hamlin-Wilson, Gail, ed. *Biographical Dictionary of the Indians of the Americas.* 2 vols. Newport Beach, Calif.: American Indian Publishers, 1991.

Harmon, Alexandra. *Indians in the Making: Ethnic Relations and Indian Identities Around Puget Sound.* Berkeley: University of California Press, 1998.

Harris, R. Cole, ed. *Historical Atlas of Canada: From the Beginning to 1800.* Toronto: University of Toronto Press, 1987.

Hart, Paula. _Native American Religions_. New York: Facts on File, 1997.

Harvey, Karen D. _How to Teach About American Indians: A Guide for the School Library Media Specialist_. Westport, Conn.: Greenwood Press, 1995.

Hauptman, Laurence M. _Tribes and Tribulations: Misconceptions About American Indians and Their Histories_. Albuquerque: University of New Mexico Press, 1995.

Heard, J. Norman. _Handbook of the American Frontier: Four Centuries of Indian-White Relations_. 3 vols. Metuchen, N.J.: Scarecrow Press, 1987-1992.

Hill, Edward E., comp. _Guide to the Records of the National Archives of the United States Relating to American Indians_. Washington, D.C.: National Archives and Records Service, 1981.

Hill, Tom, ed. _Creation's Journey: Native American Identity and Belief_. Washington, D.C.: Smithsonian Institution Press, 1994.

Hinton, Leane, and Pamela Munro, eds. _Studies in American Indian Languages: Description and Theory_. Berkeley: University of California Press, 1998.

Hirschfelder, Arlene B., ed. _Native Heritage: Personal Accounts by American Indians, 1790 to the Present_. New York: Macmillan, 1995.

Hirschfelder, Arlene B., et al. _Guide to Research on North American Indians_. Chicago: American Library Association, 1983.

Hirschfelder, Arlene B., and Paulette Molin, comps. _The Encyclopedia of Native American Religions: An Introduction_. New York. Facts on File, 1992.

Hodge, Frederick W., ed. _Handbook of American Indians North of Mexico_. 2 vols. Washington, D.C.: U.S. Government Printing Office, 1907-1910.

Horr, David A., comp. and ed. _American Indian Ethnohistory_. 118 vols. New York: Garland, 1974.

Hoxie, Frederick E., ed. _Encyclopedia of North American Indians_. Boston: Houghton Mifflin, 1996.

Hoxie, Frederick E. _Indians in American History: An Introduction_. Arlington Heights, Ill.: Harlan Davidson, 1988.

Hoxie, Frederick E, and Harvey Markowitz, comps. _Native Americans: An Annotated Bibliography_. Pasadena, Calif.: Salem Press, 1990.

Hultkrantz, Ake. _The Religions of the American Indians_. Translated by Monica Setterwall. Berkeley: University of California Press, 1967.

Hurt, R. Douglas. _Indian Agriculture in America: Prehistory to the Present_. Lawrence: University Press of Kansas, 1987.

Jenness, Diamond. _The Indians of Canada_. Ottawa: F. A. Acland, 1932.

Johansen, Bruce E. _The Encyclopedia of Native American Economic History_. Westport, Conn.: Greenwood Press, 1999.

_____. Native America and the Evolution of Democracy: A Supplementary Bibliography_. Westport, Conn.: Greenwood Press, 1999.

_____, ed. Encyclopedia of Native American Legal Tradition_. Westport, Conn.: Greenwood Press, 1998.

Johansen, Bruce E., and Donald Grinde, Jr. _The Encyclopedia of Native American Biography: Six Hundred Life Stories of Important People from Powhatan to Wilma Mankiller_. New York: Henry Holt, 1997.

Johnson, Michael. _Macmillan Encyclopedia of Native American Tribes_. New York: Macmillan Library Reference, 1999.

Johnson, Steven L. _Guide to American Indian Documents in the Congressional Series Set, 1817-1899_. New York: Clearwater, 1977.

Johnson, Troy R., Joane Nagel, and Duane Champagne, eds. *American Indian Activism: Alcatraz to the Longest Walk.* Urbana: University of Illinois Press, 1997.

Josephy, Alvin M., Jr. *500 Nations: An Illustrated History of North American Indians.* New York: Alfred A. Knopf, 1994.

_____. *The Patriot Chiefs: A Chronicle of American Indian Resistance.* Rev. ed. New York: Penguin Books, 1993.

Josephy, Alvin M., Jr., ed., and William Brandon. *The American Heritage Book of Indians.* New York: American Heritage, 1961.

Josephy, Alvin M., Jr., Joane Nagel, and Troy R. Johnson. *Red Power: The American Indians' Fight for Freedom.* 2d ed. Lincoln: University of Nebraska Press, 1999.

Kapplar, Charles. *Indian Affairs: Laws and Treaties.* 2 vols. Washington, D.C.: U.S. Government Printing Office, 1904-1941.

Karr, Ronald D., ed. *Indian New England, 1524-1674: A Compendium of Eyewitness Accounts of Native American Life.* Pepperell, Mass.: Branch Line Press, 1999.

Keeling, Richard. *North American Indian Music: A Guide to Published Sources and Selected Recordings.* New York: Garland, 1997.

Keenan, Jerry. *Encyclopedia of American Indian Wars, 1492-1890.* Santa Barbara, Calif.: ABC-CLIO, 1997.

Keller, Robert H., and Michael F. Turek. *American Indians and National Parks.* Tucson: University of Arizona Press, 1998.

Kilpatrick, Jacquelyn. *Celluloid Indians: Native Americans and Film.* Lincoln: University of Nebraska Press, 1999.

King, J. C. H. *First Peoples, First Contacts: Native Peoples of North America.* Cambridge, Mass.: Harvard University Press, 1999.

Klein, Barry T., ed. *Reference Encyclopedia of the American Indian.* 2 vols. 8th ed. New York: Todd, 1998.

Klein, Laura F., and Lillian A. Ackerman, eds. *Women and Power in Native North America.* Norman: University of Oklahoma Press, 1995.

Krech, Shepard, III. *Native Canadian Anthropology and History: A Selective Bibliography.* Winnipeg: Rupert's Land Research Centre, University of Winnipeg, 1986.

Krech, Shepard, and Barbara A. Hail, eds. *Collecting Native America, 1870-1960.* Washington, D.C.: Smithsonian Institution Press, 1999.

Krupat, Arnold. *For Those Who Come After: A Study of Native American Autobiography.* Berkeley: University of California Press, 1985.

_____. *The Turn to the Native: Studies in Criticism and Culture.* Lincoln: University of Nebraska Press, 1996.

_____, ed. *Native American Autobiography: An Anthology.* Madison: University of Wisconsin Press, 1994.

Lake-Thom, Bobby. *Spirits of the Earth: A Guide to Native American Nature Symbols, Stories, and Ceremonies.* New York: Plume, 1997.

Langer, Howard J. *American Indian Quotations.* Westport, Conn.: Greenwood Press, 1996.

Laubin, Reginald, and Gladys Laubin. *Indian Dances of North America.* Norman: University of Oklahoma Press, 1977.

Leacock, Eleanor Burke, and Nancy O. Lurie, eds. *North American Indians in Historical Perspective.* Prospect Heights, Ill.: Waveland Press, 1988.

Legters, Lyman H. *American Indian Policy: Self-governance and Economic Development.* Westport, Conn.: Greenwood Press, 1994.

Leitch, Barbara A. *A Concise Dictionary of Indian Tribes of North America.*

Algonac, Mich.: Reference Publications, 1979.

Lester, David. *Crime and the Native American.* Springfield, Ill.: Charles C. Thomas, 1999.

_____. *Suicide in American Indians.* Commack, N.Y.: Nova Science Publishers, 1997.

Lester, Patrick D. *Biographical Dictionary of Native American Painters.* Tulsa, Olka.: Sir Publications, 1995.

Lewis, David R. *Neither Wolf Nor Dog: American Indians, Environment, and Agrarian Change.* New York: Oxford University Press, 1994.

Liberty, Margot, ed. *American Indian Intellectuals.* St. Paul, Minn.: West, 1978.

Littlefield, Daniel F., Jr., and James W. Parin. *A Biobibliography of Native American Writers, 1772-1924.* Metuchen, N.J.: Scarecrow Press, 1981.

Lobo, Susan, and Steve Talbot, eds. *Native American Voices: A Reader.* New York: Longman, 1998.

Lyon, William S. *Encyclopedia of Native American Healing.* Santa Barbara, Calif.: ABC-CLIO, 1996.

_____. *Encyclopedia of Native American Shamanism: Sacred Ceremonies of North America.* Santa Barbara, Calif.: ABC-CLIO, 1998.

Madsen, Brigham D. *The Bannock of Idaho.* Moscow: University of Idaho Press, 1996.

Malinowski, Sharon, et al., eds. *The Gale Encyclopedia of Native American Tribes.* 4 vols. Detroit: Gale Research, 1998.

Malinowski, Sharon, and Simon Glickman, eds. *Native North American Biography.* 2 vols. New York: U.X.L., 1996.

Markowitz, Harvey, and McCrea Adams, eds. *Magill's Choice: American Indian Biographies.* Pasadena, Calif.: Salem Press, 1999.

Marks, Paula M. *In a Barren Land: American Indian Dispossession and Survival.* New York: William Morrow, 1998.

Marriott, Alice Lee, and Carol Rachlin. *American Indian Mythology.* New York: Thomas Y. Crowell, 1964.

Martin, Joel W. *Native American Religion.* New York: Oxford University Press, 1999.

Matuz, Roger, ed. *St. James Guide to Native North American Artists.* Detroit: St. James Press, 1998.

Meiners, Phyllis A. *National Directory of Foundation Grants for Native Americans.* Kansas City, Mo.: Eagle Rock Books, 1998.

Meredith, Howard L. *Modern American Indian Tribal Government and Politics.* Tsaile, Ariz.: Navajo Community College Press, 1993.

Mihesuah, Devon A. *Natives and Academics: Researching and Writing About American Indians.* Lincoln: University of Nebraska Press, 1998.

Monture-Angus, Patricia, and Renee Hulan, eds. *Native North America: Critical and Cultural Perspectives: Essays.* Toronto: ECW Press, 1999.

Moore, John J. *The Political Economy of North American Indians.* Norman: University of Oklahoma Press, 1993.

Murdock, George Peter, and Timothy J. O'Leary. *Ethnographic Bibliography of North America.* 4th ed. 5 vols. New Haven, Conn.: Human Relations Area Files Press, 1975.

Nabokov, Peter. *Native American Testimony.* New York: Harper & Row, 1979.

Nabokov, Peter, and Robert Easton. *Native American Architecture.* New York: Oxford University Press, 1989.

National Museum of the American Indian, and Tim Johnson, eds. *Spirit Capture: Photographs from the National Museum of the American Indian.* Washington, D.C.: Smithsonian Institution Press, 1998.

National Native American
Co-operative. *Native American
Directory: Alaska, Canada, United
States*. San Carlos, Ariz.: National
Native American Cooperative, 1996.

Nielsen, Marianne O., ed. *Native
Americans, Crime, and Justice*.
Boulder, Colo.: Westview Press, 1996.

Nielsen, Nancy J. *Reformer and
Activists*. New York: Facts on File,
1997.

Nies, Judith. *Native American History: A
Chronology of the Vast Achievements of
a Culture and Their Links to World
Events*. New York: Ballantine Books,
1996.

Oakly, Ruth, ed. *The North American
Indian*. 6 vols. New York: Marshall
Cavendish, 1991.

Olson, James S., and Mark Baxter, eds.
*Encyclopedia of American Indian Civil
Rights*. Westport, Conn.: Greenwood
Press, 1997.

Orchard, William C. *Beads and
Beadwork of the American Indian*.
New York: Museum of the
American Indian, Heye Foundation,
1929.

_____. *The Technique of Porcupine-Quill
Decoration Among the North American
Indians*. New York: Museum of the
American Indian, Heye Foundation,
1971.

Osterreich, Shelley Anne. *Native North
American Shamanism: An Annotated
Bibliography*. Westport, Conn.:
Greenwood Press, 1998.

Paterek, Josephine. *Encyclopedia of
American Indian Costume*. Santa
Barbara, Calif.: ABC-CLIO, 1994.

Patterson, Lotsee. *Directory of Native
American Tribal Libraries*. Norman:
University of Oklahoma, 1995.

Peltier, Leonard, and Harvey Arden.
*Prison Writings: My Life Is My Sun
Dance*. New York: St. Martin's Press,
1999.

Philip, Kenneth R. *Termination
Revisited: American Indians on the
Trail to Self-determination, 1933-1953*.
Lincoln: University of Nebraska
Press, 1999.

Phillips, Charles, and Alan Axelrod,
eds. *Encyclopedia of the American
West*. 4 vols. New York: Simon &
Schuster/Macmillan, 1996.

Pritchard, Evan T. *No Word for Time:
The Way of the Algonquin People*.
Tulsa, Okla.: Council Oaks Books,
1997.

Pritzker, Barry. *Native Americans: An
Encyclopedia of History, Culture, and
People*. 2 vols. Santa Barbara, Calif.:
ABC-CLIO, 1998.

_____. *Native America Today: A Guide to
Community Politics and Culture*. Santa
Barbara, Calif.: ABC-CLIO, 1999.

Prucha, Francis P. *A Bibliographical
Guide to the History of Indian-White
Relations in the United States*.
Chicago: University of Chicago
Press, 1977.

_____. *Indian-White Relations in the
United States: A Bibliography of Works
Published 1975-1980*. Lincoln:
University of Nebraska Press, 1982.

_____, ed. *Documents of United States
Indian Policy*. 2d ed., expanded.
Lincoln: University of Nebraska
Press, 1990.

Ray, Roger B. *Indians of Maine: A
Bibliographic Guide*. 4th ed. Portland,
Maine: Maine Historical Society,
1994.

Reddy, Marlita A., ed. *Statistical Record
of Native North Americans*. 2d ed.
Detroit: Gale Research, 1995.

Revard, Carter. *Family Matters, Tribal
Affairs*. Tucson: University of
Arizona Press, 1998.

Rockefeller-MacArthur, Elizabeth.
*American Indian Library Services in
Perspective: From Petroglyphs to
Hypertext*. Jefferson, N.C.:
McFarland, 1998.

Roemer, Kenneth M. *Native American Writers of the United States*. Detroit: Gale Research, 1997.

Roleff, Tamara L., ed. *Native American Rights*. San Diego, Calif.: Green-haven Press, 1998.

Rollins, Peter C., and John E. O'Connor, eds. *Hollywood's Indian: The Portrayal of the Native American in Film*. Lexington: University Press of Kentucky, 1998.

Ronda, James, and James Axtell. *Indian Missions: A Critical Bibliography*. Newberry Library Center for the History of the American Indian Bibliographical Series. Bloomington: Indiana University Press, 1978.

Ruoff, A. Lavonne, and Karl Kroeber. *American Indian Literatures in the United States: A Basic Bibliography for Teachers*. New York: Association for the Study of American Indian Literature, 1983.

Sandefur, Gary D. *Changing Numbers, Changing Needs: American Indian Demography and Public Health*. Washington, D.C.: National Academy Press, 1996.

Schusky, Ernest L., ed. *Political Organization of Native North Americans*. Washington, D.C.: University of America Press, 1980.

Schweitzer, Marjorie M., ed. *American Indian Grandmothers: Traditions and Transitions*. Albuquerque: University of New Mexico Press, 1999.

Shoemaker, Nancy. *American Indian Population Recovery in the Twentieth Century*. Albuquerque: University of New Mexico Press, 1999.

_____, ed. *Negotiators of Change: Historical Perspectives on Native American Women*. New York: Routledge, 1995.

Smith, Jane F., and Robert M. Kvasnicka, eds. *Indian-White Relations*. Washington, D.C.: Howard University Press, 1976.

Smith, Paul C., and Robert A. Warrior. *Like a Hurricane: The Indian Movement from Alcatraz to Wounded Knee*. New York: New Press, 1996.

Snipp, C. Mathew. *American Indians: The First of This Land*. New York: Russell Sage Foundation, 1989.

Snow, Dean R. *The American Indians: Their Archaeology and Prehistory*. New York: Thames and Hudson, 1976.

_____. *Native American Prehistory: A Critical Bibliography*. Newberry Library Center for the History of the American Indian Bibliographical Series. Bloomington: Indiana University Press, 1979.

Sonneborn, Liz. *A to Z of Native American Women*. New York: Facts on File, 1998.

Spencer, Robert F., Jesse D. Jennings, et al. *The Native Americans*. New York: Harper & Row, 1977.

Starr, Glenn Ellen. *Lumbee Indians: An Annotated Bibliography with Chronology and Index*. Jefferson, N.C.: McFarland, 1994.

Stern, Kenneth S. *Loud Hawk: The United States Versus the American Indian Movement*. Norman: University of Oklahoma Press, 1994.

Stewart, Omer C. *Peyote Religion: A History*. Norman: University of Oklahoma Press, 1987.

Stuart, Paul. *Nations Within a Nation: Historic Statistics of American Indians*. Westport, Conn.: Greenwood Press, 1987.

Sturtevant, William C., gen. ed. *Handbook of North American Indians*. Washington, D.C.: U.S. Government Printing Office, 1978.

Sullivan, Lawrence E., ed. *Native American Religions: North America*. New York: Macmillan, 1987.

Swann, Brian. *Smoothing the Ground: Essays on Native American Oral Literature*. Berkeley: University of California Press, 1983.

Swisher, Karen G. and AnCita Benally. *Native North American Firsts*. Detroit: Gale Research, 1998.

Taylor, Colin F. *Native American Life: The Family, the Hunt, Pastimes and Cere-monies*. New York: Smithmark, 1996.

Tedlock, Dennis, and Barbara Tedlock, eds. *Teachings from the American Earth: Indian Religion and Philosophy*. New York: Liveright Press, 1975.

Thomas, David D. *The Skull Wars: Kennewick Man, Archaeology, and the Battle for Native American Identity*. New York: Basic Books, 2000.

Thomas, David H., Betty Ballantine, and Ian Ballantine. *The Native Americans: An Illustrated History*. Atlanta, Ga.: Turner, 1993.

Thompson, William N. *Native American Issues: A Reference Handbook*. Santa Barbara, Calif.: ABC-CLIO, 1996.

Thornton, Russell, and Mary K. Gramsmick. *Sociology of American Indians: A Critical Bibliography*. Newberry Library Center for the History of the American Indian Bibliographical Series. Bloomington: Indiana University Press, 1980.

Thornton, Russell, ed. *Studying Native America: Problems and Prospects*. Madison: University of Wisconsin Press, 1998.

Tiller, Veronica E. Velarde. *Tiller's Guide to Indian Country: Economic Profiles of American Indian Reservations*. 2d ed. Albuquerque, N.Mex.: BowArrow, 2000.

Tyler, S. Lyman. *A History of Indian Policy*. Washington, D.C.: U.S. Department of the Interior, Bureau of Indian Affairs, 1973.

Ullom, Judith C., ed. *Folklore of the North American Indians: An Annotated Bibliography*. Washington, D.C.: Library of Congress, 1969.

Underhill, Ruth M. *Red Man's Religion*. Chicago: University of Chicago Press, 1965.

Utley, Robert M., and Wilcomb B. Washburn. *The American Heritage History of the Indian Wars*. New York: American Heritage, 1977.

Vogel, Virgil. *American Indian Medicine*. Norman: University of Oklahoma Press, 1970.

Waldman, Carl. *Atlas of the North American Indians*. New York: Facts on File, 1985.

_____. *Word Dance: The Language of Native American Culture*. New York: Facts on File, 1994.

Warhus, Mark. *Another America: Native American Maps and the History of Our Land*. New York: St. Martin's Press, 1997.

Warrior, Robert A. *Tribal Secrets: Recovering American Indian Intellectual Traditions*. Minneapolis: University of Minnesota Press, 1995.

Washburn, Wilcomb E., ed. *The American Indian and the United States*. 4 vols. New York: Random House, 1973.

Washburn, Wilcomb E. *History of Indian-White Relations*. Vol.4 in *Handbook of North American Indians*. Washington, D.C.: U.S. Government Printing Office, 1988.

Weaver, Jace. *Native American Religious Identity: Unforgotten Gods*. Mary-knoll, N.Y.: Orbis Books, 1998.

Weston, Mary Ann. *Native Americans in the News: Images of Indians in the Twentieth Century Press*. Westport, Conn.: Greenwood Press, 1996.

White, Philip M. *American Indian Studies: A Bibliographic Guide*. Englewood, Colo.: Libraries Unlimited, 1995.

_____. *The Kickapoo Indians, Their History and Culture: An Annotated Bibliography*. Westport, Conn.: Greenwood Press, 1999.

_____. *The Native American Sun Dance Religion and Ceremony: An Annotated Bibliography*. Westport, Conn.:

　　　　　　　　　　　　　American Indian Tribes

Greenwood Press, 1998.

Wishart, David J. *An Unspeakable Sadness: The Dispossession of the Nebraska Indians*. Lincoln: University of Nebraska Press, 1995.

Wolfson, Evelyn. *From Abenaki to Zuni: A Dictionary of Native American Tribes*. New York: Walker, 1988.

Wright, David A., Michael W. Hirlinger, and Robert E. England. *The Politics of Second Generation Discrimination in American Indian Education: Incidence, Explanation, and Mitigating Strategies*. Westport, Conn.: Bergen & Garvey, 1998.

Wunder, John R., ed. *Native American Cultural and Religious Freedoms*. New York: Garland, 1996.

_____. *Native American Sovereignty*. New York: Garland, 1996.

Zimmerman, Larry J. *Native North America*. Boston: Little, Brown, 1996.

HISTORY

Adler, Michael A., ed. *The Prehistoric Pueblo World, A.D. 1150-1350*. Tucson: University of Arizona Press, 1996.

Adams, Howard. *Prison of Grass: Canada from the Native Point of View*. Toronto: New Press, 1975.

Allen, Charles W., and Richard E. Jensen. *From Fort Laramie to Wounded Knee: In the West That Was*. Lincoln: University of Nebraska Press, 1997.

Anderson, Terry Lee. *Sovereign Nations or Reservations?: An Economic History of American Indians*. San Francisco: Pacific Research Institute for Public Policy, 1995.

Axtell, James. *The European and the Indian: Essays in the Ethnohistory of Colonial North America*. New York: Oxford University Press, 1981.

Barrington, Linda, ed. *The Other Side of the Frontier: Economic Explorations into Native American History*.

Boulder, Colo.: Westview Press, 1999.

Berkhofer, Robert F., Jr. *Salvation and the Savage: An Analysis of Protestant Missions and American Indian Response 1787-1862*. Lexington: University of Kentucky Press, 1965.

Britten, Thomas A. *American Indians in World War I: At Home and at War*. Albuquerque: University of Alabama Press, 1997.

_____. *A Brief History of the Seminole-Negro Indian Scouts*. Lewiston, N.Y.: Edwin Mellen Press, 1999.

Brown, Dee A. *Bury My Heart at Wounded Knee: An Indian History of the American West*. New York: Henry Holt, 1970.

Brown, Jennifer S. H. *Strangers in Blood: Fur Trade Company Families in Indian Country*. Vancouver: University of British Columbia Press, 1980.

Brown, Jennifer S. H., and Elizabeth Vibert, eds. *Reading Beyond Words: Contexts for Native History*. Orchard Park, N.Y.: Broadview Press, 1996.

Burt, Larry W. *Tribalism in Crisis: Federal Indian Policy, 1953-1961*. Albuquerque: University of New Mexico Press, 1982.

Calloway, Colin G. *The American Revolution in Indian Country: Crisis and Diversity in Native American Communities*. New York: Cambridge University Press, 1995.

_____. *Crown and Calumet: British-Indian Relations, 1783-1815*. Norman: University of Oklahoma Press, 1987.

_____. *First Peoples: A Documentary Survey of American Indian History*. Boston: Bedford/St. Martin's, 1999.

_____. *New Worlds for All: Indians, Europeans, and the Remaking of Early America*. Baltimore, Md.: Johns Hopkins University Press, 1997.

_____. *The Western Abenakis of Vermont, 1600-1800: War, Migration, and the*

Survival of an Indian People. Norman: University of Oklahoma Press, 1990.
_____, ed. *The World Turned Upside Down: Indian Voices from Early America.* Boston: St. Martin's Press, 1994.

Coe, Joffre L., and Thomas D. Burke. *Town Creek Indian Mound: A Native American Legacy.* Chapel Hill: University of North Carolina Press, 1995.

Cook, Sherburne F. *The Conflict Between the California Indian and White Civilization.* Berkeley: University of California Press, 1974.

Coward, John M. *The Newspaper Indian: Native American Identity in the Press, 1820-90.* Urbana: University of Illinois Press, 1999.

Cowger, Thomas W. *The National Congress of American Indians: The Founding Years.* Lincoln: University of Nebraska Press, 1999.

Cronon, William. *Changes in the Land: Indians, Colonists, and the Ecology of New England.* New York: Hill & Wang, 1983.

Crosby, Alfred W., Jr. *The Columbian Exchange: Biological and Cultural Consequences of 1492.* Westport, Conn.: Greenwood Press, 1972.

Curtis, Edward S. *In a Sacred Manner We Live.* Barre, Mass.: Barre Publishers, 1972.

Debo, Angie. *The Rise and Fall of the Choctaw Republic.* 2d ed. Norman: University of Oklahoma Press, 1967.

Deloria, Vine, and Raymond J. DeMallie. *Documents of American Indian Diplomacy: Treaties, Agreements, and Conventions, 1775-1979.* Norman: University of Oklahoma Press, 1999.

Dickason, Olive P. *The Myth of the Savage and the Beginnings of French Colonialism in the Americas.* Edmonton: University of Alberta Press, 1984.

Dippie, Brian W. *The Vanishing American: White Attitudes and U.S. Indian Policy.* Middletown, Conn.: Wesleyan University Press, 1982.

Fixico, Donald L. *The Invasion of Indian Country in the Twentieth Century: American Capitalism and Tribal Natural Resources.* Niwot: University Press of Colorado, 1998.

_____. *Termination and Relocation: Federal Indian Policy, 1945-1966.* Albuquerque: University of New Mexico Press, 1986.

Foreman, Grant. *Indian Removal: The Emigration of the Five Civilized Tribes of Indians.* Norman: University of Oklahoma Press, 1932.

Francis, Lee. *A Historical Time Line of Native America.* New York: St. Martin's Griffin, 1996.

Franco, Jere B. *Crossing the Pond: The Native American Effort in World War II.* Denton: University of North Texas Press, 1999.

Fritz, Henry. *The Movement for Indian Assimilation, 1860-1890.* Philadelphia: University of Pennsylvania Press, 1963.

Getty, Ian A. L., and Antoine S. Lussier. *As Long as the Sun Shines and Water Flows: A Reader in Canadian Native Studies.* Vancouver: University of British Columbia Press, 1983.

Gleach, Frederic W. *Powhatan's World and Colonial Virginia: A Conflict of Cultures.* Lincoln: University of Nebraska Press, 1997.

Green, Michael D. *The Politics of Indian Removal: Creek Government and Society in Crisis.* Lincoln: University of Nebraska Press, 1982.

Greene, Jerome A. *Lakota and Cheyenne: Indian Views of the Great Sioux War, 1876-1877.* Norman: University of Oklahoma Press, 1994.

_____, ed. *Battles and Skirmishes of the Great Sioux War, 1876-1877: The Military View.* Norman: University of Oklahoma Press, 1993.

Hagan, William T. *American Indians.* Rev. ed. Chicago: University of Chicago Press, 1979.

Hardorff, Richard G. *Hokahey! A Good Day to Die!: The Indian Casualties of the Custer Fight.* Spokane, Wash.: Arthur H. Clark, 1993.

Hanke, Lewis. *Aristotle and the American Indians.* Chicago: Henry Regnery, 1959.

Hays, Robert G. *A Race at Bay: New York Times Editorials on "the Indian Problem," 1860-1900.* Carbondale, Ill.: Southern Illinois University Press, 1997.

Heizer, Robert F. *The Destruction of California Indians.* Lincoln: University of Nebraska Press, 1993.

Hilger, M. Inez. *Chippewa Families: A Social Study of White Earth Reservation, 1938.* St, Paul, Minn.: Minnesota Historical Society Press, 1998.

Horsman, Reginald. *Expansion and American Indian Policy, 1783-1812.* East Lansing: Michigan State University Press, 1967.

Hoxie, Frederick E. *A Final Promise: The Campaign to Assimilate the Indians, 1880-1920.* Lincoln: University of Nebraska Press, 1984.

Hoxie, Frederick E., Ronald Hoffman, and Peter J. Albert. *Native Americans and the Early Republic.* Charlottesville: University Press of Virginia, 1999.

Hoxie, Frederick E., and Peter Iverson. *Indians in American History: An Introduction.* 2d ed. Wheeling, Ill.: Harlan Davidson, 1998.

Huddleston, Lee Eldridge. *Origins of the American Indians: European Concepts, 1492-1729.* Austin: University of Texas Press, 1967.

Jackson, Helen Hunt. *A Century of Dishonor: A Sketch of the United States Government's Dealings with Some of the Indian Tribes.* New York:

Harper and Brothers. 1881.

_____. *The Indian Reform Letters of Helen Hunt Jackson, 1879-1885.* Norman: University of Oklahoma Press, 1998.

Jacobs, Wilbur R. *Dispossessing the American Indian: Indians and Whites on the Colonial Frontier.* New York: Charles Scribner's Sons, 1972.

Jaenen, Cornelius J. *Friend and Foe: Aspects of French- Amerindian Cultural Contact in the Sixteenth and Seventeenth Centuries.* New York: Columbia University Press, 1976.

Jennings, Francis. *The Invasion of America.* New York: W. W. Norton, 1975.

John, Elizabeth A. H. *Storms Brewed in Other Men's Worlds: The Confrontation of Indians, Spanish, and French in the Southwest, 1540-1795.* Lincoln: University of Nebraska Press, 1975.

Jones, Dorothy V. *License for Empire: Colonialism by Treaty in Early America.* Chicago: University of Chicago Press, 1982.

Keller, Robert H. *American Protestantism and United States Indian Policy, 1869-82.* Lincoln: University of Nebraska Press, 1983.

Kennedy, John H. *Jesuit and Savage in New France.* New Haven, Conn.: Yale University Press, 1950.

Kessler, Donna J. *The Making of Sacagawea: A Euro-American Legend.* Tuscaloosa: University of Alabama Press, 1996.

Knaut, Andrew L. *The Pueblo Revolt of 1680: Conquest and Resistance in Seventeenth-century New Mexico.* Norman: University of Oklahoma Press, 1995.

Krech, Shepard, III. *The Ecological Indian: Myth and History.* New York: W.W. Norton, 1999.

LePore, Jill. *The Name of War: King Philip's War and the Origins of American Identity.* New York: Alfred

A. Knopf, 1998.

Liebersohn, Harry. *Aristocratic Encounters: European Travelers and North American Indians.* New York: Cambridge University Press, 1998.

Little Bear, Leroy, and Menno Boldt, eds. *Pathways to Self-Determination.* Toronto: University of Toronto Press, 1984.

Longhena, Maria. *Ancient Mexico: The History and Culture of the Maya, Aztecs, and Other Pre-Columbian Peoples.* New York: Tabori & Chang, 1998.

McCormick, Anita L. *Native Americans and the Reservation in American History.* Springfield, N.J.: Enslow, 1996.

McCutchen, David, ed. *The Red Record: The Wallam Olum, the Oldest Native North American History.* Garden City Park, N.Y.: Avery, 1993.

McMurtry, Larry. *Crazy Horse.* New York: Viking Press, 1999.

Mancall, Peter C., and James H. Merrell. *American Encounters: Natives and Newcomers from European Contact to Indian Removal.* New York: Routledge, 1999.

Milanich, Jerald T., and Susan Milbruth, eds. *First Encounters: Spanish Explorations in the Caribbean and the United States, 1492-1570.* Gainesville: University of Florida Press, 1989.

Miller, Jay, Colin G. Calloway, and Richard A. Sattler. *Writings in Indian History, 1985-1990.* Norman: University of Oklahoma Press, 1995.

Miller, J. R. *Skyscrapers Hide the Heavens: A History of Indian-White Relations in Canada.* Toronto: University of Toronto Press, 1989.

Moeller, Bill, and Jan Moeller. *Chief Joseph and the Nez Perces: A Photographic History.* Missoula, Mont.: Mountain Press, 1995.

Mooney, James. *The Ghost-dance Religion and the Sioux Outbreak of 1890.* 1896. Reprint. Lincoln: University of Nebraska Press, 1991.

Morrison, Kenneth M. *The Embattled Northeast: The Elusive Ideal of Alliance in Abenaki-Euramerican Relations.* Berkeley: University of California Press, 1984.

Moses, L.G. *Wild West Shows and the Images of American Indians, 1883-1933.* Albuquerque: University of New Mexico Press, 1996.

Nash, Gary B. *Red, White, and Black: The Peoples of Early America.* Englewood Cliffs, N.J.: Prentice-Hall, 1974.

Parker, Arthur C. *Red Jacket: Seneca Chief.* Lincoln: University of Nebraska Press, 1998.

Priest, Loring Benson. *Uncle Sam's Stepchildren: The Reformation of United States Indian Policy, 1865-1887.* New Brunswick, N.J.: Rutgers University Press, 1942.

Prucha, Francis Paul. *The Great Father: The United States Government and the American Indians.* Lincoln: University of Nebraska Press, 1986.

Ray, Arthur J. *Indians in the Fur Trade: Their Role as Trappers, Hunters, and Middlemen in the Lands Southwest of Hudson Bay, 1660-1870.* Toronto: University of Toronto Press, 1974.

Rawls, James J. *Chief Red Fox Is Dead: A History of Native America Since 1945.* Fort Worth, Tex.: Harcourt Brace College Publishers, 1996.

Redmond, Elsa M., ed. *Chiefdoms and Chieftaincy in the Americas.* Gainesville: University Press of Florida, 1998.

Riley, Carroll L. *Rio Del Norte: People of the Upper Rio Grande from Earliest Times to the Pueblo Revolt.* Salt Lake City: University of Utah Press, 1995.

Rountree, Helen C., ed. *Powhatan Foreign Relations, 1500-1722.*

Charlottesville: University Press of Virginia, 1993.

Salisbury, Neal. *Manitou and Providence: Indians, Europeans, and the Making of New England*. New York: Oxford University Press, 1982.

Sando, Joe S. *Pueblo Nations: Eight Centuries of Pueblo Indian History*. Sante Fe, N.Mex.: Clear Light, 1992.

Sandos, James A., and Larry E. Burgess. *The Hunt for Willie Boy: Indian-hating and Popular Culture*. Norman: University of Oklahoma Press, 1994.

Satz, Ronald N. *American Indian Policy in the Jacksonian Era*. Lincoln: University of Nebraska Press, 1975.

Sheehan, Bernard W. *Savagism and Civility: Indians and Englishmen in Colonial Virginia*. New York: Cambridge University Press, 1980.

_____. *Seeds of Extinction: Jeffersonian Philanthropy and the American Indian*. Chapel Hill: University of North Carolina Press, 1973.

Sherrow, Victoria. *Cherokee Nation v. Georgia: Native American Rights*. Springfield, N.J.: Enslow, 1997.

Stannard, David E., *American Holocaust: The Conquest of the New World*. New York: Oxford University Press, 1992.

Starkey, Armstrong. *European and Native American Warfare, 1675-1815*. Norman: University of Oklahoma Press, 1998.

Stern, Theodore. *Chiefs and Change in the Oregon Country: Indian Relations at Fort Nez Perces, 1818-1855*. Corvallis: Oregon State University Press, 1996.

Sugden, John. *Tecumseh: A Life*. New York: Henry Holt, 1998.

Szasz, Margaret C. *Education and the American Indian: The Road to Self-determination Since 1928*. 3d ed. Albuquerque: University of New Mexico Press, 1999.

_____. *Indian Education in the American Colonies, 1607-1783*. Albuquerque: University of New Mexico Press, 1988.

Trennert, Robert A., Jr. *Alternative to Extinction: Federal Indian Policy and the Beginnings of the Reservation System, 1846-51*. Philadelphia: University of Pennsylvania Press, 1975.

Trigger, Bruce G. *Natives and Newcomers: Canada's "Heroic Age" Reconsidered*. Montreal: McGill-Queen's University Press, 1985.

Utley, Robert M. *The Indian Frontier of the American West, 1846-1890*. Albuquerque: University of New Mexico Press, 1984.

Viola, Herman J. *Diplomats in Buckskin: A History of the Indian Delegations in Washington City*. Washington, D.C.: Smithsonian Institution Press, 1981.

Wallace, Anthony F.C. *Jefferson and the Indians: The Tragic Fate of the First Americans*. Cambridge, Mass.: Belknap Press of Harvard University Press, 1999.

Washburn, Wilcomb E. *The Assault on Indian Tribalism: The General Allotment Law (Dawes Act) of 1887*. Philadelphia: J. B. Lippincott, 1975.

Weaver, Sally M. *Making Canadian Indian Policy: The Hidden Agenda, 1968-70*. Toronto: University of Toronto Press, 1981.

Weber, David J. *What Caused the Pueblo Revolt of 1680?* Boston: Bedford/St. Martin's Press, 1999.

White, Richard. *The Roots of Dependency: Subsistence, Environment, and Social Change Among the Choctaws, Paw-nees, and Navajos*. Lincoln: University of Nebraska Press, 1983.

Williams, Robert A. *Linking Arms Together: American Indian Treaty Visions of Law and Peace, 1600-1800*. New York: Oxford University Press,

1997.

Wilson, James. *The Earth Shall Weep: A History of Native America.* New York: Atlantic Monthly Press, 1999.

Wright, J. Leitch, Jr., and James H. Merrell. *The Only Land They Knew: American Indians in the Old South.* Lincoln: University of Nebraska Press, 1999.

CULTURE AREAS

ARCTIC AND SUBARCTIC

Boas, Franz. *The Central Eskimo.* Bureau of American Ethnology, Annual Report 6 (1884-1885). Washington, D.C.: U.S. Government Printing Office. 1888.

Catton, Theodore. *Inhabited Wilderness: Indians, Eskimos, and National Parks in Alaska.* Albuquerque: University of New Mexico Press, 1997.

Chance, Norman A. *The Eskimo of North Alaska.* New York: Holt, Rinehart and Winston, 1966.

Condon, Richard G. *Inuit Youth: Growth and Change in the Canadian Arctic.* New Brunswick, N.J.: Rutgers University Press, 1987.

Damas, David. *Arctic.* Vol. 5 in *Handbook of North American Indians.* Washington, D.C.: Smithsonian Institution Press, 1984.

Dumond, Don E. *The Eskimos and Aleuts.* Rev. ed. London: Thames and Hudson, 1987.

Fienup-Riordan, Ann. *Boundaries and Passages: Rule and Ritual in Yup'ik Eskimo Oral Tradition.* Norman: University of Oklahoma Press, 1994.

Helm, June. *The Indians of the Subarctic: A Critical Bibliography.* Newberry Library Center for the History of the American Indian Bibliographical Series. Bloomington: Indiana University Press, 1976.

_____. *Prophecy and Power Among the Dogrib Indians.* Lincoln: University of Nebraska Press, 1994.

_____, ed. *Subarctic.* Vol. 6 in *Handbook of North American Indians.* Washington, D.C.: Smithsonian Institution Press, 1981.

Hensel, Chase. *Telling Our Selves: Ethnicity and Discourse in Southwestern Alaska.* New York: Oxford University Press, 1996.

Ives, John W. *A Theory of Northern Athapaskan Prehistory.* Boulder, Colo.: Westview Press, 1990.

Kohlhoff, Dean. *When the Wind Was a River: Aleut Evacuation in World War II.* Seattle: University of Washington Press, 1995.

Krech, Shepard, III, ed. *The Subarctic Fur Trade: Native Social and Economic Adaptations.* Vancouver: University of British Columbia Press, 1984.

Lowry, Shannon. *Natives of the Far North: Alaska's Vanishing Culture in the Eye of Edward Sheriff Curtis.* Mechanicsburg, Pa.: Stackpole Books, 1994.

Mitchell, Donald. *Sold American: The Story of Alaska Natives and Their Land, 1867-1959: The Army to Statehood.* Hanover, N.H.: University Press of New England, 1997.

Nelson, Richard K. *Hunters of the Northern Forest.* Chicago: University of Chicago Press, 1973.

_____. *Hunters of the Northern Ice.* Chicago: University of Chicago Press, 1969.

Olson, Wallace M. *The Tlingit: an Introduction to Their Culture and History.* 3d ed. Auke Bay, Alaska: Heritage Research, 1997.

Oswalt, Wendell H. *Eskimos and Explorers.* Novato, Calif.: Chandler and Sharp, 1979.

Ray, Dorothy J. *Aleut and Eskimo Art: Tradition and Innovation in South Alaska.* Seattle: University of Washington Press, 1981.

Simeone, William E. *Rifles, Blankets, and Beads: Identity, History, and the Northern Athapaskan Potlatch.* Norman: University of Oklahoma Press, 1995.

Skinner, Ramona E. *Alaska Native Policy in the Twentieth Century.* New York: Garland, 1997.

VanStone, James W. *Athapaskan Adaptations: Hunters and Fishermen of the Subarctic Forests.* Chicago: Aldine, 1974.

CALIFORNIA

Bahr, Diana M. *From Mission to Metropolis: Cupeno Indian Women in Los Angeles.* Norman: University of Oklahoma Press, 1993.

Bean, Lowell J. *Mukat's People: The Cahuilla Indians of Southern California.* Berkeley: University of California Press, 1973.

Chartkoff, Joseph L., and Kerry K. Chartkoff. *The Archaeology of California.* Stanford, Calif.: Stanford University Press, 1984.

Davis-Kimball, Jeannine. *Finding Guide to the California Indian Library Collections: California State Library.* 8 vols. Berkeley: University of California Press, 1993.

Grant, Campbell. *The Rock Painting of the Chumash: A Study of a California Indian Culture.* Berkeley: University of California Press, 1965.

Heizer, Robert F. *The Destruction of California Indians.* Lincoln: University of Nebraska Press, 1993.

_____. *The Indians of California: A Critical Bibliography.* Newberry Library Center for the History of the American Indian Bibliographical Series. Bloomington: Indiana University Press, 1976.

_____, ed. *California.* Vol. 8 in *Handbook of North American Indians.* Washington, D.C.: Smithsonian Institution Press, 1978.

Heizer, Robert F., and Albert B. Elsasser, comps. *A Bibliography of California Indians: Archaeology, Ethnography, and Indian History.* New York: Garland, 1977.

Heizer, Robert F., and Theodora Kroeber, eds. *Ishi, the Last Yahi: A Documentary History.* Berkeley: University of California Press, 1979.

Heizer, Robert F., and Mary A. Whipple, eds. *The California Indians: A Source Book.* 2d rev. ed. Berkeley: University of California Press, 1971.

Holmes, Marie S., and John R. Johnson. *The Chumash and Their Predecessors: An Annotated Bibliography.* Santa Barbara, Calif.: Santa Barbara Museum of Natural History, 1998.

Keeling, Richard. *Cry for Luck: Sacred Song and Speech Among the Yurok, Hupa, and Karok Indians of Northwestern California.* Berkeley: University of California Press, 1992.

Kroeber, Theodora, and Robert F. Heizer. *Almost Ancestors: The First Californians,* edited by F. David Hales. San Francisco: Sierra Club Books, 1968.

Lee, Gaylen D. *Walking Where We Lived: Memoirs of a Mono Indian Family.* Norman: University of Oklahoma Press, 1998.

McCawley, William. *The First Angelinos: The Gabrielino Indians of Los Angeles.* Novato, Calif.: Ballena Press, 1996.

Ray, Verne F. *Primitive Pragmatists: The Modoc Indians of Northern California.* Seattle: University of Washington Press, 1963.

Shipek, Florence C. *Pushed into the Rocks: Southern California Indian Land Tenure, 1769-1986.* Lincoln: University of Nebraska Press, 1987.

White, Phillip M., and Stephen D. Fitt. *Bibliography of the Indians of San Diego County: The Kumeyaay,*

Diegueno, Luiseno, and Cupeno. Lanham, Md.: Scarecrow Press, 1998.

GREAT BASIN

Beck, Charlotte, ed. *Models for the Millennium: Great Basin Anthropology Today.* Salt Lake City: University of Utah Press, 1999.

Bunte, Pamela A., and Robert J. Franklin. *From the Sands to the Mountain: Change and Persistence in a Southern Paiute Community.* Lincoln: University of Nebraska Press, 1987.

Crum, Steven J. *The Road on Which We Came = Po'i pentun tammen kimmappeh: A History of the Western Shoshone.* Salt Lake City: University of Utah Press, 1994.

D'Azevedo, Warren L. *Great Basin.* Vol. 11 in *Handbook of North American Indians.* Washington, D.C.: Smithsonian Institution Press, 1986.

_____, ed. and comp. *The Washo Indians of California and Nevada.* University of Utah Anthropological Papers 67. Salt Lake City: University of Utah Press, 1963.

Densmore, Frances. *Northern Ute Music.* Bureau of American Ethnology, Bulletin 75. Washington, D.C.: U.S. Government Printing Office, 1922.

Fowler, Don D., ed. *Great Basin Cultural Ecology: A Symposium.* Desert Research Institute Publications in the Social Sciences 8. Reno, Nev.: Publications Office of the Desert Research Institute, 1972.

Grayson, Donald K. *The Desert's Past: A Natural Prehistory of the Great Basin.* Washington: Smithsonian Institution Press, 1993.

Hopkins, Sarah Winnemucca. *Life Among the Piutes: Their Wrongs and Claims.* New York: G. P. Putnam's Sons, 1883.

Knack, Martha. *Life Is with People.* Socorro, N.Mex.: Ballena Press, 1980.

Knack, Martha, and Omer C. Stewart. *As Long as the River Shall Run: An Ethnohistory of Pyramid Lake Indian Reservation.* Berkeley: University of California Press. 1984.

Laird, Carobeth. *Mirror and Pattern: George Laird's World of Chemehuevi Mythology.* Banning, Calif.: Malki Museum Press, 1984.

Madsen, Brigham D. *The Bannock of Idaho.* Caldwell, Idaho: Caxton Printers, 1958.

Steward, Julian H. *Basin-Plateau Aboriginal Sociopolitical Groups.* Bureau of American Ethnology, Bulletin 120. Washington, D.C.: U.S. Government Printing Office, 1938.

Stewart, Omer C. *Indians of the Great Basin: A Critical Bibliography.* Newberry Library Center for the History of the American Indian Bibliographical Series. Bloomington: Indiana University Press, 1982.

NORTHEAST

Anson, Bert. *The Miami Indians.* Norman: University of Oklahoma Press, 1970.

Barnouw, Victor. *Wisconsin Chippewa Myths and Tales and Their Relation to Chippewa Life.* Madison: University of Wisconsin Press, 1977.

Black Hawk (Ma-ka-tai-me-she-kia-kiak). *An Autobiography,* edited by Donald Jackson. Urbana: University of Illinois Press, 1955.

Brose, David S., et al. *Ancient Art of the American Woodlands Indians.* New York: Harry N. Abrams, in association with the Detroit Institute of Arts, 1985.

Calloway, Colin G., ed. *After King Philip's War: Presence and Persistence in Indian New England.* Hanover, N.H.: University Press of New England, 1997.

_____, ed. *Dawnland Encounters: Indians and Europeans in Northern*

New England. Hanover, N.H.: University Press of New England, 1991.

Clifton, James A. *The Prairie People: Continuity and Change in Potawatomi Indian Culture, 1665-1965*. Lawrence, Kans.: Regents Press of Kansas, 1977.

Densmore, Frances. *Chippewa Customs*. Bureau of American Ethnology, Bulletin 86. Washington, D.C.: U.S. Government Printing Office, 1929.

_____. *Chippewa Music*. 2 vols. Bureau of American Ethnology, Bulletins 45 and 53. Washington, D.C.: U.S. Government Printing Office, 1910-1913.

_____. *Uses of Plants by the Chippewa Indians*. Bureau of American Ethnology, Annual Report 44 (1926-1927). Washington, D.C.: U.S. Government Printing Office, 1928.

Edmunds, R. David. *Kinsmen Through Time: An Annotated Bibliography of Potawatomi History*. Metuchen, N.J.: Scarecrow Press, 1987.

_____. *The Potawatomis: Keepers of the Fire*. Norman: University of Oklahoma Press, 1978.

Gibson, Arrell M. *The Kickapoos: Lords of the Middle Border*. Norman: University of Oklahoma Press, 1963.

Grumet, Robert S. *Historic Contact: Indian People and Colonists in Today's Northeastern United States in the Sixteenth Through Eighteenth Centuries*. Norman: University of Oklahoma Press, 1995.

Hagan, William T. *The Sac and the Fox Indians*. Norman: University of Oklahoma Press, 1958.

Hale, Horatio E., ed. *The Iroquois Book of Rites*. Brinton's Library of Aboriginal American Literature 11. Philadelphia: D. G. Brinton, 1883.

Hauptman, Laurence M., and James Wherry. *The Pequots in Southern New England: The Fall and Rise of an American Indian Nation*. Norman:

University of Oklahoma Press, 1990.

Hickerson, Harold. *The Chippewa and Their Neighbors: A Study in Ethnohistory*. Prospect Heights, Ill.: Waveland Press, 1988.

Kinietz, W. Vernon. *The Indians of the Western Great Lakes, 1615-1760*. Ann Arbor: University of Michigan Press, 1940.

Landes, Ruth. *Ojibwa Religion and the Mdewiwin*. Madison: University of Wisconsin Press, 1968.

_____. *Ojibwa Sociology*. Columbia University Contributions to Anthropology 29. New York: Columbia University Press, 1937.

Lyford, Carrie A. *Iroquois Crafts*. Lawrence, Kans.: Haskell Institute Press, 1945.

_____. *Ojibway Crafts*. Lawrence, Kans.: Haskell Institute Press, 1943.

Mandell, Daniel R. *Behind the Frontier: Indians in Eighteenth Century Eastern Massachusetts*. Lincoln: University of Nebraska Press, 1996.

Mason, Ronald J. *Great Lakes Archaeology*. New York: Academic Press, 1981.

Morgan, Lewis Henry. *League of the Ho-de-no-sau-nee or Iroquois*. Rochester, N.Y.: Sage and Brothers, 1851.

Morgan, William N. *Prehistoric Architecture in the Eastern United States*. Cambridge, Mass.: MIT Press, 1980.

Mountain Wolf Woman. *Mountain Wolf Woman, Sister of Crashing Thunder: The Autobiography of a Winnebago Indian*, edited by Nancy O. Lurie. Ann Arbor: University of Michigan Press, 1961.

Quimby, George I. *Indian Life in the Upper Great Lakes: 11,000 B.C. to A.D. 1800*. Chicago: University of Chicago Press, 1960.

Radin, Paul, ed. *The Autobiography of a Winnebago Indian*. University of California Publications in American

Archaeology and Ethnology, vol. 16, no. 7. Berkeley: University of California Press, 1920.

Radin, Paul. *The Winnebago Tribe.* Bureau of American Ethnology, Annual Report 37 (1915-1916). Washington, D.C.: U.S. Government Printing Office, 1923.

Ritzenthaler, Robert E., and Pat Ritzenthaler. *The Woodland Indians of the Western Great Lakes.* Garden City, N.Y.: Natural History Press, 1970.

Salisbury, Neal. *The Indians of New England: A Critical Bibliography.* Newberry Library Center for the History of the American Indian Bibliographical Series. Bloomington: Indiana University Press, 1982.

Snow, Dean R. *The Archaeology of New England.* New York: Academic Press, 1980.

Strong, John A. *"We Are Still Here!":* *The Algonquian Peoples of Long Island Today.* 2d ed. Interlaken, N.Y.: Empire State Books, 1998.

Tanner, Helen Hornbeck, et al. *Atlas of Great Lakes Indian History.* Norman: University of Oklahoma Press, 1986.

Time-Life Books. *Algonquians of the East Coast.* Alexandria, Va.: Time-Life Books, 1995.

Tooker, Elisabeth. *The Indians of the Northeast: A Critical Bibliography.* Newberry Library Center for the History of the American Indian Bibliographical Series. Bloomington: Indiana University Press, 1978.

_____, ed. *Native North American Spirituality of the Eastern Woodlands: Sacred Myths, Dreams, Visions, Speeches, Healing Formulas, Rituals, and Ceremonies.* Mahwah, N.J.: Paulist Press, 1979.

Trigger, Bruce G. *The Huron: Farmers of the North.* New York: Holt, Rinehart and Winston, 1969.

_____, ed. *Northeast.* Vol. 15 in *Handbook of North American Indians.*

Washington, D.C.: Smithsonian Institution Press, 1978.

Vennum, Thomas, Jr. *Wild Rice and the Ojibway People.* St. Paul: Minnesota Historical Society, 1988.

Wallace, Anthony F. C. *The Death and Rebirth of the Seneca.* New York: Alfred A. Knopf, 1969.

Webb, William S., and Charles E. Snow. *The Adena People.* Knoxville: University of Tennessee Press, 1974.

NORTHWEST COAST AND PLATEAU

Amoss, Pamela. *Coast Salish Spirit Dancing: The Survival of an Ancestral Religion.* Seattle: University of Washington Press, 1978.

Boas, Franz. *Kwakiutl Ethnography,* edited by Helen Codere. Chicago: University of Chicago Press, 1966.

Codere, Helen. *Fighting with Property: A Study of Kwakiutl Potlatching and Warfare 1792-1930.* New York: J. J. Augustin, 1950.

Drucker, Philip. *Cultures of the North Pacific Coast.* San Francisco: Chandler, 1965.

Fahey, John. *The Flathead Indians.* Norman: University of Oklahoma Press, 1974.

Grumet, Robert S. *Native Americans of the Northwest Coast: A Critical Bibliography.* Newberry Library Center for the History of the American Indian Bibliographical Series. Bloomington: Indiana University Press, 1979.

Haines, Francis. *The Nez Percé: Tribesmen of the Columbian Plateau.* Norman: University of Oklahoma Press, 1955.

Harkin, Michael E. *The Heiltsuks: Dialogues of Culture and History on the Northwest Coast.* Lincoln: University of Nebraska Press, 1997.

Inverarity, Robert B. *Art of the Northwest Coast Indians.* Berkeley: University of California Press, 1950.

Kirk, Ruth, and Richard D. Daughtery. *Exploring Washington Archaeology.* Seattle: University of Washington Press, 1978.

Miller, Jay. *Tsimshian Culture: A Light Through the Ages.* Lincoln: University of Nebraska Press, 1997.

Miller, Jay, and Carol Eastman, ed. *The Tsimshian and Their Neighbors on the North Pacific Coast.* Seattle: University of Washington Press, 1984.

Mourning Dove (Humishuma). *Coyote Stories*, edited by Jay Miller. Lincoln: University of Nebraska Press, 1990.

_____. *Mourning Dove: A Salishan Autobiography*, edited by Jay Miller. Lincoln: University of Nebraska Press, 1990.

People of 'Ksan. *Gathering What the Great Nature Provided: Food Traditions of the Gitksan.* Seattle: University of Washington Press, 1980.

Quinn, Arthur. *Hell with the Fire Out: A History of the Modoc War.* Boston: Faber & Faber, 1997.

Ruby, Robert H., and John A. Brown. *A Guide to the Indian Tribes of the Pacific Northwest.* Norman: University of Oklahoma Press, 1986.

Samuel, Cheryl. *The Chilkat Dancing Blanket.* Seattle: Pacific Search Press, 1982.

Smyth, Willie, and Esme Ryan, eds. *Spirit of the First People: Native American Music Traditions of Washington State.* Seattle: University of Washington Press, 1999.

Spradley, James, ed. *Guests Never Leave Hungry: The Autobiography of James Sewid, a Kwakiutl Indian.* New Haven, Conn.: Yale University Press, 1969.

Stewart, Hilary. *Artifacts of the Northwest Coast Indians.* Saanichton, British Columbia: Hancock House Publishers, 1973.

_____. *Cedar: Tree of Life to the Northwest Coast Indians.* Seattle: University of Washington Press, 1984.

_____. *Indian Fishing: Early Methods on the Northwest Coast.* Seattle: University of Washington Press, 1977.

Trafzer, Clifford E. *Yakima, Palouse, Cayuse, Umatilla, Walla Walla, and Wanapum Indians: An Historical Bibliography.* Metuchen, N.J.: Scarecrow Press, 1992.

_____, ed. *Northwestern Tribes in Exile: Modoc, Nez Perce, and Palouse Removal to the Indian Territory.* Sacramento, Calif.: Sierra Oaks, 1987.

PLAINS

Ahler, Stanley A., Thomas D. Thiessen, and Michael K. Trimble. *People of the Willows: The Prehistory and Early History of the Hidatsa Indians.* Grand Forks: University of North Dakota Press, 1991.

Albers, Patricia, and Beatrice Medicine. *The Hidden Half: Studies in Plains Indian Women.* Lanham, Md.: University Press of America, 1983.

Baird, W. David. *The Quapaw Indians: A History of the Downstream People.* Norman: University of Oklahoma Press, 1981.

Berthrong, Donald J. *The Southern Cheyennes.* Norman: University of Oklahoma Press, 1963.

Black Elk, as told to John G. Neihardt. *Black Elk Speaks.* New York: William Morrow, 1932.

Blaine, Martha R. *The Pawnees: A Critical Bibliography.* Newberry Library Center for the History of the American Indian Bibliographical Series. Bloomington: Indiana University Press, 1980.

Blish, Helen H. *A Pictographic History of the Oglala Sioux, Drawings by Amos Bad Heart Bull.* Lincoln: University of Nebraska Press, 1967.

Bowers, Alfred W. *Mandan Social and Ceremonial Organization*. Chicago: University of Chicago Press, 1950.

Brown, Joseph E. *The Sacred Pipe: Black Elk's Account of the Seven Rites of the Oglala Sioux*. Norman: University of Oklahoma Press, 1953.

Calloway, Colin G., ed. *Our Hearts Fell to the Ground: Plains Indian Views of How the West Was Lost*. Boston: Bedford Books of St. Martin's Press, 1996.

Carlson, Paul H. *The Plains Indians*. College Station: Texas A&M University Press, 1998.

Carter, Cecile E. *Caddo Indians: Where We Come From*. Norman: University of Oklahoma Press, 1995.

DeMallie, Raymond, ed. *The Sixth Grandfather: Black Elk's Teachings Given to John G. Neihardt*. Lincoln: University of Nebraska Press, 1984.

DeMallie, Raymond, and Douglas R. Parks, eds. *Sioux Indian Religion*. Norman: University of Oklahoma Press, 1987.

Densmore, Frances. *Cheyenne and Arapaho Music*. Southwest Museum Papers 10. Los Angeles: Southwest Museum, 1936.

_____. *Mandan and Hidatsa Music*. Bureau of American Ethnology, Bulletin 80. Washington, D.C.: U.S. Government Printing Office, 1923.

_____. *Pawnee Music*. Bureau of American Ethnology, Bulletin 93. Washington, D.C.: U.S. Government Printing Office, 1929.

_____. *Teton Sioux Music*. Bureau of American Ethnology, Bulletin 61. Washington, D.C.: Government Printing Office, 1918.

Dorsey, George A. *The Cheyenne*. Field Columbian Museum Anthropological Series, vol. 9, nos. 1 and 2. Chicago: The Museum, 1905.

Ewers, John C. *The Blackfeet: Raiders on the Northwestern Plains*. Norman: University of Oklahoma Press, 1958.

_____. *Blackfoot Crafts*. Lawrence, Kans.: Haskell Institute Printing Department, 1945.

_____. *The Horse in Blackfoot Culture*. Bureau of American Ethnology, Bulletin 159. Washington, D.C.: U.S. Government Printing Office, 1955.

_____. *Plains Indian History and Culture: Essays on Continuity and Change*. Norman: University of Oklahoma Press, 1997.

Fenelon, James V. *Culturicide, Resistance, and Survival of the Lakota "Sioux Nation"*. New York: Garland, 1998.

Feraca, Stephen E. *Wakinyan: Lakota Religion in the Twentieth Century*. Lincoln: University of Nebraska Press, 1998.

Fletcher, Alice C. *The Hako: A Pawnee Ceremony*. Bureau of American Ethnology, Annual Report 22. (1900-1901). Washington, D.C.: U.S. Government Printing Office, 1904.

Fletcher, Alice C., and Francis La Flesche. *The Omaha Tribe*. 2 vols. Bureau of American Ethnology, Annual Report 27 (1905-1906). Washington, D.C.: U.S. Government Printing Office, 1911.

Fowler, Loretta. *Arapahoe Politics, 1851-1978*. Lincoln: University of Nebraska Press, 1982.

Frison, George. *Prehistoric Hunters of the High Plains*. New York: Academic Press, 1978.

Gilmore, Melvin R. *Uses of Plants by the Indians of the Missouri River Region*. Bureau of American Ethnology, Annual Report 33 (1911-1912). Washington, D.C.: U.S. Government Printing Office, 1919.

Gonzalez, Mario, and Elizabeth Cook-Lynn. *The Politics of Hallowed Ground: Wounded Knee and the Struggle for Indian Sovereignty*. Urbana: University of Illinois Press, 1999.

Grinnell, George B. *The Cheyenne Indians: Their History and Ways of*

Life. 2 vols. New Haven, Conn.: Yale University Press, 1923.

Hassrick, Royal B. *The Sioux: Life and Customs of a Warrior Society*. Norman: University of Oklahoma Press, 1964.

Hoebel, E. Adamson. *The Plains Indians: A Critical Bibliography*. Newberry Library Center for the History of the American Indian Bibliographical Series. Bloomington: Indiana University Press, 1979.

Holder, Preston. *The Hoe and the Horse on the Plains*. Lincoln: University of Nebraska Press, 1970.

Hyde, George E.. *Spotted Tail's Folk: A History of the Brule Sioux*. Norman: University of Oklahoma Press, 1961.

Iverson, Peter, ed. *The Plains Indians of the Twentieth Century*. Norman: University of Oklahoma Press, 1985.

Llewellen, Karl N., and E. Adamson Hoebel. *The Cheyenne Way: Conflict and Case Law in Primitive Jurisprudence*. Norman: University of Oklahoma Press, 1941.

Lowie, Robert H. *The Crow Indians*. New York: Farrar and Rinehart, 1935.

_____. *Indians of the Plains*. New York: McGraw-Hill, 1954.

_____. *Myths and Traditions of the Crow Indians*. Anthropological Papers of the American Museum of Natural History, vol. 25, pt. 1. New York: Order of Trustees, 1918.

_____. *Social Life of the Crow Indians*. Anthropological Papers of the American Museum of Natural History, vol. 9, pt. 2. New York: Order of Trustees, 1912.

Lyford, Carrie A. *Quill and Beadwork of the Western Sioux*. Lawrence, Kans.: Printing Department, Haskell Institute, 1940.

Mandelbaum, David G. *The Plains Cree*. Anthropological Papers of the American Museum of Natural History, vol. 37, pt. 2. New York: Order of Trustees, 1940.

Meyer, Roy W. *History of the Santee Sioux: United States Indian Policy on Trial*. Rev. ed. Lincoln: University of Nebraska Press, 1993.

Murie, James R. *Ceremonies of the Pawnee*. 2 parts, edited by Douglas R. Parks. 2 vols. Washington, D.C.: Smithsonian Institution Press, 1981.

Newkumet, Vynola Beaver, and Howard L. Meridith. *Hasinai: A Traditional History of the Caddo Confederacy*. College Station: Texas A&M University Press, 1988.

Petersen, Karen D. *Plains Indian Art from Fort Marion*. Norman: University of Oklahoma Press, 1971.

Plenty Coups. *American: The Life Story of a Great Indian, Plenty-coups, Chief of the Crows*, edited by Frank B. Linderman. Chicago, N.Y.: World Book, 1930.

Powell, Peter J. *The Cheyennes, Ma'heo'o's People: A Critical Bibliography*. Newberry Library Center for the History of the American Indian Bibliographical Series. Bloomington: Indiana University Press, 1980.

_____. *People of the Sacred Mountain: A History of the Northern Cheyenne Chiefs and Warrior Societies, 1830-1879*. 2 vols. San Francisco: Harper & Row, 1981.

Powers, William K. *Yuwipi: Vision and Experience in Oglala Ritual*. Lincoln: University of Nebraska Press, 1982.

Standing Bear, Luther. *My People the Sioux*. Boston: Houghton Mifflin, 1928.

Stands in Timber, John, and Margot Liberty. *Cheyenne Memories*. New Haven, Conn.: Yale University Press, 1967.

Unrau, William E. *The Emigrant Indians of Kansas: A Critical Bibliography*. Newberry Library Center for the History of the American Indian Bibliographical Series. Bloomington:

Indiana University Press, 1979.

Voget, Fred W. *The Shoshoni-Crow Sun Dance.* Norman: University of Oklahoma Press, 1984.

Walker, James R. *Lakota Belief and Ritual,* edited by Raymond J. DeMallie and Elaine A. Jahner. Lincoln: University of Nebraska Press, 1980.

_____. *Lakota Myth,* edited by Elaine A. Jahner. Lincoln: University of Nebraska Press, 1983.

_____. *Lakota Society,* edited by Raymond J. DeMallie. Lincoln: University of Nebraska Press, 1982.

Wedel, Waldo R., ed. *A Plains Archaeology Source Book: Selected Papers of the Nebraska Historical Society.* New York: Garland, 1985.

Weist, Katherine M., and Susan R. Sharrock. *An Annotated Bibliography of Northern Plains Ethnohistory.* Missoula: Department of Anthropology, University of Montana, 1985.

Wildschut, W., and John C. Ewers. *Crow Indian Beadwork.* New York: Museum of the American Indian, Heye Foundation, 1959.

Will, George F., and George E. Hyde. *Corn Among the Indians of the Upper Missouri.* St. Louis, Mo.: William Harvey Minor Co., 1917.

Wissler, Clark, ed. *Societies of the Plains Indians.* American Museum of Natural History, Anthropological Papers, vol. 11., pts. 1-13. New York: The Trustees, 1912-1916.

Wolferman, Kristie C. *The Osage in Missouri.* Columbia: University of Missouri Press, 1997.

Wood, W. Raymond, and Margot Liberty, eds. *Anthropology on the Great Plains.* Lincoln: University of Nebraska Press, 1980.

Zimmerman, Larry J. *Peoples of Prehistoric South Dakota.* Lincoln: University of Nebraska Press, 1985.

SOUTHEAST

Axtell, James. *The Indians' New South: Cultural Change in the Colonial Southeast.* Baton Rouge: Louisiana State University Press, 1997.

Baird, W. David. *The Chickasaw People.* Phoenix: Indian Tribal Series, 1974.

_____. *The Choctaw People.* Phoenix: Indian Tribal Series, 1973.

_____. *Peter Pitchlynn: Chief of the Choctaws.* Norman: University of Oklahoma Press, 1972.

Blu, Karen I. *The Lumbee Problem: The Making of an American Indian People.* Cambridge, England: Cambridge University Press, 1980.

Densmore, Frances. *Choctaw Music.* Bureau of American Ethnology, Bulletin 136. Washington, D.C.: U.S. Government Printing Office, 1943.

_____. *Seminole Music.* Bureau of American Ethnology, Bulletin 161. Washington, D.C.: U.S. Government Printing Office, 1956.

Edmunds, R. David. *The Shawnee Prophet.* Lincoln: University of Nebraska Press, 1983.

Fogelson, Raymond D. *The Cherokees: A Critical Bibliography.* Newberry Library Center for the History of the American Indian Bibliographical Series. Bloomington: Indiana University Press, 1978.

Gilliland, Marion Spjut. *The Material Culture of Key Marco, Florida.* Gainesville: University Presses of Florida, 1975.

Green, Michael D. *The Creeks: A Critical Bibliography.* Newberry Library Center for the History of the American Indian Bibliographical Series. Bloomington: Indiana University Press, 1979.

Hann, John H. *A History of the Timucua Indians and Missions.* Gainesville: University Press of Florida, 1996.

Hann, John H., and Bonnie G. McEwan. *The Apalachee Indians and*

Mission San Luis. Gainesville: University Press of Florida, 1998.

Hudson, Charles M., ed. *Ethnology of the Southeastern Indians*. New York: Garland, 1985.

_____. *The Southeastern Indians*. Knoxville: University of Tennessee Press, 1976.

Kidwell, Clara Sue, and Charles Roberts. *The Choctaws: A Critical Bibliography*. Newberry Library Center for the History of the American Indian Bibliographical Series. Bloomington: Indiana University Press, 1980.

King, Duane H., ed. *The Cherokee Indian Nation: A Troubled History*. Knoxville: University of Tennessee Press, 1979.

McReynolds, Edwin C. *The Seminoles*. Norman: University of Oklahoma Press, 1957.

Merrell, James H. *The Indians' New World: Catawbas and Their Neighbors from European Contact Through the Era of Removal*. Chapel Hill: University of North Carolina Press, for the Institute of Early American History and Culture, Williamsburg, Virginia, 1989.

Milanich, Jerald T. *The Timucua*. Cambridge, Mass.: Blackwell Publishers, 1996.

Milanich, Jerald T., and Charles H. Fairbanks. *Florida Archaeology*. New York: Academic Press, 1980.

Mooney, James. *Myths of the Cherokee*. Bureau of American Ethnology, Annual Report 19 (1897-1898). Washington, D.C.: U.S. Government Printing Office, 1900.

_____. *The Sacred Formulas of the Cherokees*. Bureau of American Ethnology, Annual Report 7 (1885-1886). Washington, D.C.: U.S. Government Printing Office, 1891.

Rountree, Helen C. *The Powhatan Indians of Virginia: Their Traditional Culture*. Norman: University of Oklahoma Press, 1989.

Swanton, John R. *The Indians of the Southeastern United States*. Bureau of American Ethnology, Bulletin 137. Washington, D.C.: U.S. Government Printing Office, 1946.

_____. *Myths and Tales of the Southeastern Indians*. Bureau of American Ethnology, Bulletin 88. Washington, D.C.: U.S. Government Printing Office, 1929.

Usner, Daniel H. *American Indians in the Lower Mississippi Valley: Social and Economic Histories*. Lincoln: University of Nebraska Press, 1998.

Walthall, John A. *Prehistoric Indians of the Southeast: Archaeology of Alabama and the Middle South*. Tuscaloosa: University of Alabama Press, 1980.

Worth, John E. *The Timucuan Chiefdoms of Spanish Florida*. 2 vols. Gainesville: University Press of Florida, 1998.

SOUTHWEST

Anderson, Gary C. *The Indian Southwest, 1580-1830: Ethnogenesis and Reinvention*. Norman: University of Oklahoma Press, 1999.

Basso, Keith H., ed. *Western Apache Raiding and Warfare, from the Notes of Grenville Goodwin*. Tucson: University of Arizona Press, 1971.

Benedict, Ruth. *Zuni Mythology*. 2 vols. New York: Columbia University Press, 1935.

Bunzel, Ruth L. *The Pueblo Potter: A Study of Creative Imagination in Primitive Art*. New York: Columbia University Press, 1929.

Cordell, Linda S. *Prehistory of the Southwest*. Orlando, Fla.: Academic Press, 1984.

Densmore, Frances. *Papago Music*. Bureau of American Ethnology, Bulletin 90. Washington, D.C.: U.S. Government Printing Office, 1929.

Dilworth, Leah. *Imagining Indians in the Southwest: Persistent Visions of a Primitive Past.* Washington, D.C.: Smithsonian Institution Press, 1996.

Dobyns, Henry F., and Robert C. Euler. *Indians of the Southwest.* Newberry Library Center for the History of the American Indian Bibliographical Series. Bloomington: Indiana University Press, 1980.

Dozier, Edward P. *Hano: A Tewa Indian Community in Arizona.* New York: Holt, Rinehart and Winston, 1966.

Eggan, Fred. *Social Organization of the Western Pueblos.* Chicago: University of Chicago Press, 1950.

Erickson, Winston P. *Sharing the Desert: The Tohono O'odham in History.* Tucson: University of Arizona Press, 1994.

Ferguson, T. J., and Richard E. Hart. *A Zuni Atlas.* Norman: University of Oklahoma Press, 1985.

Foster, Morris. *Being Comanche: A Social History of an American Indian Community.* Tucson: University of Arizona Press, 1991.

Frisbie, Charlotte J. *Navajo Medicine Bundles or Jish: Acquisition, Transmission, and Disposition in the Past and Present.* Albuquerque: University of New Mexico Press, 1987.

Goodman, James M. *The Navajo Atlas: Environments, Resources, People, and History of the Dine Bikeyah.* Norman: University of Oklahoma Press, 1982.

Haile, O. F. M., Fr. Berard, comp. and trans. *Navajo Coyote Tales: The Curly To Aheeddliinii Version*, edited by Karl Luckert. Lincoln: University of Nebraska Press, 1984.

Himmel, Kelly F. *The Conquest of the Karankawas and the Tonkawas, 1821-1859.* College Station: Texas A&M University Press, 1999.

Iverson, Peter. *Carlos Montezuma and the Changing World of American Indians.* Albuquerque: University of New Mexico Press, 1982.

_____. *The Navajo Nation.* Westport, Conn.: Greenwood Press, 1981.

_____. *The Navajos: A Critical Bibliography.* Newberry Library Center for the History of the American Indian Bibliographical Series. Bloomington: Indiana University Press, 1976.

Kent, Kate Peck. *Navajo Weaving: Three Centuries of Change.* Santa Fe, N.M.: School of American Research Press, 1985.

_____. *Prehistoric Textiles of the Southwest.* Santa Fe: School of American Research; and Albuquerque: University of New Mexico Press, 1983.

Kluckhohn, Clyde. *Navaho Witchcraft.* Boston: Beacon Press, 1962.

Laird, W. David. *Hopi Bibliography, Comprehensive and Annotated.* Tucson: University of Arizona Press, 1977.

Lamphere, Louise. *To Run After Them: Cultural and Social Bases of Cooperation in a Navajo Community.* Tucson: University of Arizona Press, 1977.

Leighton, Dorothea, and John Adair. *People of the Middle Place: A Study of the Zuni Indians.* New Haven, Conn.: Human Relations Area Files Press, 1966.

Lister, Robert H., and Florence C. Lister. *Chaco Canyon: Archaeology and Archaeologists.* Albuquerque: University of New Mexico Press, 1981.

Melody, Michael Edward. *The Apache: A Critical Bibliography.* Newberry Library Center for the History of the American Indian Bibliographical Series. Bloomington: Indiana University Press, 1977.

Ortiz, Alfonso, ed. *New Perspectives on the Pueblos.* Albuquerque:

University of New Mexico Press, 1972.

_____, ed. *Southwest*. Vol. 9 in *Handbook of North American Indians*. Washington: Smithsonian Institution Press, 1979.

_____, ed. *Southwest*. Vol. 10 in *Handbook of North American Indians*. Washington, D.C.: Smithsonian Institution Press, 1983.

_____. *The Tewa World: Space, Time, Being, and Becoming in a Pueblo Society*. Chicago: University of Chicago Press, 1969.

Parsons, Elsie C. *Pueblo Indian Religion*. 2 vols. Chicago: University of Chicago Press, 1939.

Plog, Stephen. *Ancient Peoples of the American Southwest*. New York: Thames and Hudson, 1997.

Reichard, Gladys A. *Navaho Indian Religion: A Study of Symbolism*. 2 vols. New York: Pantheon Books, 1950.

Ricklis, Robert A. *The Karankawa Indians of Texas: An Ecological Study of Cultural Tradition and Change*. Austin: University of Texas Press, 1996.

Stevenson, Matilda C. *The Zuni Indians: Their Mythology, Esoteric Fraternities, and Ceremonies*. Bureau of American Ethnology, Annual Report 23 (1901-1902). Washington, D.C.: U.S. Government Printing Office, 1904.

Tanner, Clara Lee. *Prehistoric Southwestern Craft Arts*. Tucson: University of Arizona Press, 1976.

_____. *Southwest Indian Painting: A Changing Art*. 2d ed. Tucson: University of Arizona Press, 1973.

Tiller, Veronica E. Velarde. *The Jicarilla Apache Tribe: A History*. Rev. ed. Albuquerque: BowArrow, 2000.

Trimble, Stephen. *The People: Indians of the American Southwest*. Santa Fe, N. Mex.: School of American Research, 1993.

Underhill, Ruth M. *Papago Woman*. New York: Holt, Rinehart and Winston, 1979.

Warren, Scott S. *Desert Dwellers: Native People of the American Southwest*. San Francisco: Chronicle Books, 1997.

Whitewolf, Jim. *The Life of a Kiowa Apache Indian*, edited by Charles S. Brant. New York: Dover, 1969.

Wills, W.H. *Early Prehistoric Agriculture in the American Southwest*. Santa Fe, N.M.: School of American Research Press, 1988.

CONTEMPORARY LIFE

Ambler, Marjane. *Breaking the Iron Bonds: Indian Control of Energy Development*. Lawrence: University Press of Kansas, 1990.

Berkhofer, Robert, Jr. *The White Man's Indian*. New York: Alfred A. Knopf, 1978.

Bordewich, Fergus M. *Killing the White Man's Indian: Reinventing Native Americans at the End of the Twentieth Century*. New York: Doubleday, 1996.

Browne, Donald R. *Electronic Media and Indigenous Peoples: A Voice of Our Own?* Ames: University of Iowa Press, 1996.

Champagne, Duane, ed. *Contemporary Native American Cultural Issues*. Walnut Creek, Calif.: AltaMira Pres, 1999.

Crozier-Hogle, Lois, Darryl B. Wilson, and Jay Leibold, ed. *Surviving in Two Worlds: Contemporary Native American Voices*. Austin: University of Texas Press, 1997.

Deloria, Vine, Jr. *Behind the Trail of Broken Treaties: An Indian Declaration of Independence*. New York: Delta, 1974.

_____. *God Is Red*. New York: Grosset & Dunlap, 1973.

Everton, Macduff. *The Modern Maya: A Culture in Transition*. Albuquerque:

University of New Mexico Press, 1991.

Frazier, Ian. *On the Rez.* New York: Farrar, Straus & Giroux, 2000.

Fuchs, Estelle, and Robert Havighurst. *To Live on This Earth.* Garden City, N.Y.: Doubleday, 1972.

Grobsmith, Elizabeth S. *Indians in Prison: Incarcerated Native Americans in Nebraska.* Lincoln: University of Nebraska Press, 1994.

Guyette, Susan. *Planning for Balanced Development: A Guide for Native American and Rural Communities.* Santa Fe: Clear Light Publishers, 1996.

Hertzberg, Hazel W. *The Search for an American Indian Identity: Modern Pan-Indian Movements.* Syracuse, N.Y.: Syracuse University Press, 1971.

Highwater, Jamake. *The Sweet Grass Lives On: Fifty Contemporary North American Indian Artists.* New York: Lippincott and Thomas Y. Crowell, 1980.

Hirchsfelder, Arlene, and Martha K. de Montaño. *The Native North American Almanac: A Portrait of Native America Today.* New York: Prentice-Hall, 1993.

Hobson, Geary, ed. *The Remembered Earth: An Anthology of Contemporary Native American Literature.* Albuquerque: University of New Mexico Press, 1979.

Holm, Tom. *Strong Hearts, Wounded Souls: Native American Veterans of the Vietnam War.* Austin: University of Texas Press, 1996.

Hotvedt, Kris. *Pueblo and Navajo Indian Life Today.* Rev. ed. Sante Fe, N.Mex.: Sunstone Press, 1993.

Iverson, Peter. *We Are Still Here: American Indians in the Twentieth Century.* Wheeling, Ill.: Harlan Davidson, 1998.

James, Caroline. *Nez Perce Women in Transition, 1877-1990.* Moscow: University of Idaho Press, 1996.

Johnson, Troy R., ed. *Contemporary Native American Political Issues.* Walnut Creek, Calif.: AltaMira Press, 1999.

Kasari, Patricia. *Impact of Occupational Dislocation: The American Indian Labor Force at the Close of the Twentieth Century.* New York: Garland, 1999.

Keith, Michael C. *Signals in the Air: Native Broadcasting in America.* Westport, Conn.: Praeger, 1995.

Lane, Ambrose I. *Return of the Buffalo: The Story Behind America's Indian Gaming Explosion.* Westport, Conn.: Bergin & Garvey, 1995.

Lang, Sabine. *Men as Women, Women as Men: Changing Gender in Native American Cultures.* Austin: University of Texas Press, 1998.

McNickle, D'Arcy. *The Surrounded.* New York: Dodd, Mead, 1936.

Mason, W. Dale. *Indian Gaming: Tribal Sovereignty and American Politics.* Norman: University of Oklahoma Press, 2000.

Momaday, N. Scott. *House Made of Dawn.* New York: Harper & Row, 1968.

Nagel, Joane. *American Indian Ethnic Renewal: Red Power and the Resurgence of Identity and Culture.* New York: Oxford University Press, 1996.

O'Brien, Sharon. *American Indian Tribal Governments.* Norman: University of Oklahoma Press, 1989.

O'Nell, Theresa D. *Disciplined Hearts: History, Identity, and Depression in an American Indian Community.* Berkeley: University of California Press, 1996.

Owens, Louis. *Mixedblood Messages: Literature, Film, Family, Place.* Norman: University of Oklahoma Press, 1998.

Paquin, Ron, and Robert Doherty. *Not First in Nobody's Heart: The Life Story of a Contemporary Chippewa*. Ames: Iowa State University Press, 1992.

Pommersheim, Frank. *Braid of Feathers: American Law and Contemporary Tribal Life*. Berkeley: University of California Press, 1995.

Red Horse, John, et al. *The American Indian Family: Strengths and Stresses*. Isleta, N.Mex.: American Indian Social Research and Development Associates, 1981.

Rosen, Kenneth. *The Man to Send Rain Clouds: Contemporary Stories by American Indians*. New York: Viking Press, 1974.

Scherer, Mark R. *Imperfect Victories: The Legal Tenacity of the Omaha Tribe, 1945-1995*. Lincoln: University of Nebraska Press, 1999.

Silko, Leslie Marmon. *Ceremony*. New York: Viking Press, 1977.

_____. *Yellow Woman and a Beauty of the Spirit: Essays on Native American Life Today*. New York: Simon & Schuster, 1996.

Snake, Reuben, and Jay C. Fikes. *Reuben Snake: Your Humble Serpent, Indian Visionary and Activist*. Santa Fe, N.Mex.: Clearlight Press, 1996.

Strickland, Rennard. *Tonto's Revenge: Reflections on American Indian Culture and Policy*. Albuquerque: University of New Mexico Press, 1997.

Tedlock, Barbara. *The Beautiful and the Dangerous: Encounters with the Zuni Indians*. New York: Viking Press, 1992.

Waddell, Jack O., and O. Michael Watson, eds. *The American Indian in Urban Society*. Boston: Little, Brown, 1971.

Warren, Kay B. *Indigenous Movements and Their Critics: Pan-Maya Activism in Guatemala*. Princeton, N.J.: Princeton University Press, 1998.

Washburn, Wilcomb E. *Red Man's Land/White Man's Law: The Past and Present State of the American Indian*. 2d ed. Norman: University of Oklahoma Press, 1995.

Weibel-Orlando, Joan. *Indian Country, L.A.: Maintaining Ethnic Community in Complex Society*. Rev. ed. Urbana: University of Illinois Press, 1999.

Welch, James. *Winter in the Blood*. New York: Harper & Row, 1974.

INDEX

Sliammon, 206
Smallpox, 16, 48, 82, 89, 93, 122, 131-132, 143, 154, 158-159, 175, 185, 188, 198, 211, 214, 223, 241, 261, 269-270, 308, 311, 322-323, 355, 359, 362, 402, 410, 415, 424-425, 442, 454-455, 463, 465, 481, 505, 507, 512, 528, 536-537, 546, 561
Smith, Jedediah, 407, 410
Smith, John, 323, 500
Snohomish, 495-496
Snoqualmie, 496-497
Social organization; California, 21; Great Basin, 28; Northeast, 8, 33; Northwest Coast, 40; Plateau, 53; Southeast, 59, 61
Societies, non-kin-based, Arapaho, 114
Sooke, 497
Southeast culture area, 9, 57-66
Southern Cult, 341
Southern Paiute. See Paiute, Southern
Southwest culture area, 5, 7, 67-73
Spiro, 148, 341
Spokane, 497-498
Squamish, 499
Standing Bear, 432
Stevens, Isaac, 414
Stillaguamish, 494
Stockbridge, 315
Stoneys. See Assiniboine
Strange Woman religion, 435
Sturgeon War, 333
Subarctic culture area, 4, 74-78
Sullivan, John, 525
Sumass, 210
Sun Dance, 115, 141
Sunghees, 497
Sunset Crater, 482
Suquamish, 500
Susquehannock, 500-502
Sutaio Cheyenne, 176
Swallah, 502-503
Swampy Cree, 213
Swanton, 81
Swinomish, 493
Sycamore Shoals Treaty, 169
Syphilis, 505

Tahltan, 503-504
Tanaina, 504-505
Tanana, 505-506
Tanoan, 70, 440, 443, 445
Tappan, 306
Tattoos and tattooing, 511
Tauitau, Chief, 163
Tawakoni, 545
Tayovaya, 545
Tecumseh, 34, 218, 245, 476; and Potawatomi, 435
Teepee. See Tipi
Tenino, 506
Tenochtitlán, 126
Teotihuacán, 181, 344, 517; and Zapotecs, 569
Tete de Boule Cree, 213
Teton, 485
Tewa, 442
Texcoco, 128
Thompson, 507
Thoreau, Henry David, 423
Thule, 272, 508-509
Tillamook, 481, 509-510
Timucua, 510-511
Tin-ne-áh (Apache), 102
Tintatuwan, 485
Tionontati (Peton), 425
Tiou, 511-512
Tipai, 285
Tipis, 5, 46; Apache, 104; Arapaho, 113-115; Assiniboine, 121; Bannock, 131; Blackfoot, 142; Cheyenne, 176; Coeur d'Alene, 198; Comanche, 203; Crow, 226; Hare, 258; Iowa, 275; Kiowa, 295; Nez Perce, 375; Okanagan, 388; Omaha, 393; Oto, 403; Ponca, 431; Sarsi, 464; Sioux, 484; Ute, 530; Wichita, 546
Tippecanoe, Battle of, 476
Tlacopán, 128
Tlallum, 194
Tlatocan, 127
Tlingit, 512-513
Tobacco, 9, 33, 40, 86, 120, 124, 150, 156, 160, 181, 190, 197, 226, 244, 246-247, 260, 290, 307-308, 321, 374, 397, 404, 425, 539, 545, 553